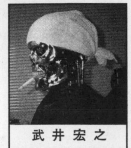

武井宏之

It's 2002. I turn 30 this year. Only ten years until I hit the venerable age of 40. Just a little more effort.

—Hiroyuki Takei

Unconventional author/artist Hiroyuki Takei began his career by winning the coveted Hop Step Award (for new manga artists) and the Osamu Tezuka Award (named after the famous artist of the same name). After working as an assistant to famed artist Nobuhiro Watsuki, Takei debuted in **Weekly Shonen Jump** in 1997 with **Butsu Zone**, an action series based on Buddhist mythology. His multi-cultural adventure manga **Shaman King**, which debuted in 1998, became a hit and was adapted into an anime TV series. Takei lists Osamu Tezuka, American comics and robot anime among his many influences.

SHAMAN KING VOL. 18
The SHONEN JUMP Manga Edition

STORY AND ART BY
HIROYUKI TAKEI

English Adaptation/Lance Caselman
Translation/Lillian Olsen
Touch-up Art & Lettering/John Hunt
Design/Nozomi Akashi
Editor/Carol Fox

Editor in Chief, Books/Alvin Lu
Editor in Chief, Magazines/Marc Weidenbaum
VP of Publishing Licensing/Rika Inouye
VP of Sales/Gonzalo Ferreyra
Sr. VP of Marketing/Liza Coppola
Publisher/Hyoe Narita

Printed in the U.S.A.

Published by VIZ Media, LLC
P.O. Box 77010
San Francisco, CA 94107

SHONEN JUMP Manga Edition
10 9 8 7 6 5 4 3 2 1
First printing, September 2008

T 252532

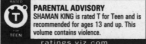

PARENTAL ADVISORY
SHAMAN KING is rated T for Teen and is
recommended for ages 13 and up. This
volume contains violence.
ratings.viz.com

www.viz.com

THE WORLD'S
MOST POPULAR MANGA

www.shonenjump.com

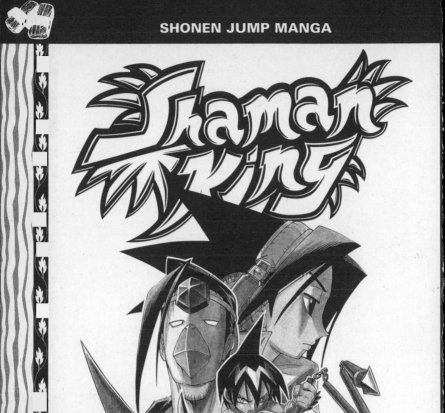

SHAMAN KING

VOL. 18
THE MASK RESTORED

STORY AND ART BY
HIROYUKI TAKEI

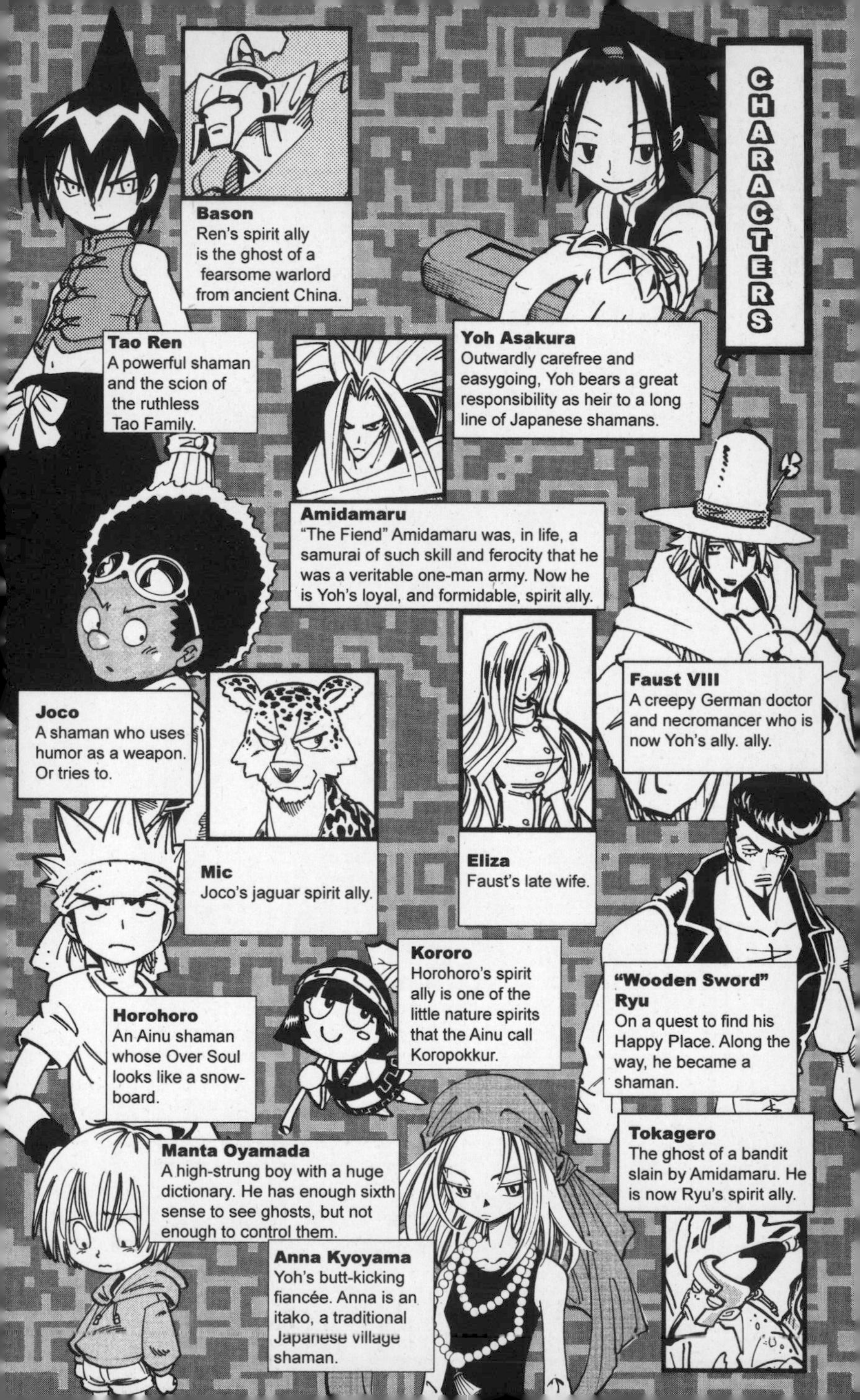

CHARACTERS

Yoh Asakura
Outwardly carefree and easygoing, Yoh bears a great responsibility as heir to a long line of Japanese shamans.

Bason
Ren's spirit ally is the ghost of a fearsome warlord from ancient China.

Tao Ren
A powerful shaman and the scion of the ruthless Tao Family.

Amidamaru
"The Fiend" Amidamaru was, in life, a samurai of such skill and ferocity that he was a veritable one-man army. Now he is Yoh's loyal, and formidable, spirit ally.

Faust VIII
A creepy German doctor and necromancer who is now Yoh's ally. ally.

Eliza
Faust's late wife.

Mic
Joco's jaguar spirit ally.

Joco
A shaman who uses humor as a weapon. Or tries to.

"Wooden Sword" Ryu
On a quest to find his Happy Place. Along the way, he became a shaman.

Kororo
Horohoro's spirit ally is one of the little nature spirits that the Ainu call Koropokkur.

Horohoro
An Ainu shaman whose Over Soul looks like a snow-board.

Tokagero
The ghost of a bandit slain by Amidamaru. He is now Ryu's spirit ally.

Anna Kyoyama
Yoh's butt-kicking fiancée. Anna is an itako, a traditional Japanese village shaman.

Manta Oyamada
A high-strung boy with a huge dictionary. He has enough sixth sense to see ghosts, but not enough to control them.

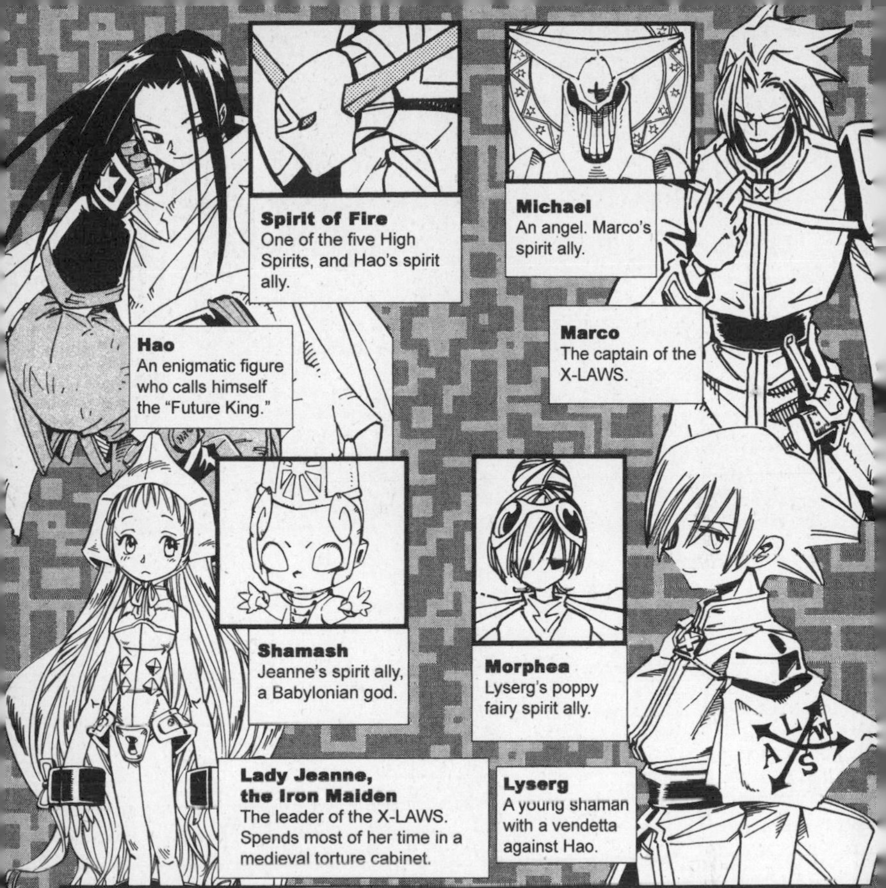

Spirit of Fire
One of the five High Spirits, and Hao's spirit ally.

Michael
An angel. Marco's spirit ally.

Hao
An enigmatic figure who calls himself the "Future King."

Marco
The captain of the X-LAWS.

Shamash
Jeanne's spirit ally, a Babylonian god.

Morphea
Lyserg's poppy fairy spirit ally.

Lady Jeanne, the Iron Maiden
The leader of the X-LAWS. Spends most of her time in a medieval torture cabinet.

Lyserg
A young shaman with a vendetta against Hao.

THE STORY THUS FAR

Yoh Asakura not only sees dead people, he talks and fights with them, too. That's because Yoh is a shaman, a traditional holy man able to interact with the spirit world. Yoh is now a competitor in the "Shaman Fight," a tournament held every 500 years to decide who will become the Shaman King and shape humanity's future.

As the tournament progresses, Yoh's father gives Ren a lesson in humility and offers to teach him the secrets of the Ultra Senji Ryakketsu. But further instruction is interrupted when Hao's minions attack. Shaken by the revelation that one of the attackers is the brother of a man he killed, Ren is mortally wounded, and only Yoh's last-minute intervention saves Team Ren from annihilation. Now, with Ren's life slipping away, Yoh is faced with a momentous decision.

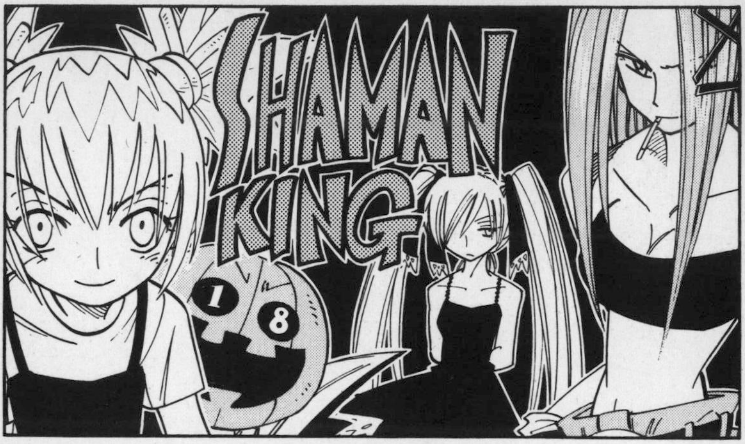
SHAMAN
KING

VOL. 18

THE MASK RESTORED

CONTENTS

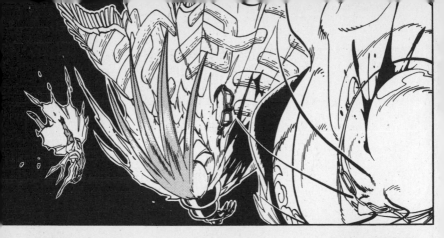

YOH...

Reincarnation 153: The Old Ren Is Gone

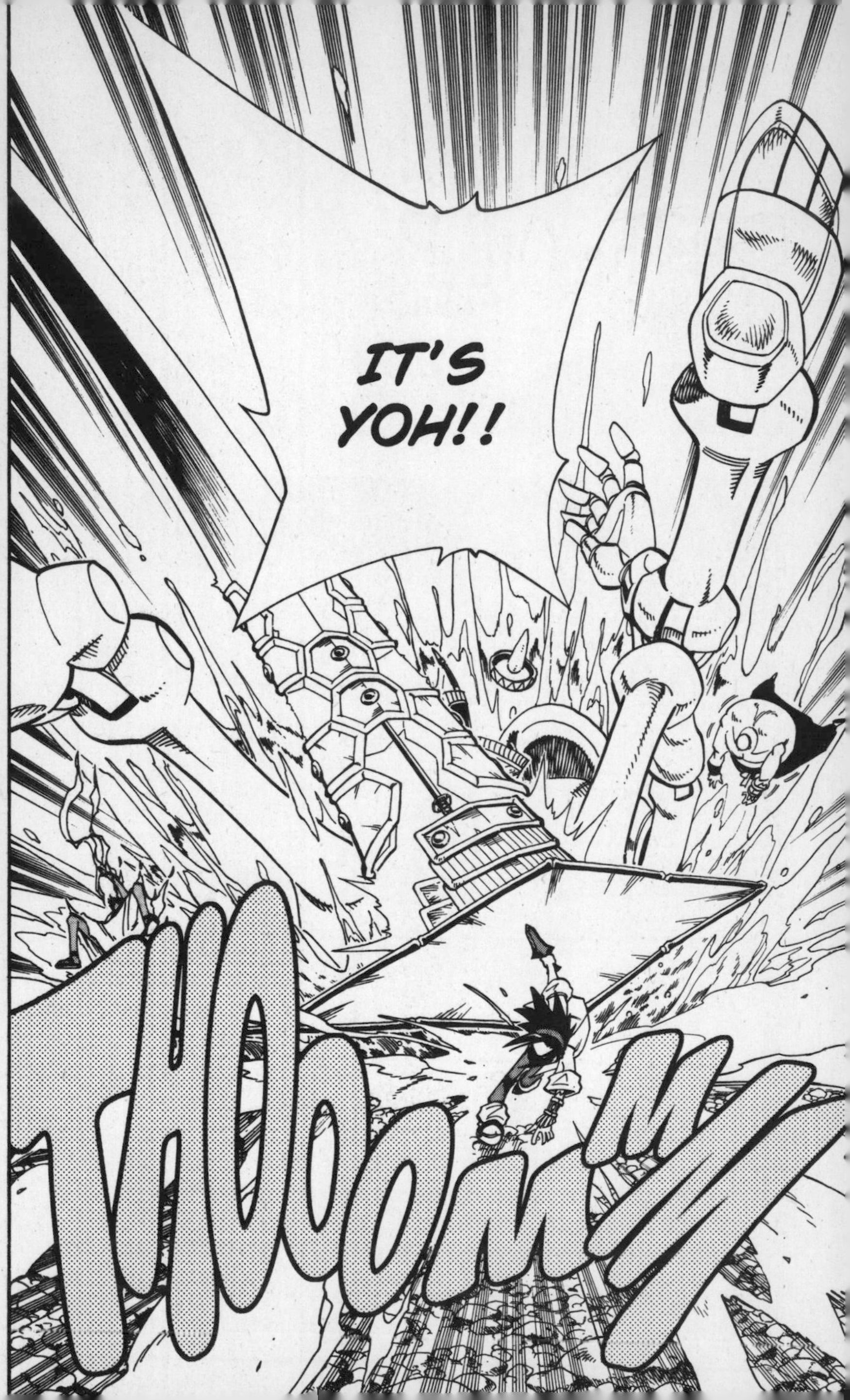
IT'S YOH!!
THOOMMM

Reincarnation 153: The Old Ren is Gone

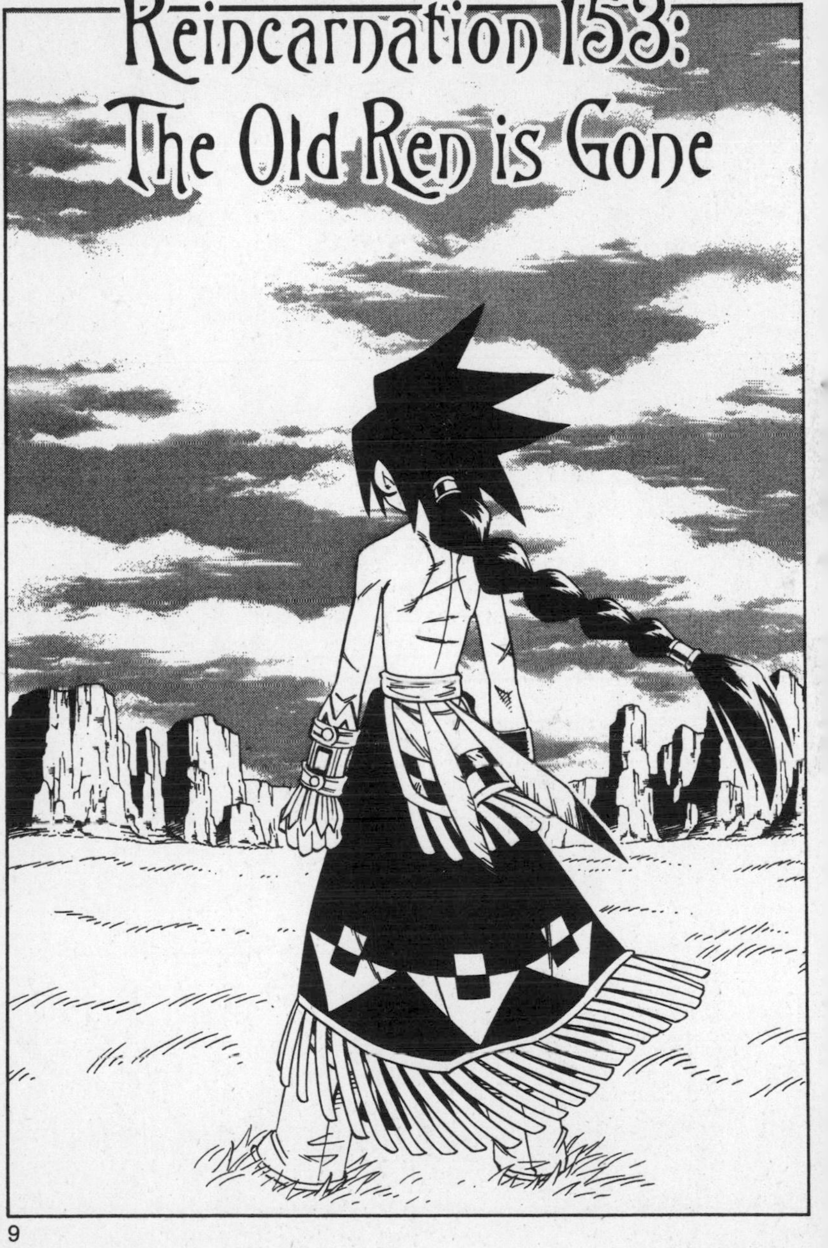

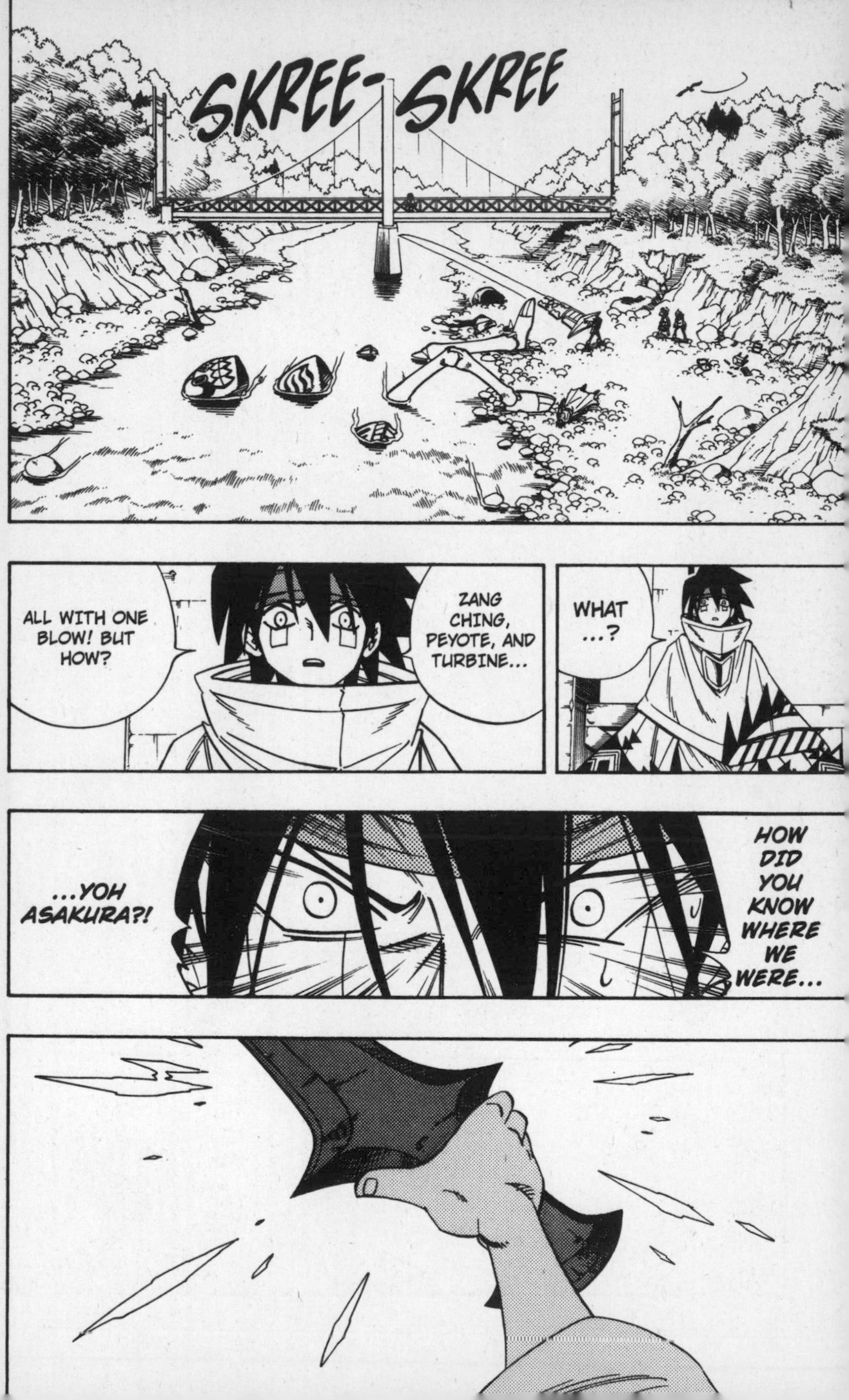
SKREE-SKREE
WHAT ...?
ZANG CHING, PEYOTE, AND TURBINE...
ALL WITH ONE BLOW! BUT HOW?
HOW DID YOU KNOW WHERE WE WERE...
...YOH ASAKURA?!

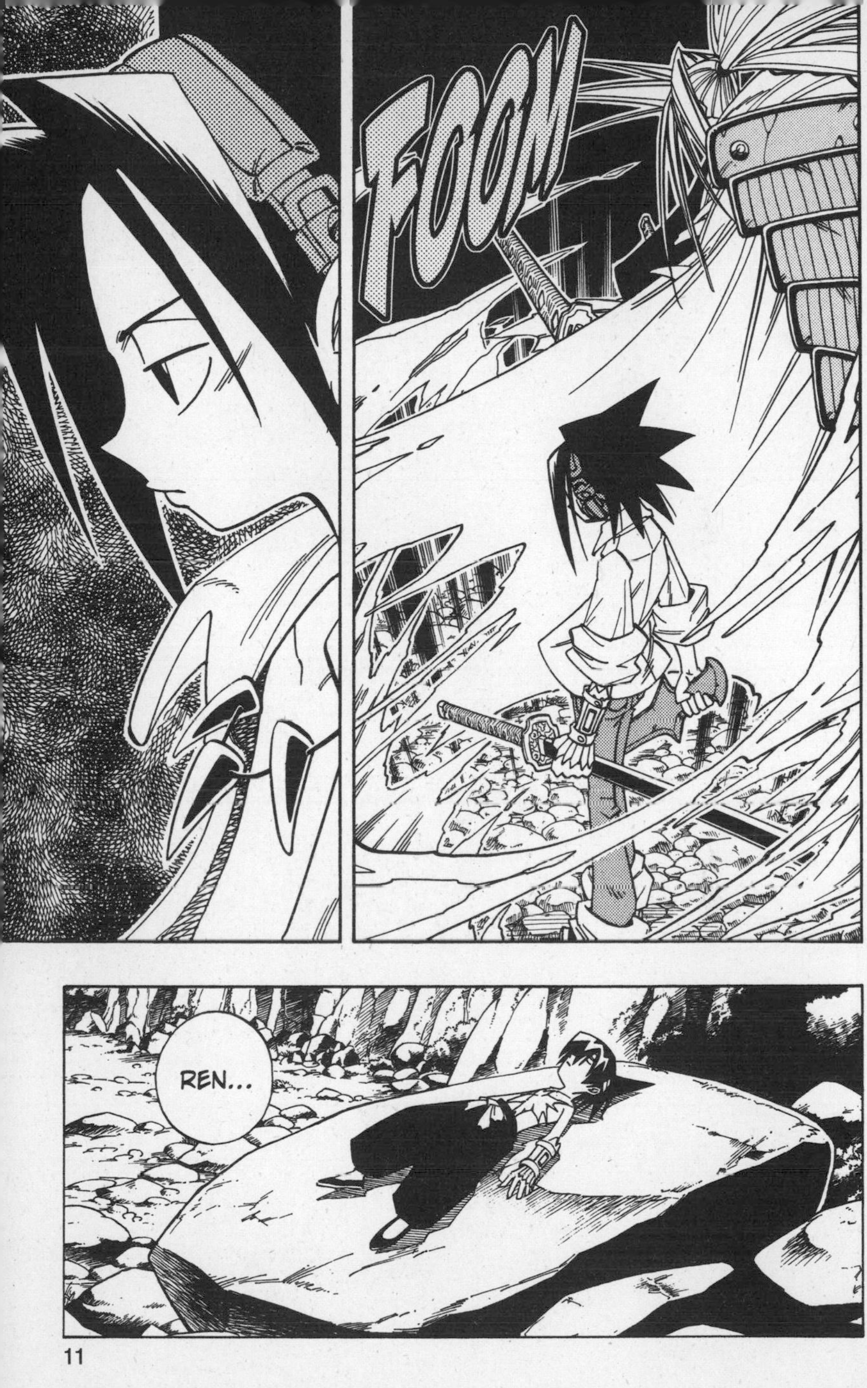
FOOM
REN...

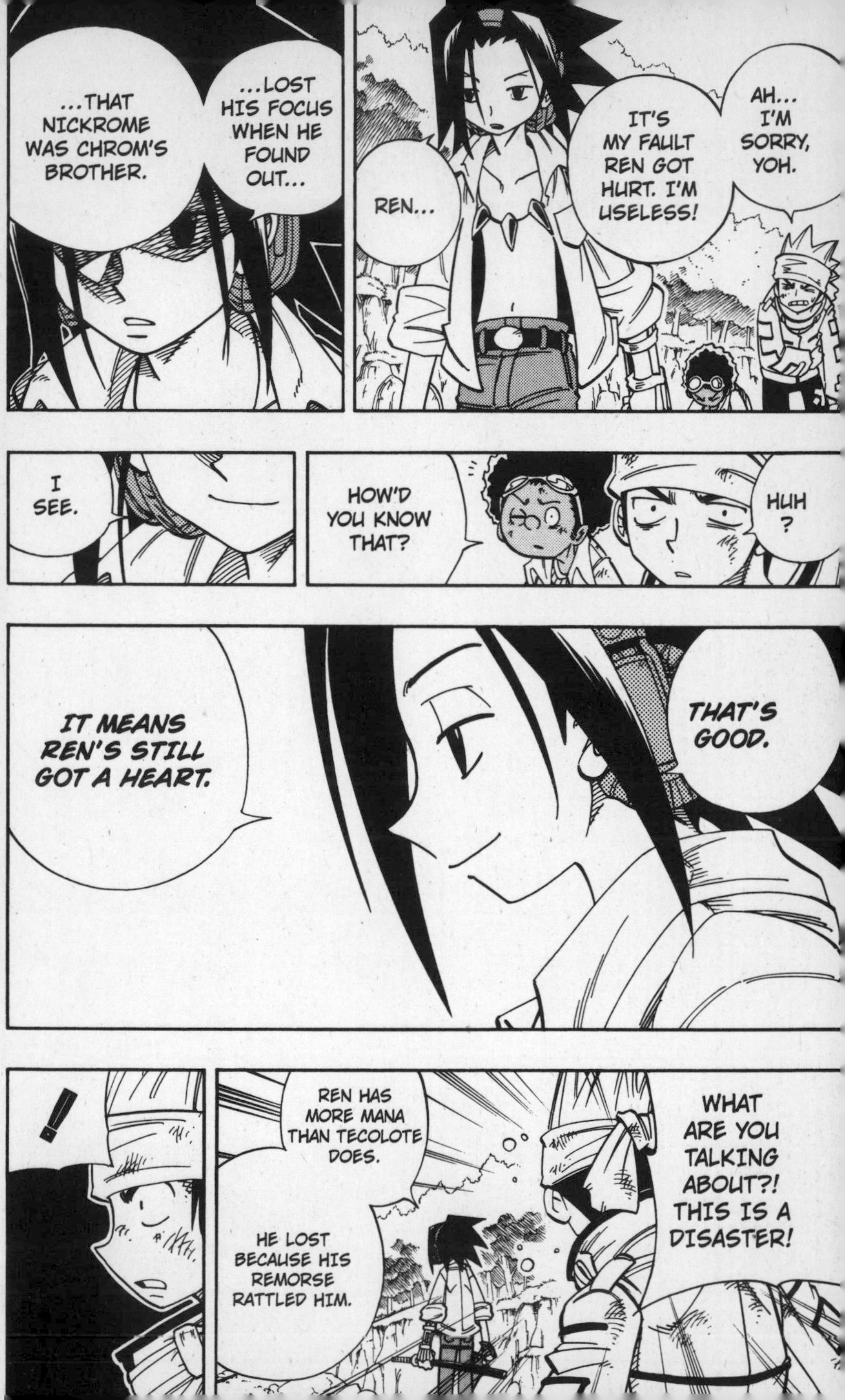
AH... I'M SORRY, YOH.
IT'S MY FAULT REN GOT HURT. I'M USELESS!
REN...
...LOST HIS FOCUS WHEN HE FOUND OUT...
...THAT NICKROME WAS CHROM'S BROTHER.
HUH?
HOW'D YOU KNOW THAT?
I SEE.
THAT'S GOOD.
IT MEANS REN'S STILL GOT A HEART.
WHAT ARE YOU TALKING ABOUT?! THIS IS A DISASTER!
REN HAS MORE MANA THAN TECOLOTE DOES.
HE LOST BECAUSE HIS REMORSE RATTLED HIM.
!

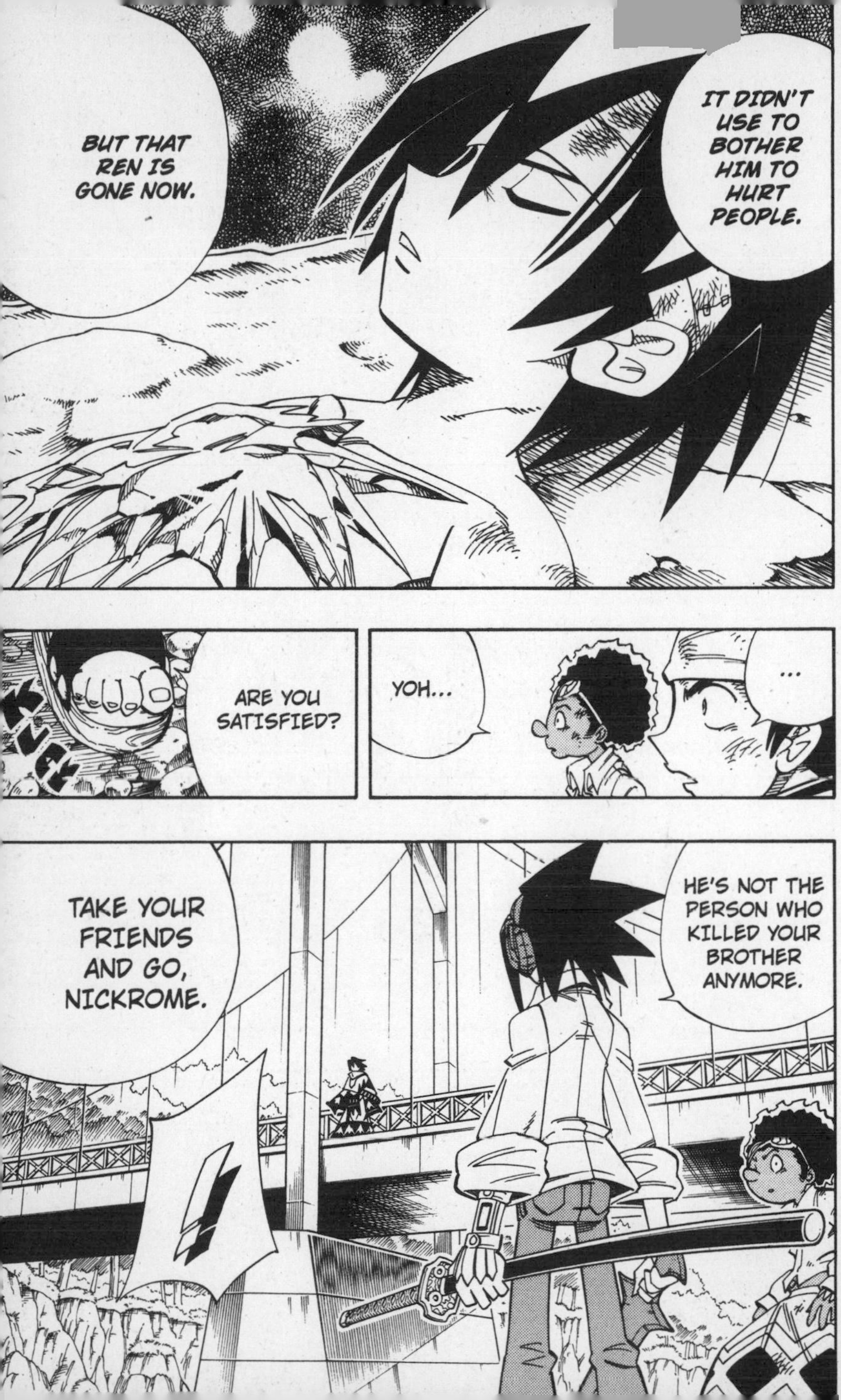
IT DIDN'T USE TO BOTHER HIM TO HURT PEOPLE.
BUT THAT REN IS GONE NOW.
...
YOH...
ARE YOU SATISFIED?
HE'S NOT THE PERSON WHO KILLED YOUR BROTHER ANYMORE.
TAKE YOUR FRIENDS AND GO, NICKROME.

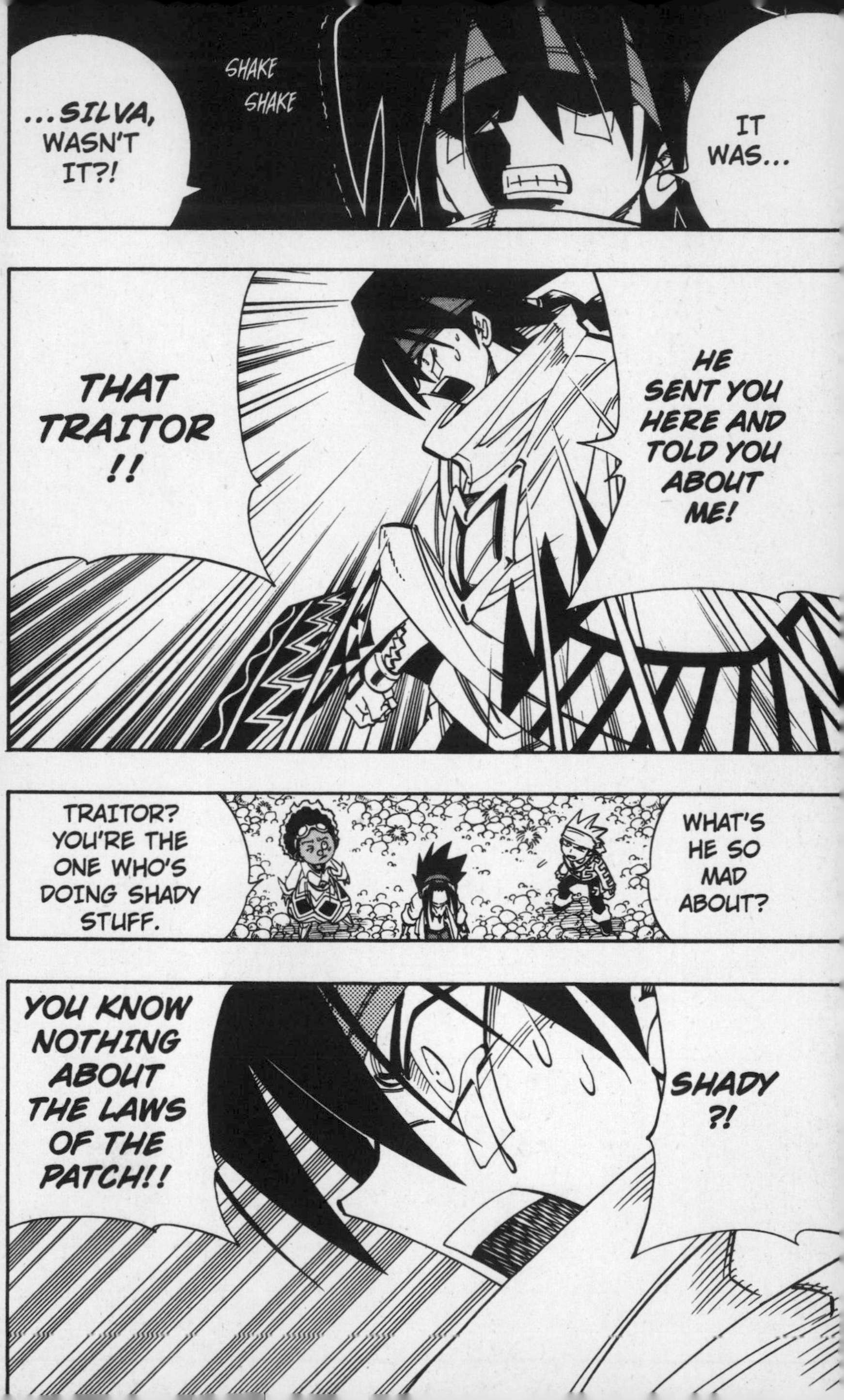
IT WAS...
SHAKE SHAKE
...SILVA, WASN'T IT?!
HE SENT YOU HERE AND TOLD YOU ABOUT ME!
THAT TRAITOR!!
WHAT'S HE SO MAD ABOUT?
TRAITOR? YOU'RE THE ONE WHO'S DOING SHADY STUFF.
SHADY?!
YOU KNOW NOTHING ABOUT THE LAWS OF THE PATCH!!

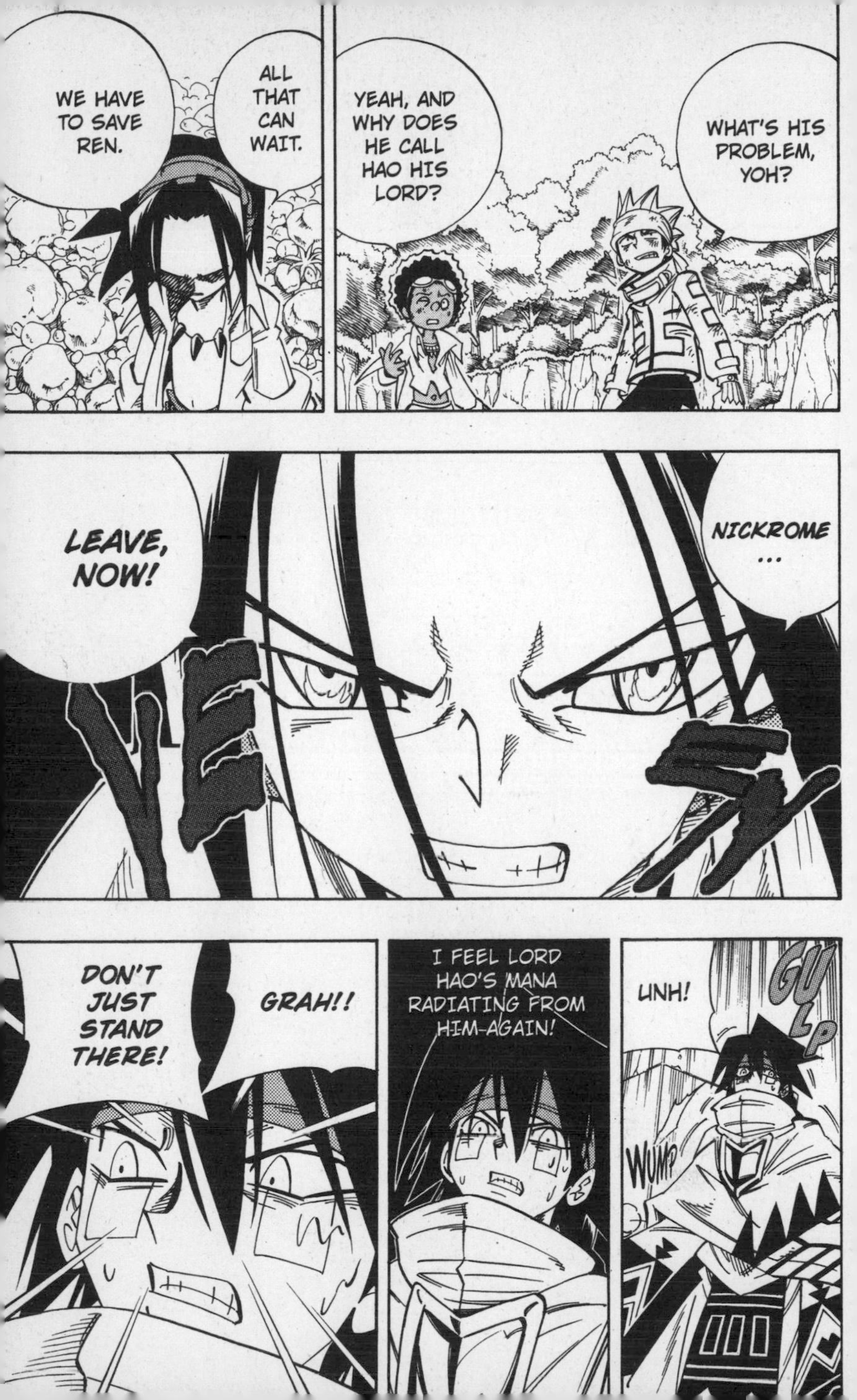
WHAT'S HIS PROBLEM, YOH?
YEAH, AND WHY DOES HE CALL HAO HIS LORD?
ALL THAT CAN WAIT.
WE HAVE TO SAVE REN.
NICKROME ...
LEAVE, NOW!
GULP
UNH!
WUMP
I FEEL LORD HAO'S MANA RADIATING FROM HIM AGAIN!
GRAH!!
DON'T JUST STAND THERE!

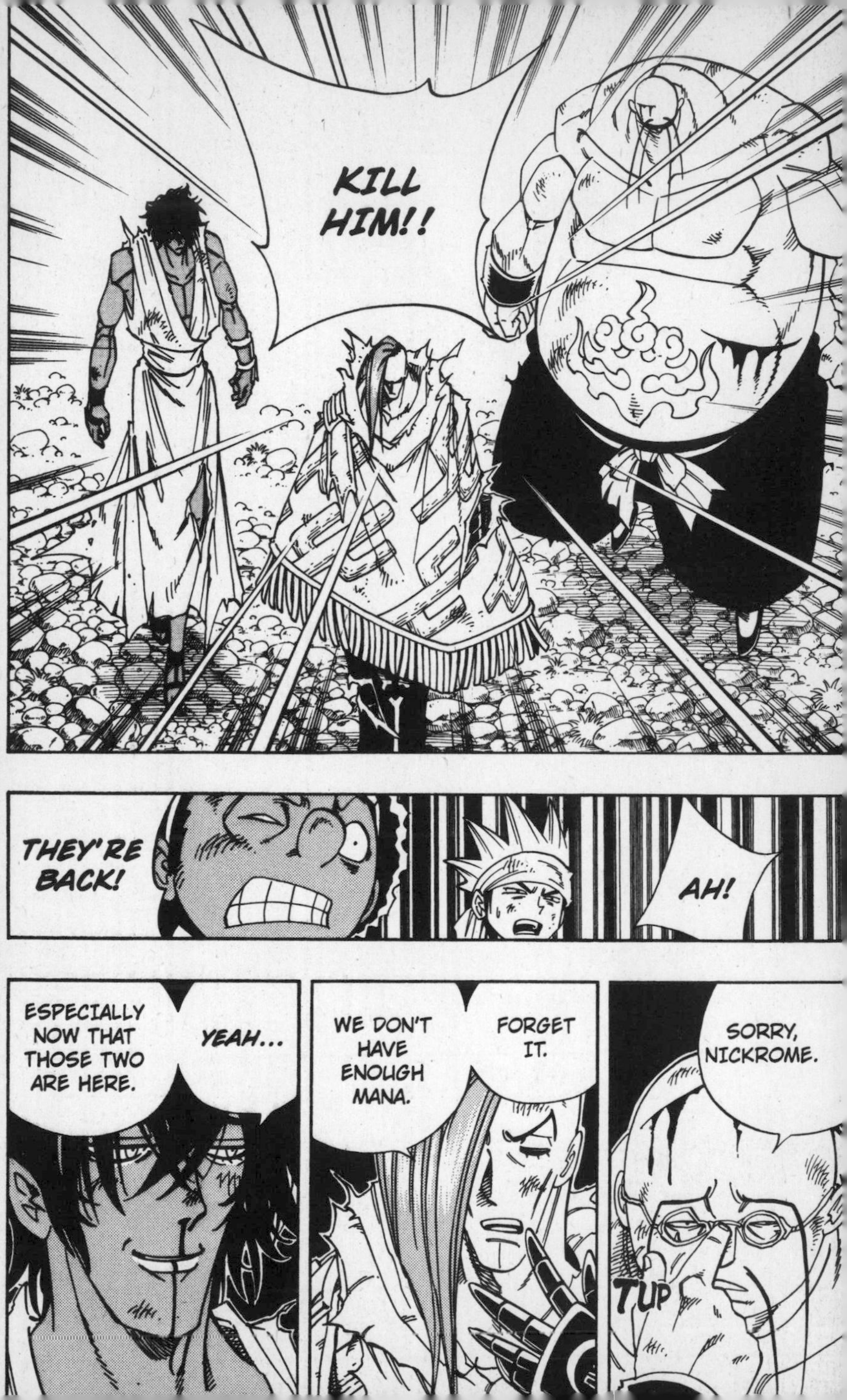
KILL HIM!!
AH!
THEY'RE BACK!
SORRY, NICKROME.
TUP
FORGET IT.
WE DON'T HAVE ENOUGH MANA.
YEAH...
ESPECIALLY NOW THAT THOSE TWO ARE HERE.

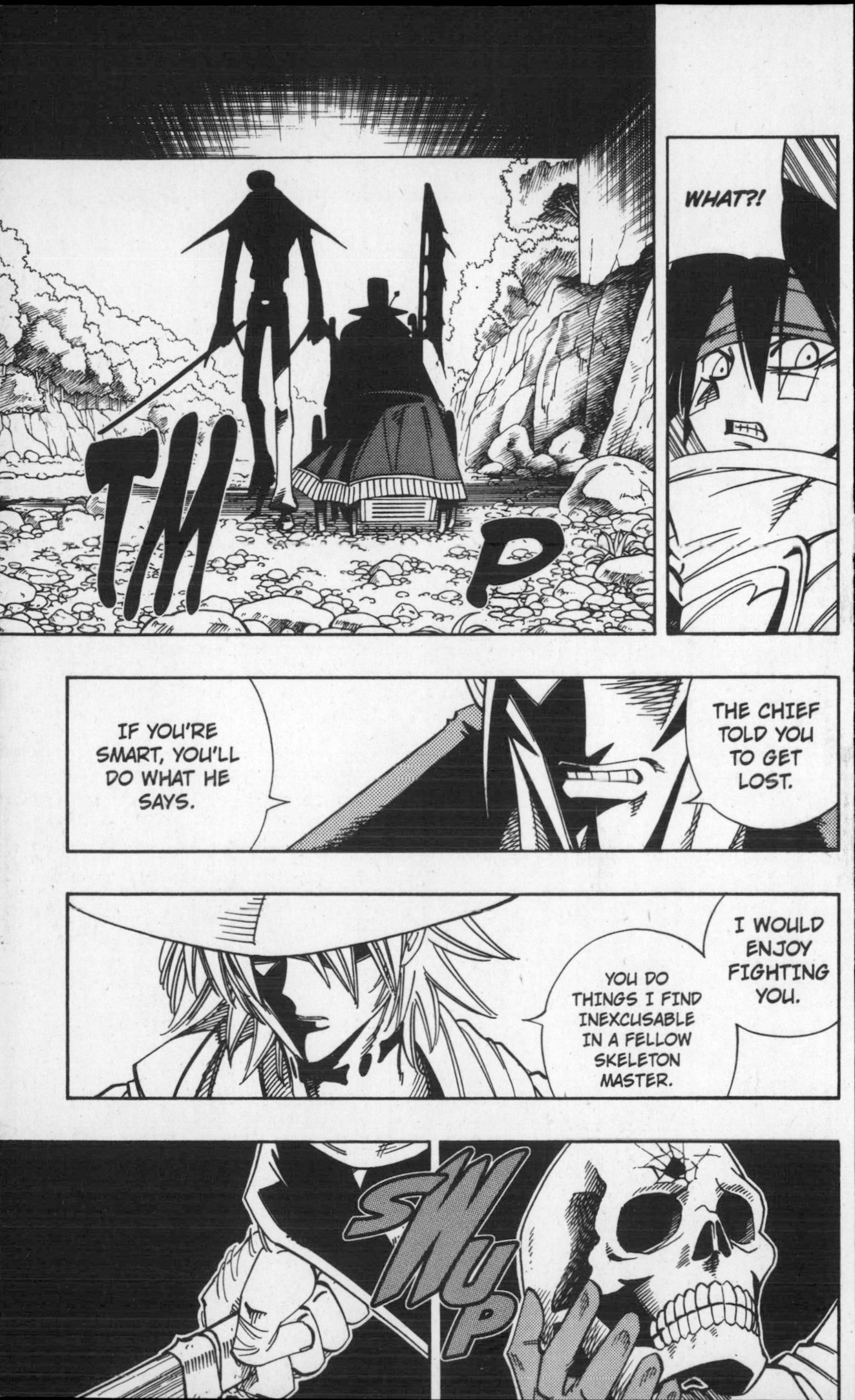
WHAT?!
TMP
THE CHIEF TOLD YOU TO GET LOST.
IF YOU'RE SMART, YOU'LL DO WHAT HE SAYS.
I WOULD ENJOY FIGHTING YOU.
YOU DO THINGS I FIND INEXCUSABLE IN A FELLOW SKELETON MASTER.
SHUP

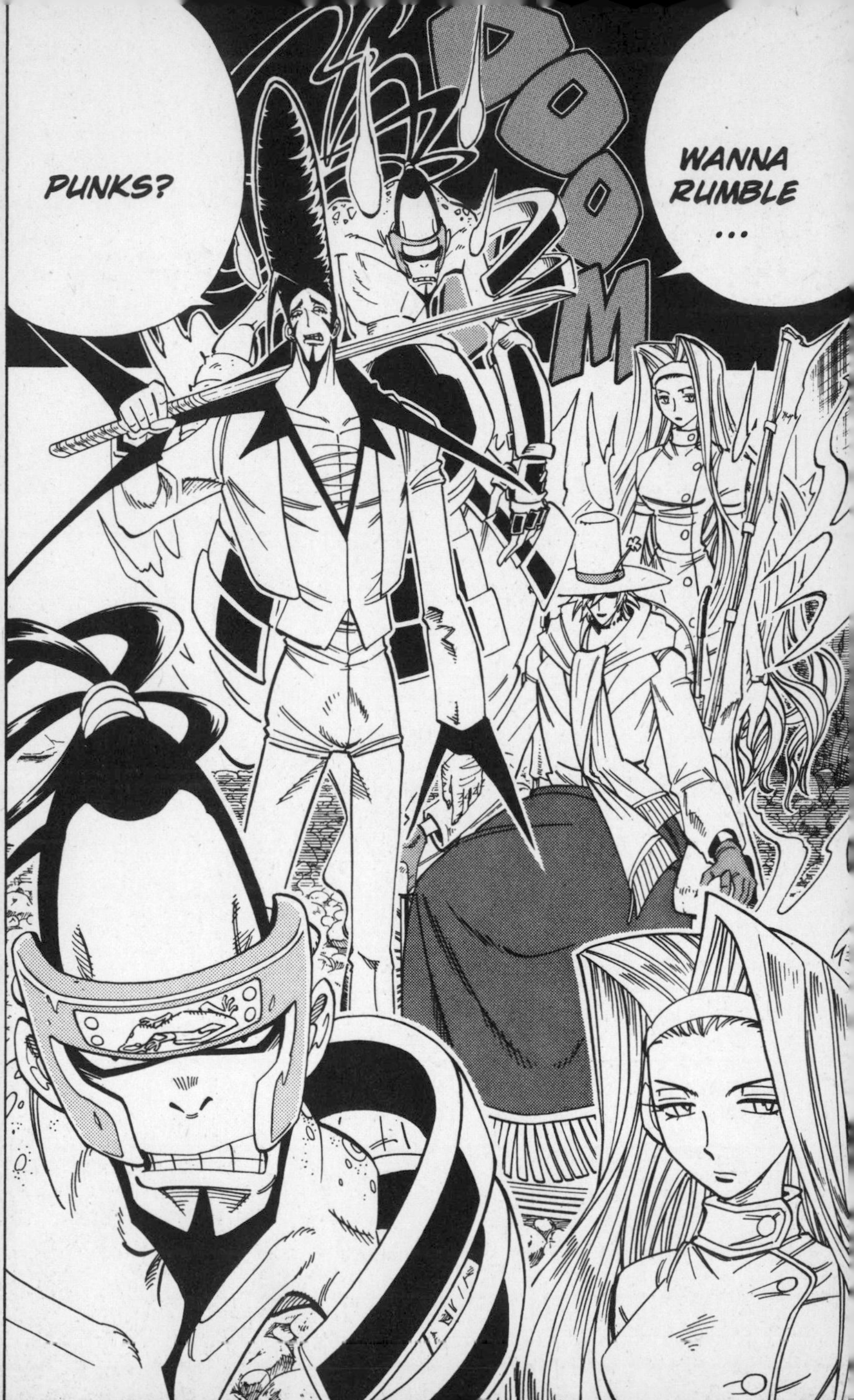
WANNA RUMBLE ...
DOOM
PUNKS?

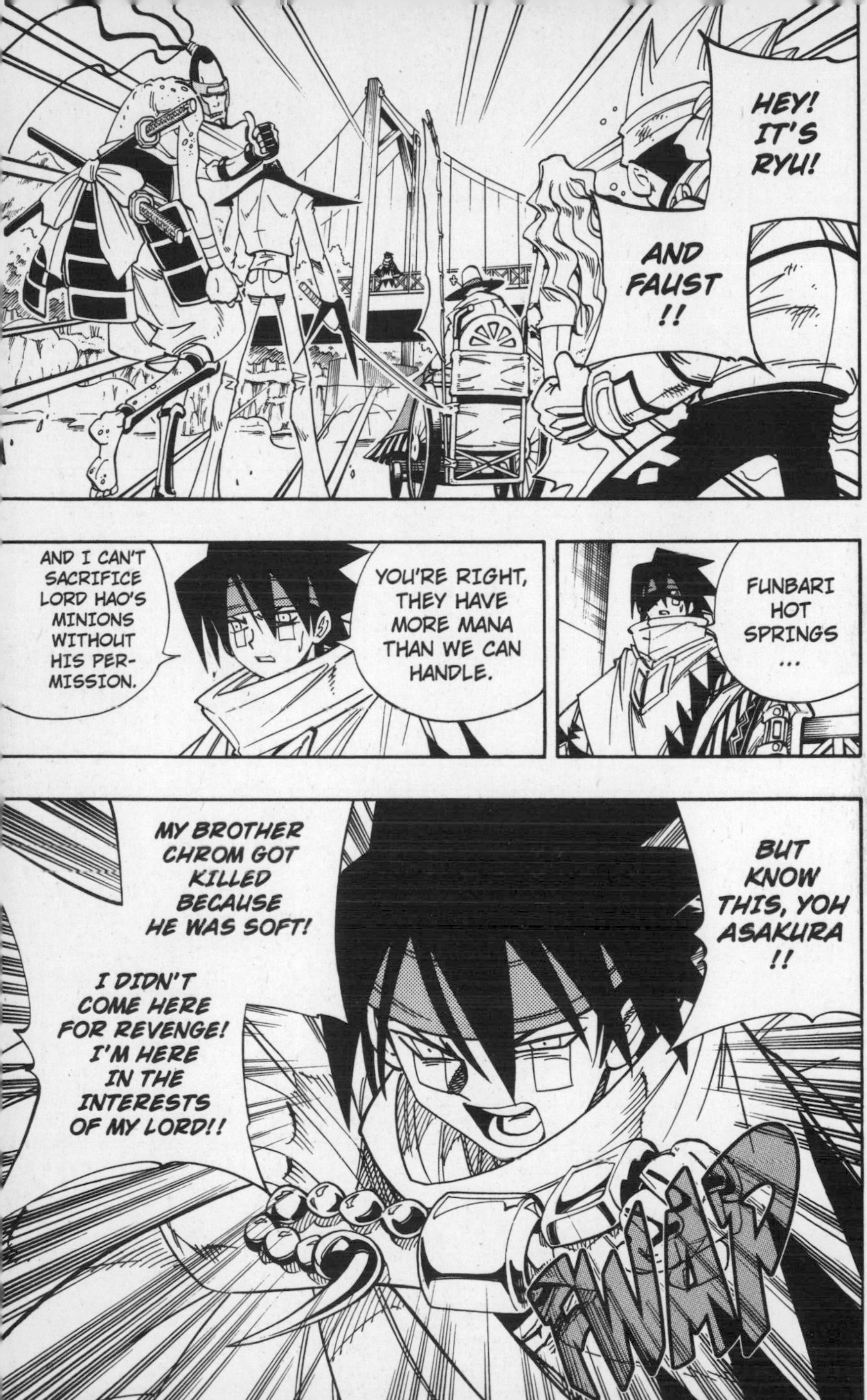
HEY! IT'S RYU!
AND FAUST !!
FUNBARI HOT SPRINGS ...
YOU'RE RIGHT, THEY HAVE MORE MANA THAN WE CAN HANDLE.
AND I CAN'T SACRIFICE LORD HAO'S MINIONS WITHOUT HIS PER-MISSION.
BUT KNOW THIS, YOH ASAKURA !!
MY BROTHER CHROM GOT KILLED BECAUSE HE WAS SOFT!
I DIDN'T COME HERE FOR REVENGE! I'M HERE IN THE INTERESTS OF MY LORD!!

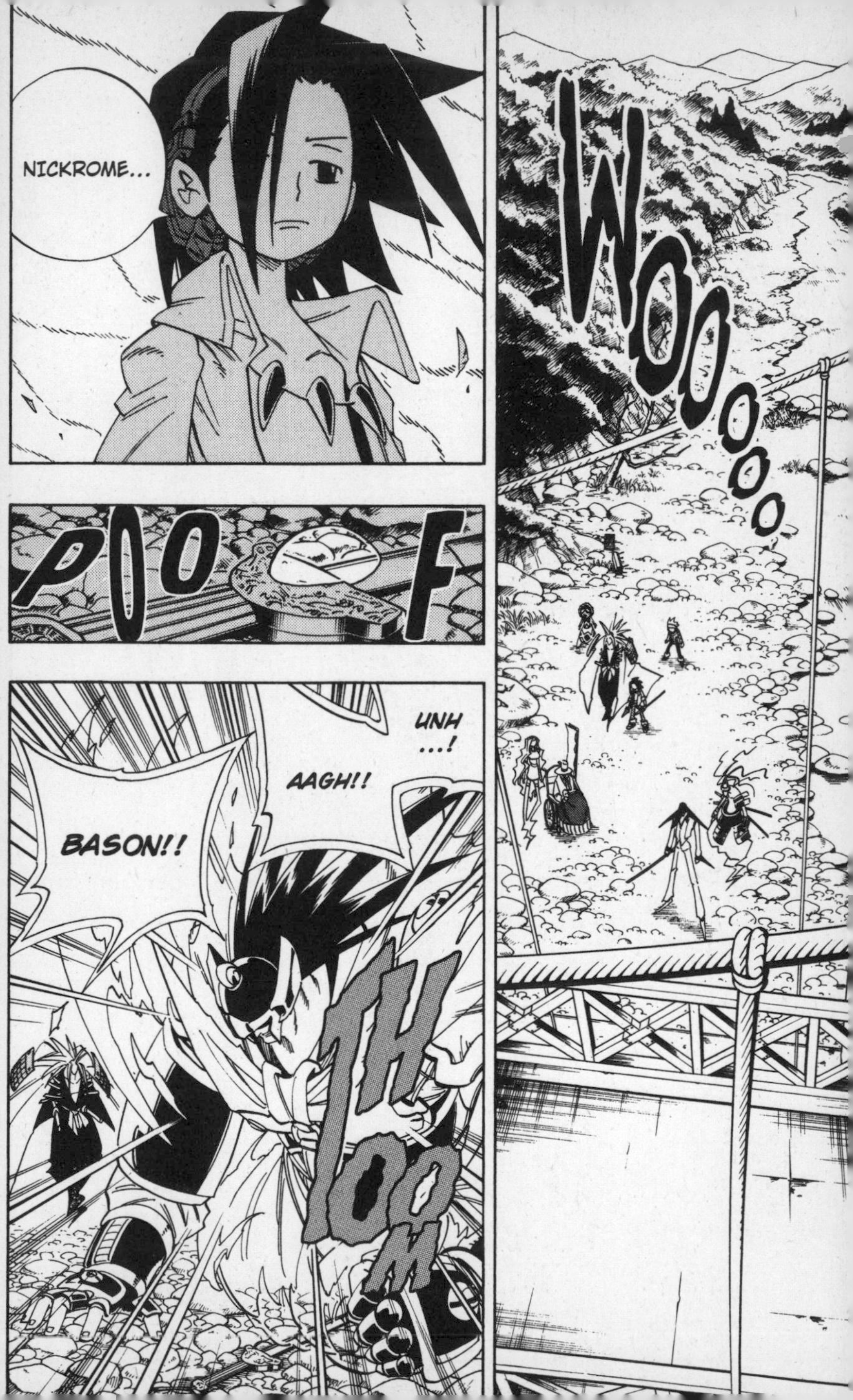
WOOOOOOOO
NICKROME...
POOF
UNH ...!
AAGH!!
BASON!!
THOOM

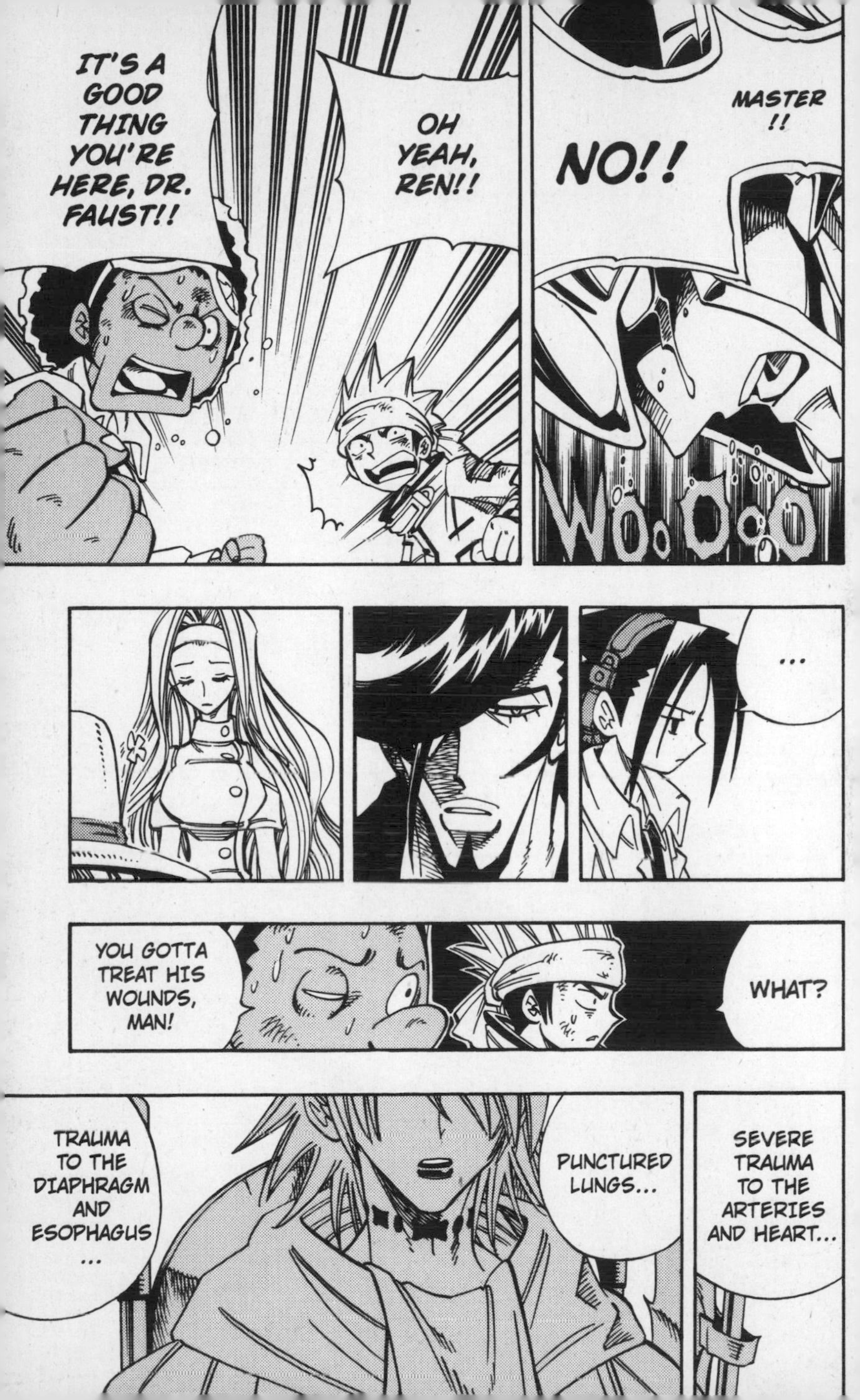

MASTER !!
NO!!
WOOOO
OH YEAH, REN!!
IT'S A GOOD THING YOU'RE HERE, DR. FAUST!!
...
WHAT?
YOU GOTTA TREAT HIS WOUNDS, MAN!
SEVERE TRAUMA TO THE ARTERIES AND HEART...
PUNCTURED LUNGS...
TRAUMA TO THE DIAPHRAGM AND ESOPHAGUS ...

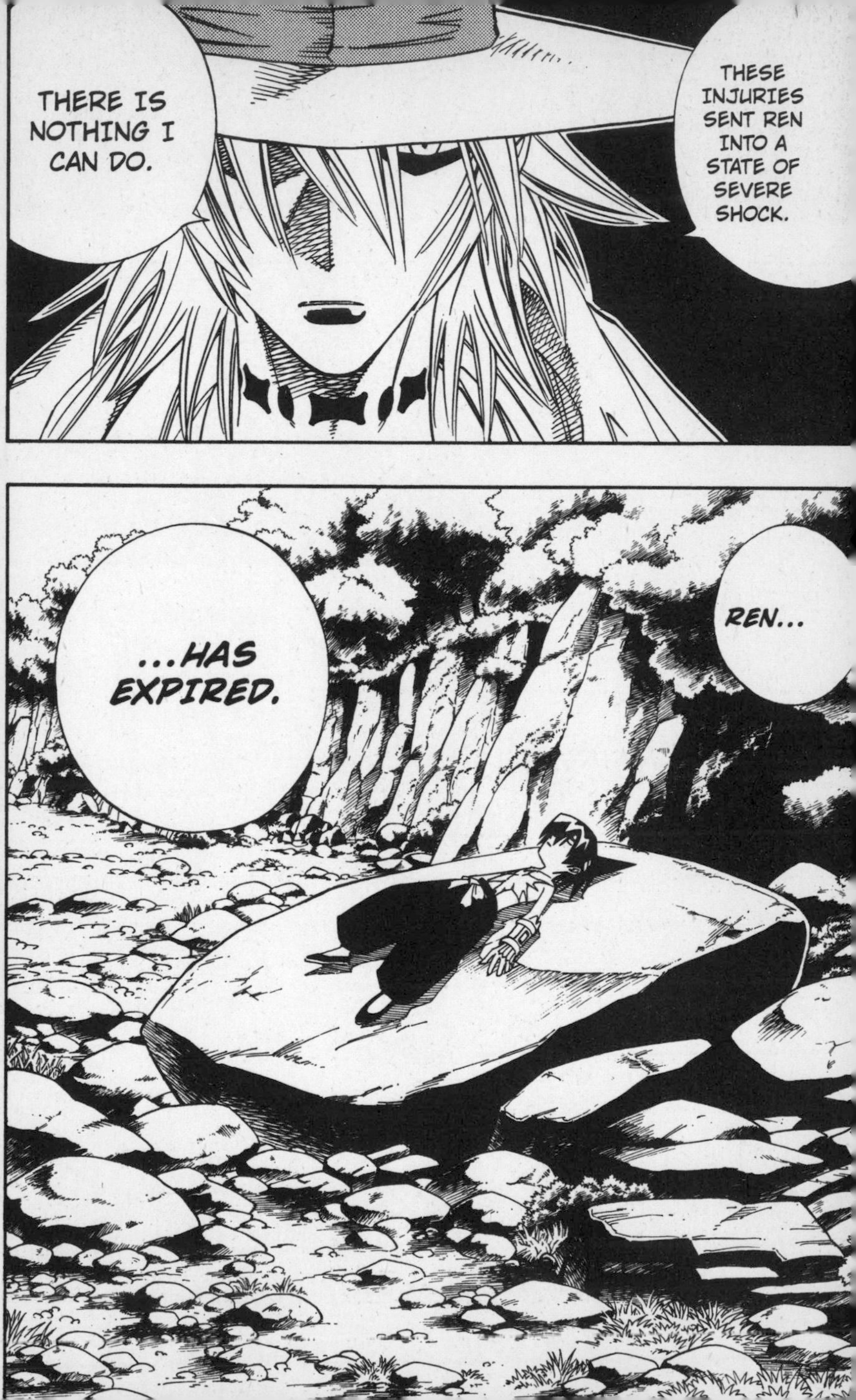
THESE INJURIES SENT REN INTO A STATE OF SEVERE SHOCK.
THERE IS NOTHING I CAN DO.
REN...
...HAS EXPIRED.

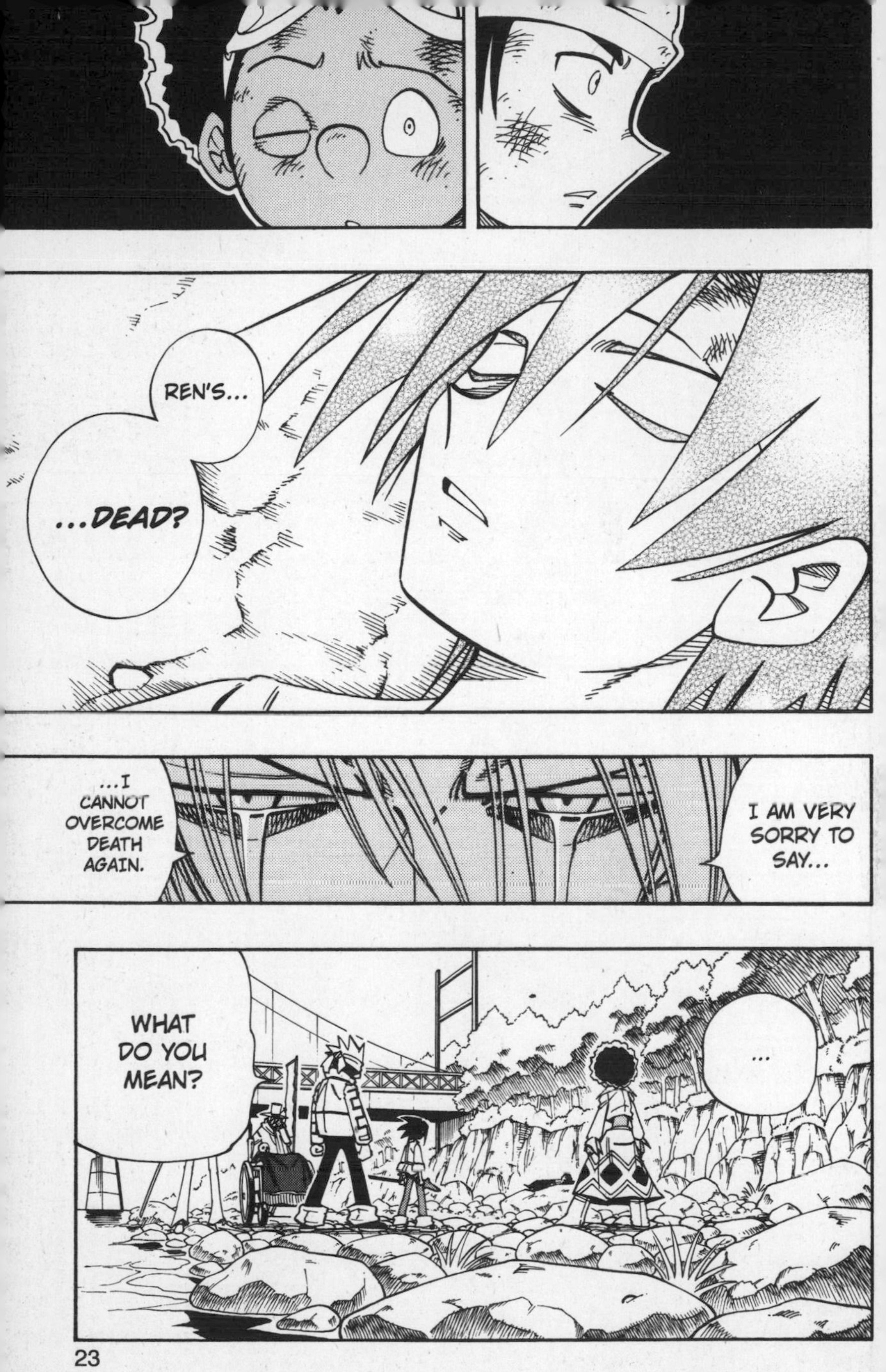
REN'S...
...DEAD?
I AM VERY SORRY TO SAY...
...I CANNOT OVERCOME DEATH AGAIN.
...
WHAT DO YOU MEAN?

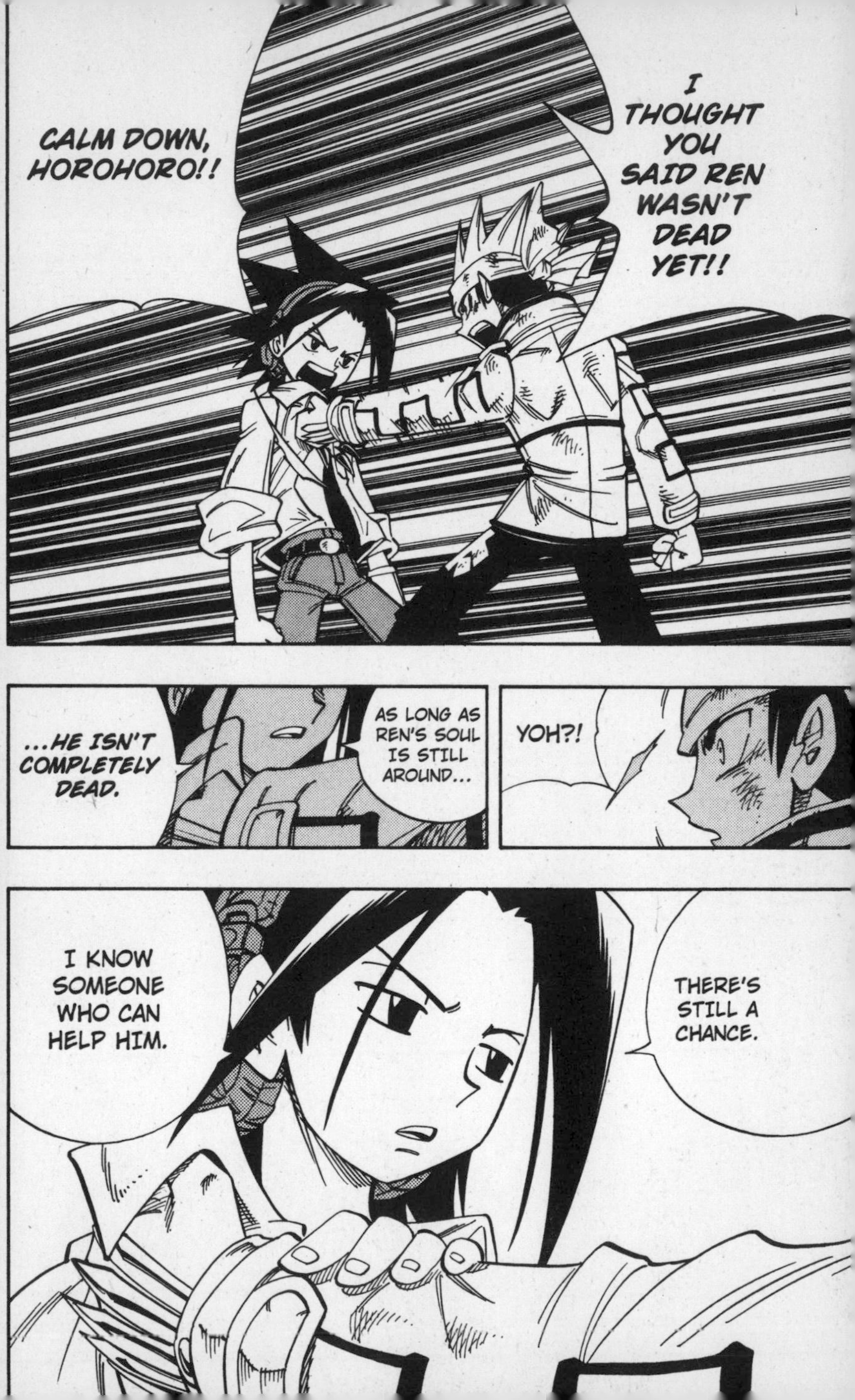
I THOUGHT YOU SAID REN WASN'T DEAD YET!!
CALM DOWN, HOROHORO!!
YOH?!
AS LONG AS REN'S SOUL IS STILL AROUND...
...HE ISN'T COMPLETELY DEAD.
THERE'S STILL A CHANCE.
I KNOW SOMEONE WHO CAN HELP HIM.

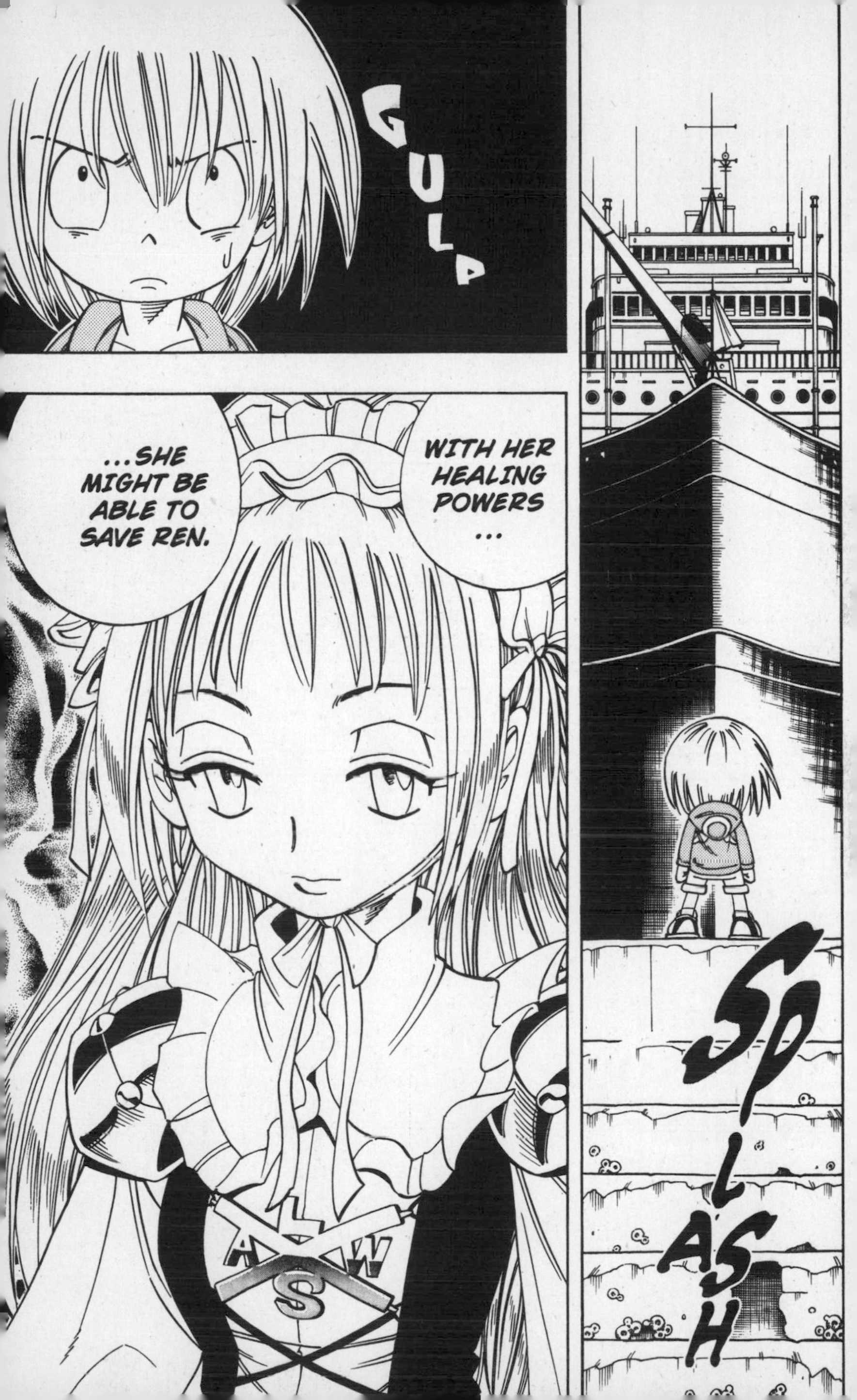
SPLASH
GULP
WITH HER HEALING POWERS ...
...SHE MIGHT BE ABLE TO SAVE REN.

SHAMAN KING CHARACTER FILE No.91

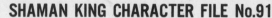

2001
(JAN)

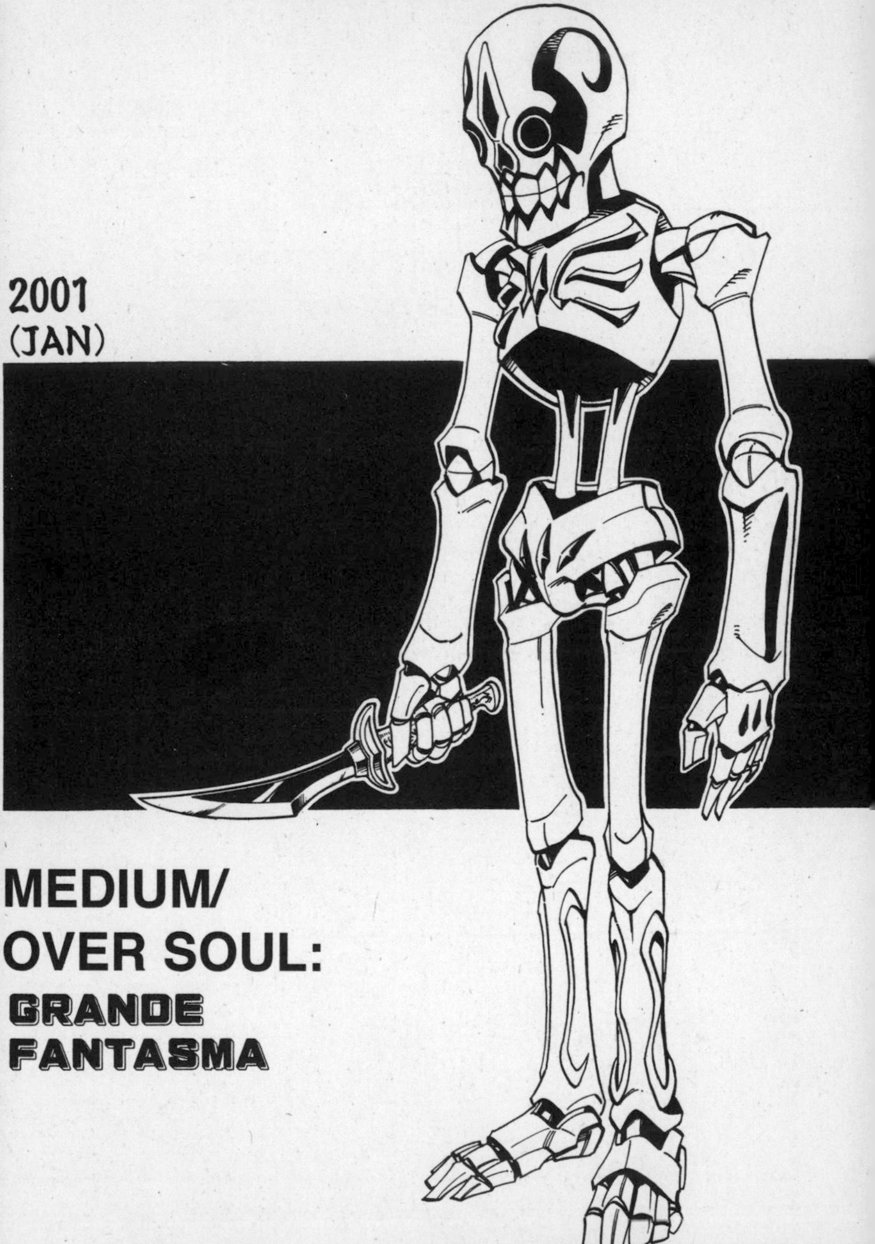

MEDIUM/
OVER SOUL:
GRANDE
FANTASMA

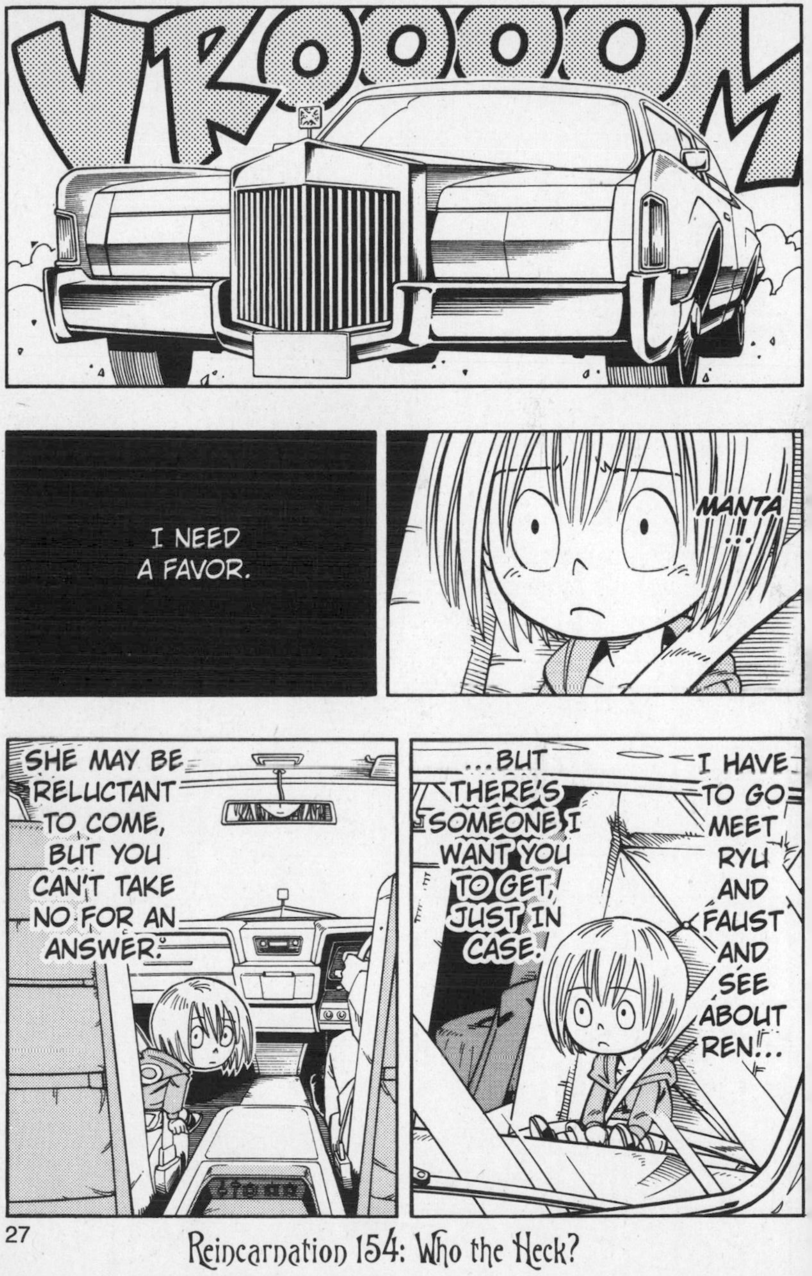
VROOOOOM
MANTA !!...
I NEED A FAVOR.
I HAVE TO GO MEET RYU AND FAUST AND SEE ABOUT REN!...
...BUT THERE'S SOMEONE I WANT YOU TO GET, JUST IN CASE.
SHE MAY BE RELUCTANT TO COME, BUT YOU CAN'T TAKE NO FOR AN ANSWER.

Reincarnation 154: Who the Heck?

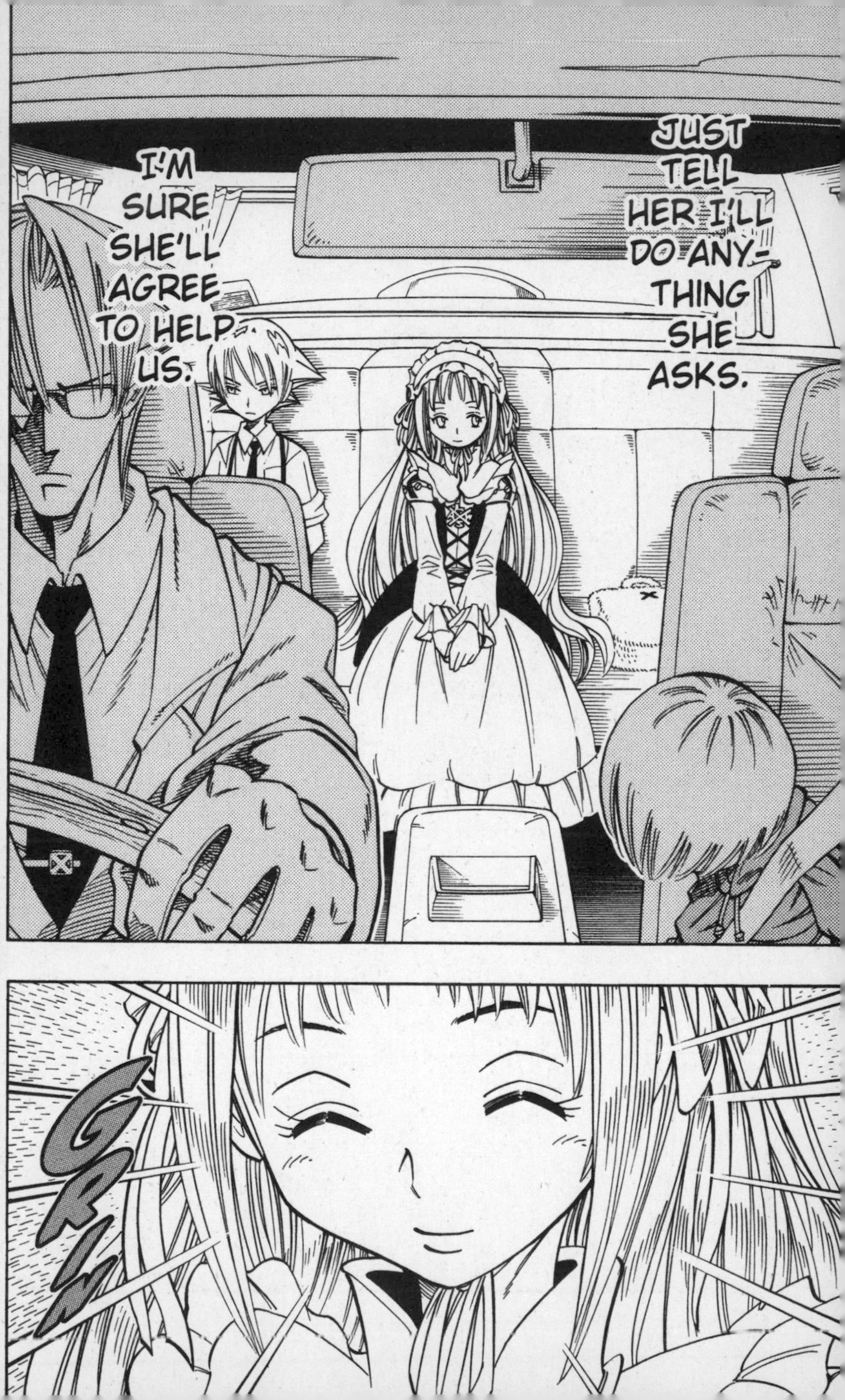
JUST TELL HER I'LL DO ANYTHING SHE ASKS.
I'M SURE SHE'LL AGREE TO HELP US.
GRIN

Reincarnation 154: Who the Heck?

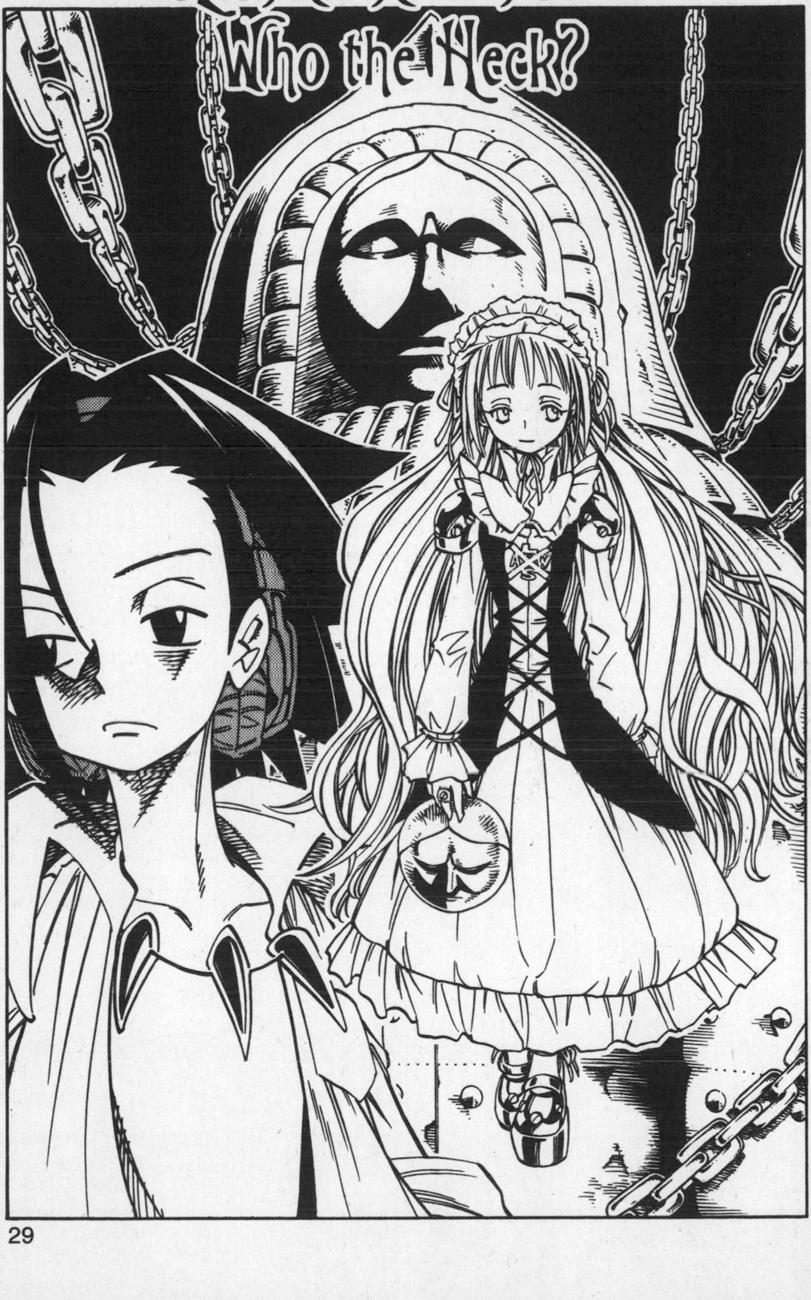

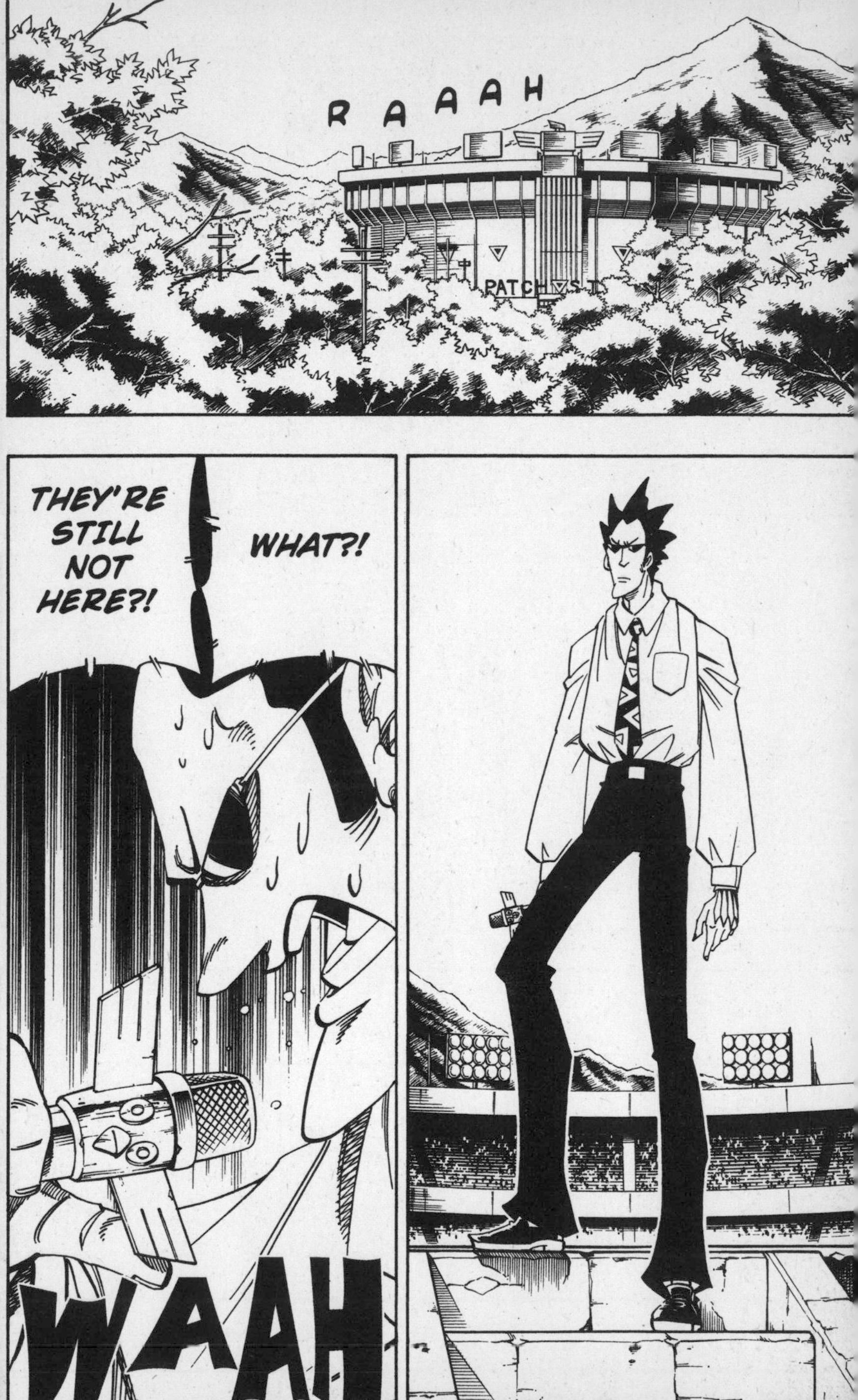
RAAAH
PATCH
THEY'RE STILL NOT HERE?!
WHAT?!
WAAH

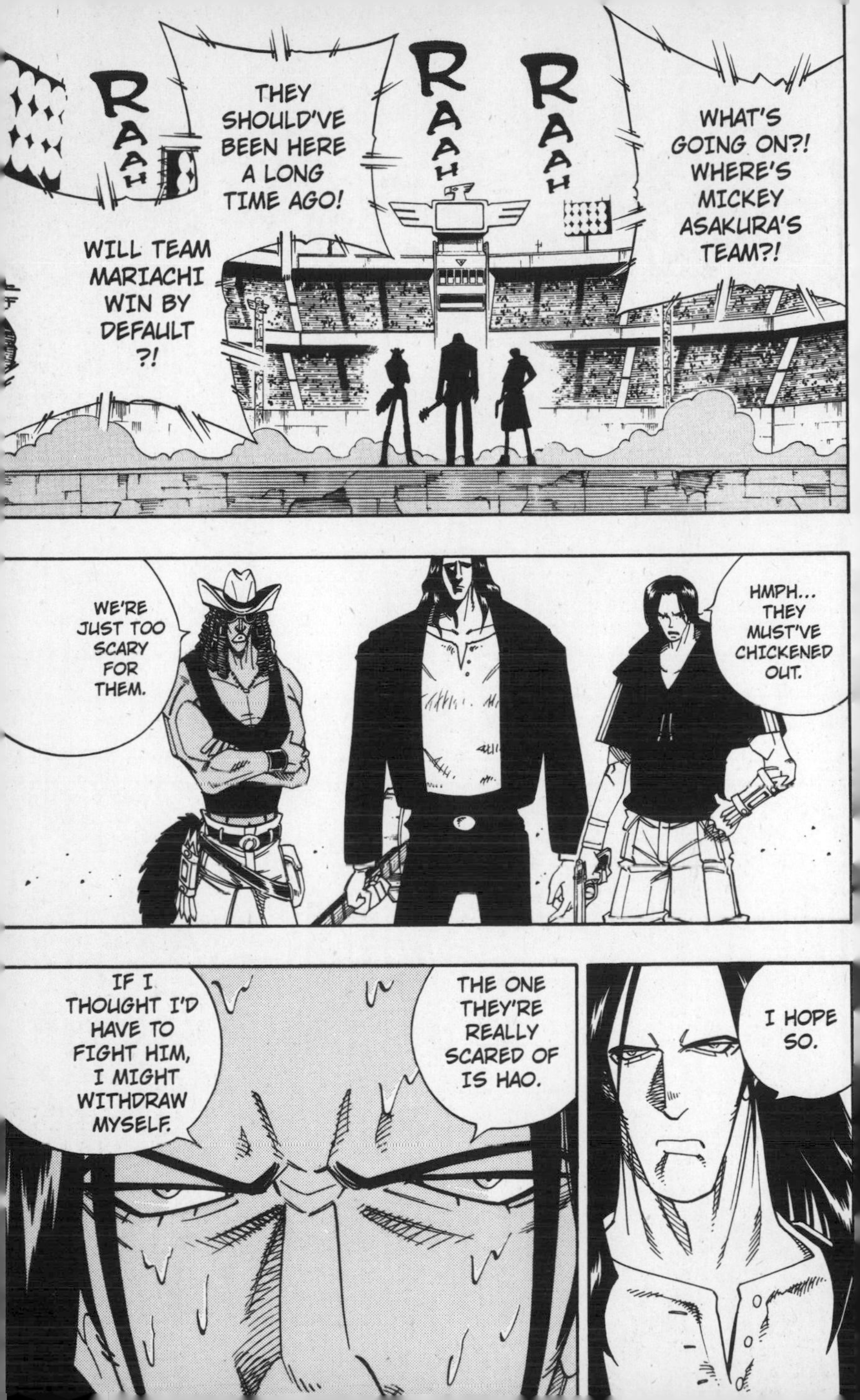
WHAT'S GOING ON?! WHERE'S MICKEY ASAKURA'S TEAM?!
RAAH
RAAH
THEY SHOULD'VE BEEN HERE A LONG TIME AGO!
RAAH
WILL TEAM MARIACHI WIN BY DEFAULT ?!
HMPH... THEY MUST'VE CHICKENED OUT.
WE'RE JUST TOO SCARY FOR THEM.
I HOPE SO.
THE ONE THEY'RE REALLY SCARED OF IS HAO.
IF I THOUGHT I'D HAVE TO FIGHT HIM, I MIGHT WITHDRAW MYSELF.

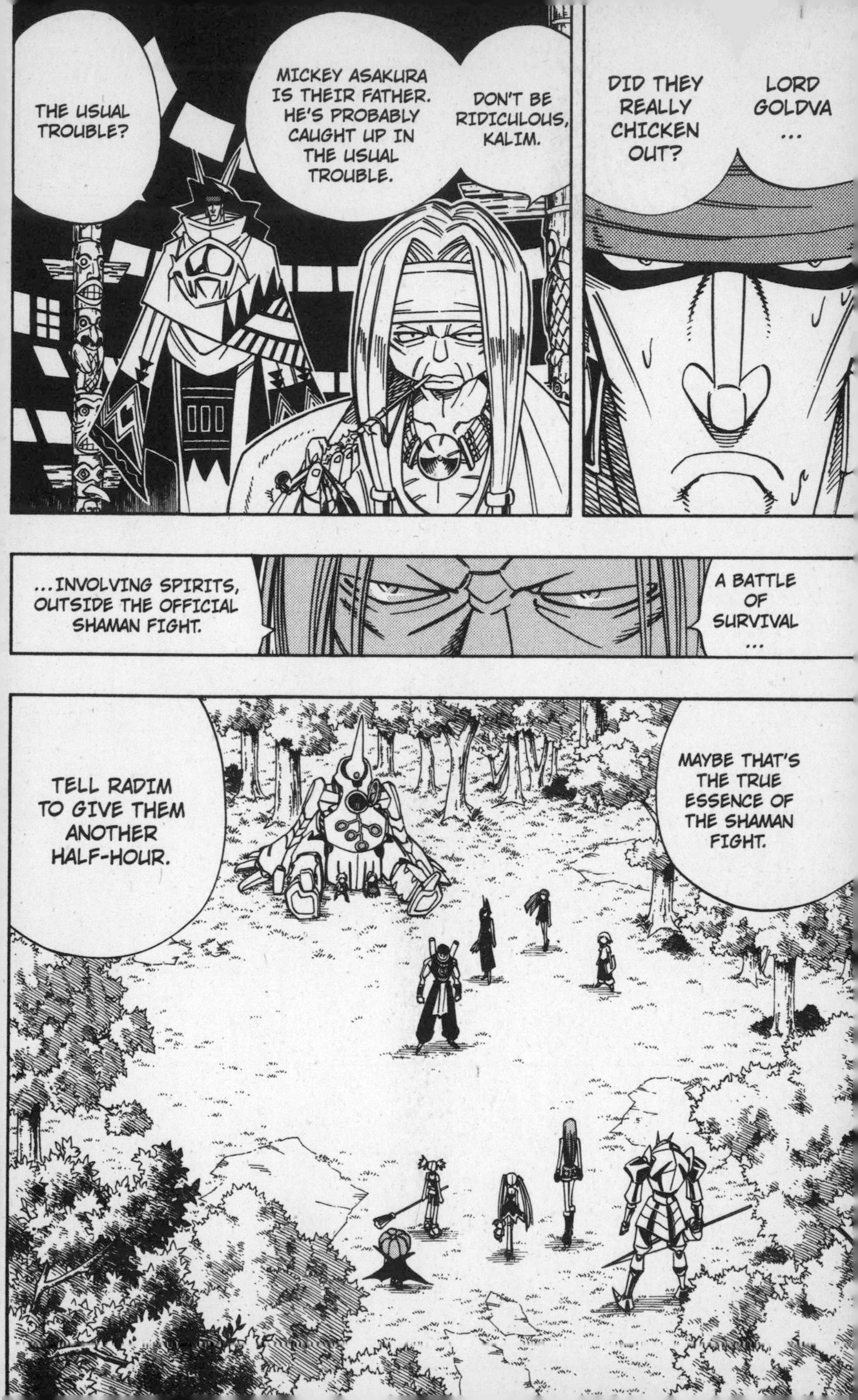
LORD GOLDVA ...
DID THEY REALLY CHICKEN OUT?
DON'T BE RIDICULOUS, KALIM.
MICKEY ASAKURA IS THEIR FATHER. HE'S PROBABLY CAUGHT UP IN THE USUAL TROUBLE.
THE USUAL TROUBLE?
A BATTLE OF SURVIVAL ...
...INVOLVING SPIRITS, OUTSIDE THE OFFICIAL SHAMAN FIGHT.
MAYBE THAT'S THE TRUE ESSENCE OF THE SHAMAN FIGHT.
TELL RADIM TO GIVE THEM ANOTHER HALF-HOUR.

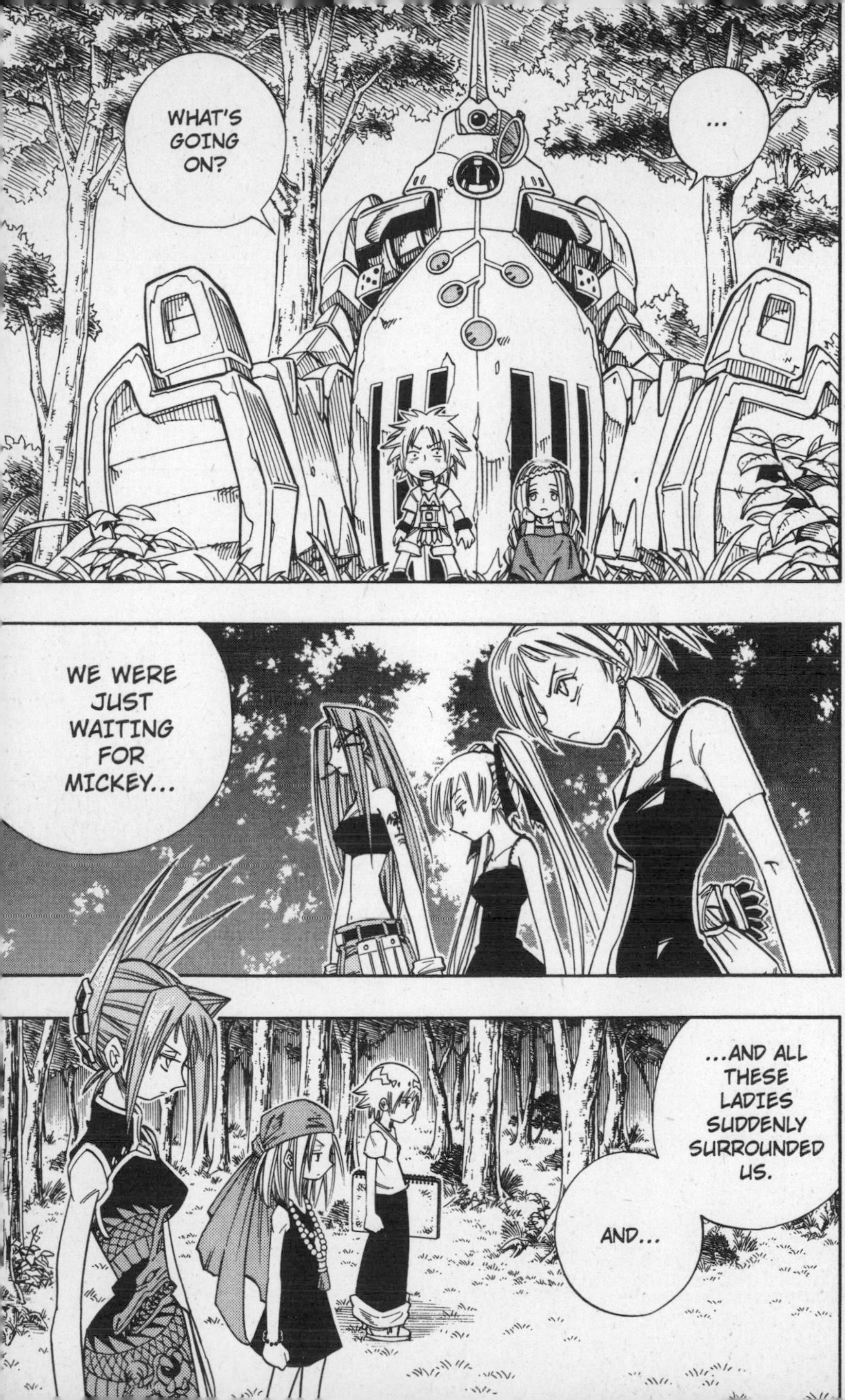
...
WHAT'S GOING ON?
WE WERE JUST WAITING FOR MICKEY...
...AND ALL THESE LADIES SUDDENLY SURROUNDED US.
AND...

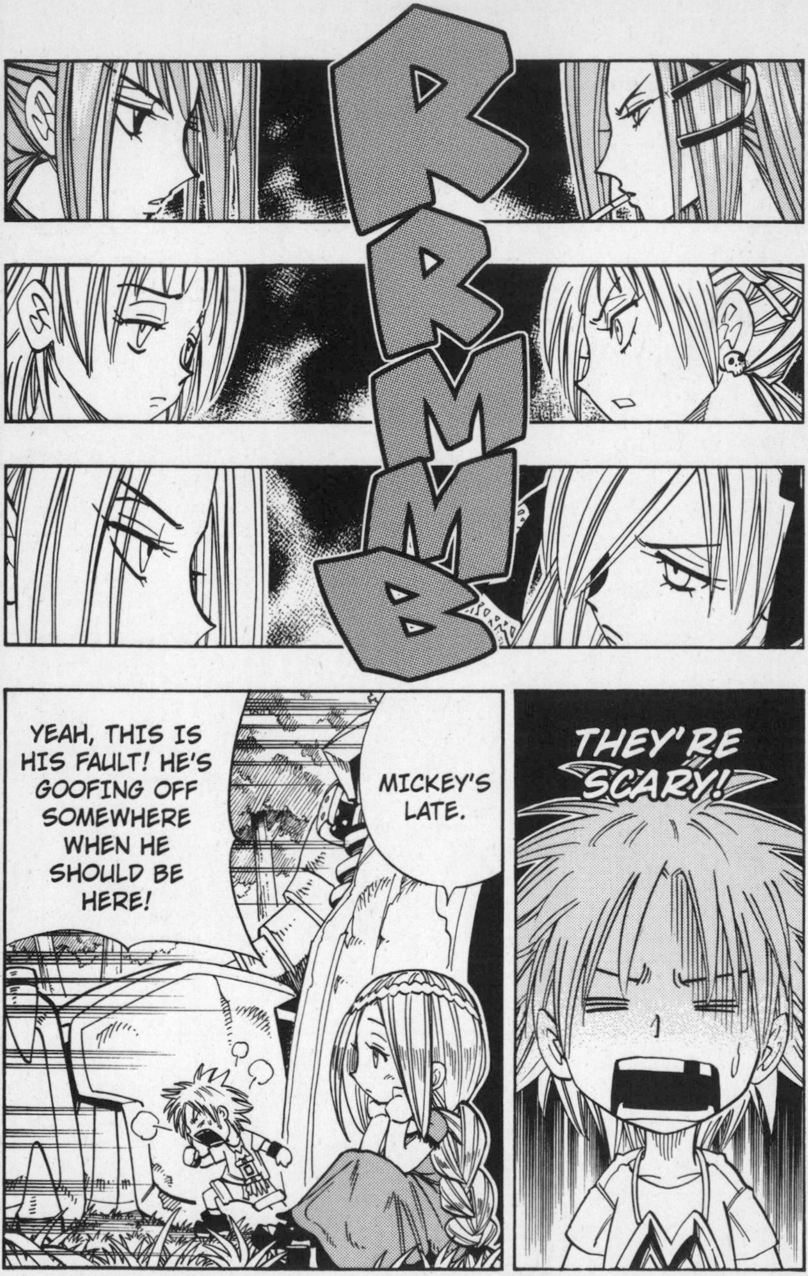
RRMMB
THEY'RE SCARY!
MICKEY'S LATE.
YEAH, THIS IS HIS FAULT! HE'S GOOFING OFF SOMEWHERE WHEN HE SHOULD BE HERE!

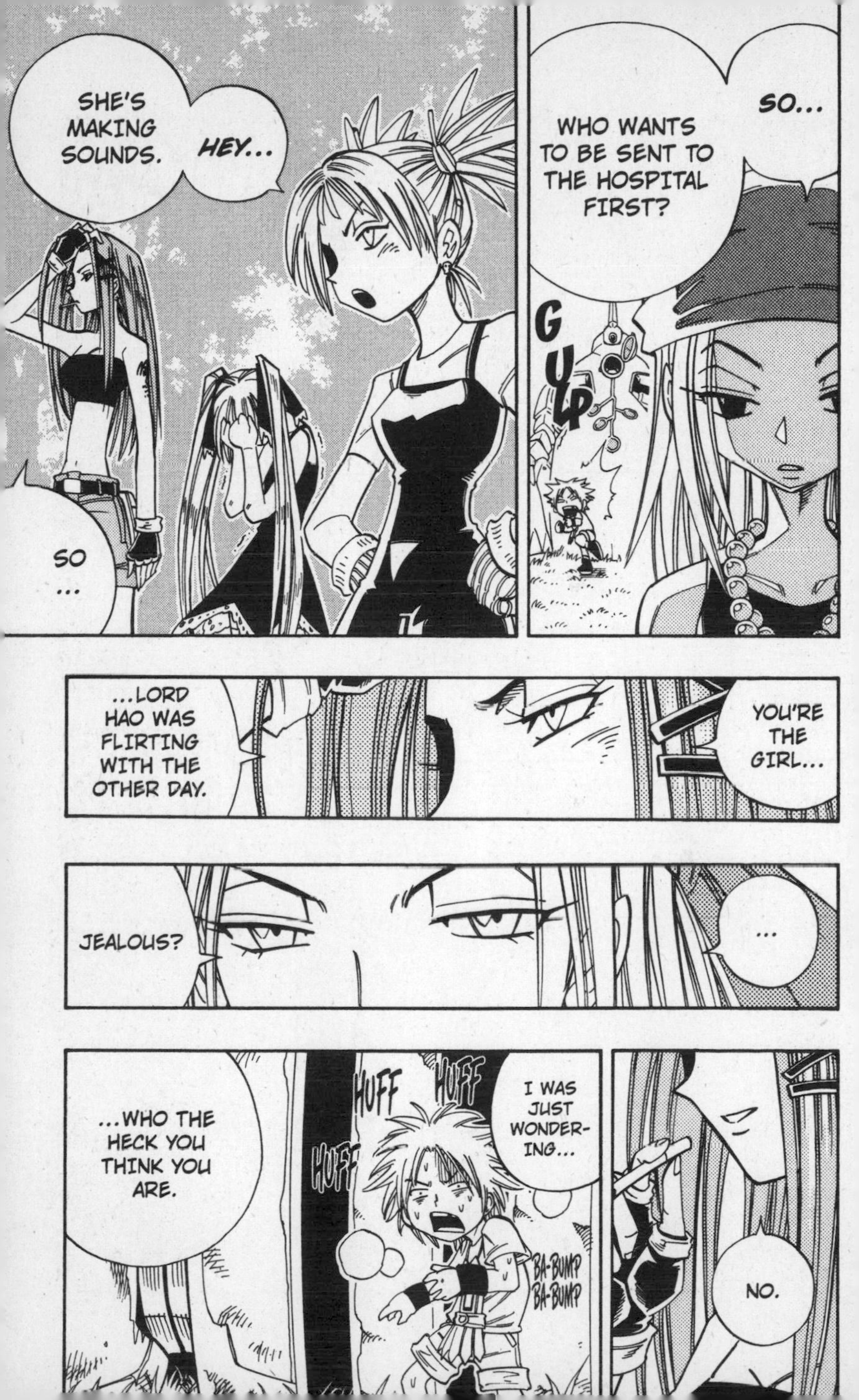
SO...
WHO WANTS TO BE SENT TO THE HOSPITAL FIRST?
GULP
HEY...
SHE'S MAKING SOUNDS.
SO ...
YOU'RE THE GIRL...
...LORD HAO WAS FLIRTING WITH THE OTHER DAY.
...
JEALOUS?
NO.
I WAS JUST WONDERING...
HUFF HUFF
HUFF
BA-BUMP BA-BUMP
...WHO THE HECK YOU THINK YOU ARE.

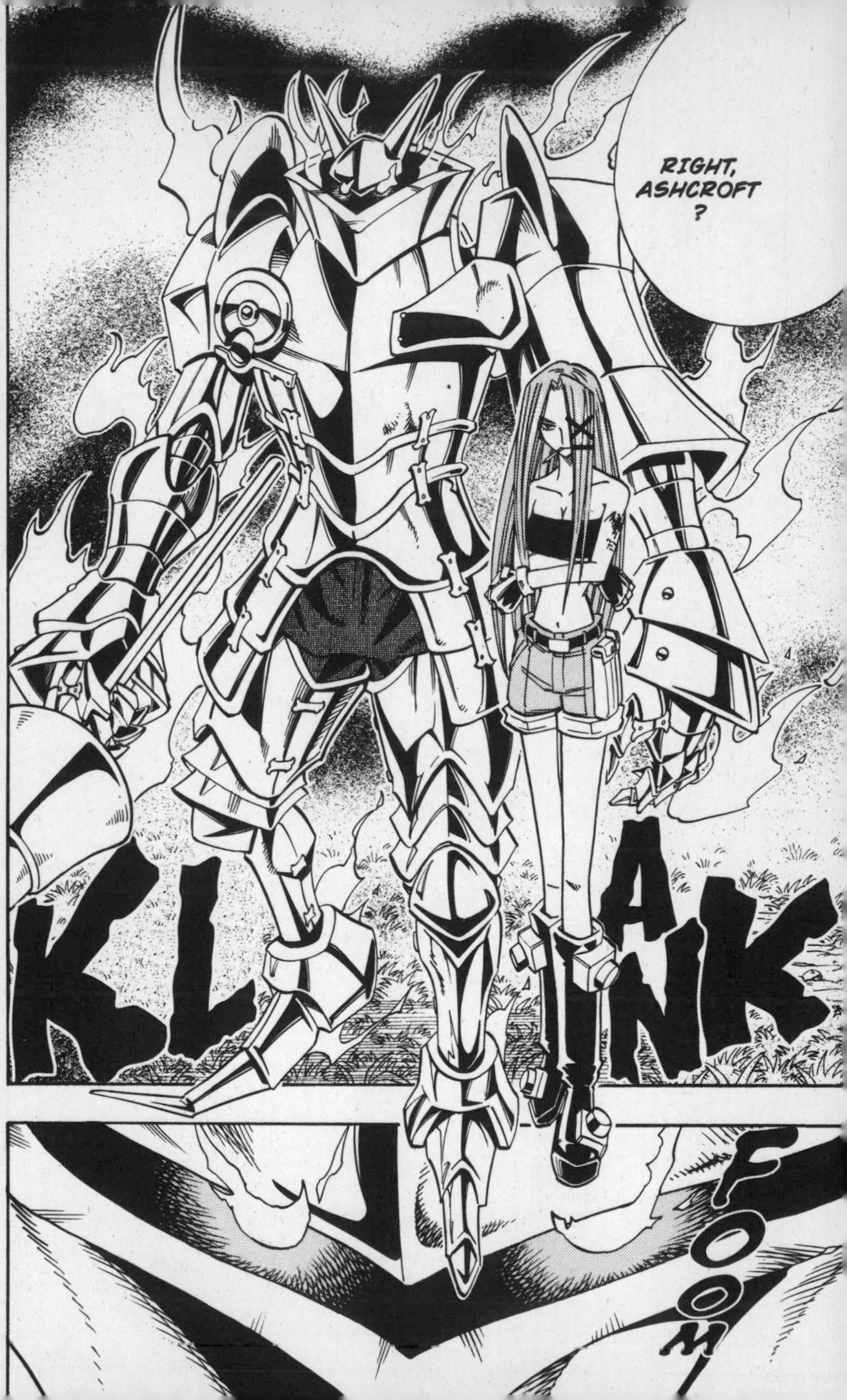
RIGHT, ASHCROFT ?
KLANK
FOOOM

READ THIS WAY

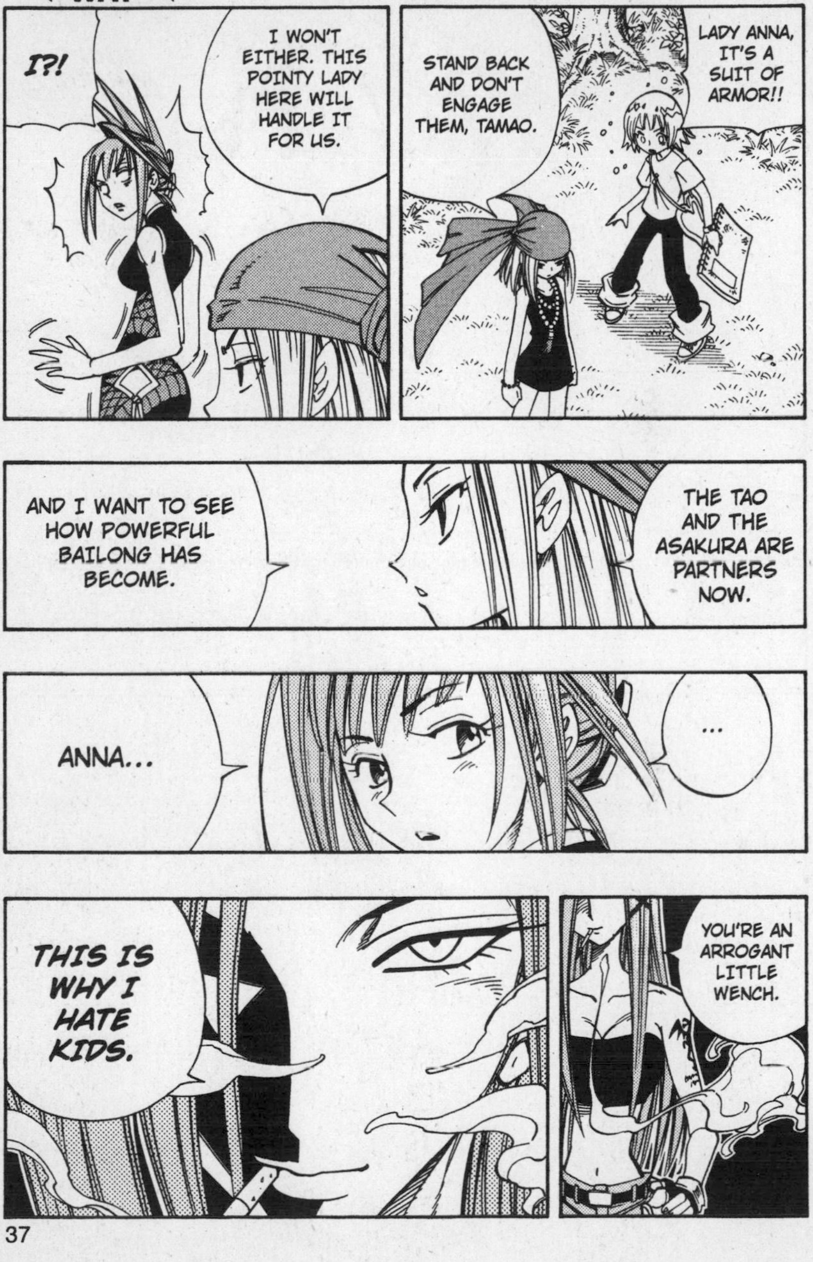
LADY ANNA, IT'S A SUIT OF ARMOR!!
STAND BACK AND DON'T ENGAGE THEM, TAMAO.
I WON'T EITHER. THIS POINTY LADY HERE WILL HANDLE IT FOR US.
I?!
THE TAO AND THE ASAKURA ARE PARTNERS NOW.
AND I WANT TO SEE HOW POWERFUL BAILONG HAS BECOME.
...
ANNA...
YOU'RE AN ARROGANT LITTLE WENCH.
THIS IS WHY I HATE KIDS.

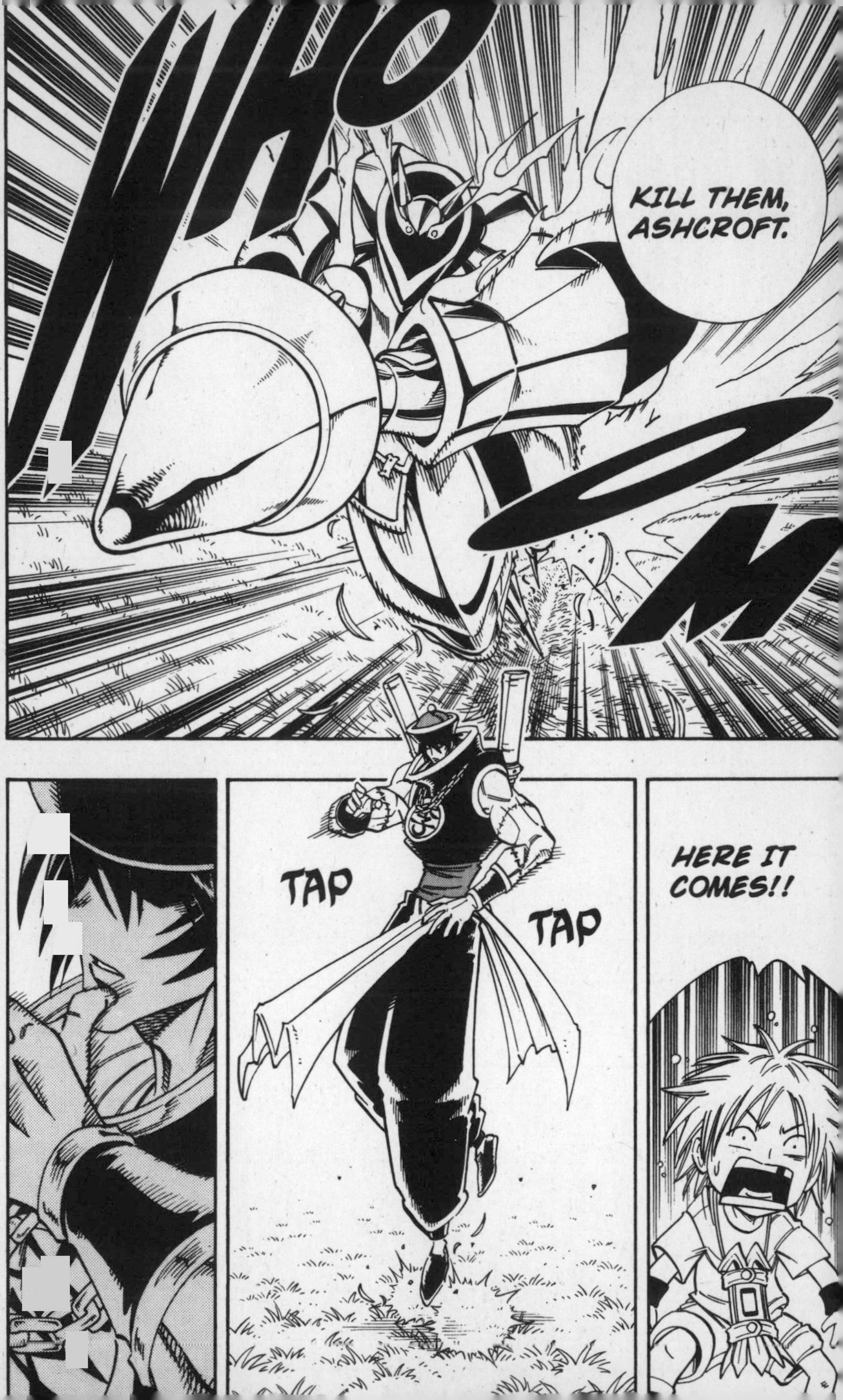
WHOOM
KILL THEM, ASHCROFT.
HERE IT COMES!!
TAP
TAP

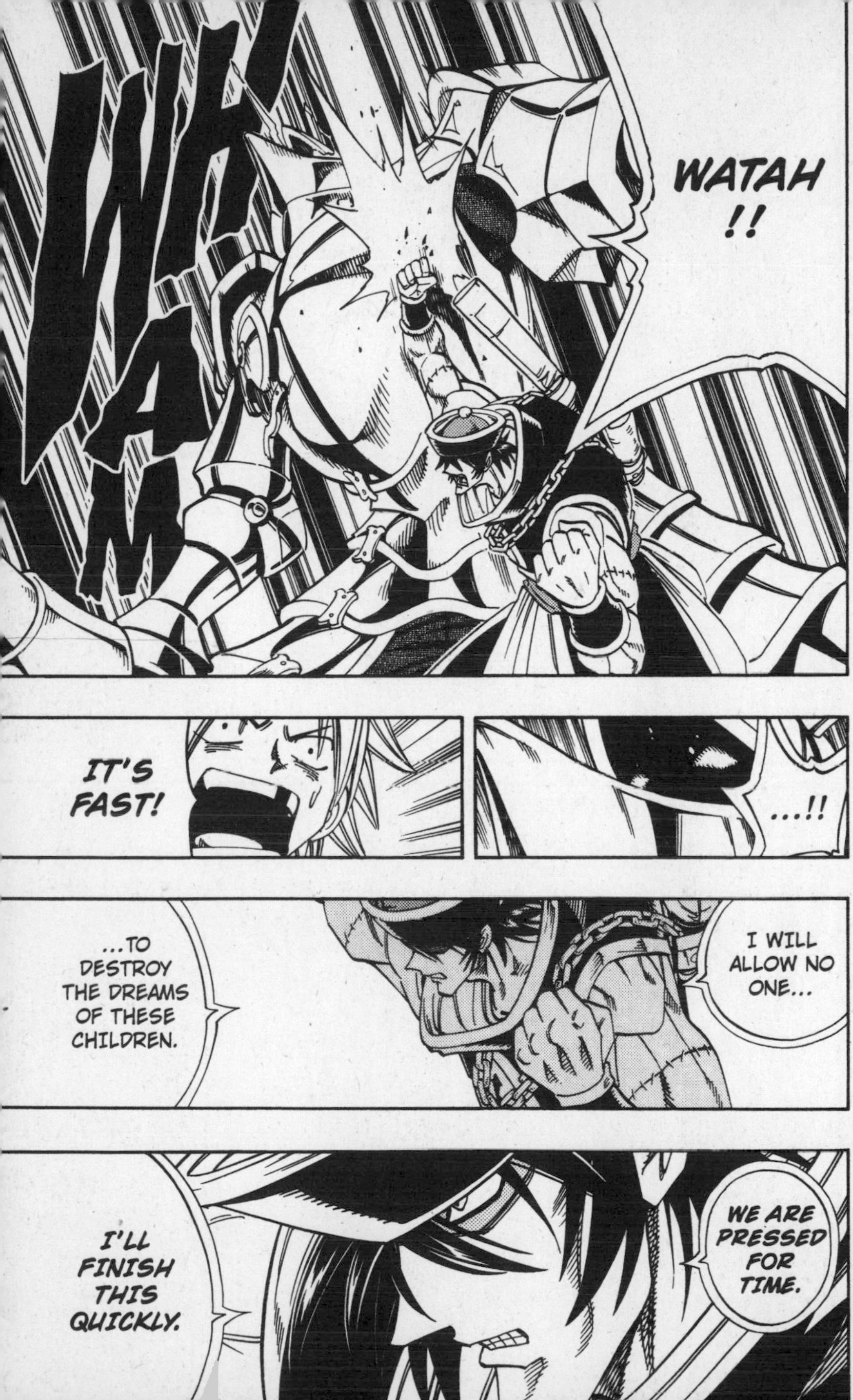
WATAH !!
...!!
IT'S FAST!
I WILL ALLOW NO ONE...
...TO DESTROY THE DREAMS OF THESE CHILDREN.
WE ARE PRESSED FOR TIME.
I'LL FINISH THIS QUICKLY.

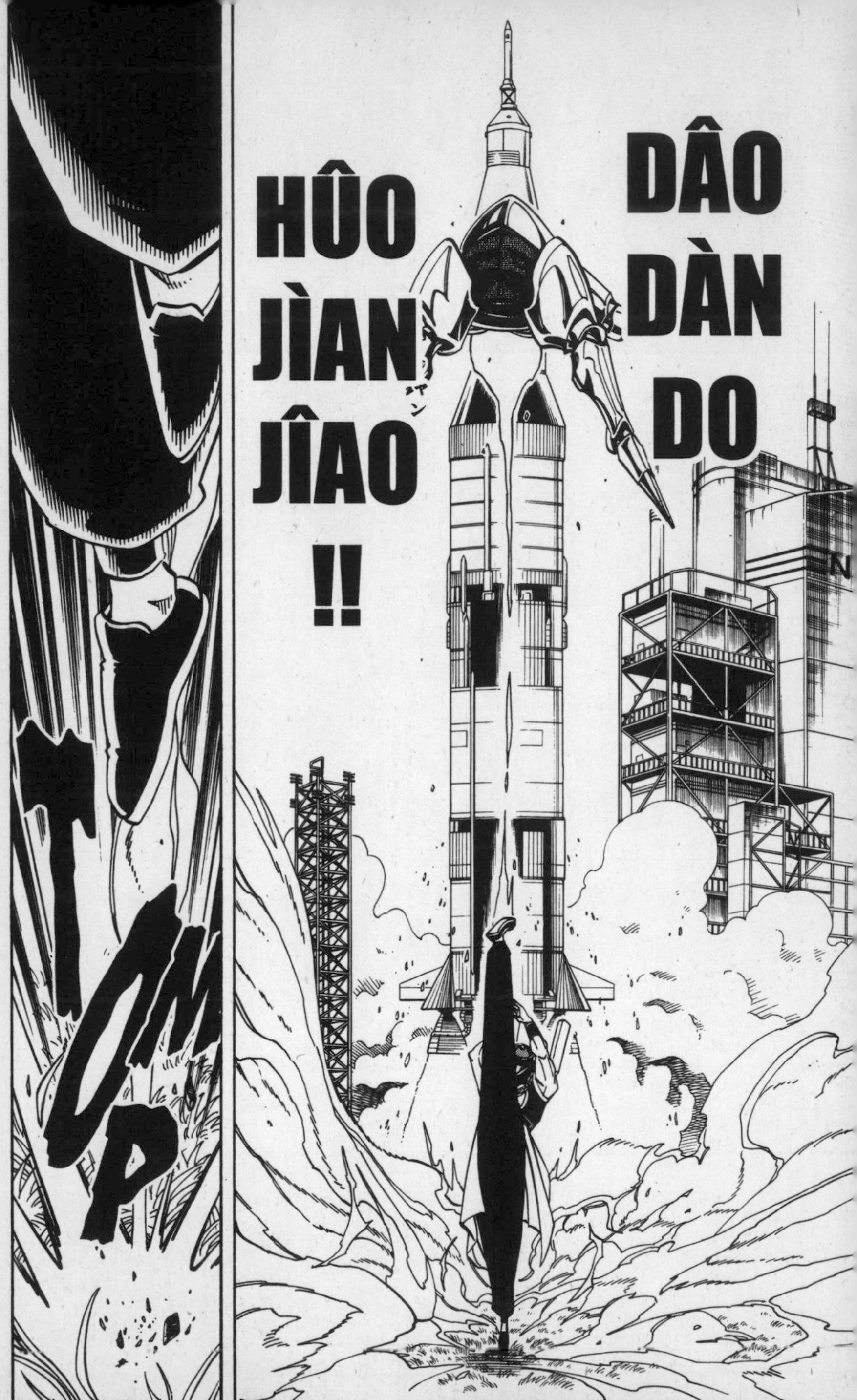
DÂO DÀN DO
HÛO JÌAN JÎAO !!

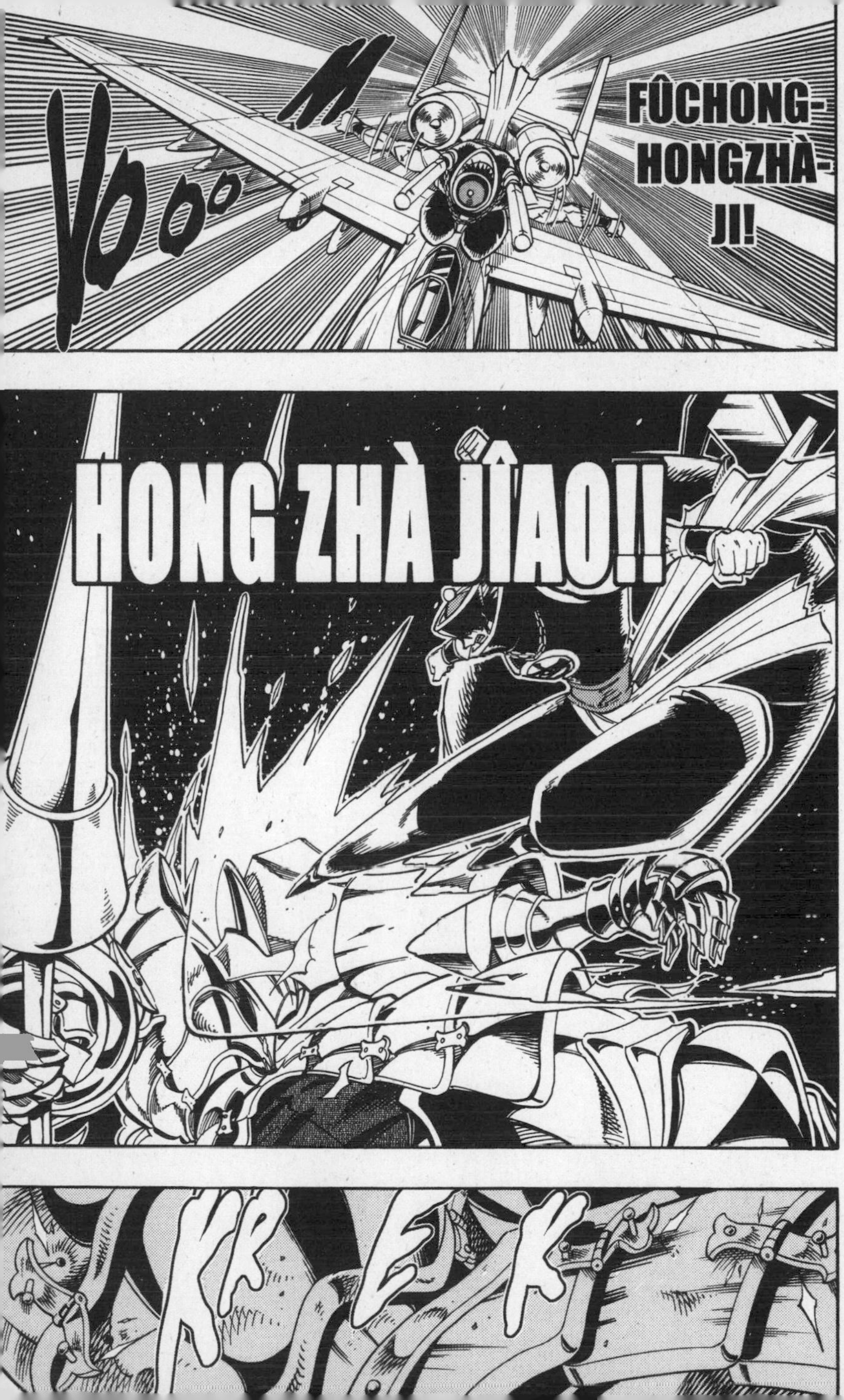
FÛCHONG-HONGZHÀ-JI!
VOOOM
HONG ZHÀ JÎAO!!
KREK

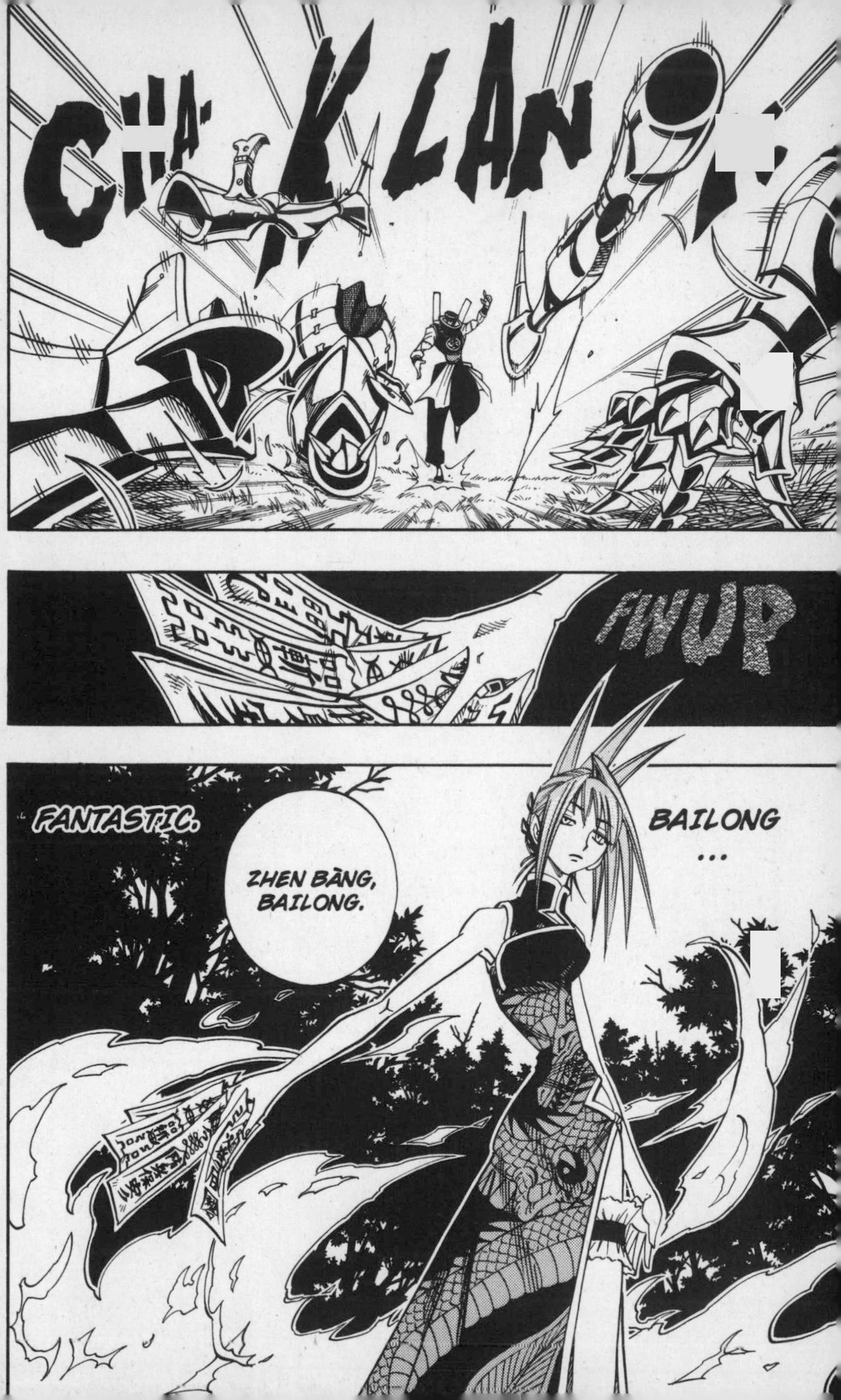
CHA-KLAN
FWUP
BAILONG ...
ZHEN BÀNG, BAILONG.
FANTASTIC.

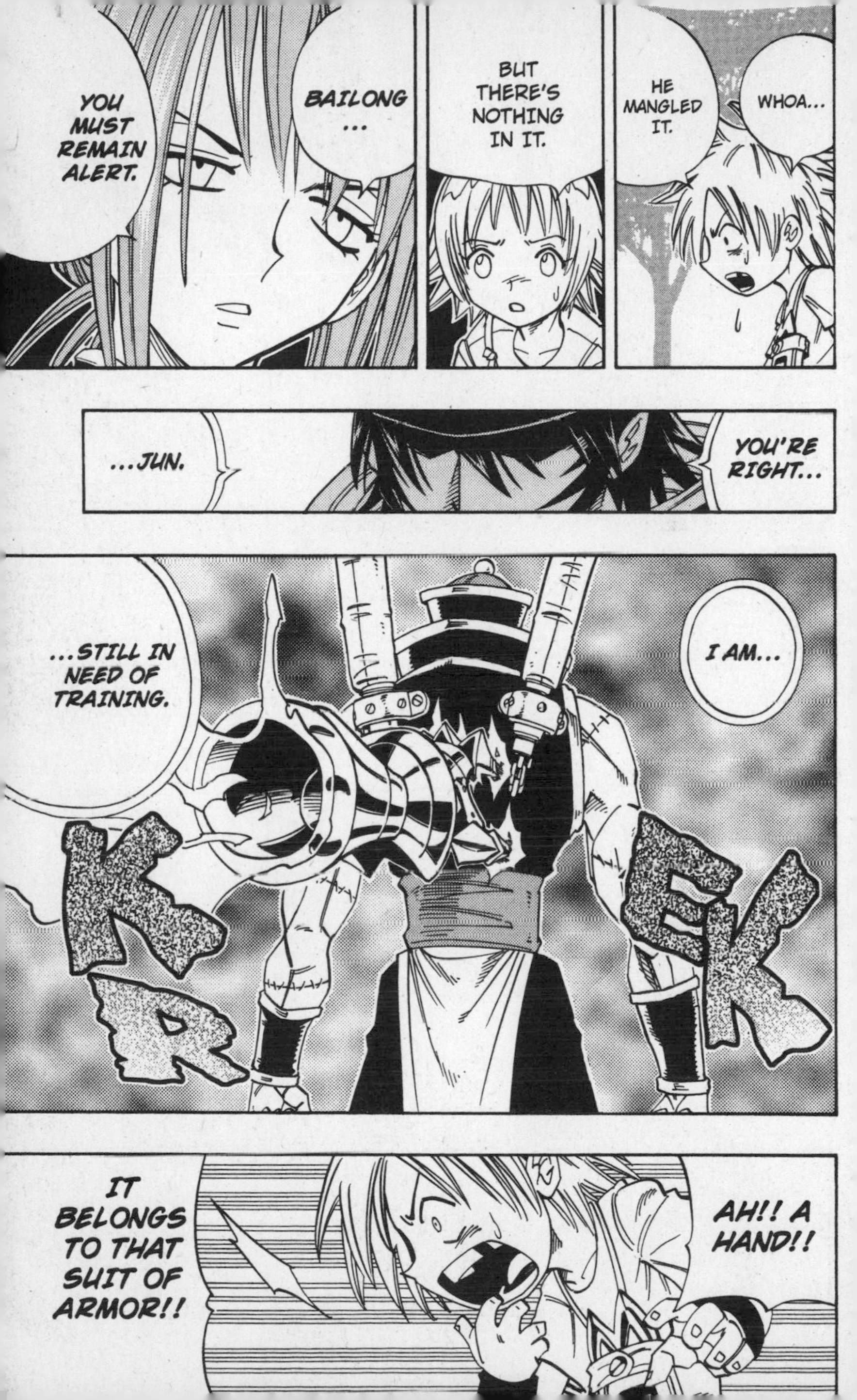
WHOA...
HE MANGLED IT.
BUT THERE'S NOTHING IN IT.
BAILONG ...
YOU MUST REMAIN ALERT.
YOU'RE RIGHT...
...JUN.
I AM...
...STILL IN NEED OF TRAINING.
KREK
AH!! A HAND!!
IT BELONGS TO THAT SUIT OF ARMOR!!

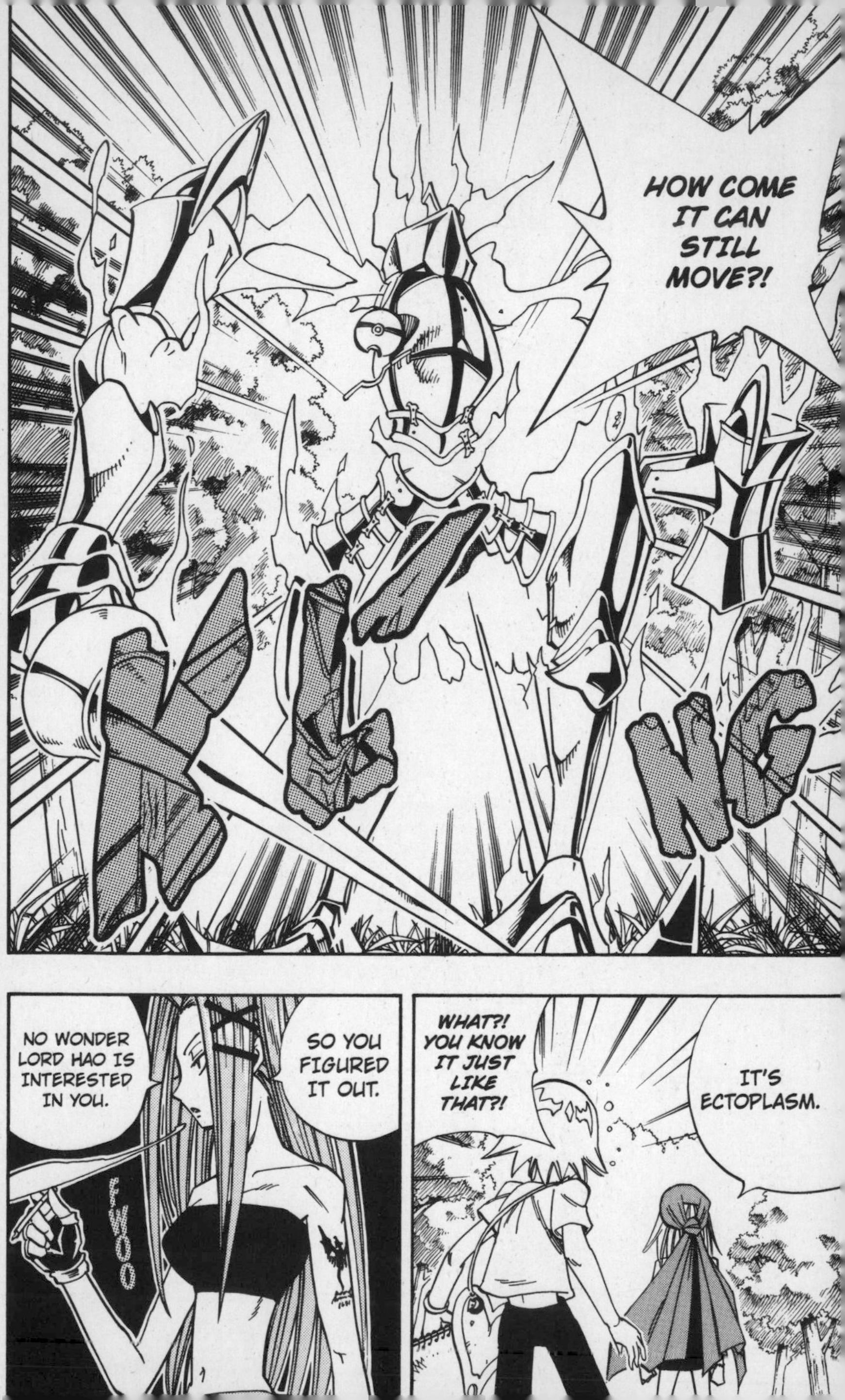
HOW COME IT CAN STILL MOVE?!
NG
IT'S ECTOPLASM.
WHAT?! YOU KNOW IT JUST LIKE THAT?!
SO YOU FIGURED IT OUT.
NO WONDER LORD HAO IS INTERESTED IN YOU.
FWOO

READ THIS WAY

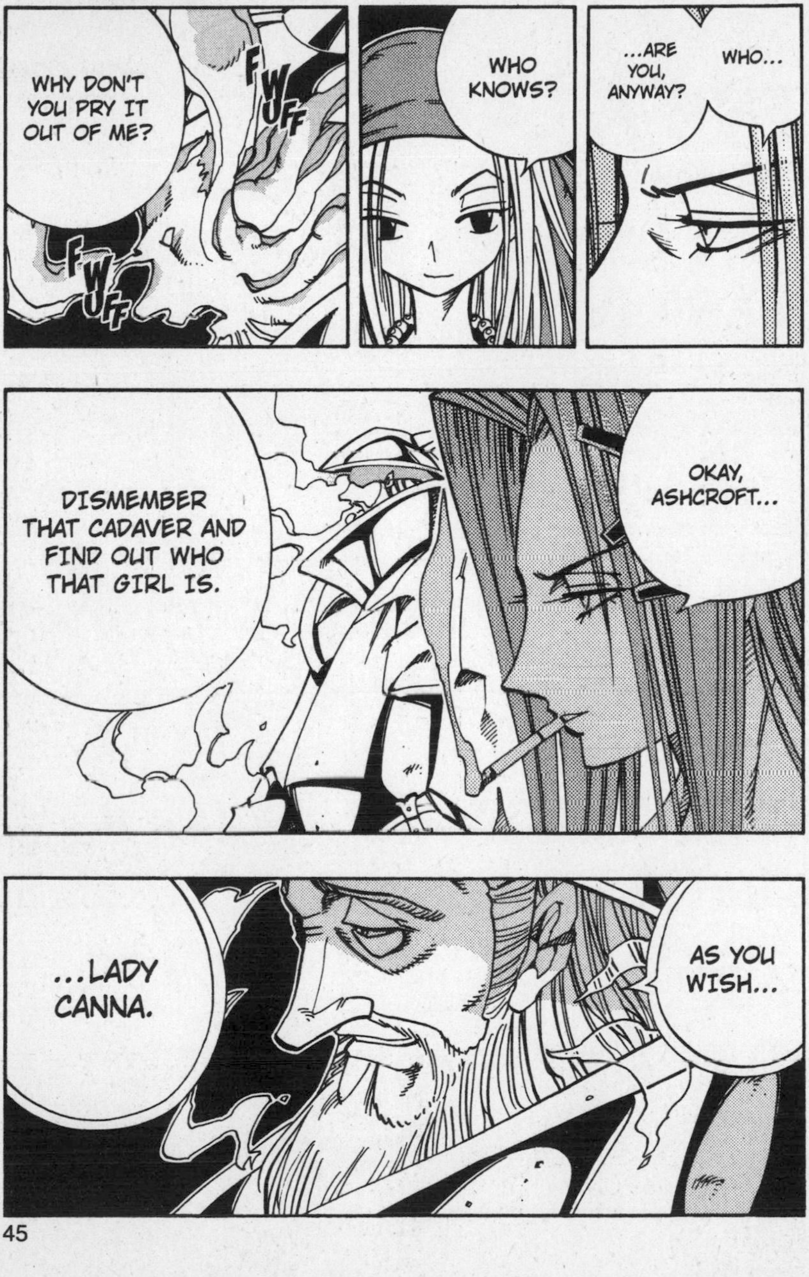
WHO... ...ARE YOU, ANYWAY?
WHO KNOWS?
WHY DON'T YOU PRY IT OUT OF ME?
FWUFF
FWUFF
OKAY, ASHCROFT...
DISMEMBER THAT CADAVER AND FIND OUT WHO THAT GIRL IS.
AS YOU WISH...
...LADY CANNA.

SHAMAN KING ITEM FILE No.51

THE X-LAWS
PRIVATE CAR, LINCOLN X
1972 LINCOLN CONTINENTAL MARK IV

2001
(JAN)

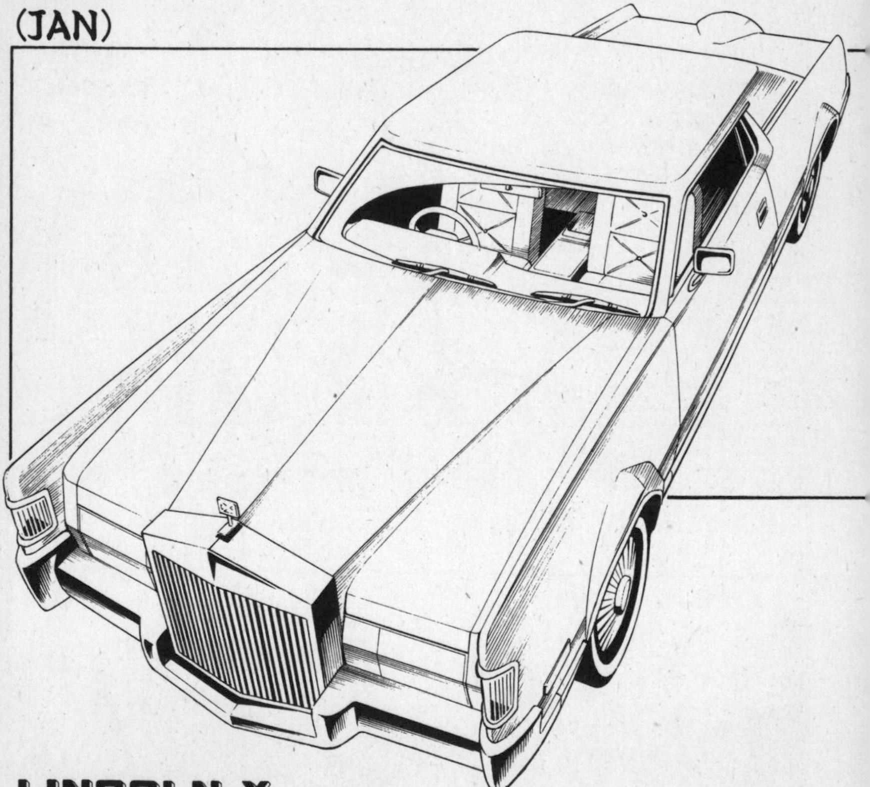

LINCOLN-X

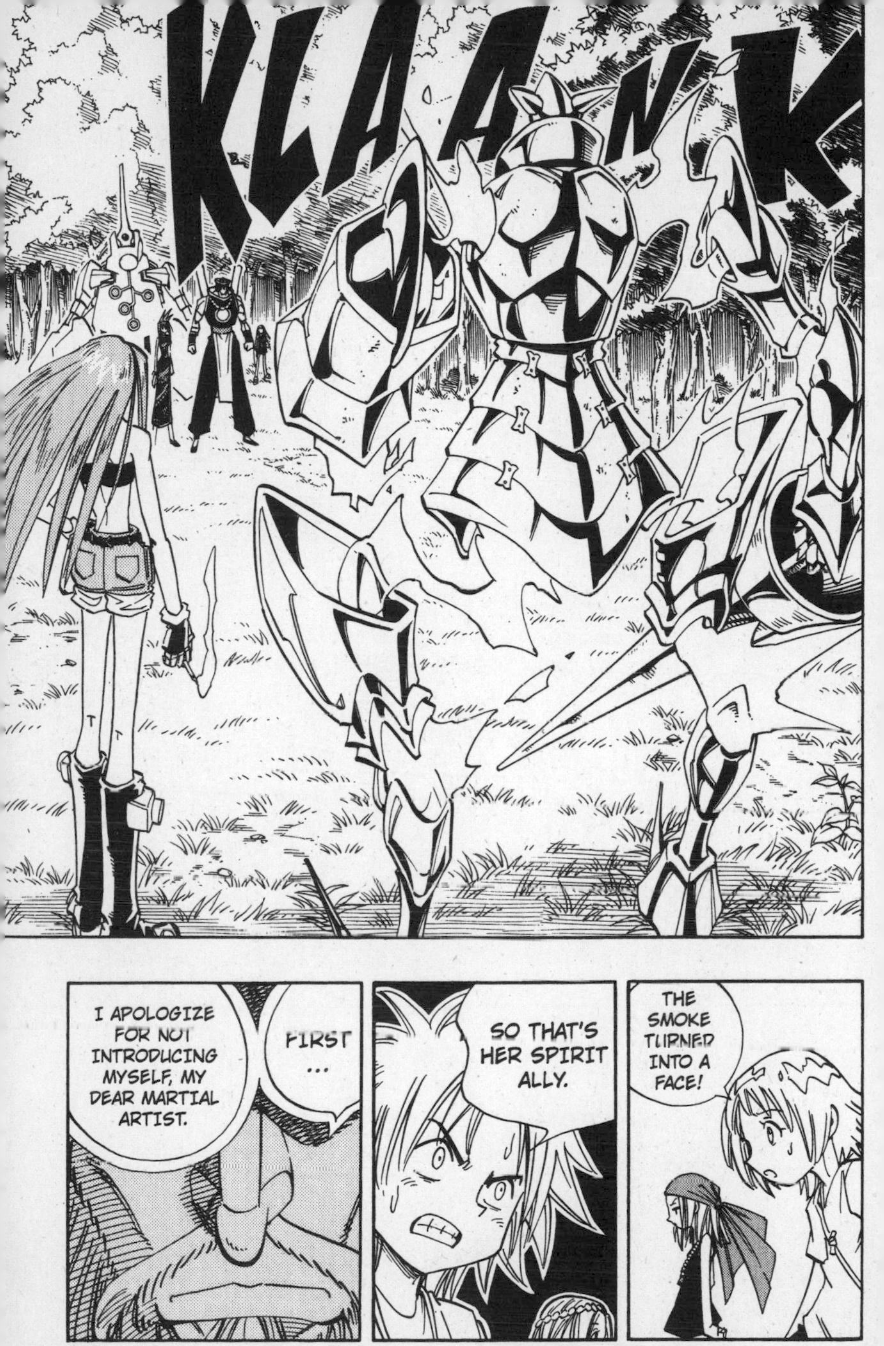
KLAANK
THE SMOKE TURNED INTO A FACE!
SO THAT'S HER SPIRIT ALLY.
FIRST...
I APOLOGIZE FOR NOT INTRODUCING MYSELF, MY DEAR MARTIAL ARTIST.

Reincarnation 155: My Terms

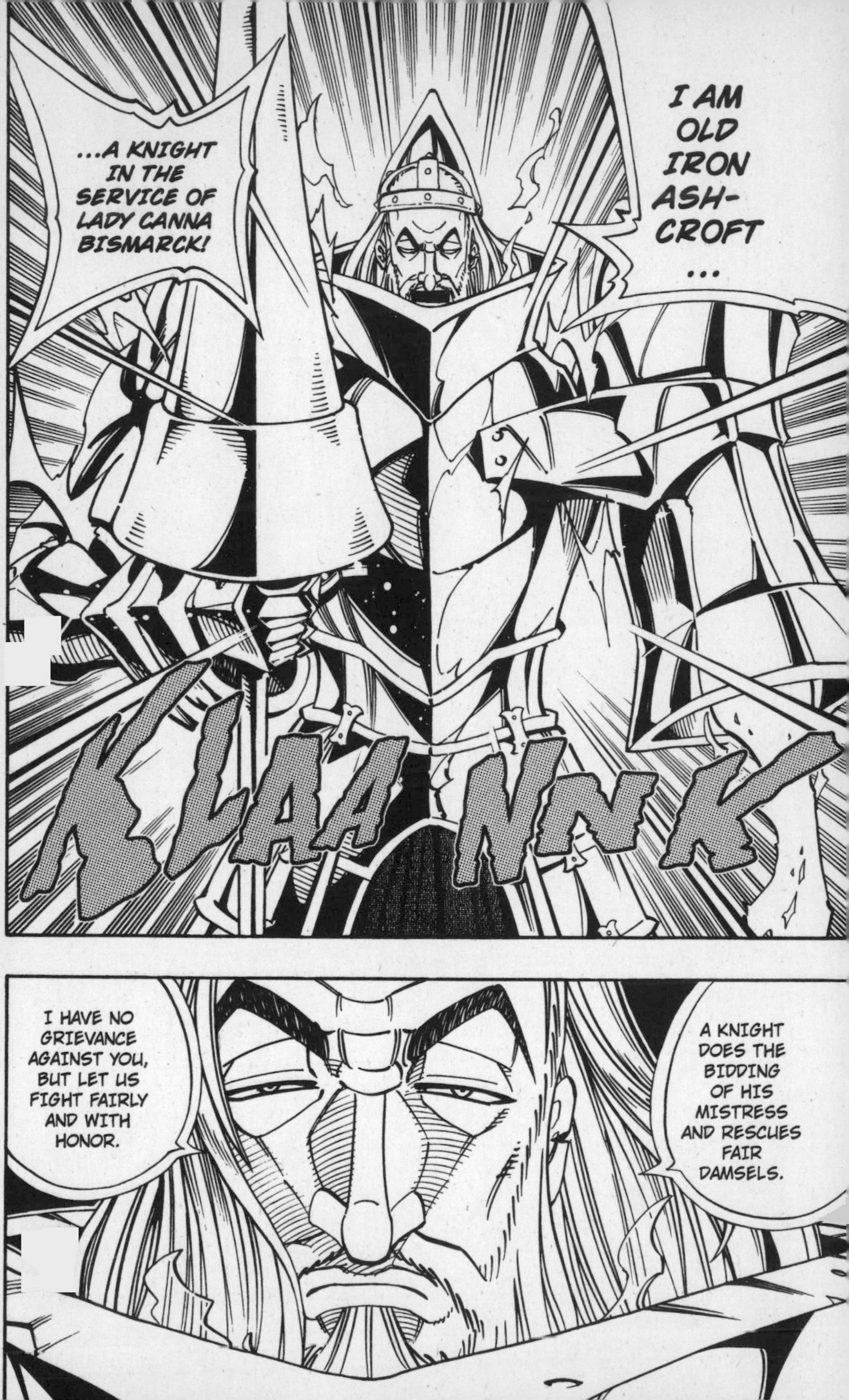
I AM OLD IRON ASH-CROFT ...
...A KNIGHT IN THE SERVICE OF LADY CANNA BISMARCK!
KLAANNK
A KNIGHT DOES THE BIDDING OF HIS MISTRESS AND RESCUES FAIR DAMSELS.
I HAVE NO GRIEVANCE AGAINST YOU, BUT LET US FIGHT FAIRLY AND WITH HONOR.

Reincarnation 155: My Terms

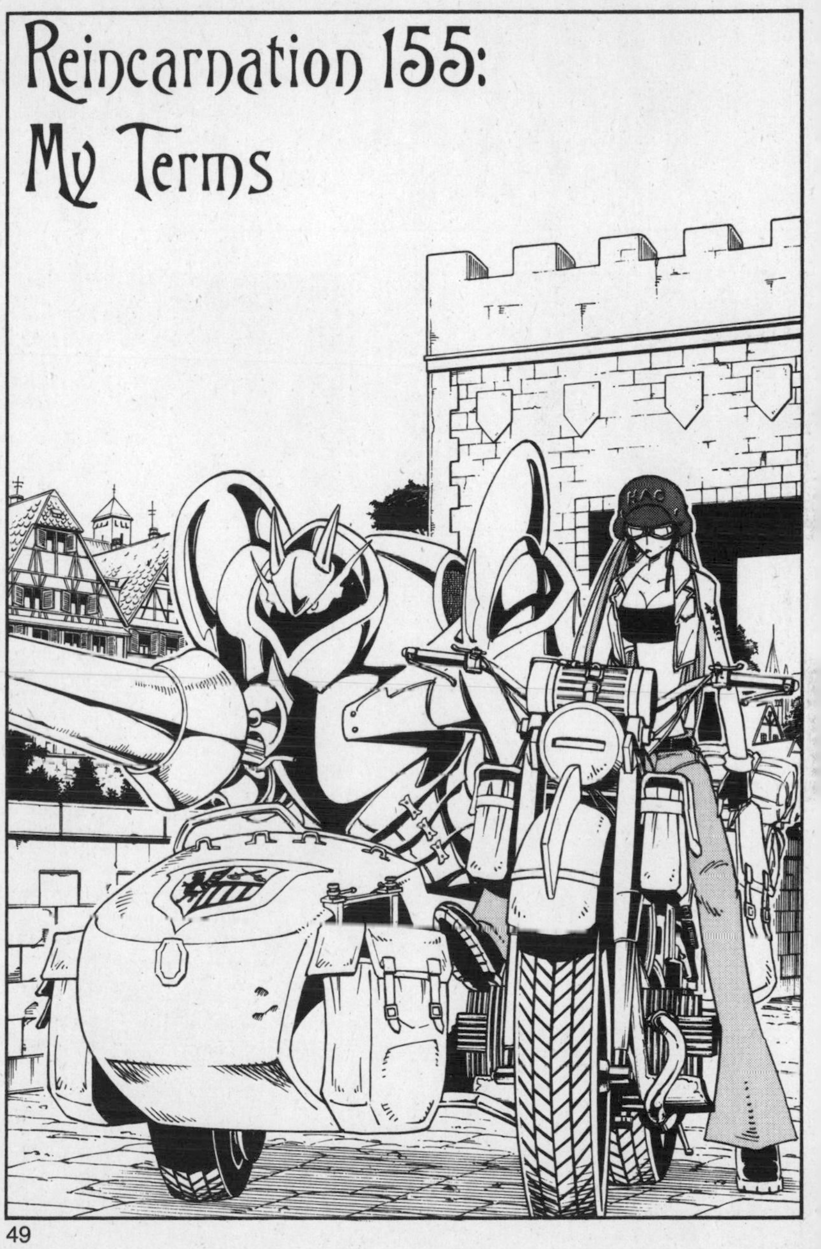

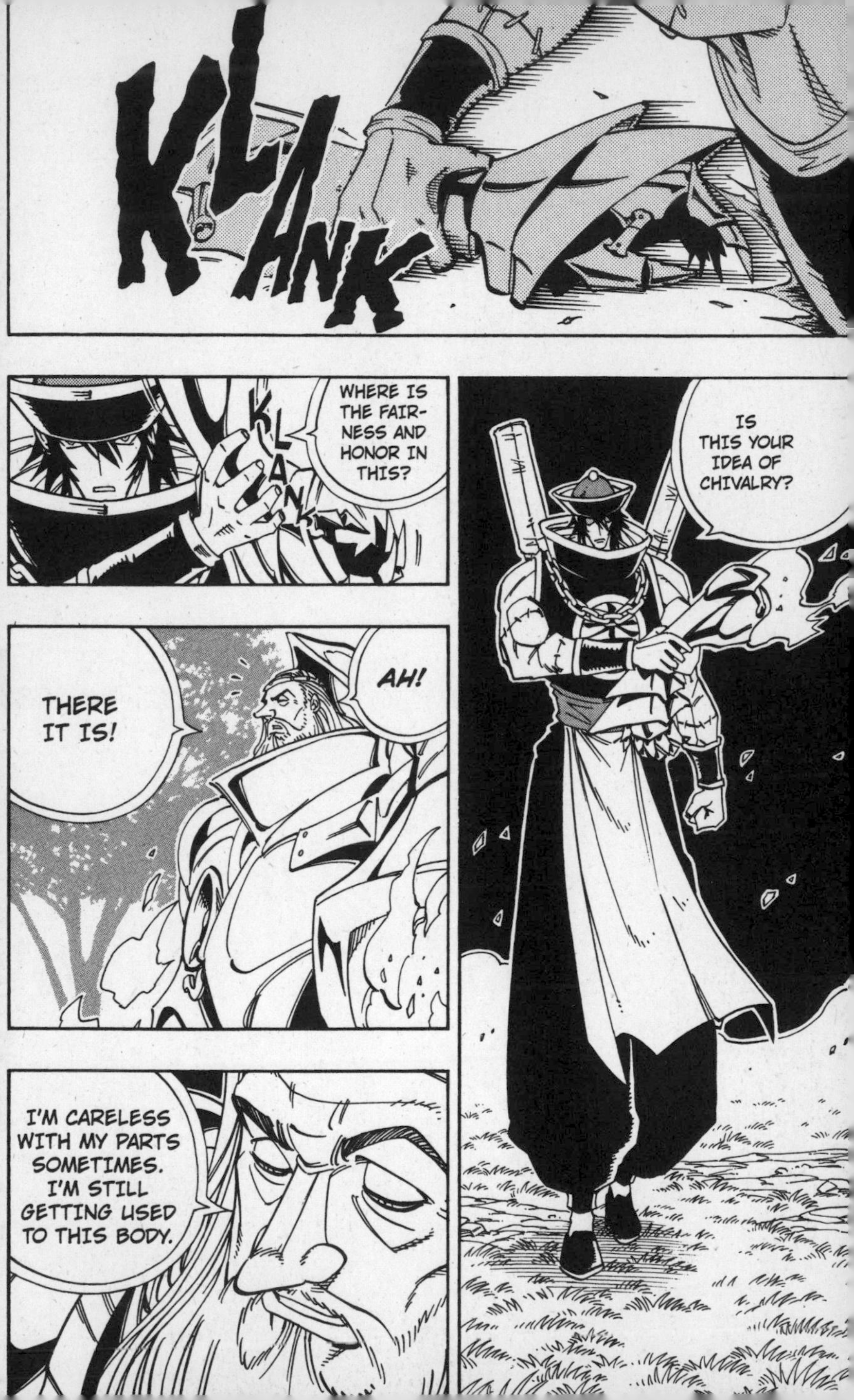
KLANK
IS THIS YOUR IDEA OF CHIVALRY?
WHERE IS THE FAIRNESS AND HONOR IN THIS?
KLANK
AH!
THERE IT IS!
I'M CARELESS WITH MY PARTS SOMETIMES. I'M STILL GETTING USED TO THIS BODY.

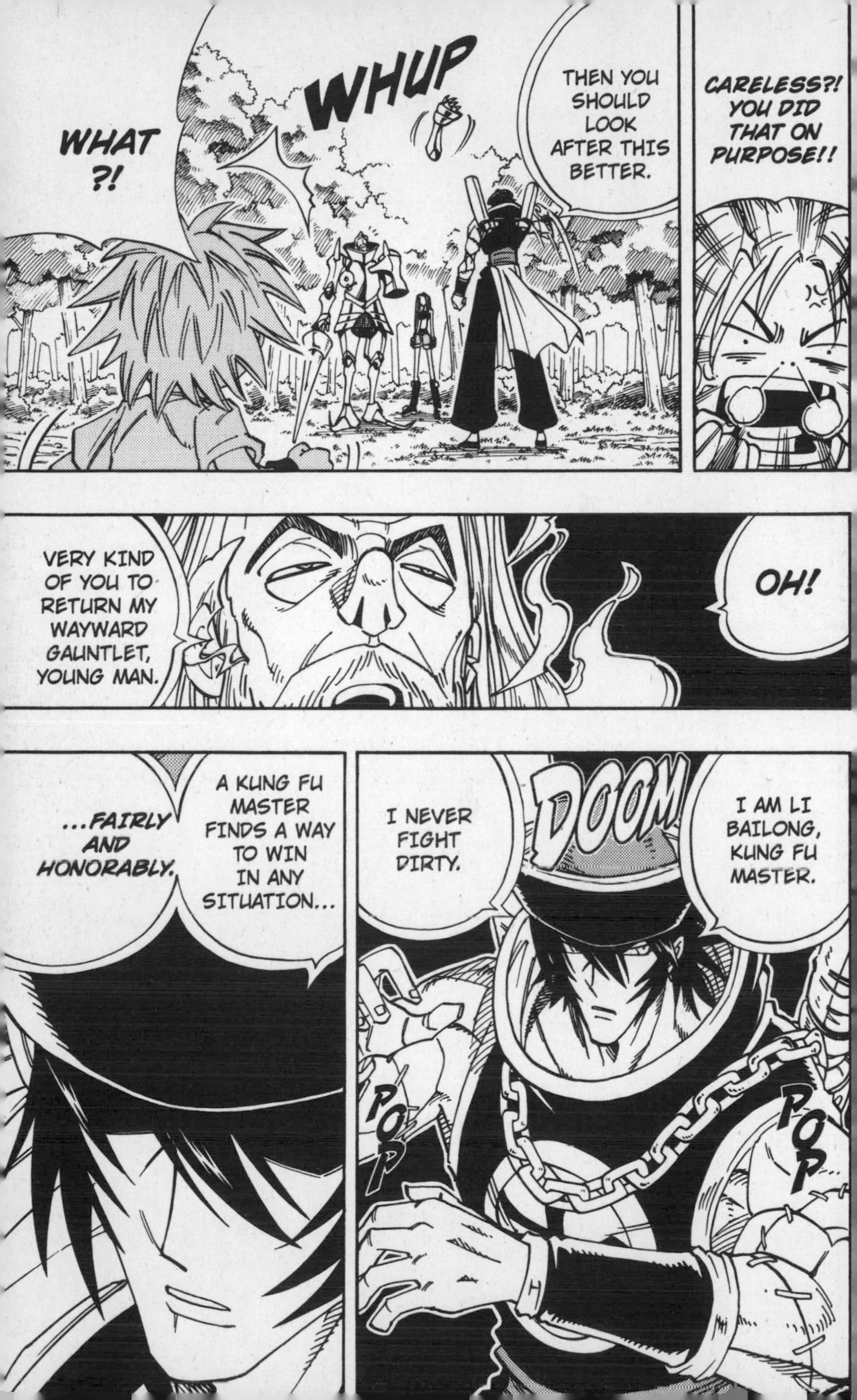
CARELESS?! YOU DID THAT ON PURPOSE!!
THEN YOU SHOULD LOOK AFTER THIS BETTER.
WHUP
WHAT ?!
OH!
VERY KIND OF YOU TO RETURN MY WAYWARD GAUNTLET, YOUNG MAN.
I AM LI BAILONG, KUNG FU MASTER.
DOOM
I NEVER FIGHT DIRTY.
POP
POP...
A KUNG FU MASTER FINDS A WAY TO WIN IN ANY SITUATION...
...FAIRLY AND HONORABLY.

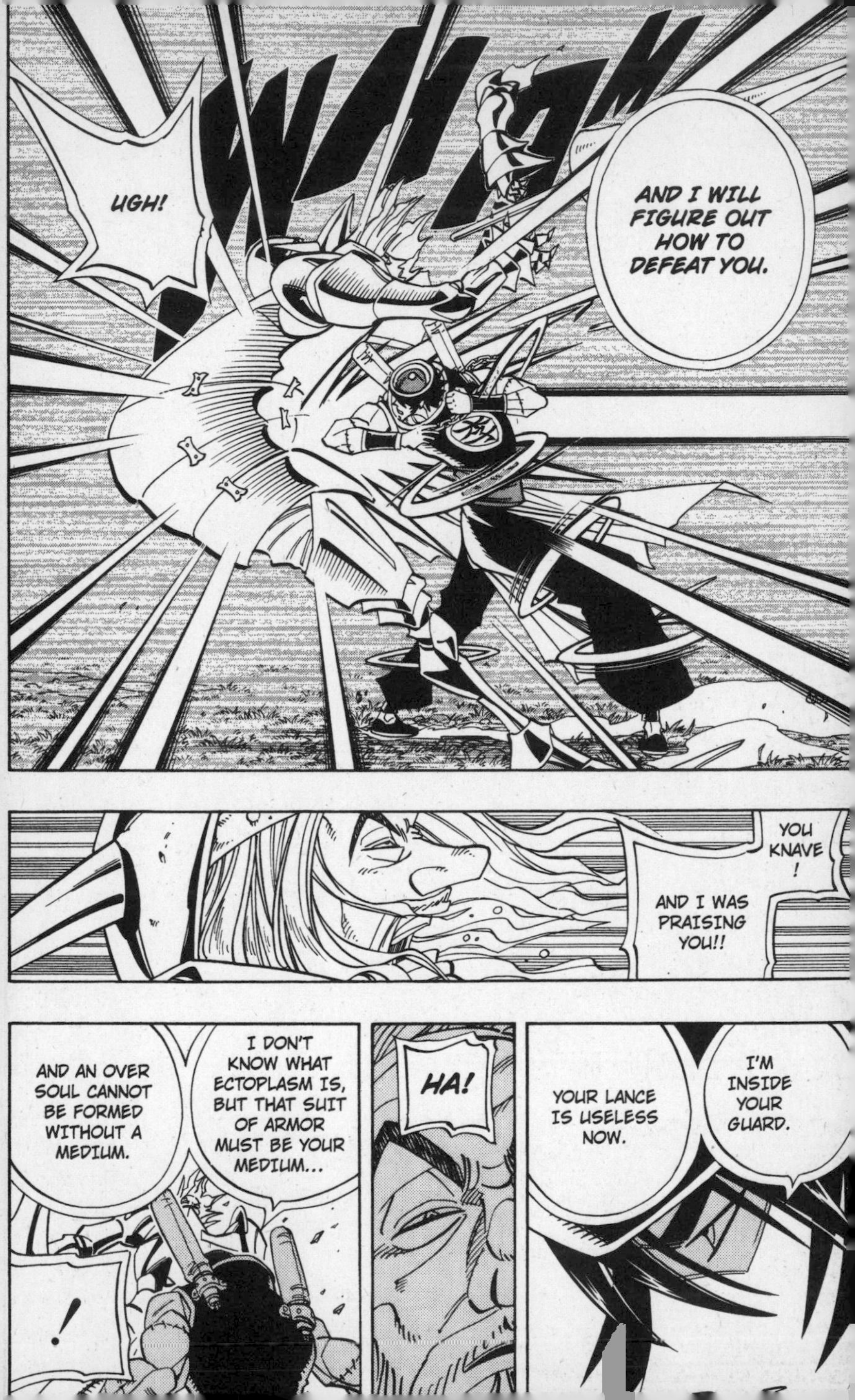
WHAM
AND I WILL FIGURE OUT HOW TO DEFEAT YOU.
UGH!
YOU KNAVE!
AND I WAS PRAISING YOU!!
I'M INSIDE YOUR GUARD.
YOUR LANCE IS USELESS NOW.
HA!
I DON'T KNOW WHAT ECTOPLASM IS, BUT THAT SUIT OF ARMOR MUST BE YOUR MEDIUM...
AND AN OVER SOUL CANNOT BE FORMED WITHOUT A MEDIUM.
!

THEREFORE...

I WILL DESTROY IT!!

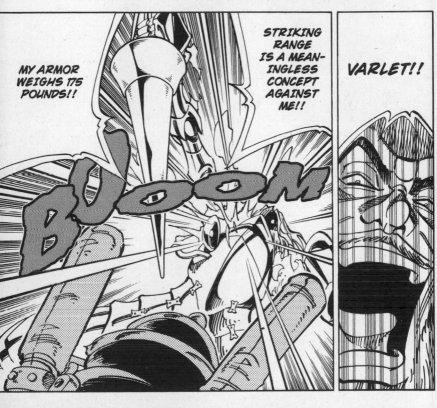

STRIKING RANGE IS A MEANINGLESS CONCEPT AGAINST ME!!

VARLET!!

MY ARMOR WEIGHS 175 POUNDS!!

FOOL!!

YOUR FISTS CAN NEVER BREAK IT!!

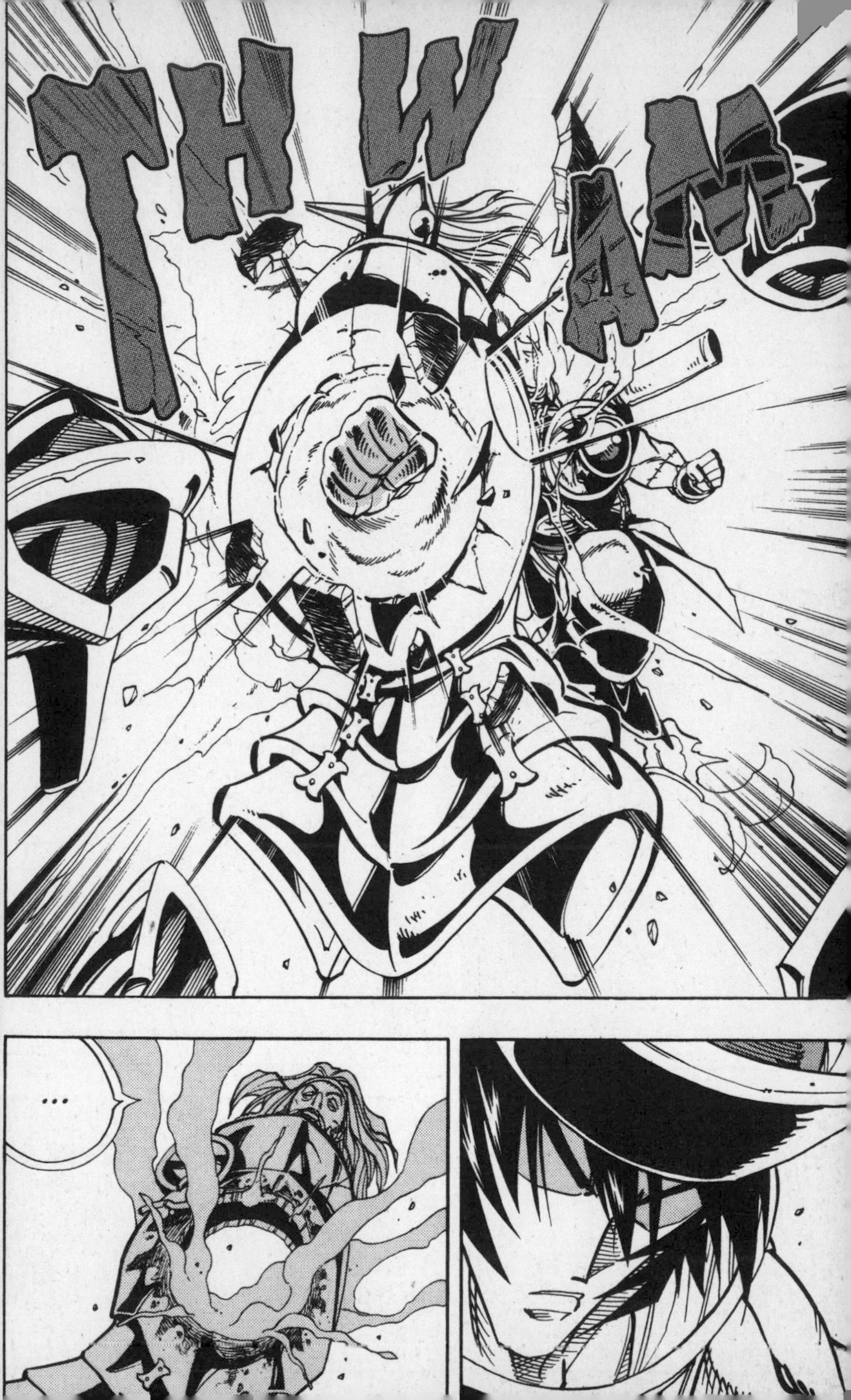
THWAM
...

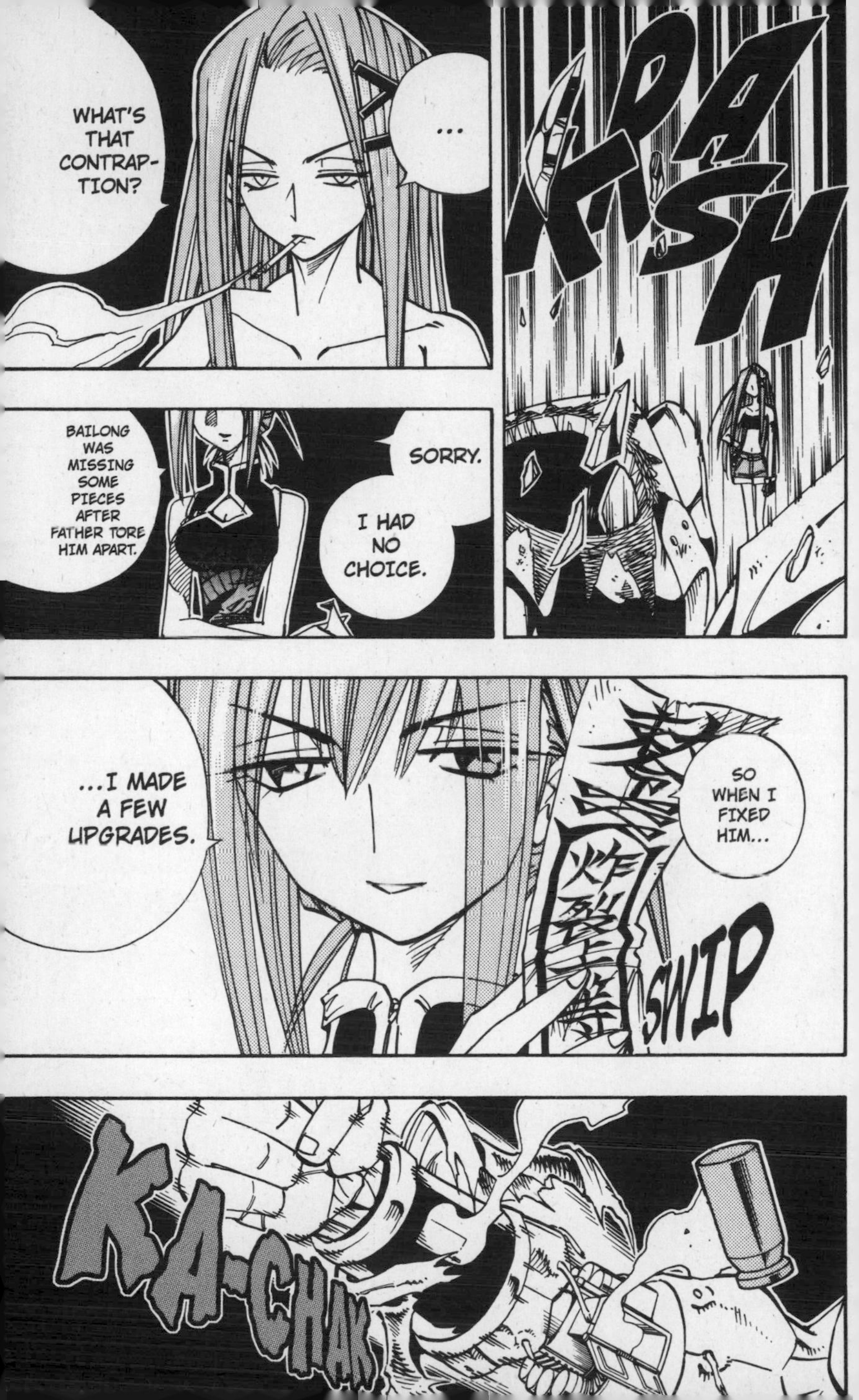
...
WHAT'S THAT CONTRAPTION?
SORRY.
I HAD NO CHOICE.
BAILONG WAS MISSING SOME PIECES AFTER FATHER TORE HIM APART.
SO WHEN I FIXED HIM...
...I MADE A FEW UPGRADES.
SWIP
KA-CHAK

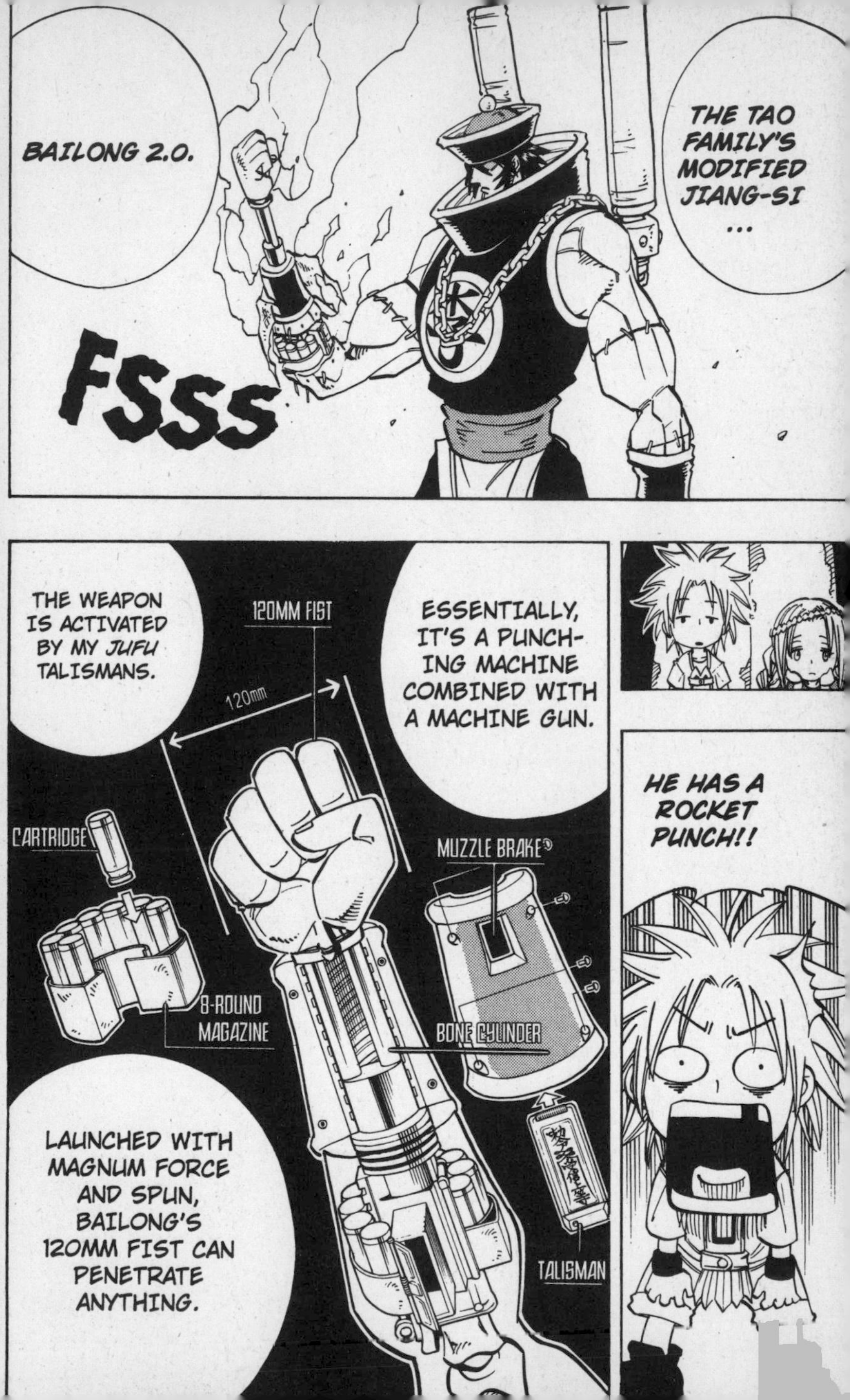
THE TAO FAMILY'S MODIFIED JIANG-SI ...
BAILONG 2.0.
FSSS
HE HAS A ROCKET PUNCH!!
ESSENTIALLY, IT'S A PUNCH-ING MACHINE COMBINED WITH A MACHINE GUN.
THE WEAPON IS ACTIVATED BY MY JUFU TALISMANS.
120MM FIST
120mm
MUZZLE BRAKE
CARTRIDGE
8-ROUND MAGAZINE
BONE CYLINDER
TALISMAN
LAUNCHED WITH MAGNUM FORCE AND SPUN, BAILONG'S 120MM FIST CAN PENETRATE ANYTHING.

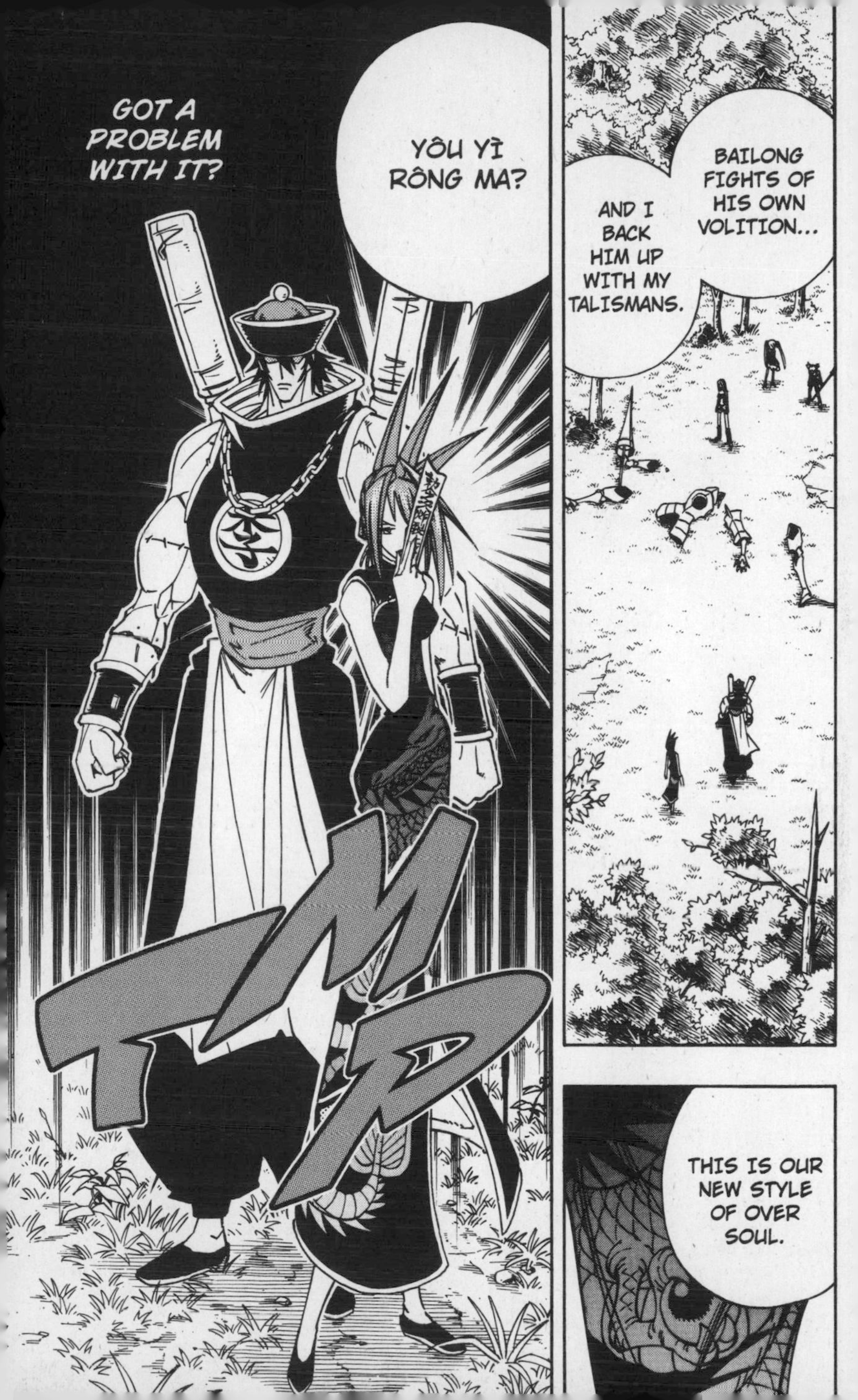
BAILONG FIGHTS OF HIS OWN VOLITION...
AND I BACK HIM UP WITH MY TALISMANS.
THIS IS OUR NEW STYLE OF OVER SOUL.
YÔU YÌ RÔNG MA?
GOT A PROBLEM WITH IT?
TMP

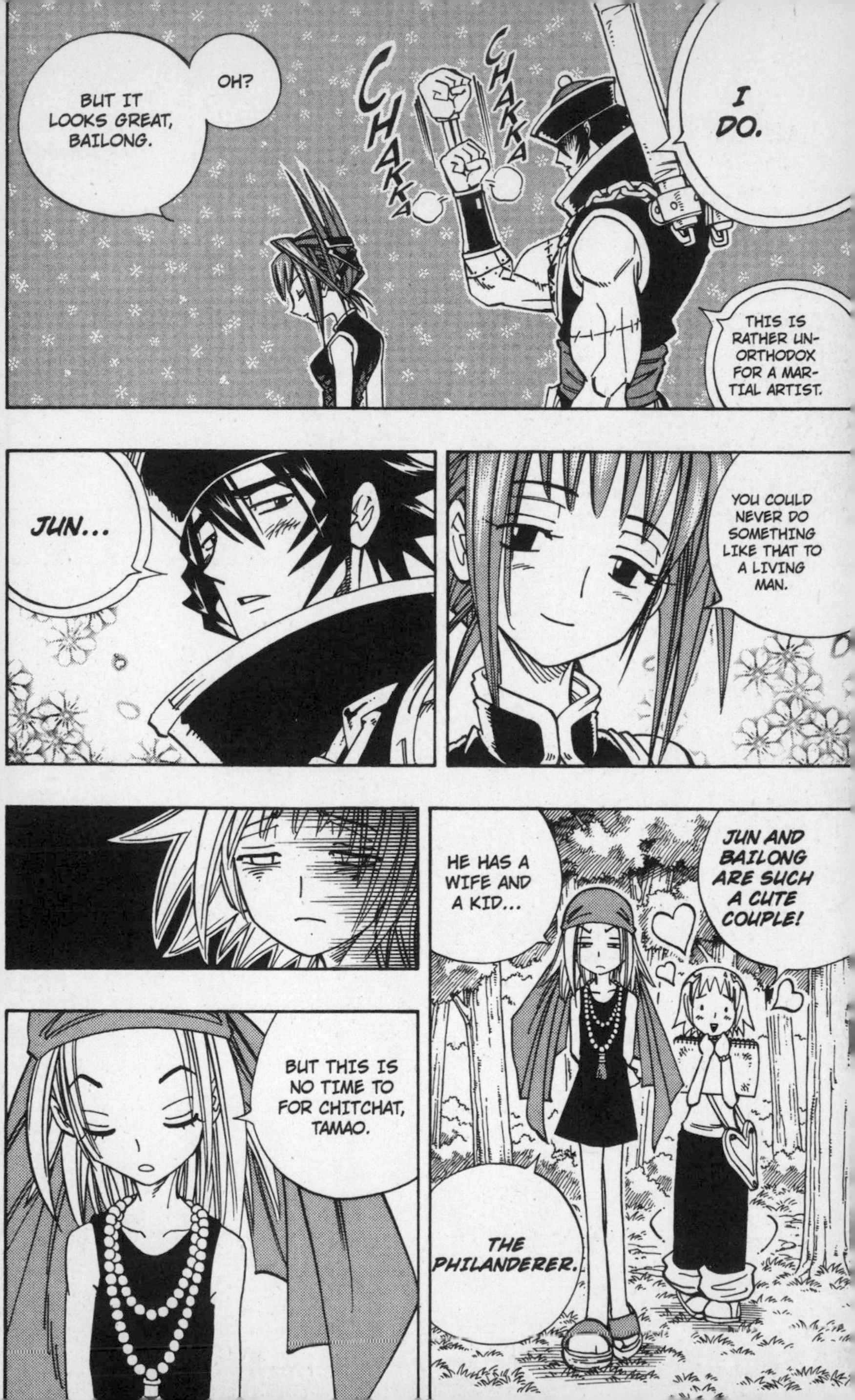
I DO.
CHAKKA
CHAKKA
OH?
BUT IT LOOKS GREAT, BAILONG.
THIS IS RATHER UN-ORTHODOX FOR A MAR-TIAL ARTIST.
YOU COULD NEVER DO SOMETHING LIKE THAT TO A LIVING MAN.
JUN...
JUN AND BAILONG ARE SUCH A CUTE COUPLE!
HE HAS A WIFE AND A KID...
THE PHILANDERER.
BUT THIS IS NO TIME TO FOR CHITCHAT, TAMAO.

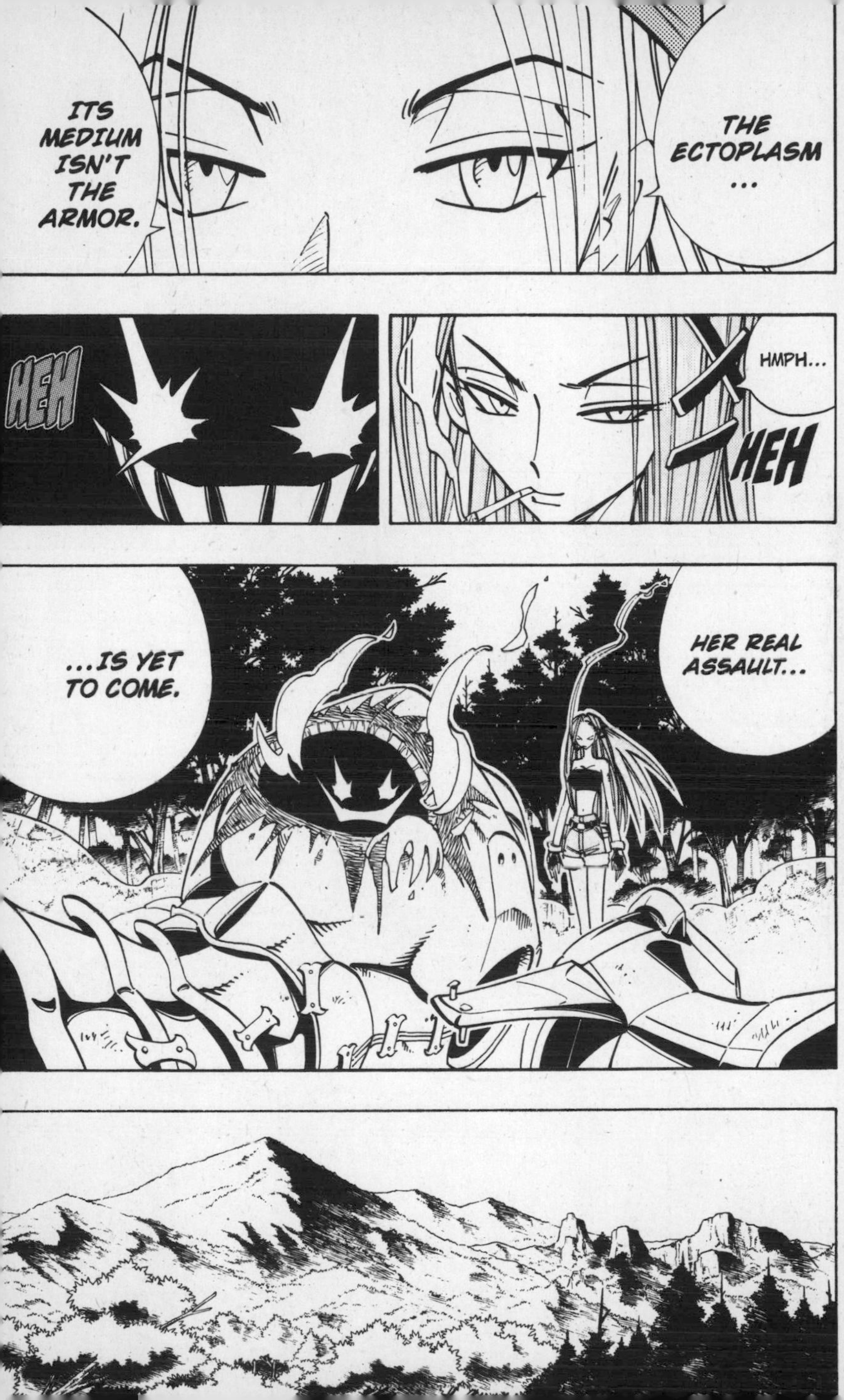
THE ECTOPLASM ...
ITS MEDIUM ISN'T THE ARMOR.
HMPH...
HEH
HEH
HER REAL ASSAULT...
...IS YET TO COME.

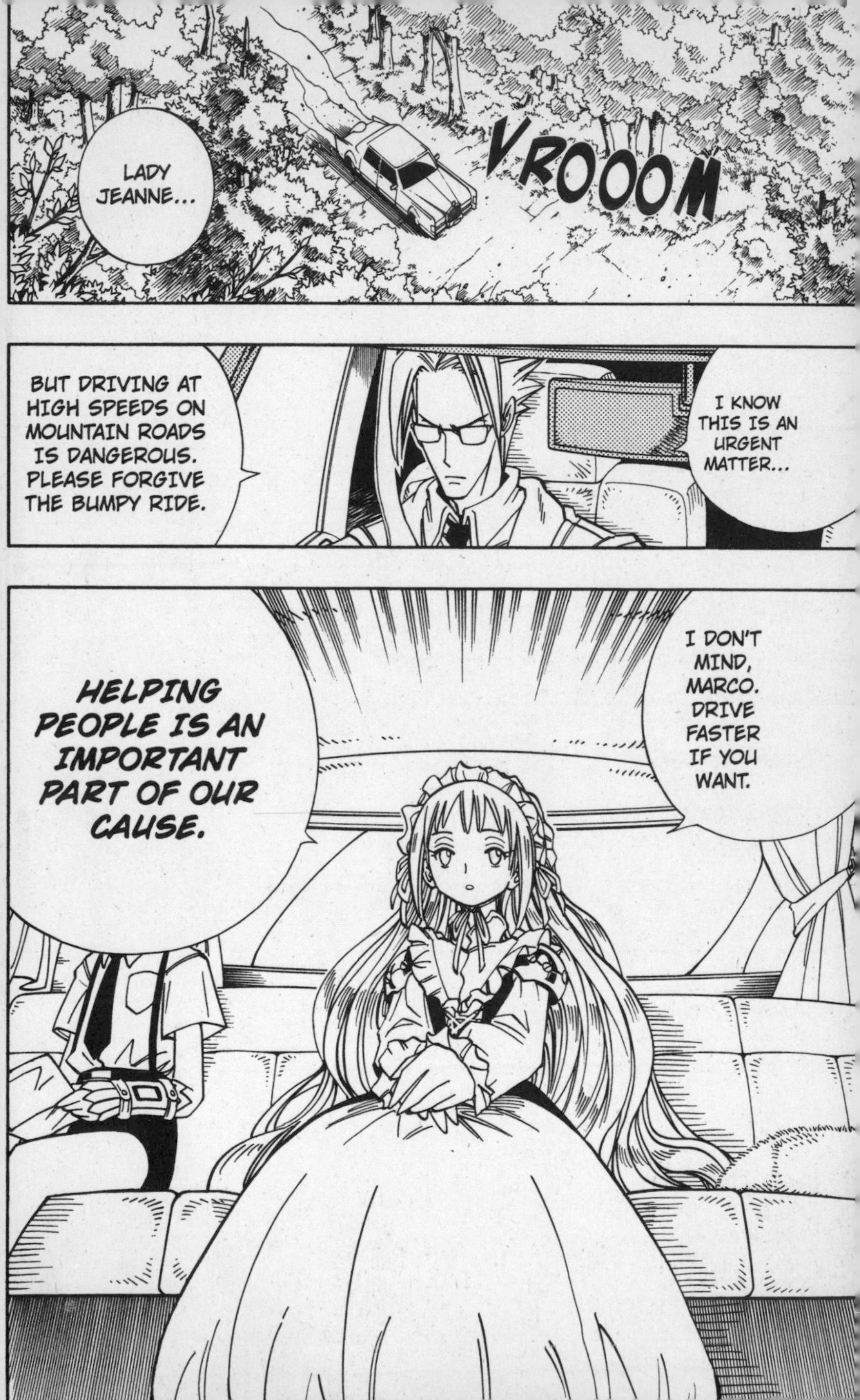
VROOOM
LADY JEANNE...
I KNOW THIS IS AN URGENT MATTER...
BUT DRIVING AT HIGH SPEEDS ON MOUNTAIN ROADS IS DANGEROUS. PLEASE FORGIVE THE BUMPY RIDE.
I DON'T MIND, MARCO. DRIVE FASTER IF YOU WANT.
HELPING PEOPLE IS AN IMPORTANT PART OF OUR CAUSE.

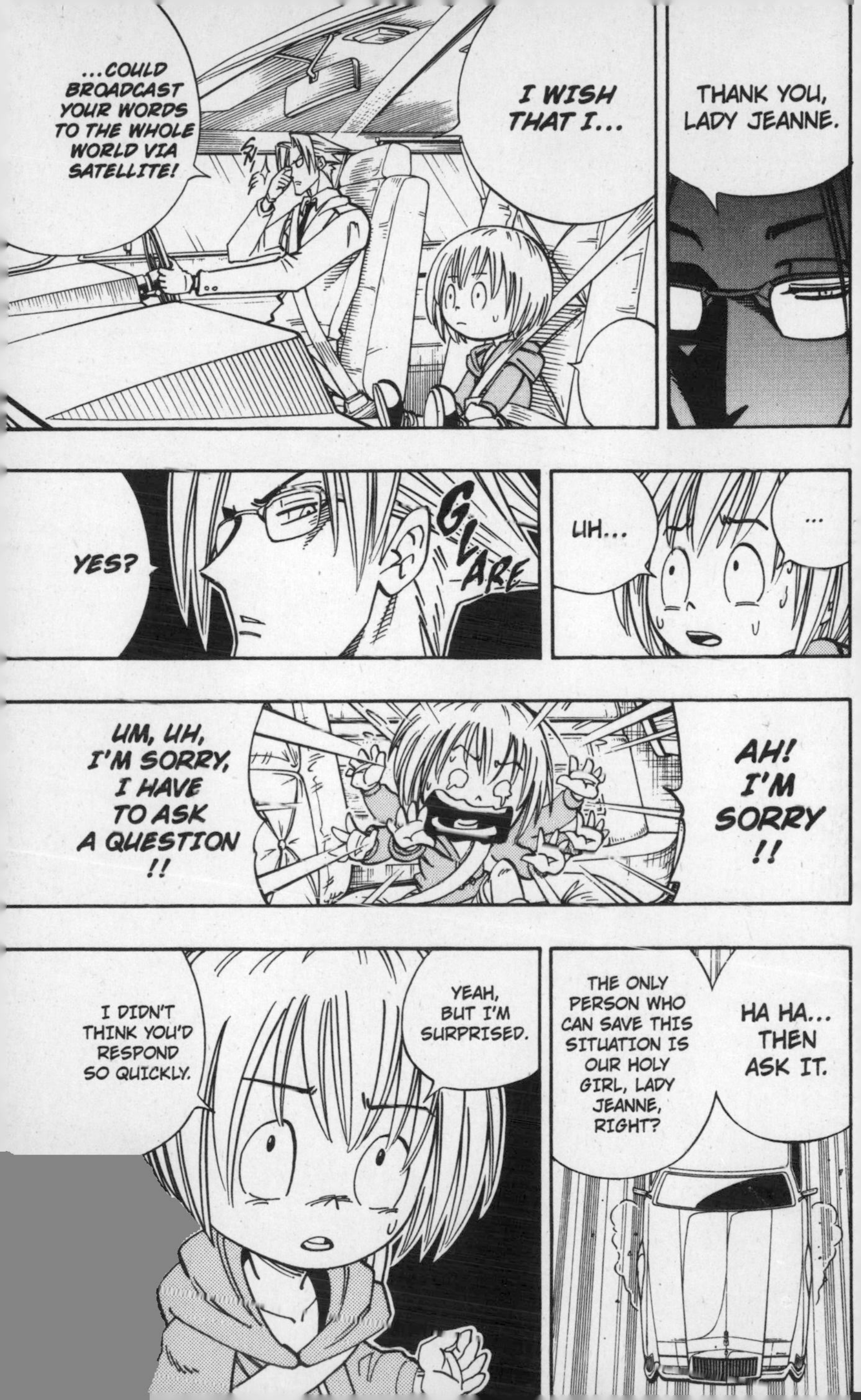
THANK YOU, LADY JEANNE.
I WISH THAT I...
...COULD BROADCAST YOUR WORDS TO THE WHOLE WORLD VIA SATELLITE!
...
UH...
YES?
GLARE
AH! I'M SORRY !!
UM, UH, I'M SORRY, I HAVE TO ASK A QUESTION !!
HA HA... THEN ASK IT.
THE ONLY PERSON WHO CAN SAVE THIS SITUATION IS OUR HOLY GIRL, LADY JEANNE, RIGHT?
YEAH, BUT I'M SURPRISED.
I DIDN'T THINK YOU'D RESPOND SO QUICKLY.

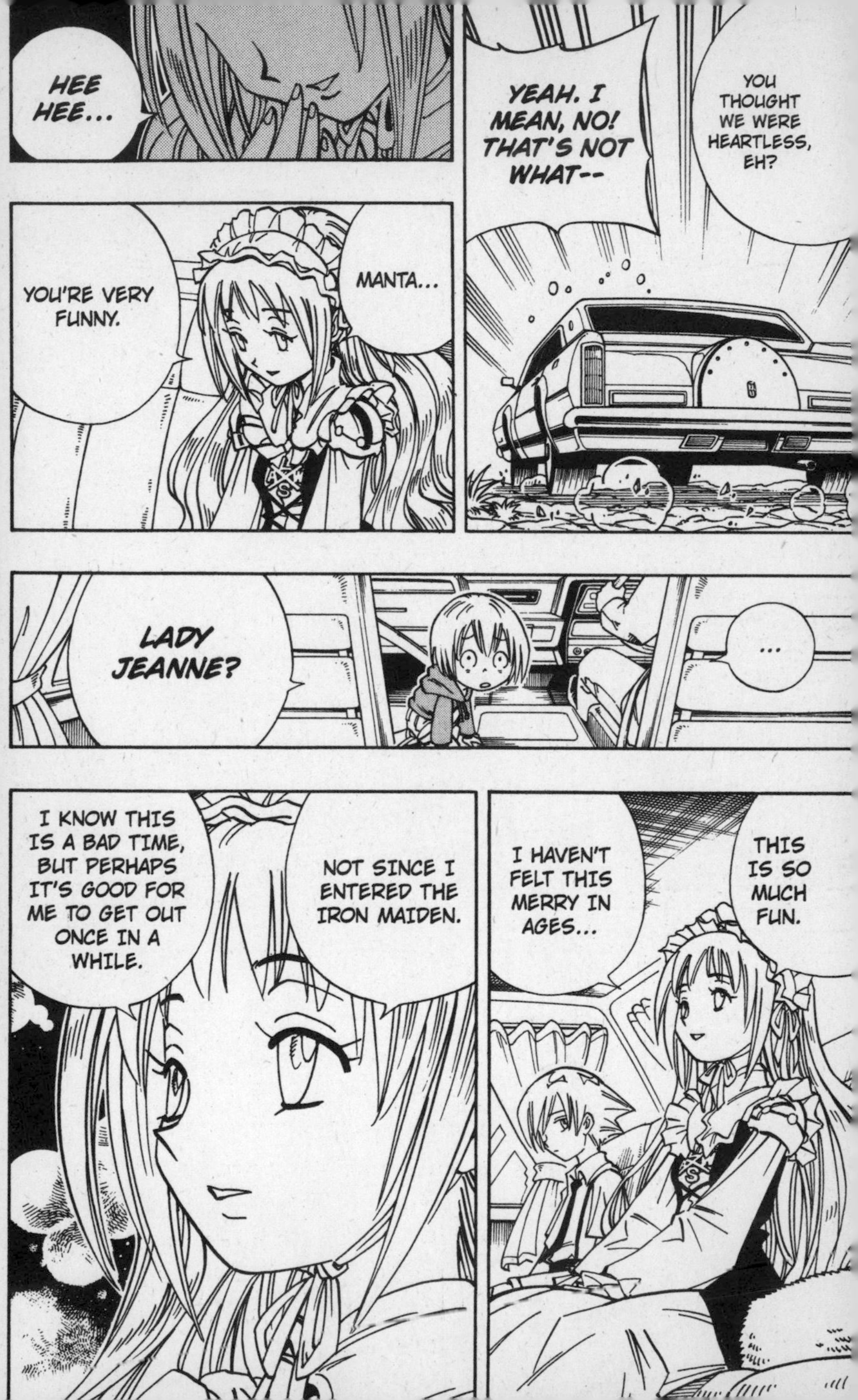
YOU THOUGHT WE WERE HEARTLESS, EH?
YEAH. I MEAN, NO! THAT'S NOT WHAT--
HEE HEE...
MANTA...
YOU'RE VERY FUNNY.
...
LADY JEANNE?
THIS IS SO MUCH FUN.
I HAVEN'T FELT THIS MERRY IN AGES...
NOT SINCE I ENTERED THE IRON MAIDEN.
I KNOW THIS IS A BAD TIME, BUT PERHAPS IT'S GOOD FOR ME TO GET OUT ONCE IN A WHILE.

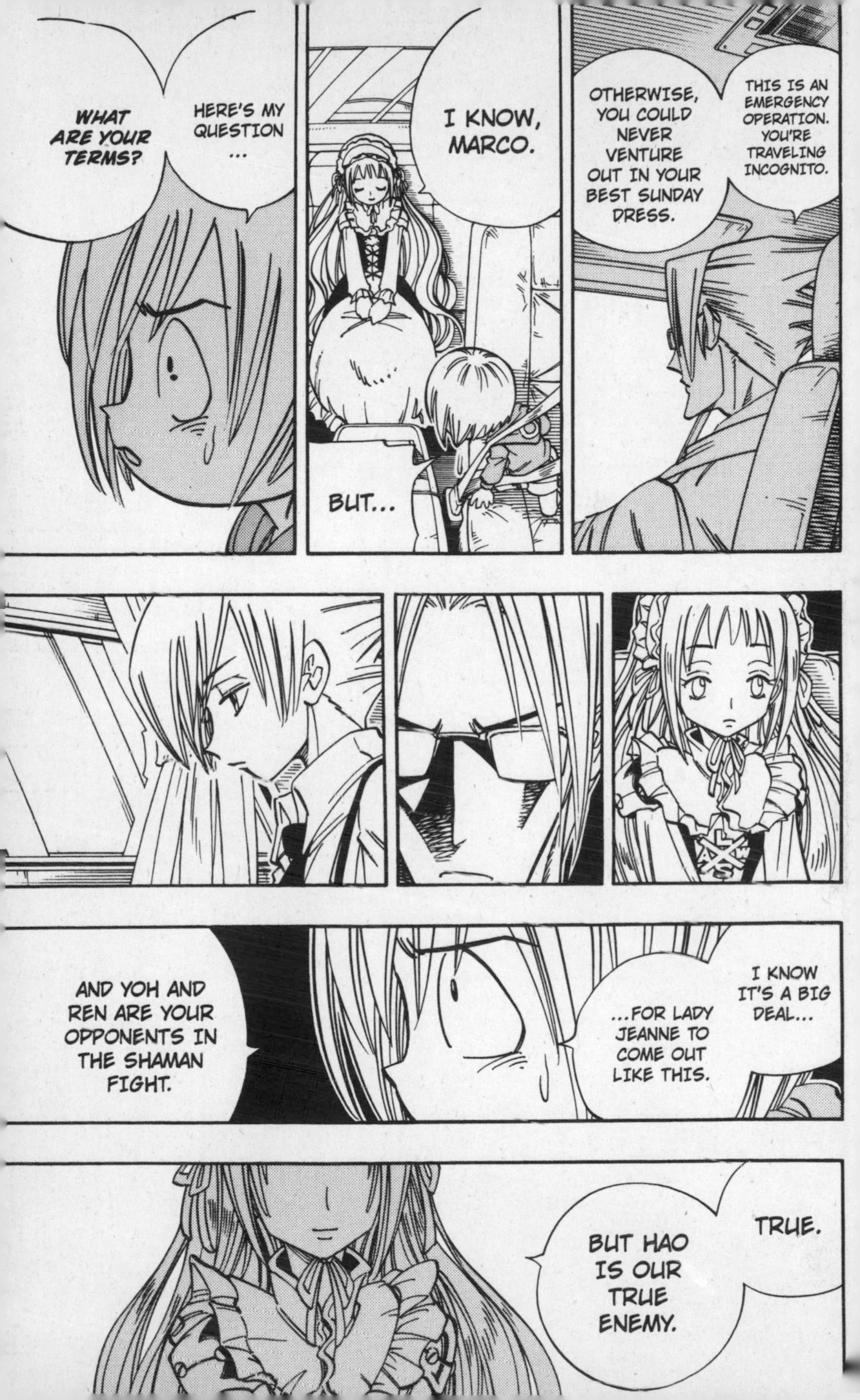
THIS IS AN EMERGENCY OPERATION. YOU'RE TRAVELING INCOGNITO.
OTHERWISE, YOU COULD NEVER VENTURE OUT IN YOUR BEST SUNDAY DRESS.
I KNOW, MARCO.
BUT...
HERE'S MY QUESTION ...
WHAT ARE YOUR TERMS?
I KNOW IT'S A BIG DEAL...
...FOR LADY JEANNE TO COME OUT LIKE THIS.
AND YOH AND REN ARE YOUR OPPONENTS IN THE SHAMAN FIGHT.
TRUE.
BUT HAO IS OUR TRUE ENEMY.

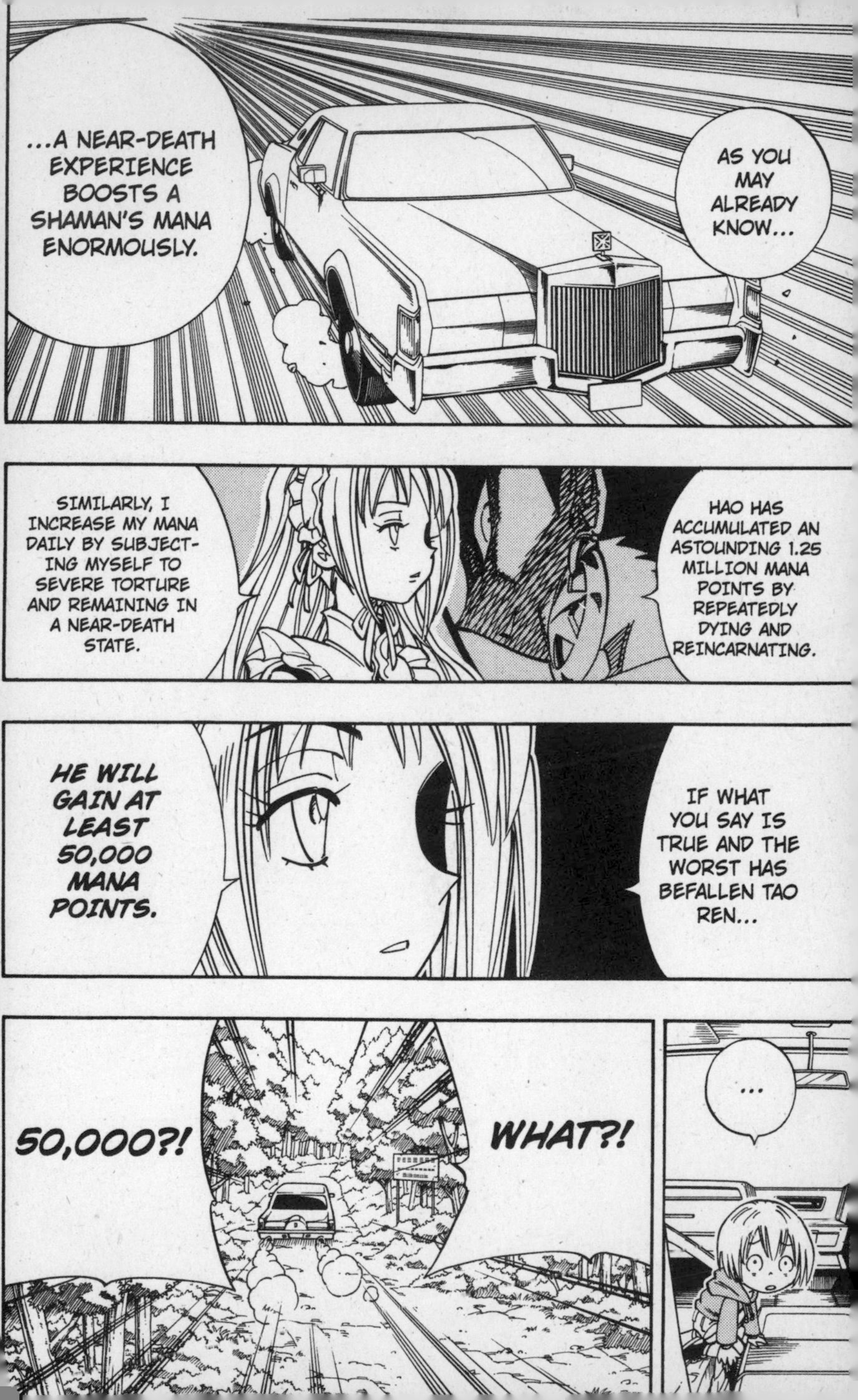
AS YOU MAY ALREADY KNOW...
...A NEAR-DEATH EXPERIENCE BOOSTS A SHAMAN'S MANA ENORMOUSLY.
HAO HAS ACCUMULATED AN ASTOUNDING 1.25 MILLION MANA POINTS BY REPEATEDLY DYING AND REINCARNATING.
SIMILARLY, I INCREASE MY MANA DAILY BY SUBJECT-ING MYSELF TO SEVERE TORTURE AND REMAINING IN A NEAR-DEATH STATE.
IF WHAT YOU SAY IS TRUE AND THE WORST HAS BEFALLEN TAO REN...
HE WILL GAIN AT LEAST 50,000 MANA POINTS.
...
WHAT?!
50,000?!

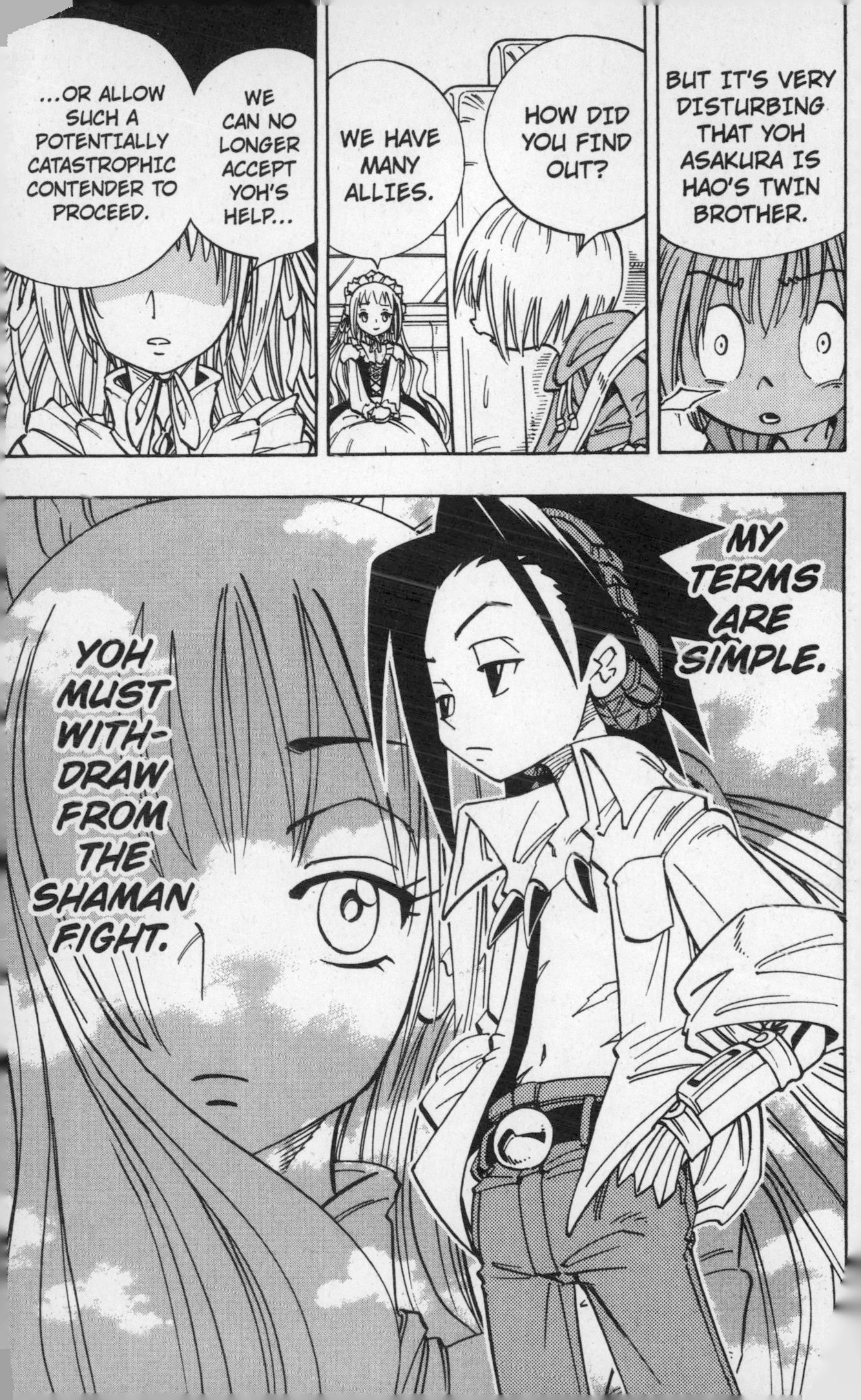
BUT IT'S VERY DISTURBING THAT YOH ASAKURA IS HAO'S TWIN BROTHER.
HOW DID YOU FIND OUT?
WE HAVE MANY ALLIES.
WE CAN NO LONGER ACCEPT YOH'S HELP...
...OR ALLOW SUCH A POTENTIALLY CATASTROPHIC CONTENDER TO PROCEED.
MY TERMS ARE SIMPLE.
YOH MUST WITH-DRAW FROM THE SHAMAN FIGHT.

SHAMAN KING ITEM FILE No.52

2001
(JAN)

パイロンバンカー

白龍蠻可亜

THE BAILONG BUNKER

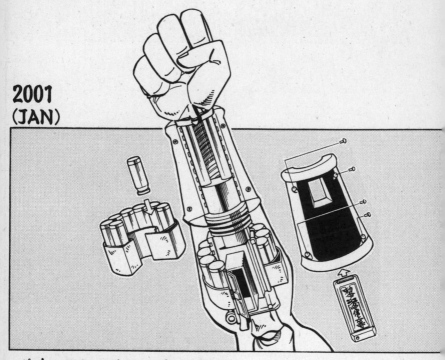

Reincarnation 156: Sorry

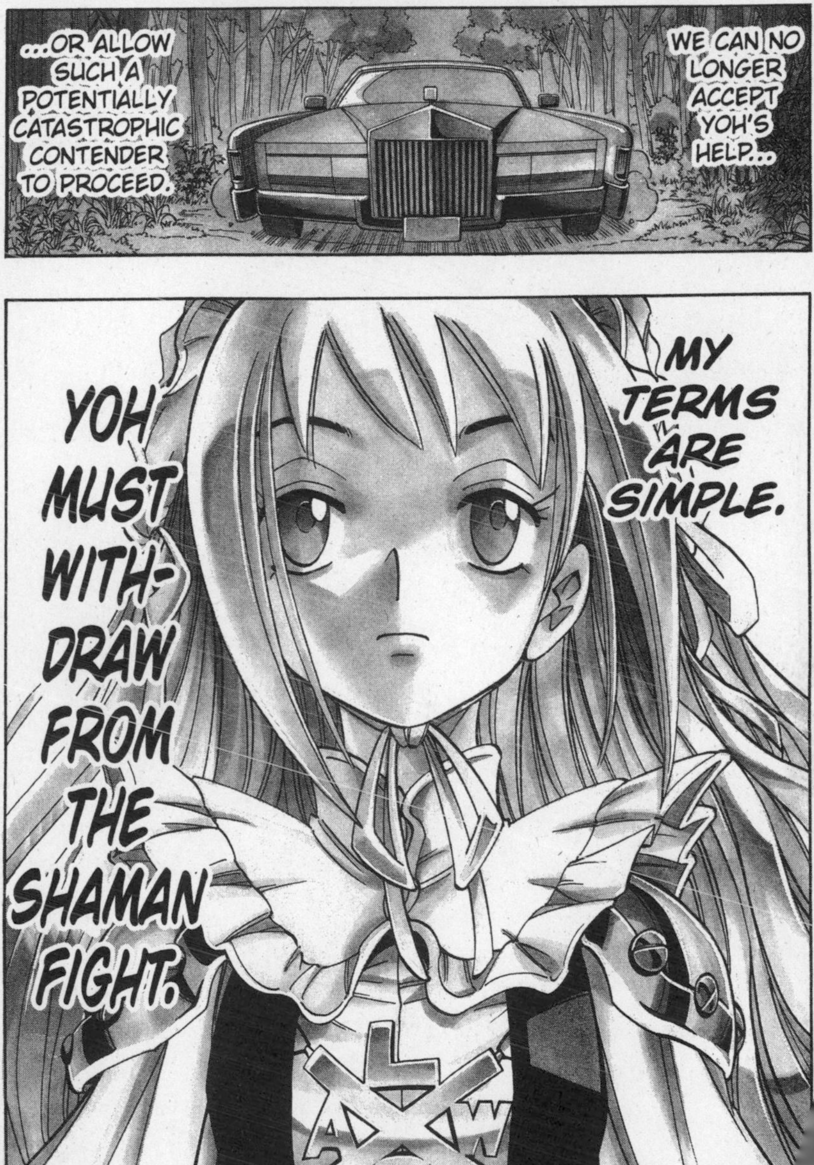
WE CAN NO LONGER ACCEPT YOH'S HELP...
...OR ALLOW SUCH A POTENTIALLY CATASTROPHIC CONTENDER TO PROCEED.
MY TERMS ARE SIMPLE.
YOH MUST WITH-DRAW FROM THE SHAMAN FIGHT.

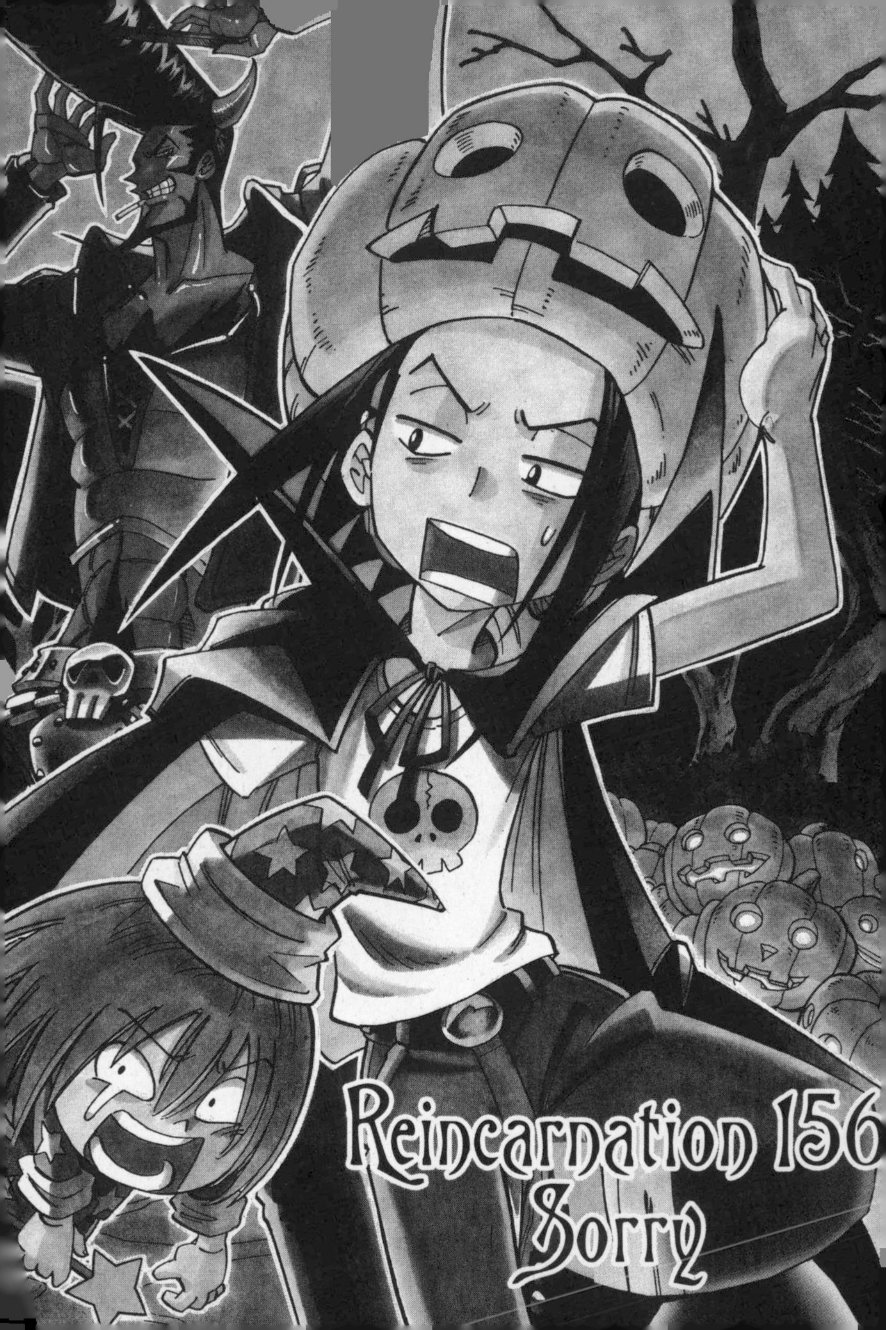
Reincarnation 156
Sorry

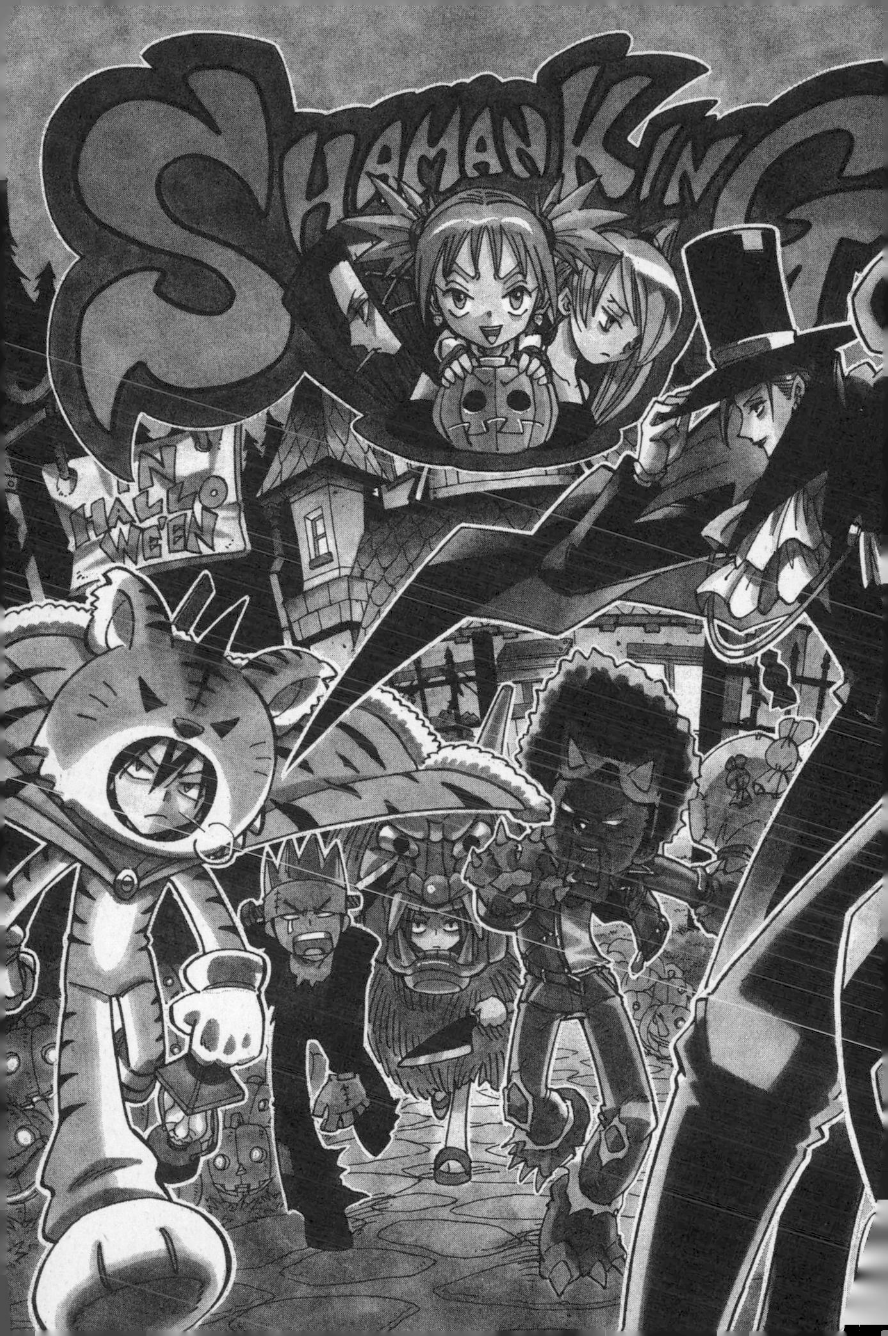
'N
HALLO
WE'EN

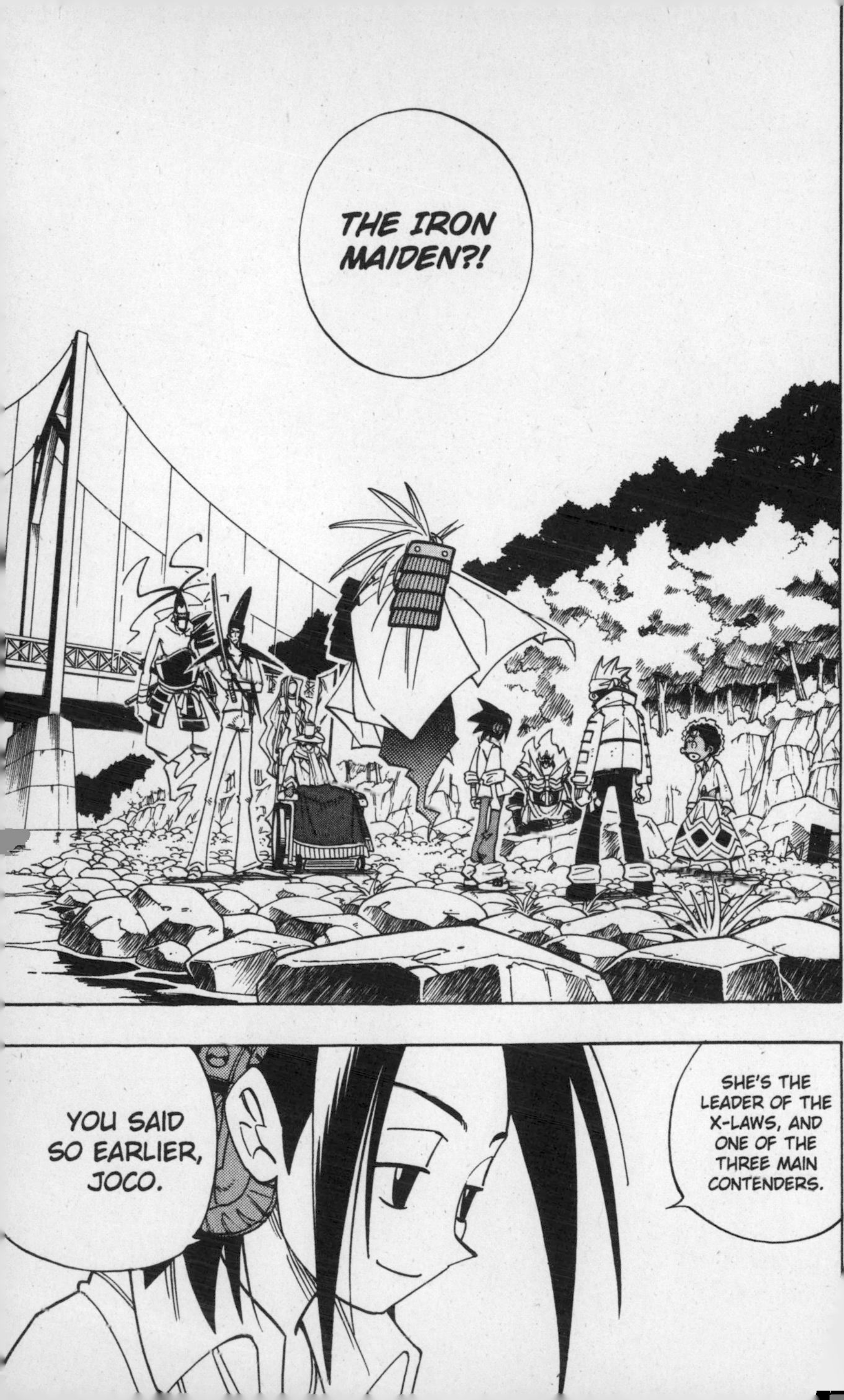
THE IRON MAIDEN?!
SHE'S THE LEADER OF THE X-LAWS, AND ONE OF THE THREE MAIN CONTENDERS.
YOU SAID SO EARLIER, JOCO.

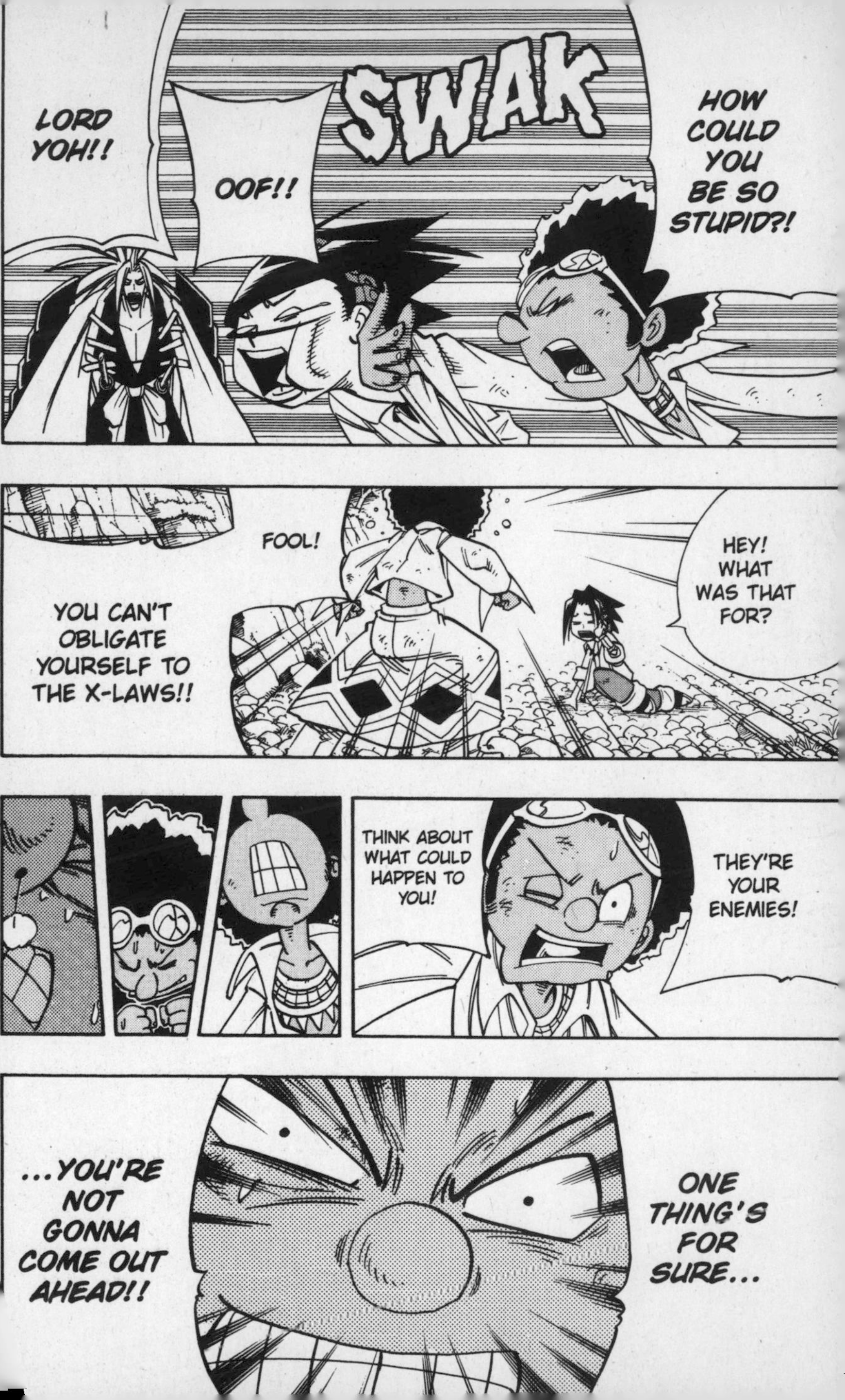
HOW COULD YOU BE SO STUPID?!
SWAK
OOF!!
LORD YOH!!
HEY! WHAT WAS THAT FOR?
FOOL!
YOU CAN'T OBLIGATE YOURSELF TO THE X-LAWS!!
THEY'RE YOUR ENEMIES!
THINK ABOUT WHAT COULD HAPPEN TO YOU!
ONE THING'S FOR SURE...
...YOU'RE NOT GONNA COME OUT AHEAD!!

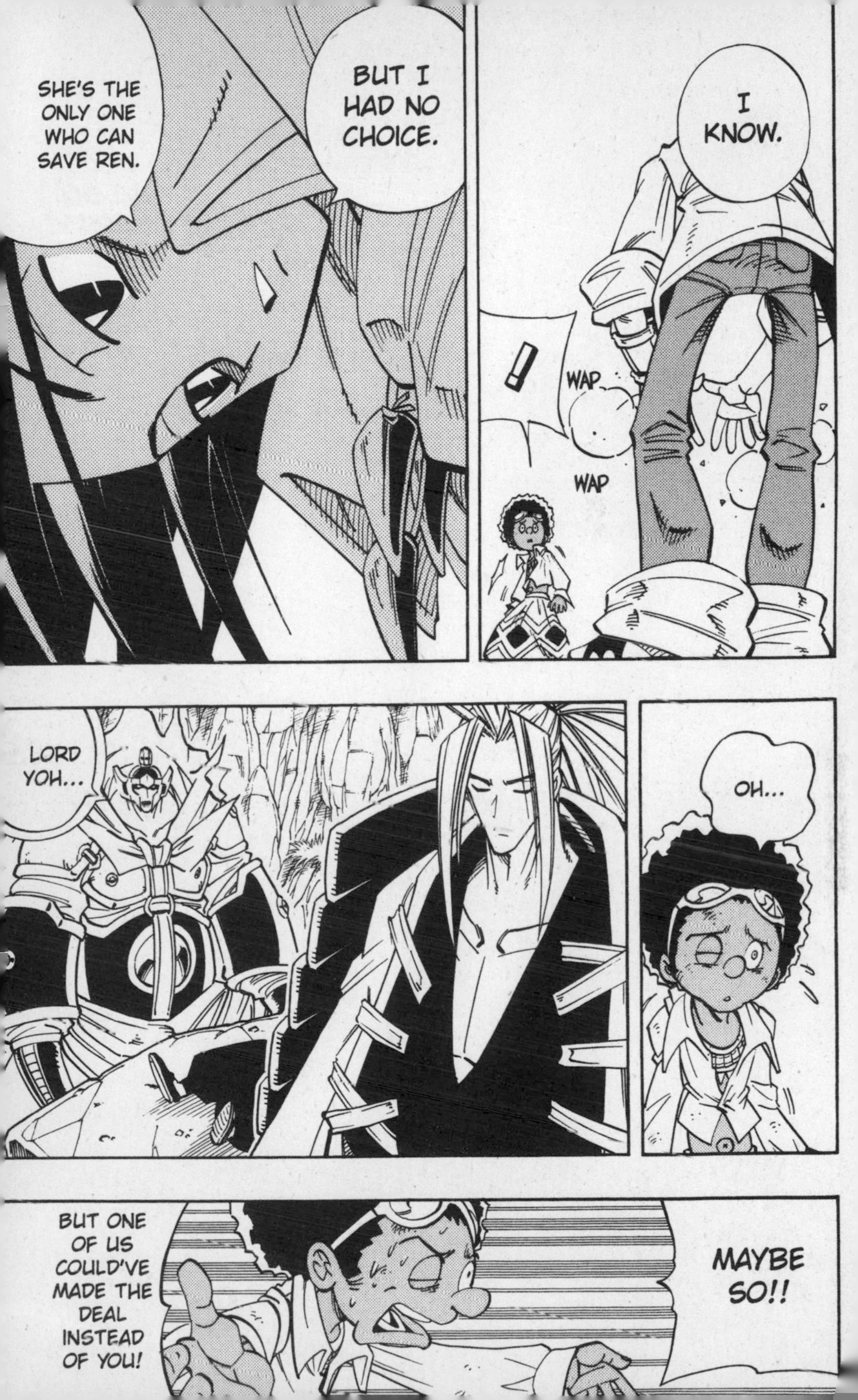
I KNOW.
!
WAP
WAP
BUT I HAD NO CHOICE.
SHE'S THE ONLY ONE WHO CAN SAVE REN.
OH...
LORD YOH...
MAYBE SO!!
BUT ONE OF US COULD'VE MADE THE DEAL INSTEAD OF YOU!

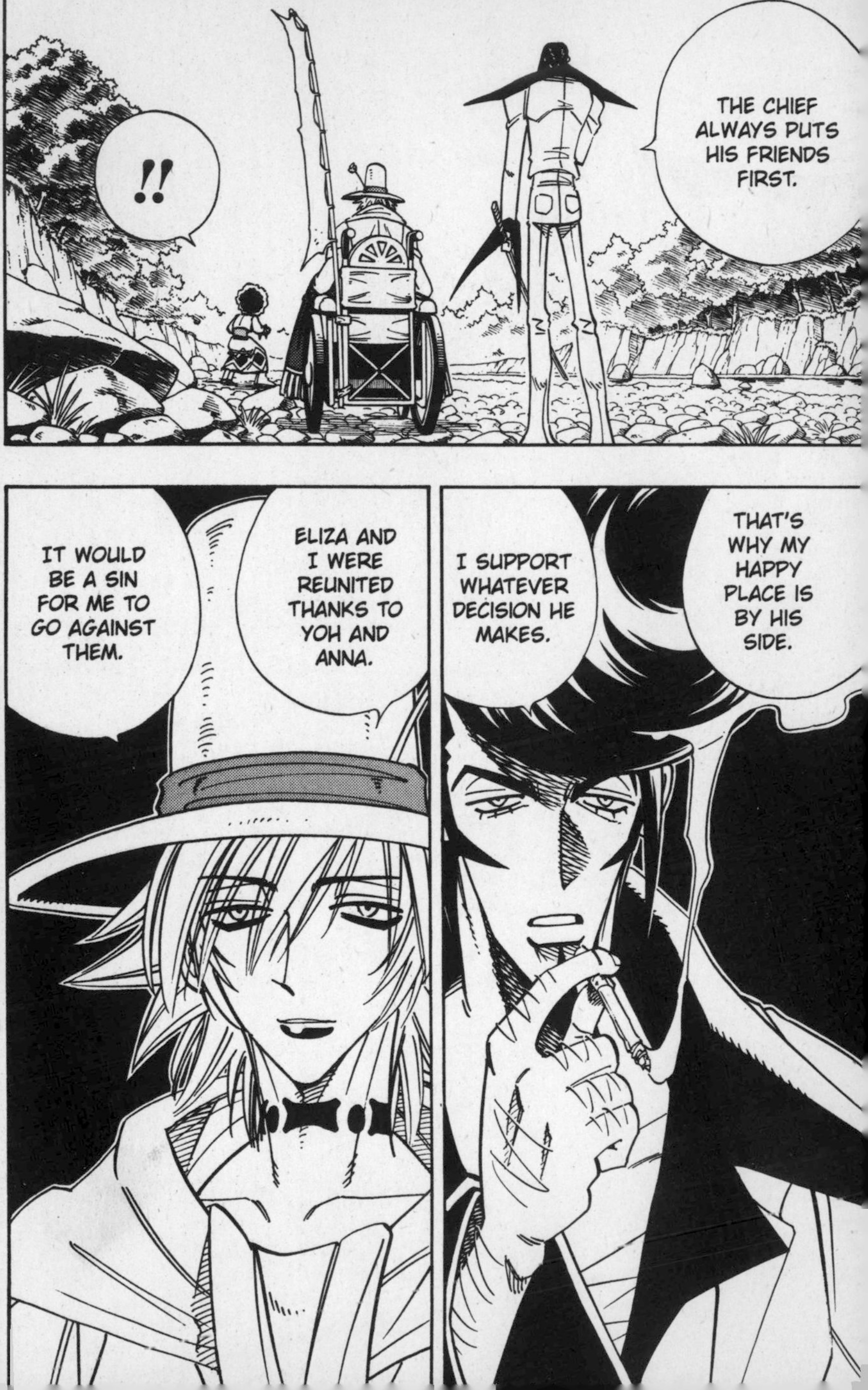
THE CHIEF ALWAYS PUTS HIS FRIENDS FIRST.
!!
THAT'S WHY MY HAPPY PLACE IS BY HIS SIDE.
I SUPPORT WHATEVER DECISION HE MAKES.
ELIZA AND I WERE REUNITED THANKS TO YOH AND ANNA.
IT WOULD BE A SIN FOR ME TO GO AGAINST THEM.

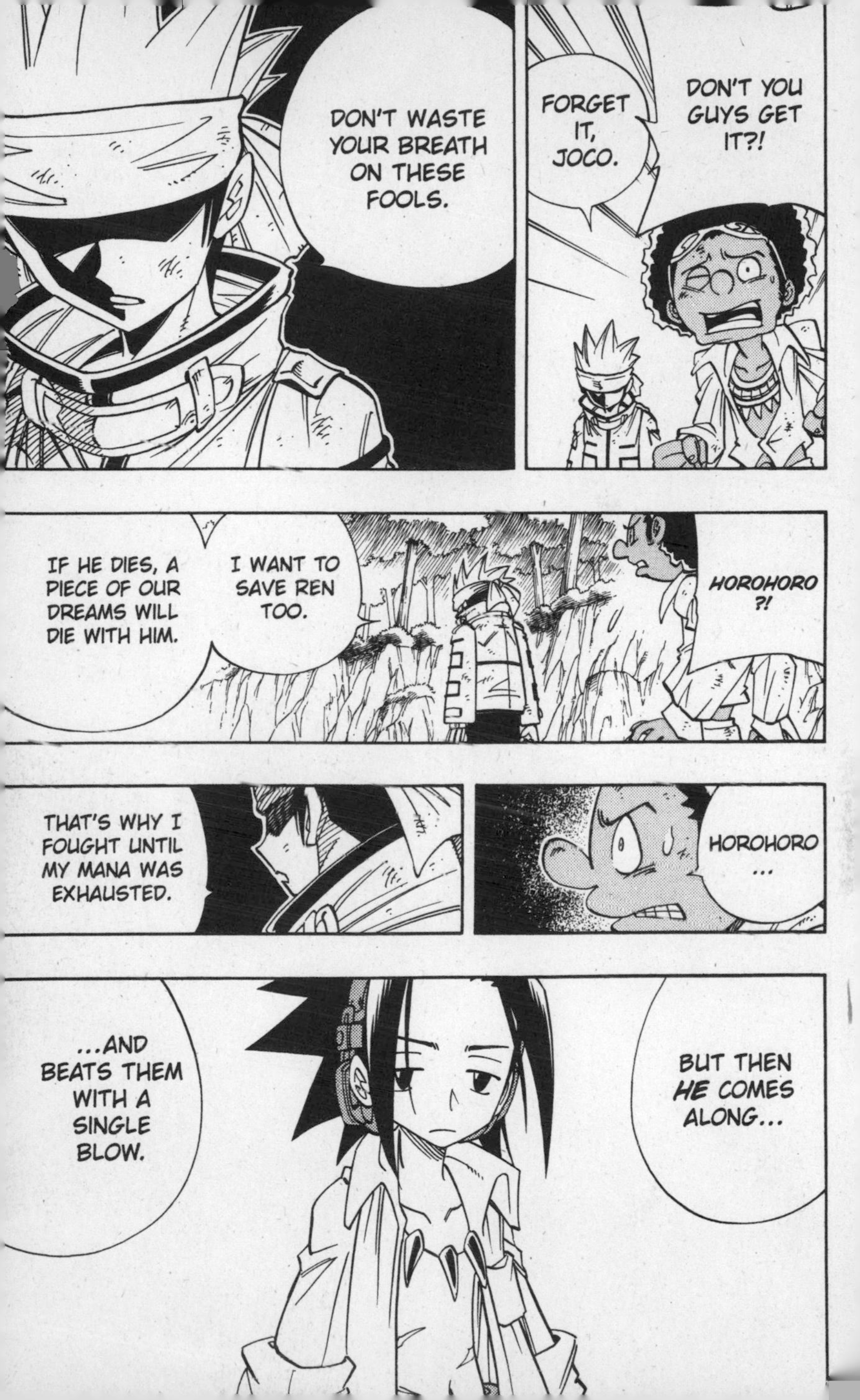

DON'T YOU GUYS GET IT?!
FORGET IT, JOCO.
DON'T WASTE YOUR BREATH ON THESE FOOLS.
HOROHORO ?!
I WANT TO SAVE REN TOO.
IF HE DIES, A PIECE OF OUR DREAMS WILL DIE WITH HIM.
HOROHORO ...
THAT'S WHY I FOUGHT UNTIL MY MANA WAS EXHAUSTED.
BUT THEN *HE* COMES ALONG...
...AND BEATS THEM WITH A SINGLE BLOW.

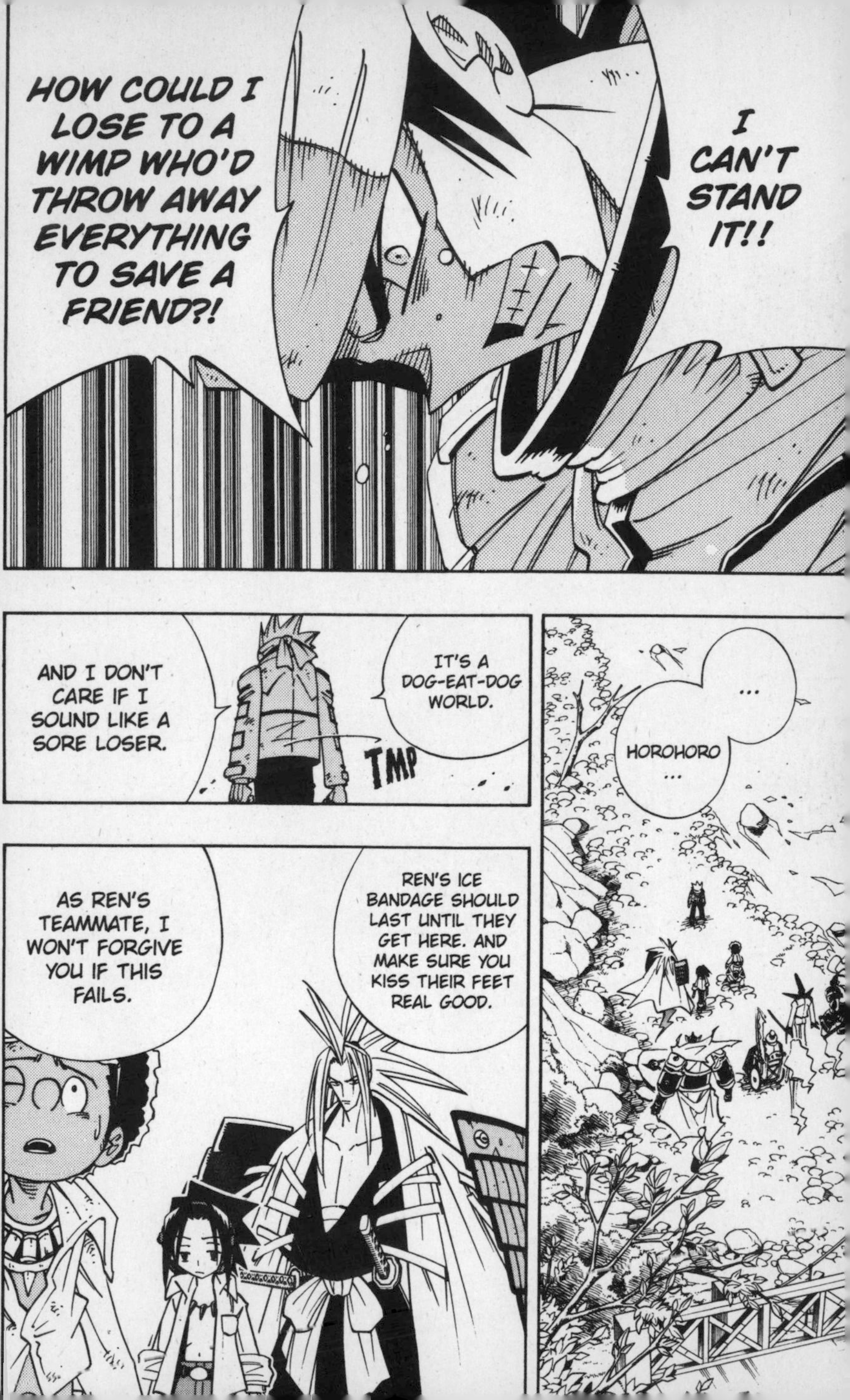
I CAN'T STAND IT!!
HOW COULD I LOSE TO A WIMP WHO'D THROW AWAY EVERYTHING TO SAVE A FRIEND?!
...
HOROHORO ...
IT'S A DOG-EAT-DOG WORLD.
AND I DON'T CARE IF I SOUND LIKE A SORE LOSER.
TMP
REN'S ICE BANDAGE SHOULD LAST UNTIL THEY GET HERE. AND MAKE SURE YOU KISS THEIR FEET REAL GOOD.
AS REN'S TEAMMATE, I WON'T FORGIVE YOU IF THIS FAILS.

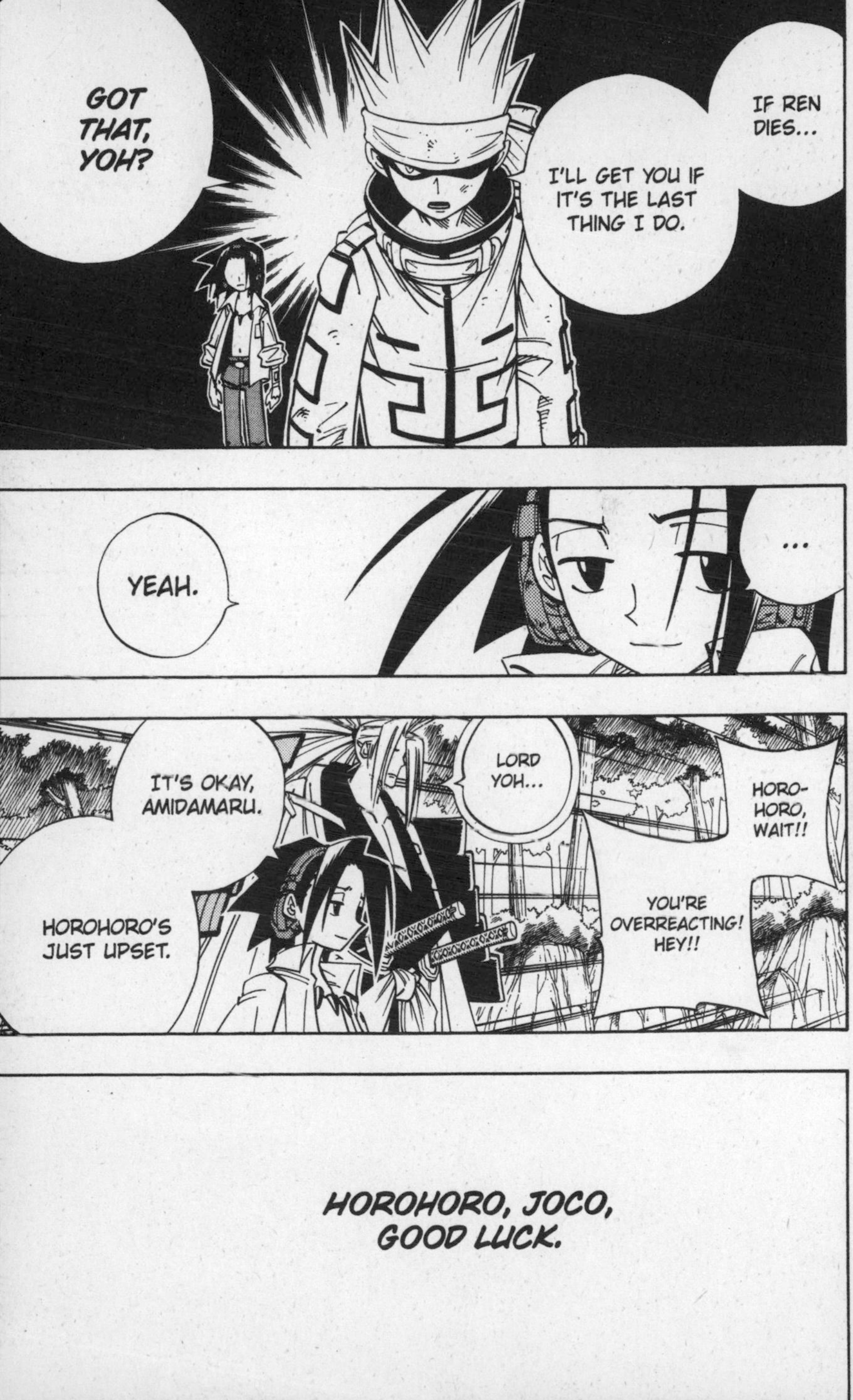
IF REN DIES...
I'LL GET YOU IF IT'S THE LAST THING I DO.
GOT THAT, YOH?
...
YEAH.
HORO-HORO, WAIT!!
YOU'RE OVERREACTING! HEY!!
LORD YOH...
IT'S OKAY, AMIDAMARU.
HOROHORO'S JUST UPSET.
HOROHORO, JOCO, GOOD LUCK.

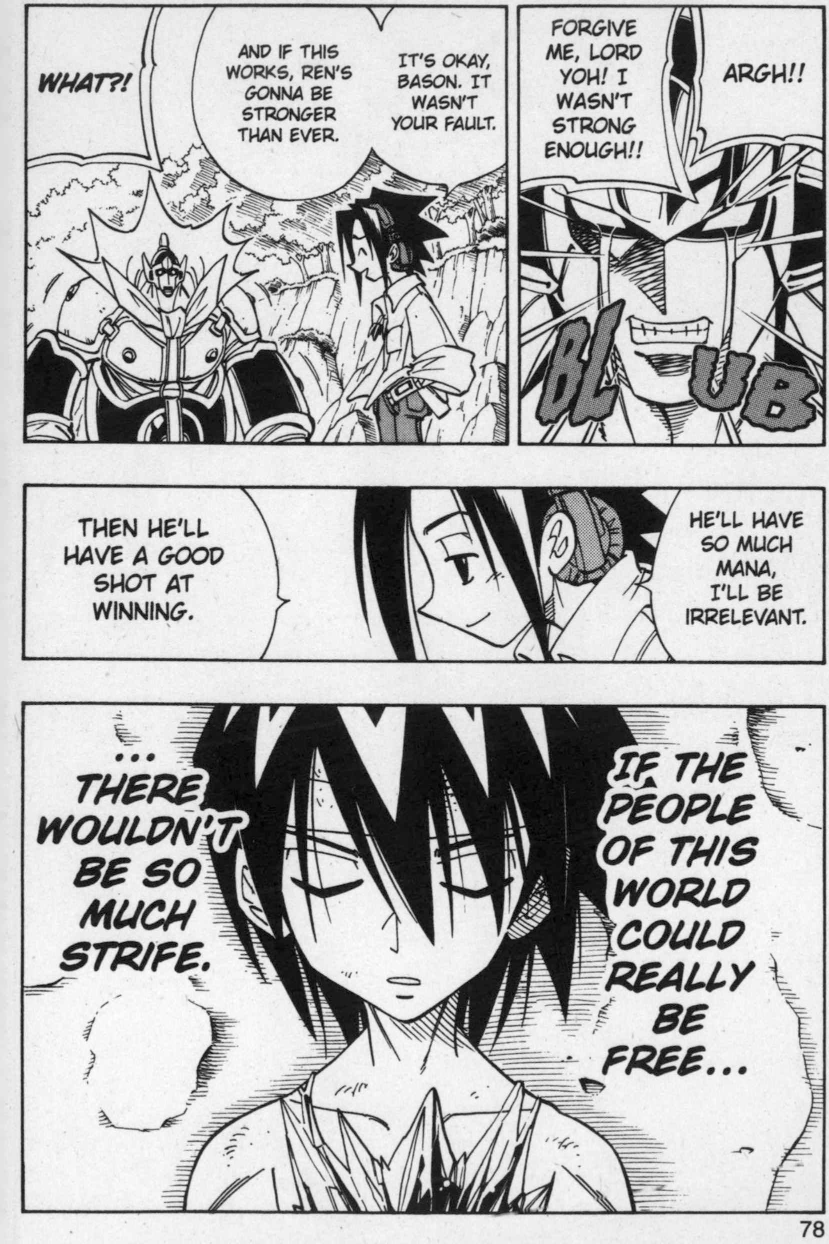
ARGH!!
FORGIVE ME, LORD YOH! I WASN'T STRONG ENOUGH!!
BLUB
IT'S OKAY, BASON. IT WASN'T YOUR FAULT.
AND IF THIS WORKS, REN'S GONNA BE STRONGER THAN EVER.
WHAT?!
HE'LL HAVE SO MUCH MANA, I'LL BE IRRELEVANT.
THEN HE'LL HAVE A GOOD SHOT AT WINNING.
IF THE PEOPLE OF THIS WORLD COULD REALLY BE FREE...
... THERE WOULDN'T BE SO MUCH STRIFE.

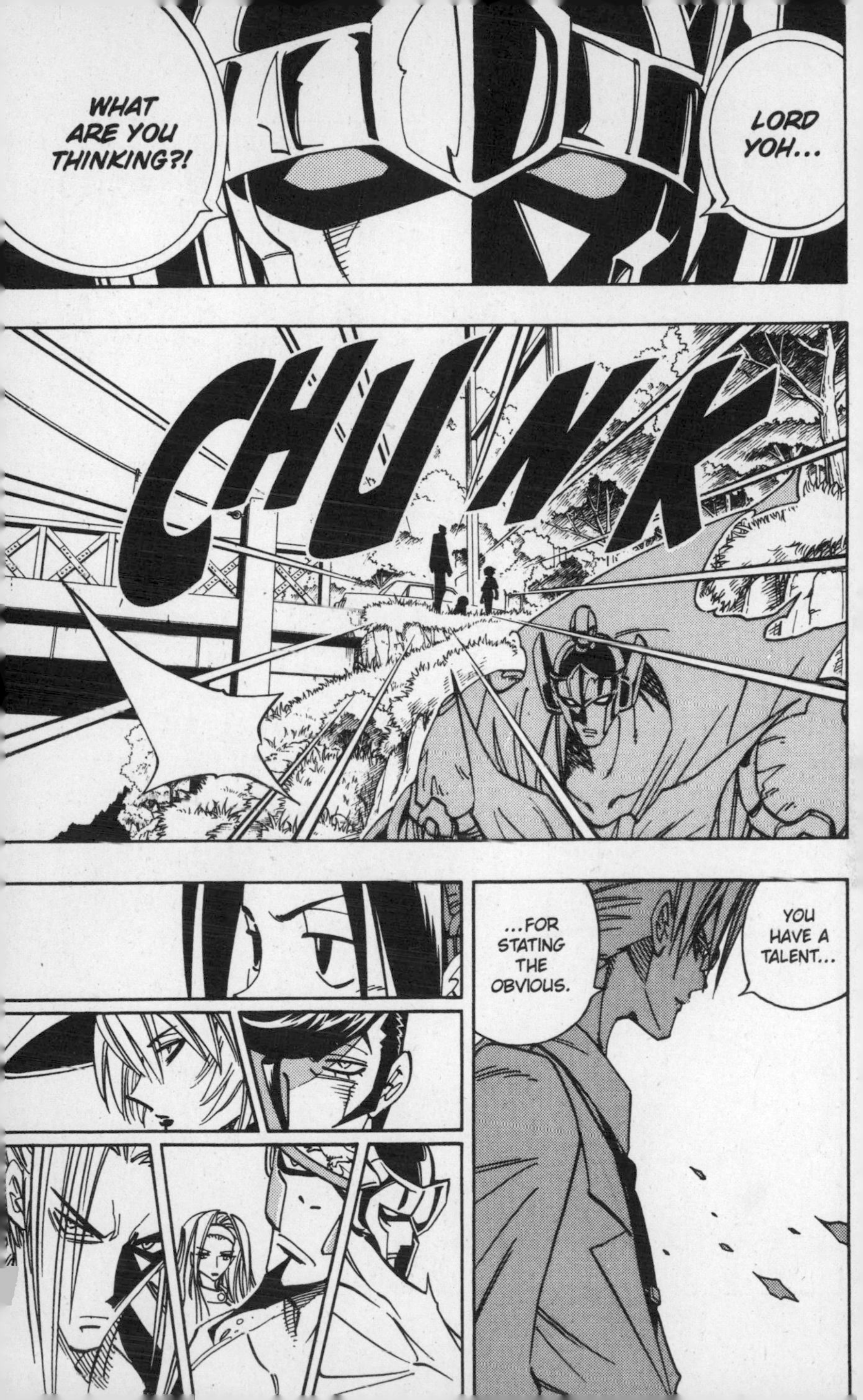
LORD YOH...
WHAT ARE YOU THINKING?!
CHUNK
YOU HAVE A TALENT...
...FOR STATING THE OBVIOUS.

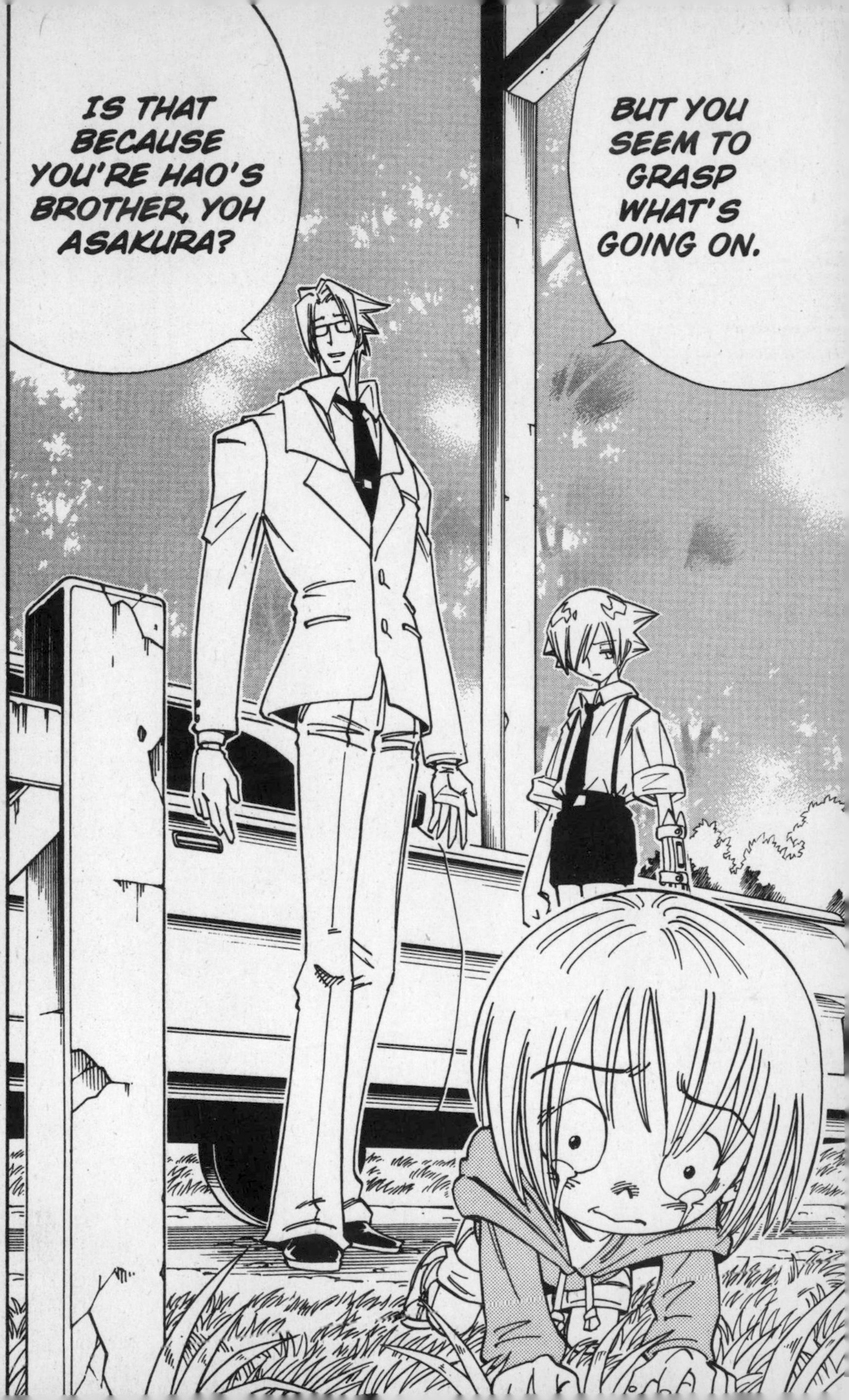
BUT YOU SEEM TO GRASP WHAT'S GOING ON.
IS THAT BECAUSE YOU'RE HAO'S BROTHER, YOH ASAKURA?

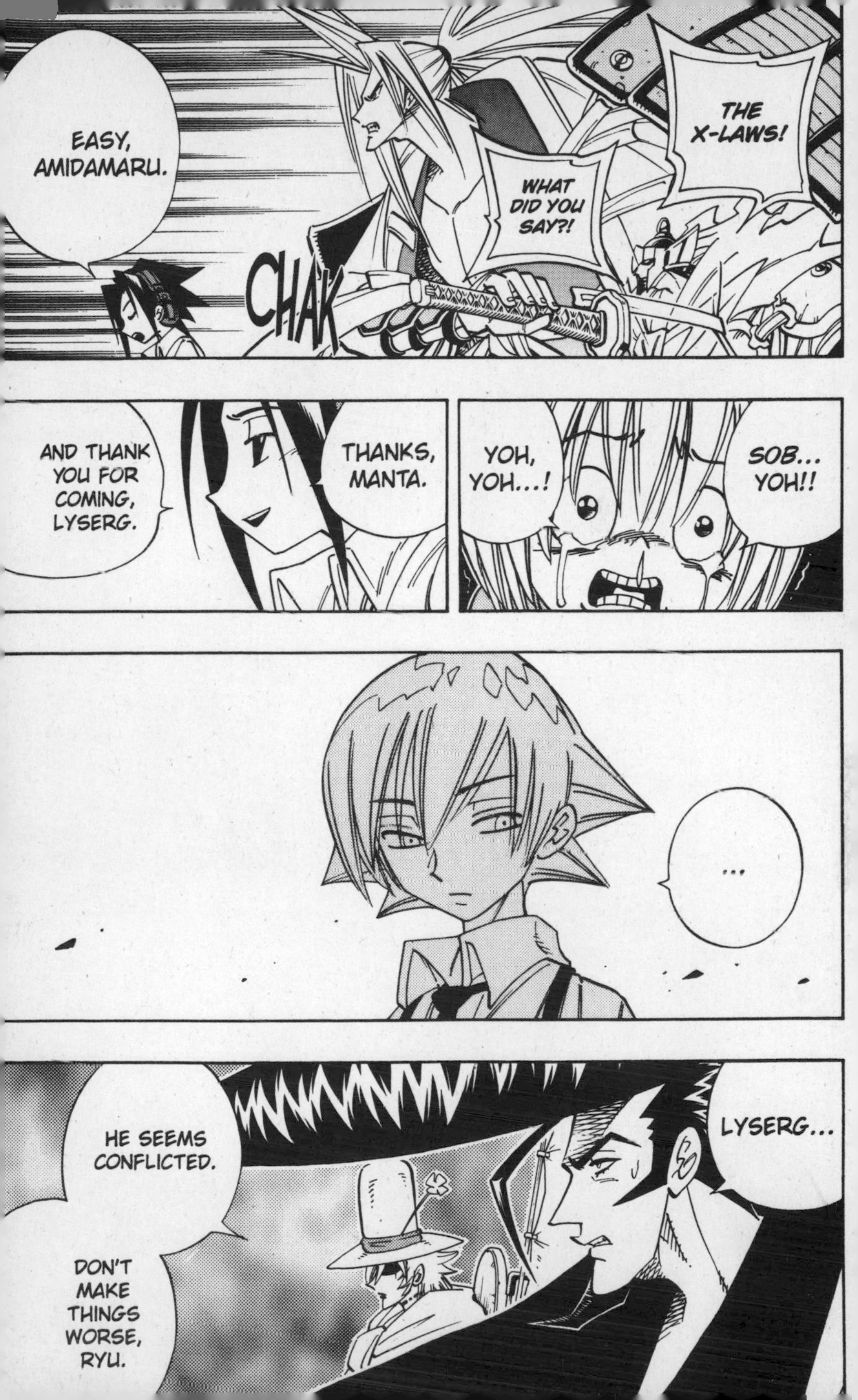
THE X-LAWS!
WHAT DID YOU SAY?!
CHAK
EASY, AMIDAMARU.
SOB... YOH!!
YOH, YOH...!
THANKS, MANTA.
AND THANK YOU FOR COMING, LYSERG.
...
LYSERG...
HE SEEMS CONFLICTED.
DON'T MAKE THINGS WORSE, RYU.

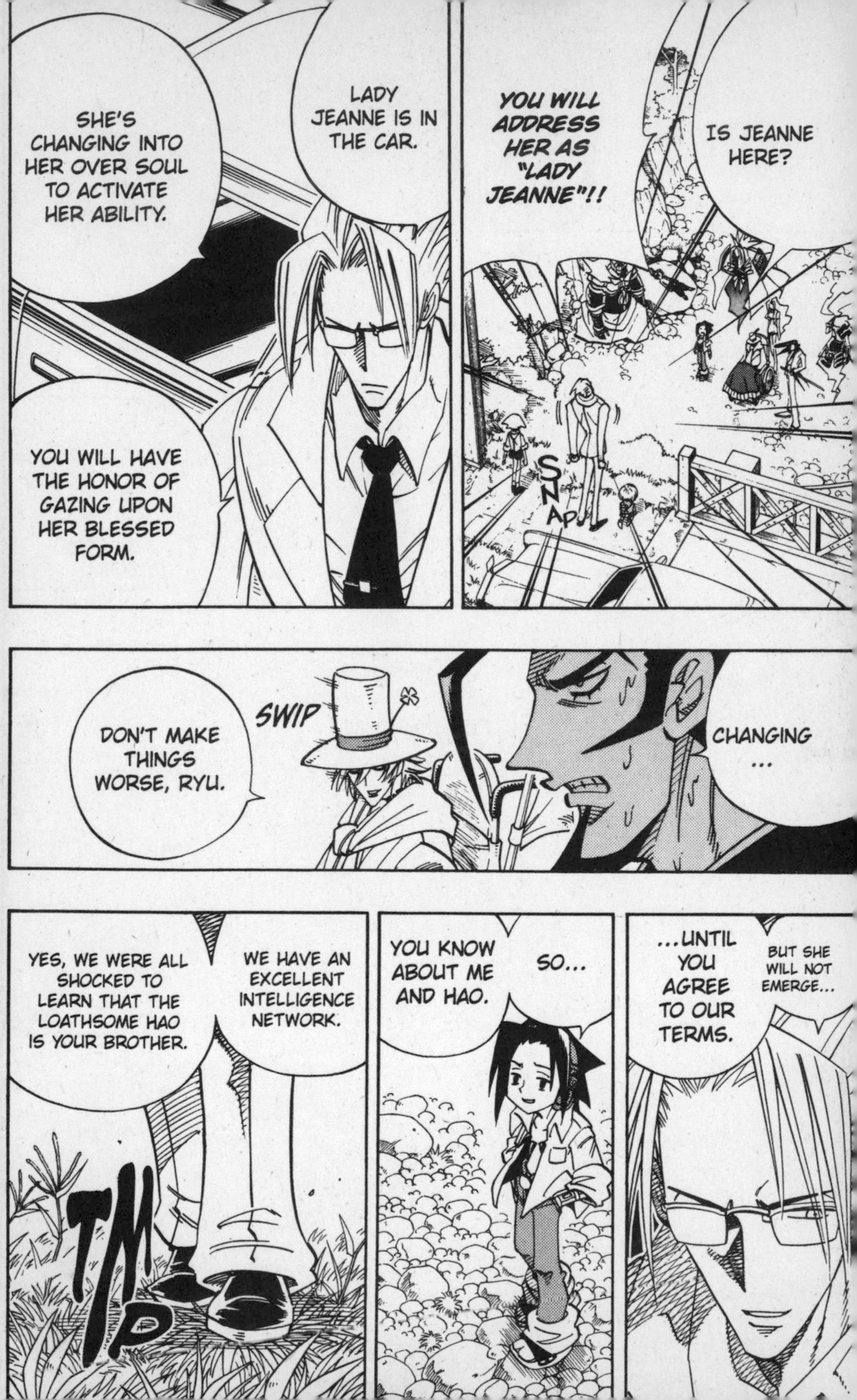
IS JEANNE HERE?
YOU WILL ADDRESS HER AS "LADY JEANNE"!!
SNAP
LADY JEANNE IS IN THE CAR.
SHE'S CHANGING INTO HER OVER SOUL TO ACTIVATE HER ABILITY.
YOU WILL HAVE THE HONOR OF GAZING UPON HER BLESSED FORM.
CHANGING ...
SWIP
DON'T MAKE THINGS WORSE, RYU.
BUT SHE WILL NOT EMERGE...
...UNTIL YOU AGREE TO OUR TERMS.
SO...
YOU KNOW ABOUT ME AND HAO.
WE HAVE AN EXCELLENT INTELLIGENCE NETWORK.
YES, WE WERE ALL SHOCKED TO LEARN THAT THE LOATHSOME HAO IS YOUR BROTHER.
TMP

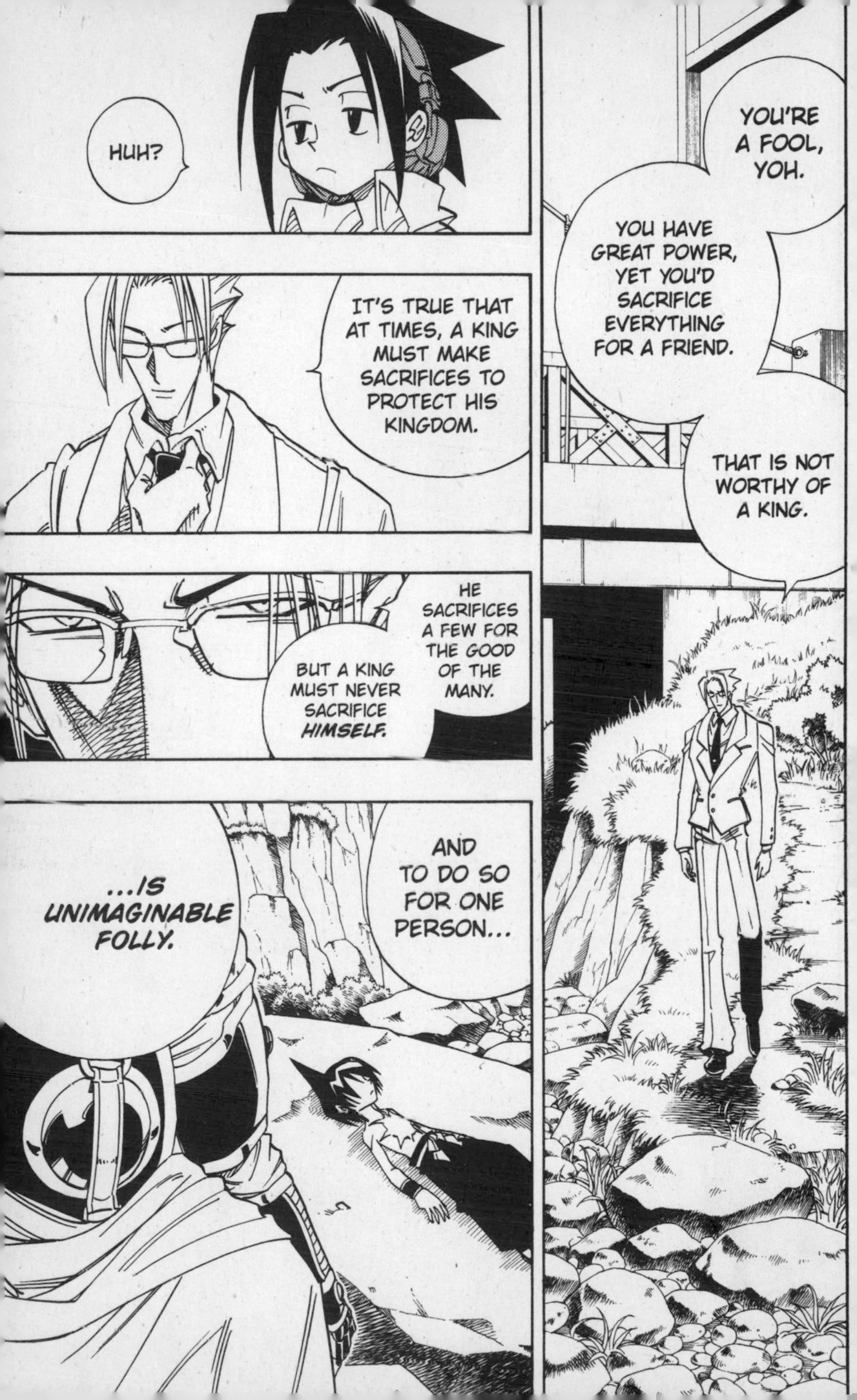
YOU'RE A FOOL, YOH.
YOU HAVE GREAT POWER, YET YOU'D SACRIFICE EVERYTHING FOR A FRIEND.
THAT IS NOT WORTHY OF A KING.
HUH?
IT'S TRUE THAT AT TIMES, A KING MUST MAKE SACRIFICES TO PROTECT HIS KINGDOM.
HE SACRIFICES A FEW FOR THE GOOD OF THE MANY.
BUT A KING MUST NEVER SACRIFICE *HIMSELF.*
AND TO DO SO FOR ONE PERSON...
...IS UNIMAGINABLE FOLLY.

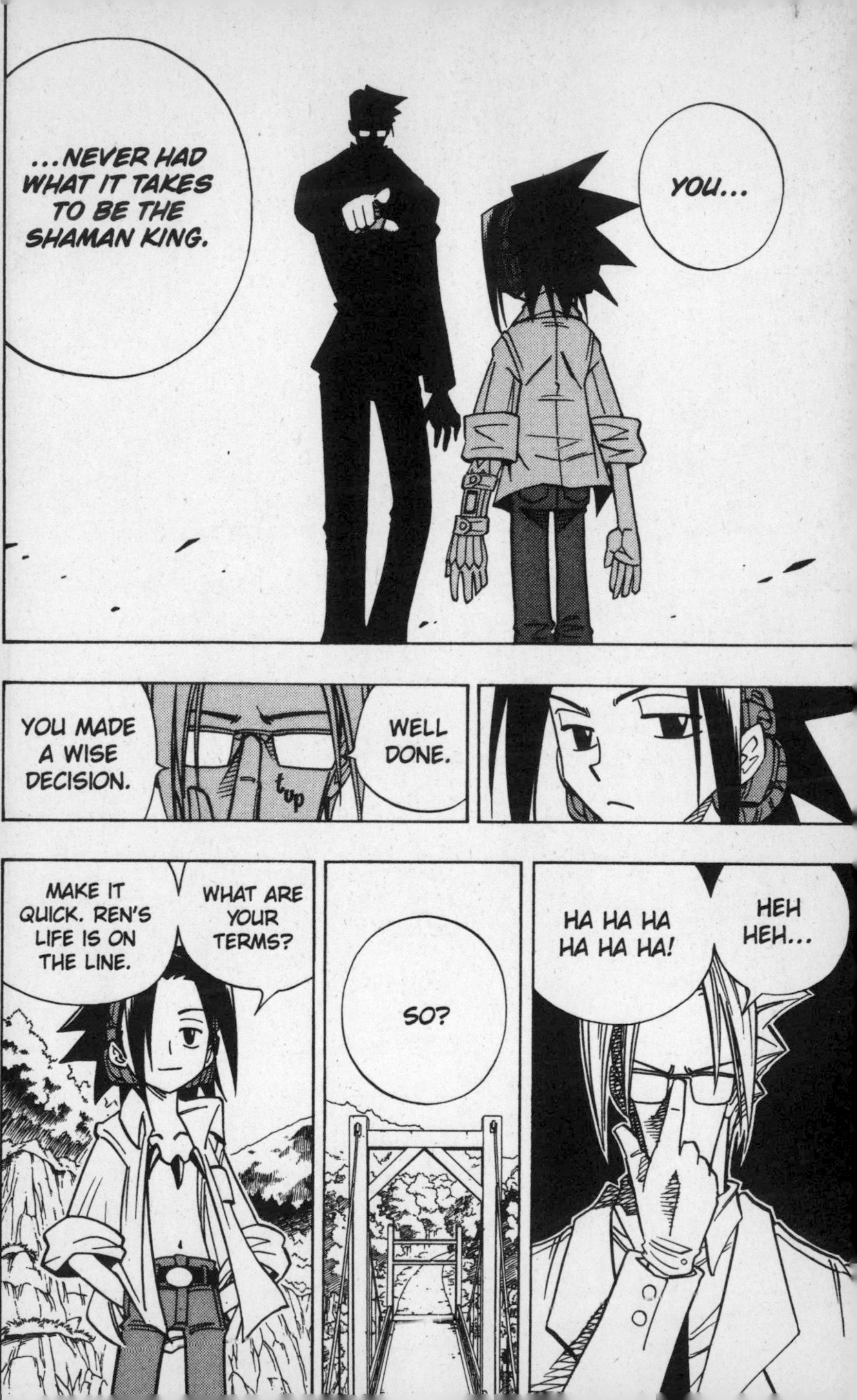
YOU...
...NEVER HAD WHAT IT TAKES TO BE THE SHAMAN KING.
WELL DONE.
YOU MADE A WISE DECISION.
tup
HEH HEH...
HA HA HA HA HA HA!
SO?
WHAT ARE YOUR TERMS?
MAKE IT QUICK. REN'S LIFE IS ON THE LINE.

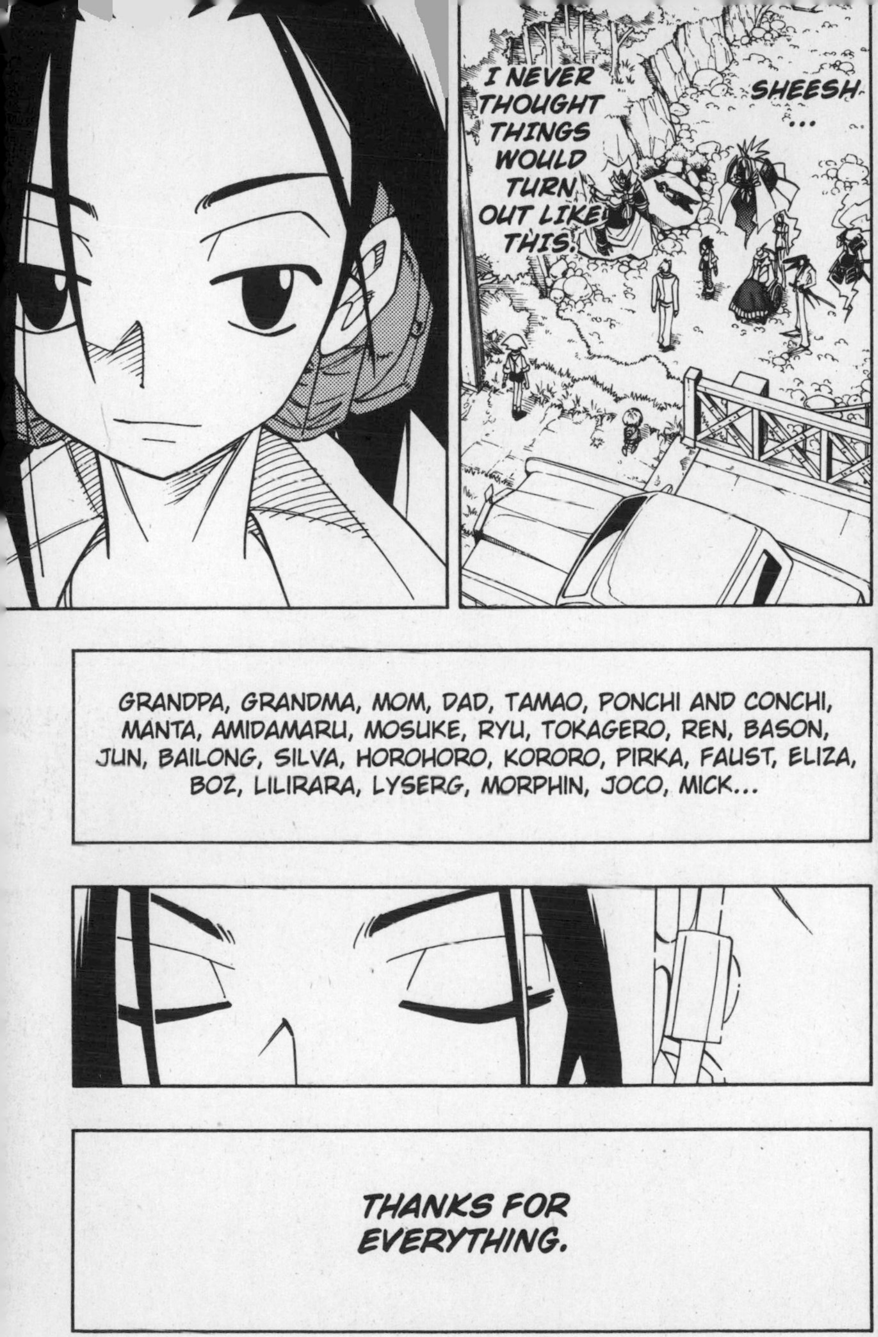
SHEESH...
I NEVER THOUGHT THINGS WOULD TURN OUT LIKE THIS.
GRANDPA, GRANDMA, MOM, DAD, TAMAO, PONCHI AND CONCHI, MANTA, AMIDAMARU, MOSUKE, RYU, TOKAGERO, REN, BASON, JUN, BAILONG, SILVA, HOROHORO, KORORO, PIRKA, FAUST, ELIZA, BOZ, LILIRARA, LYSERG, MORPHIN, JOCO, MICK...
THANKS FOR EVERYTHING.

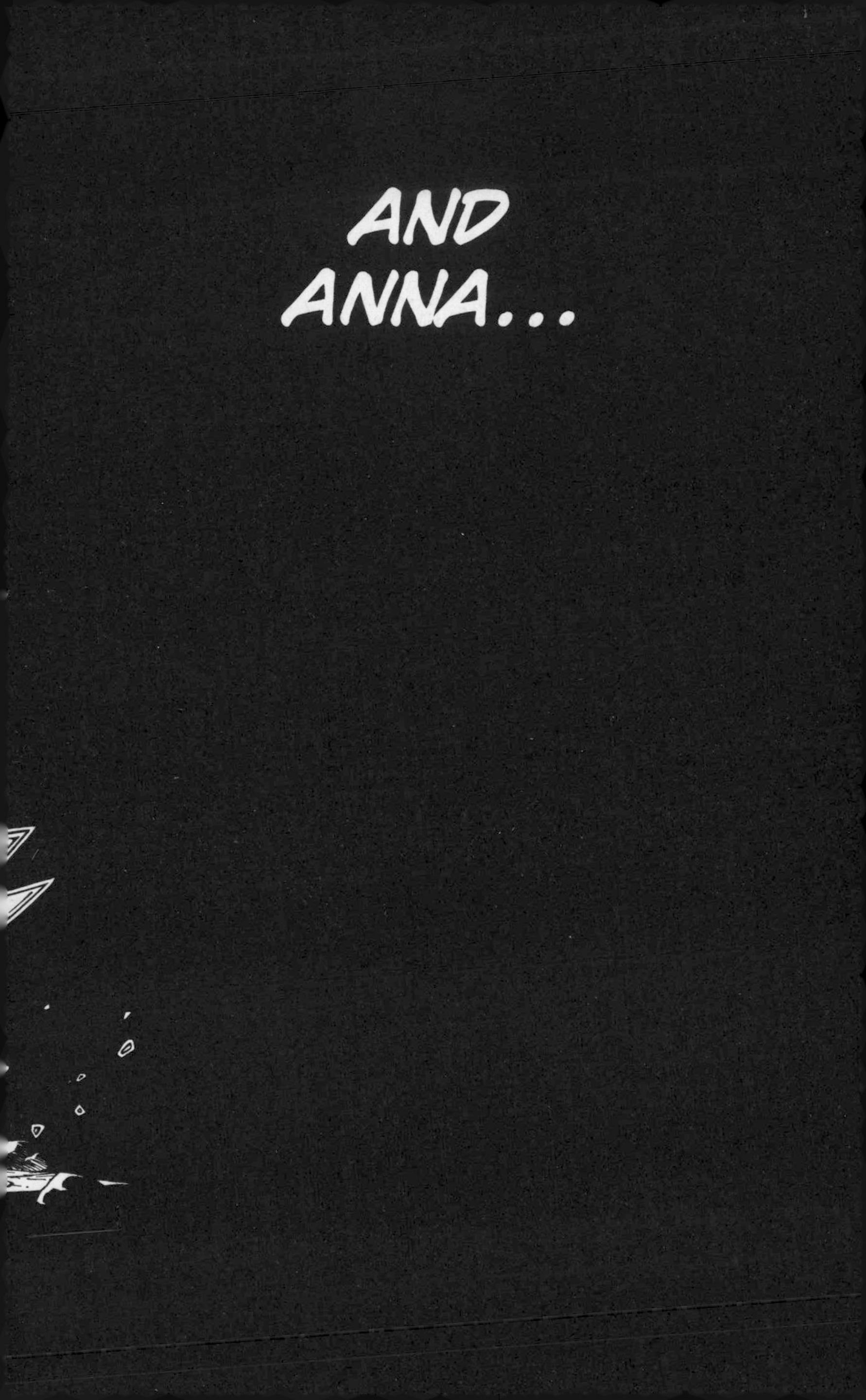
AND ANNA...

I'M SORRY.

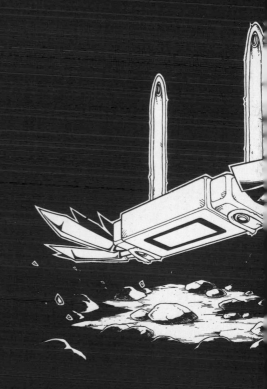

SHAMAN KING CHARACTER FILE No.92

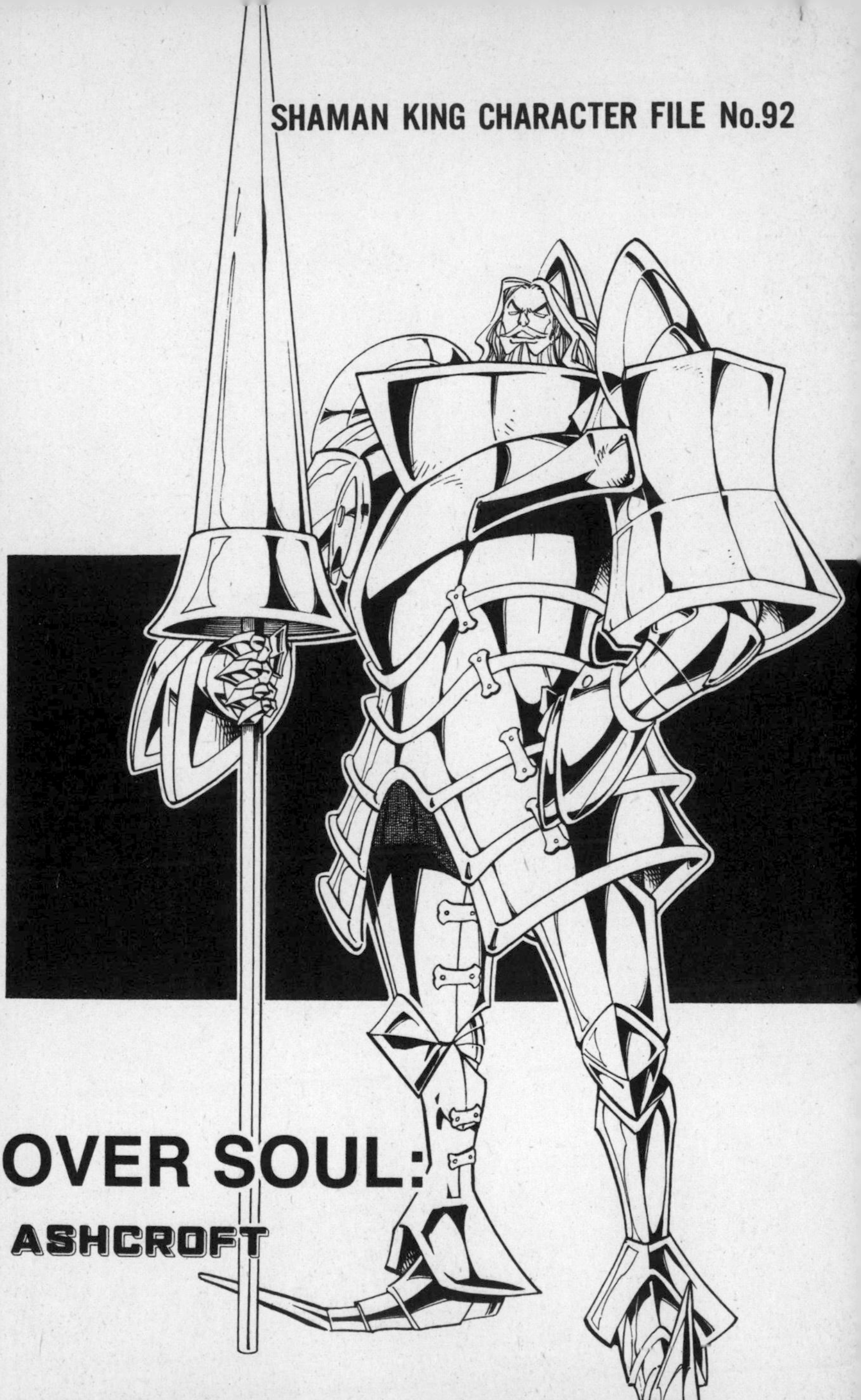

OVER SOUL:

ASHCROFT

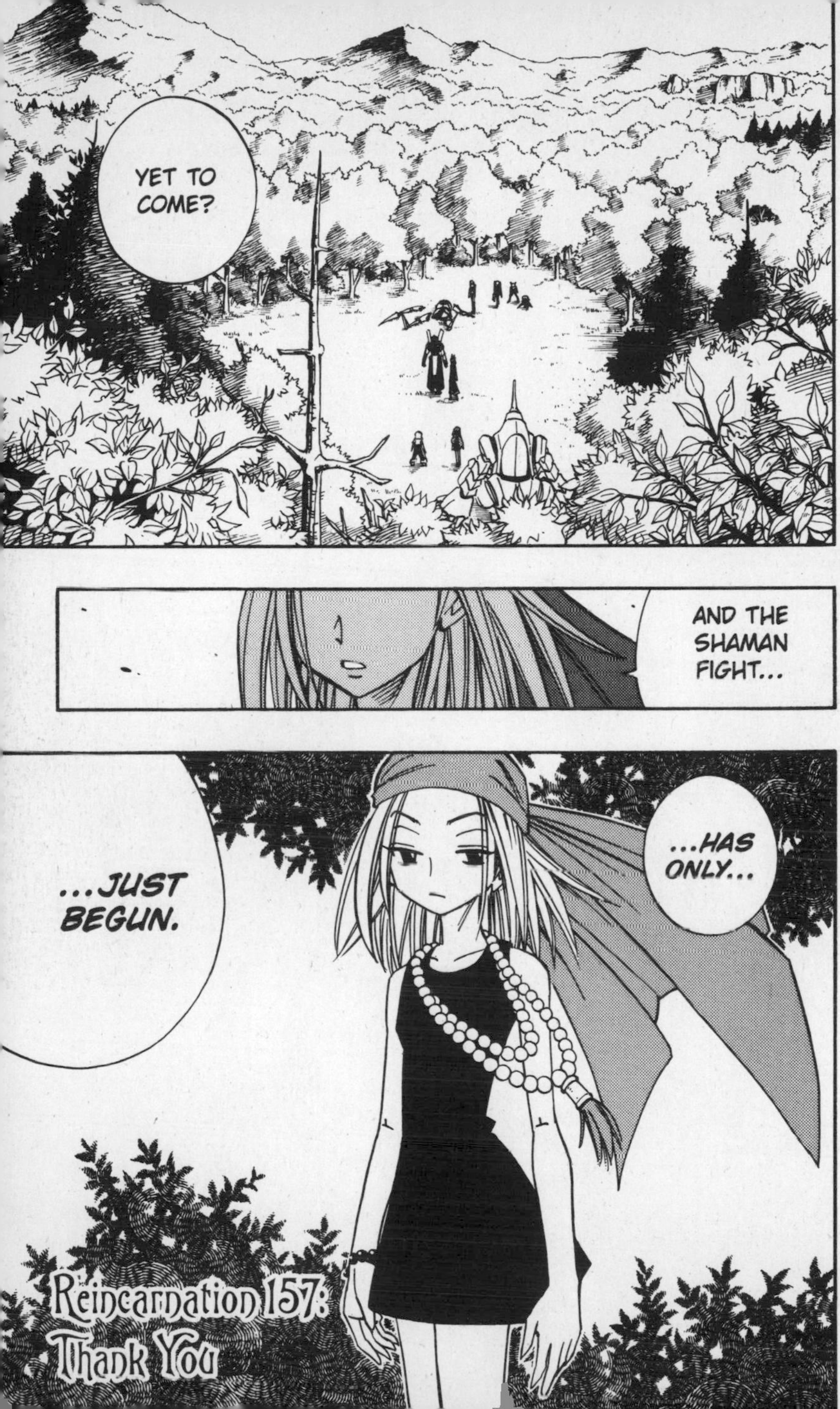
YET TO COME?
AND THE SHAMAN FIGHT...
...HAS ONLY...
...JUST BEGUN.
Reincarnation 157: Thank You

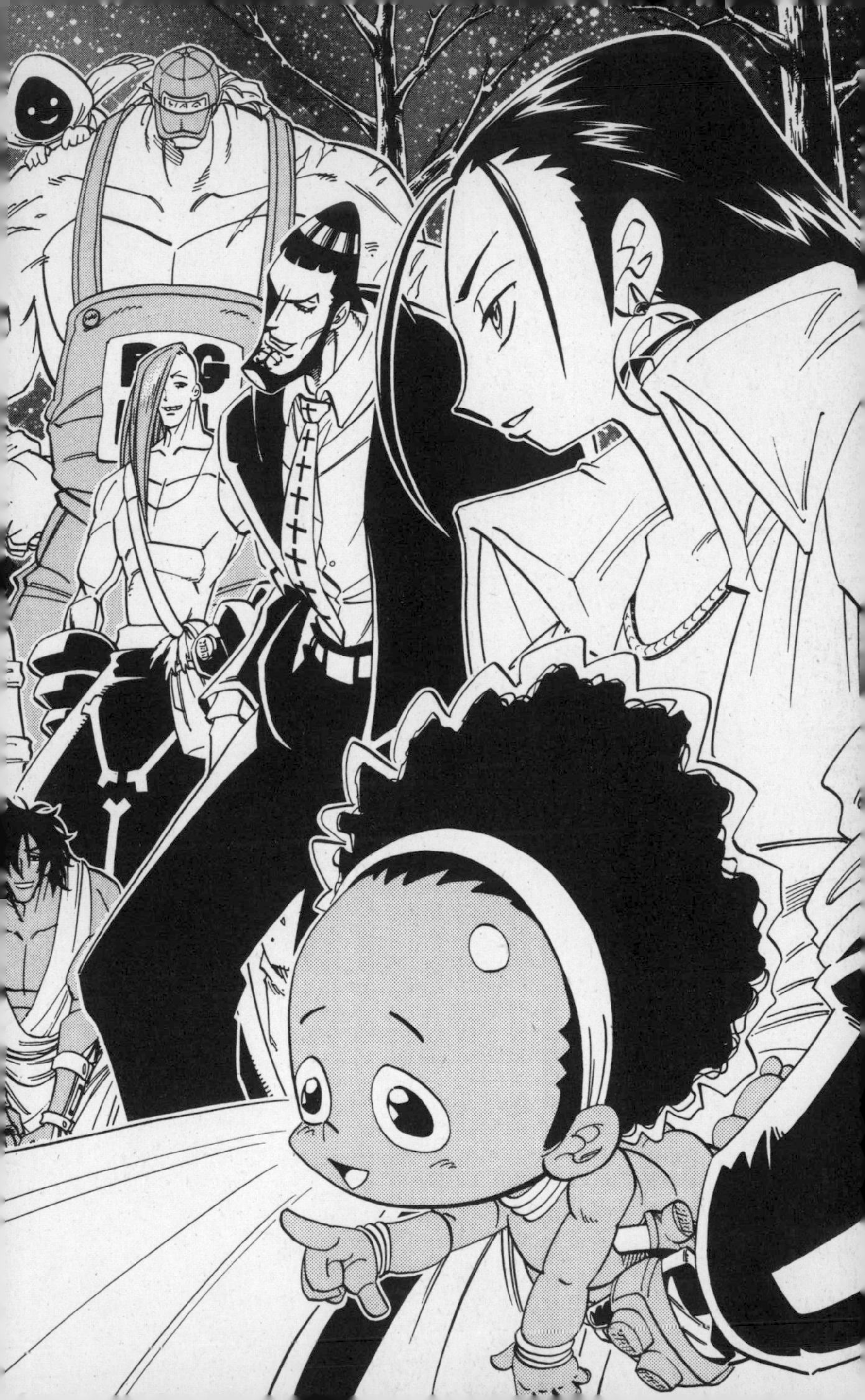

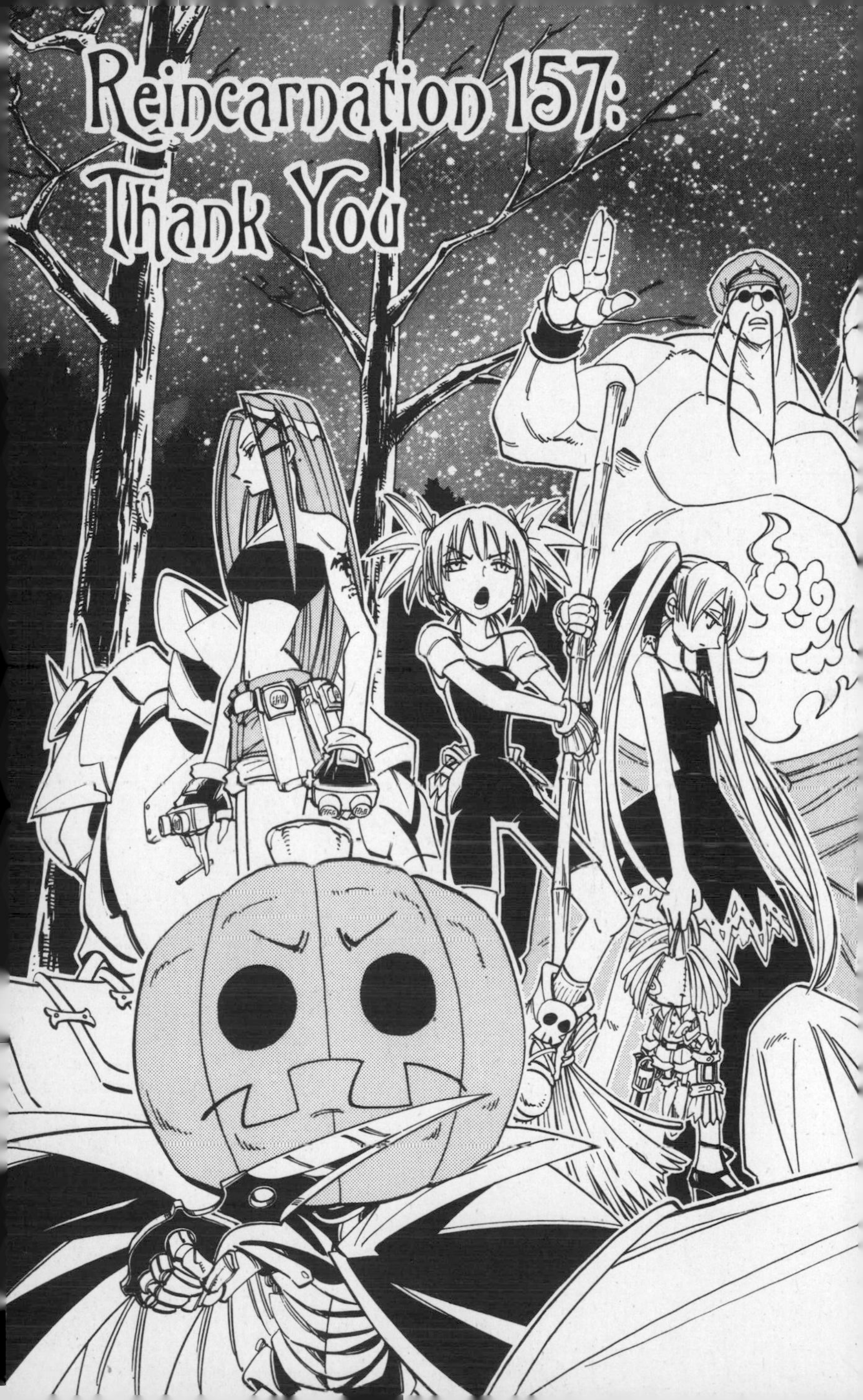
Reincarnation 157:
Thank You

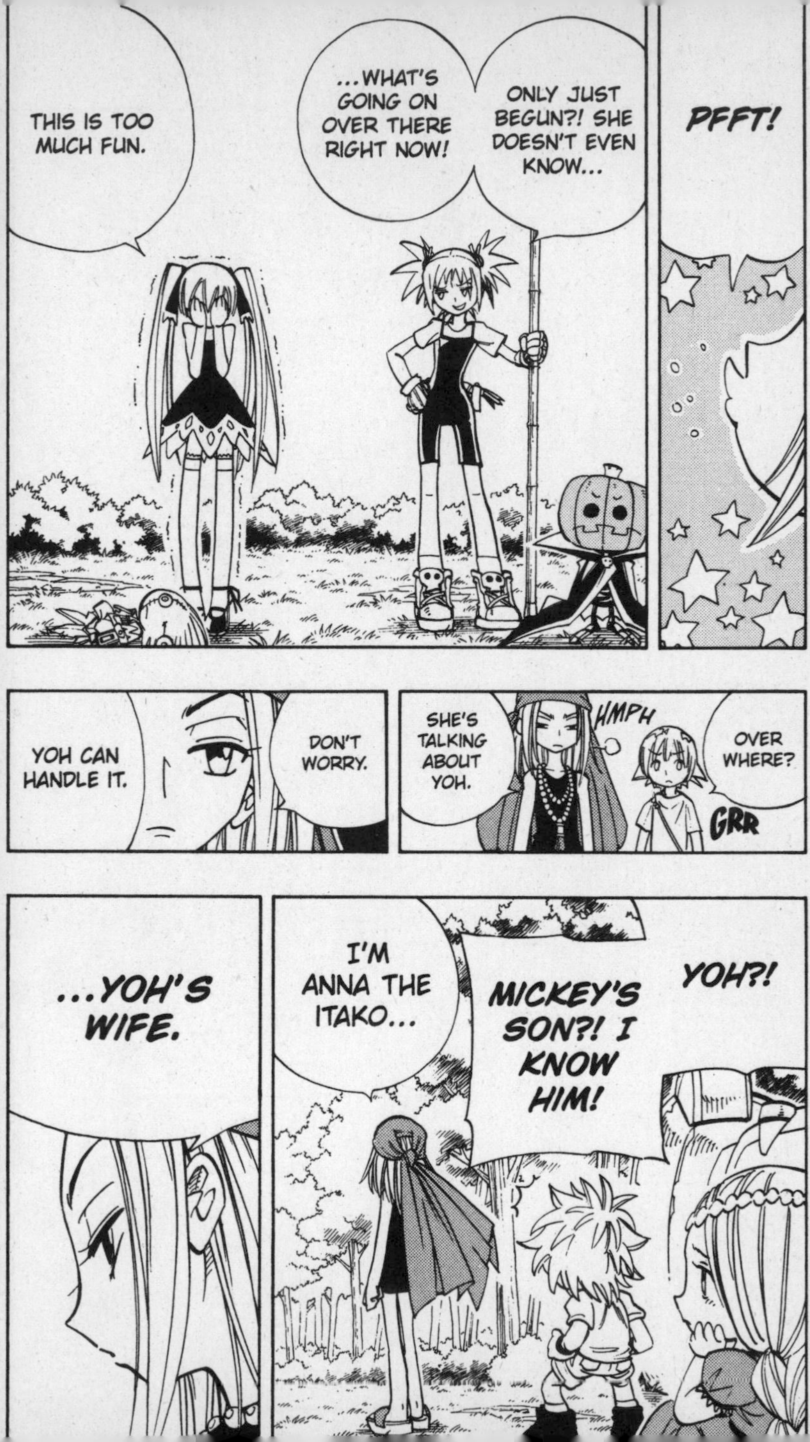
PFFT!
ONLY JUST BEGUN?! SHE DOESN'T EVEN KNOW...
...WHAT'S GOING ON OVER THERE RIGHT NOW!
THIS IS TOO MUCH FUN.
OVER WHERE?
GRR
HMPH
SHE'S TALKING ABOUT YOH.
DON'T WORRY.
YOH CAN HANDLE IT.
YOH?!
MICKEY'S SON?! I KNOW HIM!
I'M ANNA THE ITAKO...
...YOH'S WIFE.

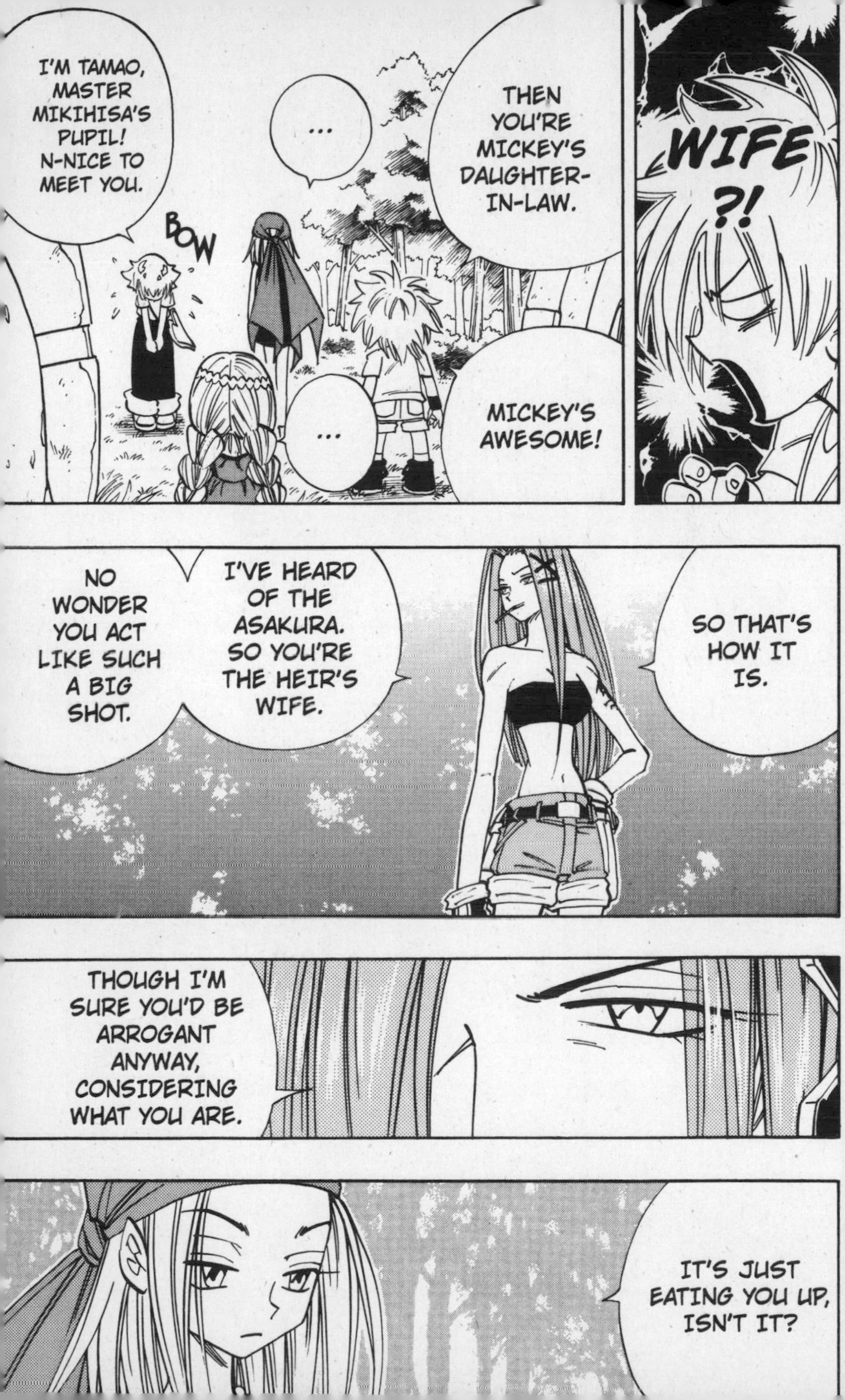
WIFE ?!
THEN YOU'RE MICKEY'S DAUGHTER-IN-LAW.
MICKEY'S AWESOME!
...
...
I'M TAMAO, MASTER MIKIHISA'S PUPIL! N-NICE TO MEET YOU.
BOW
SO THAT'S HOW IT IS.
I'VE HEARD OF THE ASAKURA. SO YOU'RE THE HEIR'S WIFE.
NO WONDER YOU ACT LIKE SUCH A BIG SHOT.
THOUGH I'M SURE YOU'D BE ARROGANT ANYWAY, CONSIDERING WHAT YOU ARE.
IT'S JUST EATING YOU UP, ISN'T IT?

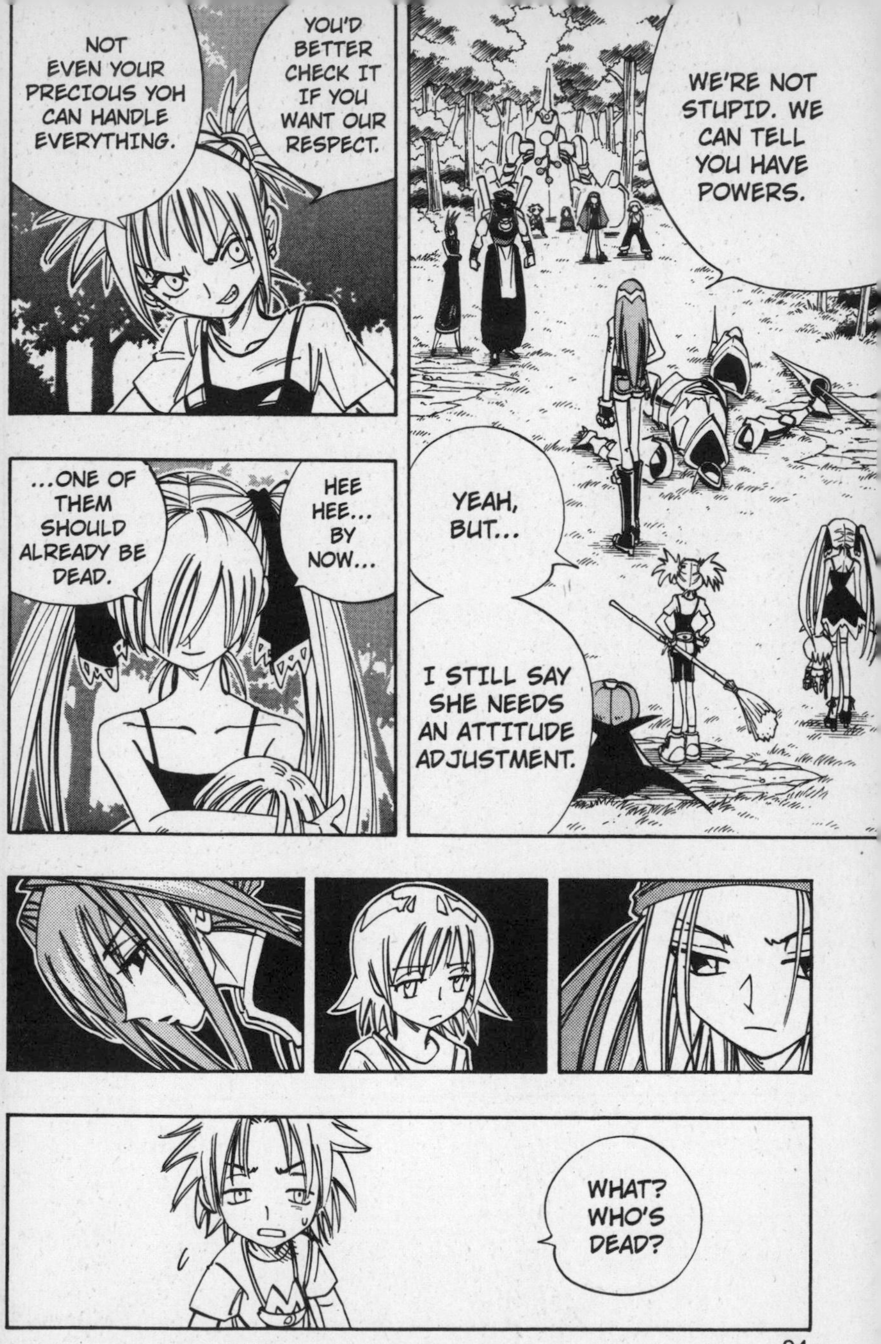
WE'RE NOT STUPID. WE CAN TELL YOU HAVE POWERS.
YEAH, BUT...
I STILL SAY SHE NEEDS AN ATTITUDE ADJUSTMENT.
YOU'D BETTER CHECK IT IF YOU WANT OUR RESPECT.
NOT EVEN YOUR PRECIOUS YOH CAN HANDLE EVERYTHING.
HEE HEE... BY NOW...
...ONE OF THEM SHOULD ALREADY BE DEAD.
WHAT? WHO'S DEAD?

READ THIS WAY

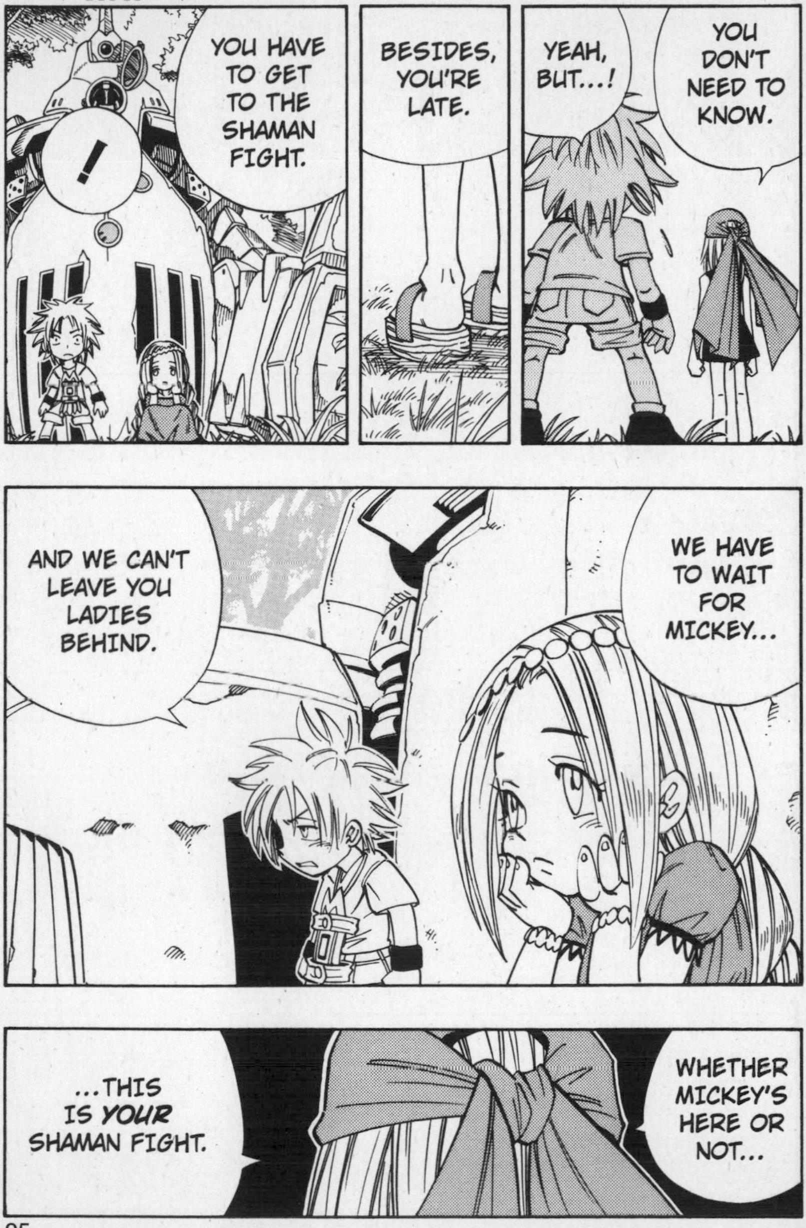
YOU DON'T NEED TO KNOW.
YEAH, BUT...!
BESIDES, YOU'RE LATE.
YOU HAVE TO GET TO THE SHAMAN FIGHT.
!
WE HAVE TO WAIT FOR MICKEY...
AND WE CAN'T LEAVE YOU LADIES BEHIND.
WHETHER MICKEY'S HERE OR NOT...
...THIS IS *YOUR* SHAMAN FIGHT.

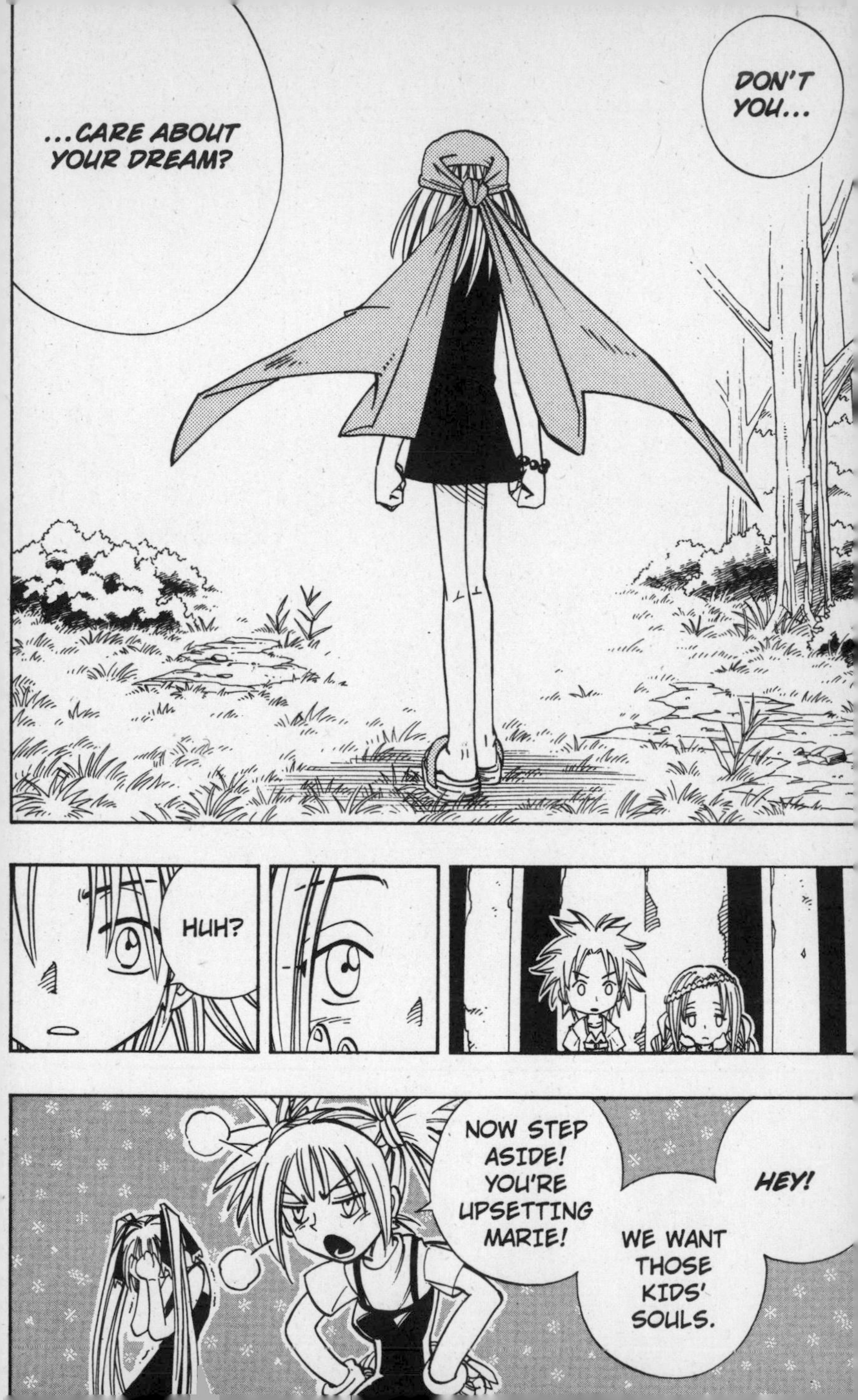
DON'T YOU...
...CARE ABOUT YOUR DREAM?
HUH?
HEY!
WE WANT THOSE KIDS' SOULS.
NOW STEP ASIDE! YOU'RE UPSETTING MARIE!

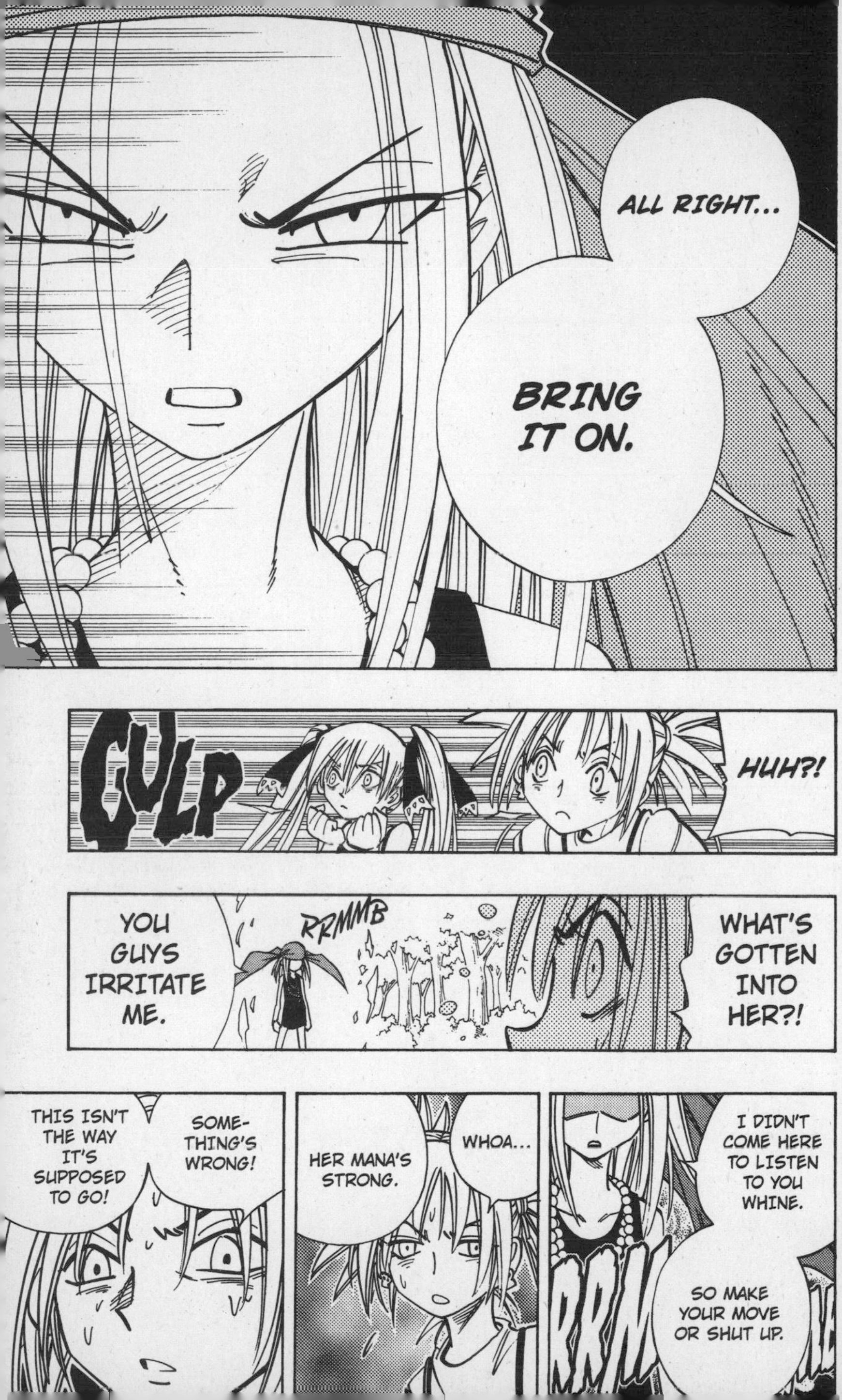
ALL RIGHT...
BRING IT ON.
HUH?!
GULP
WHAT'S GOTTEN INTO HER?!
RRMMB
YOU GUYS IRRITATE ME.
I DIDN'T COME HERE TO LISTEN TO YOU WHINE.
SO MAKE YOUR MOVE OR SHUT UP.
WHOA...
HER MANA'S STRONG.
SOME-THING'S WRONG!
THIS ISN'T THE WAY IT'S SUPPOSED TO GO!

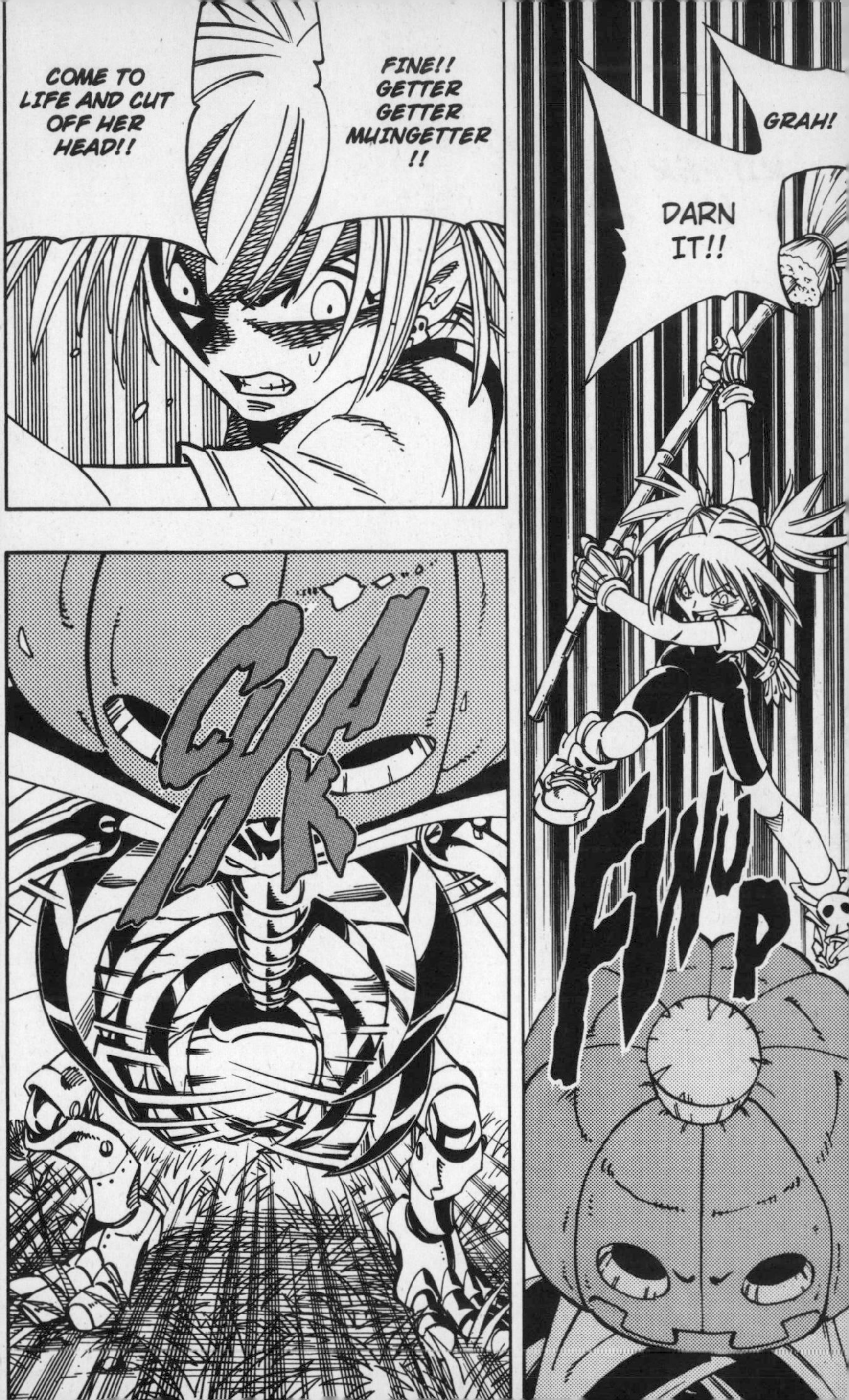
GRAH!
DARN IT!!
FWUP
FINE!! GETTER GETTER MUINGETTER !!
COME TO LIFE AND CUT OFF HER HEAD!!
GYAK

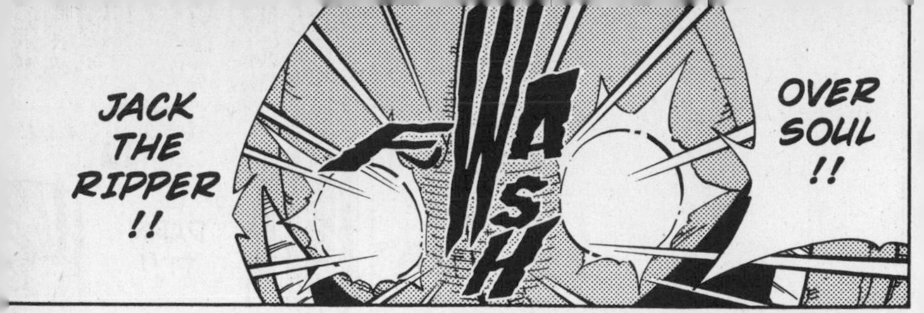
OVER SOUL !!
FWASH
JACK THE RIPPER !!

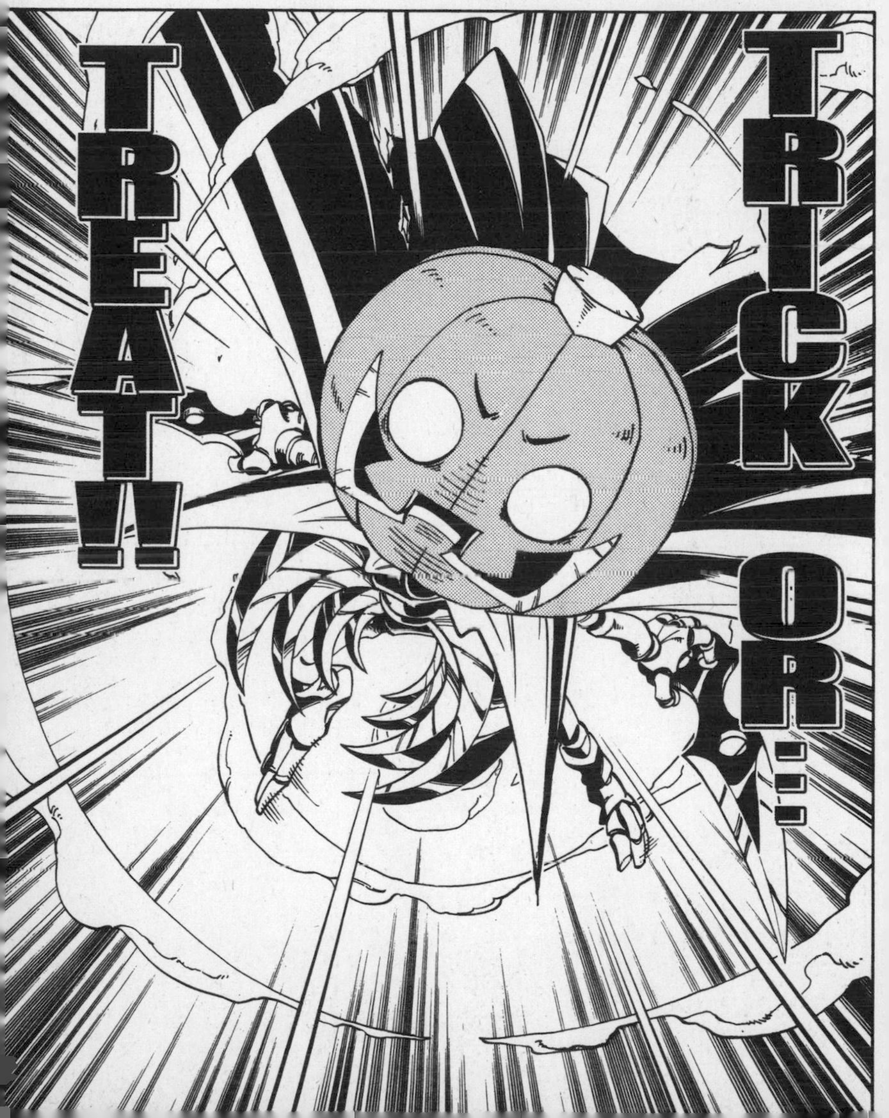
TRICK OR...
TREAT!!

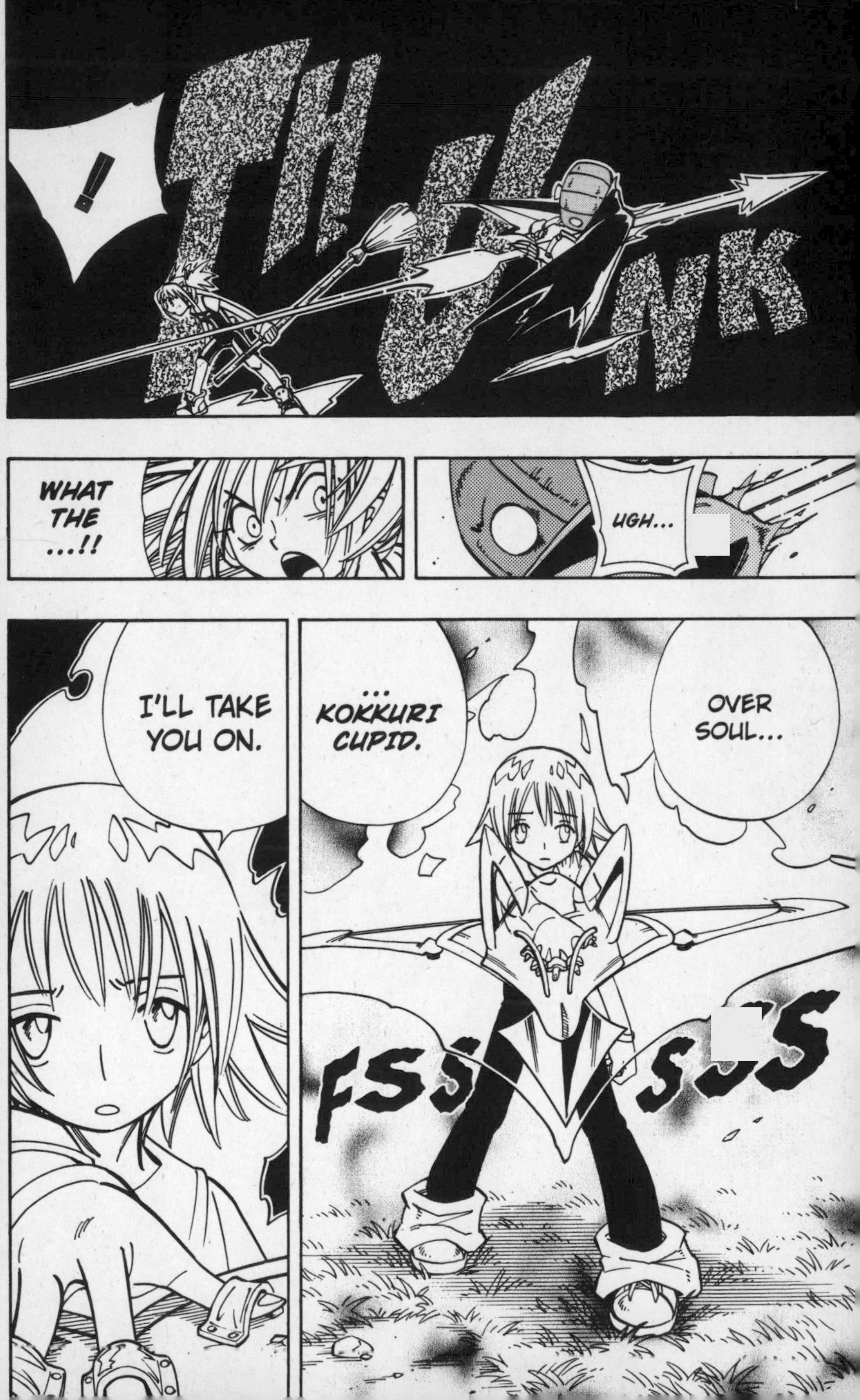
THUNK
!
UGH...
WHAT THE ...!!
OVER SOUL...
... KOKKURI CUPID.
I'LL TAKE YOU ON.
FSS

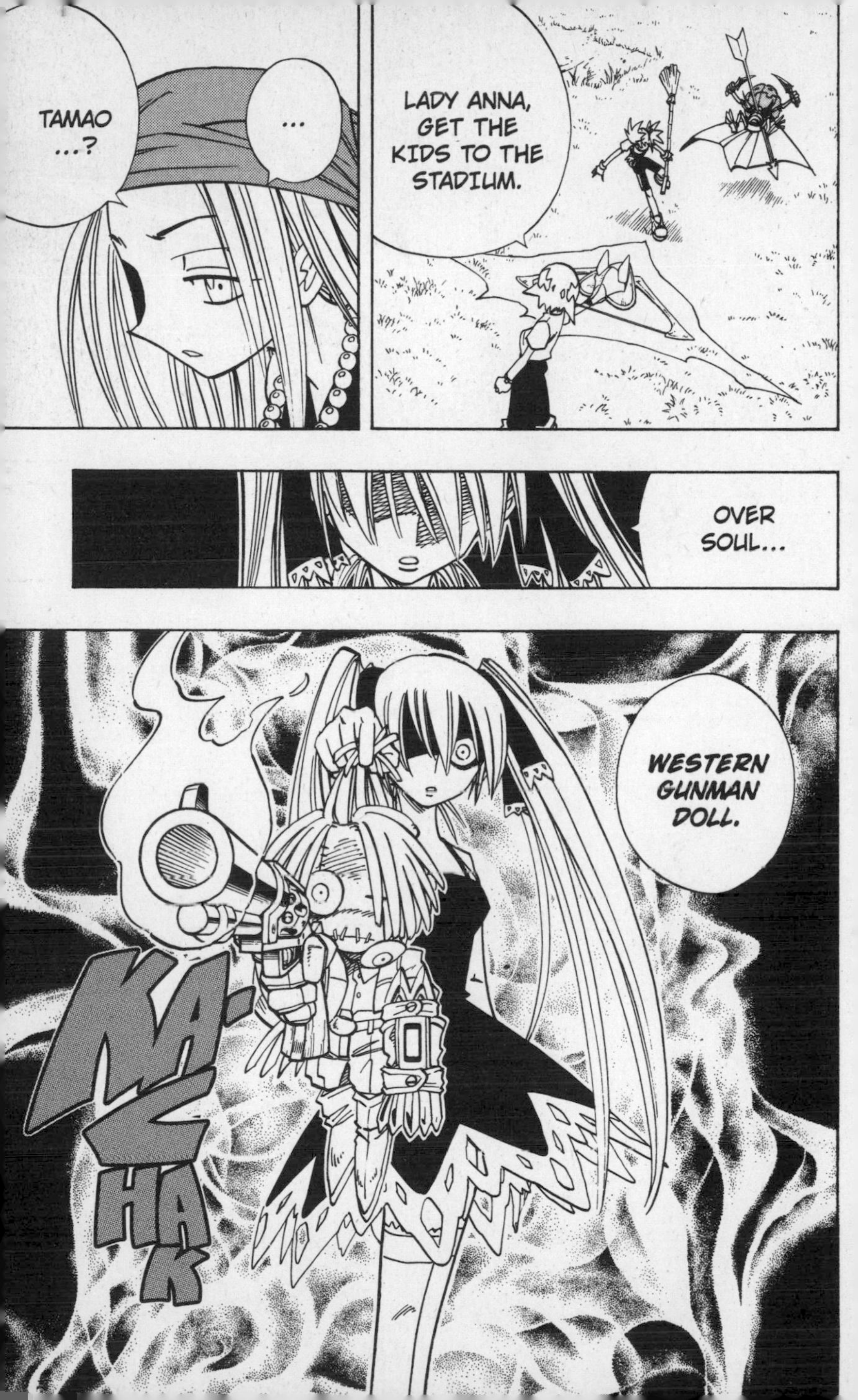
LADY ANNA, GET THE KIDS TO THE STADIUM.
...
TAMAO ...?
OVER SOUL...
WESTERN GUNMAN DOLL.
KA-CHAK

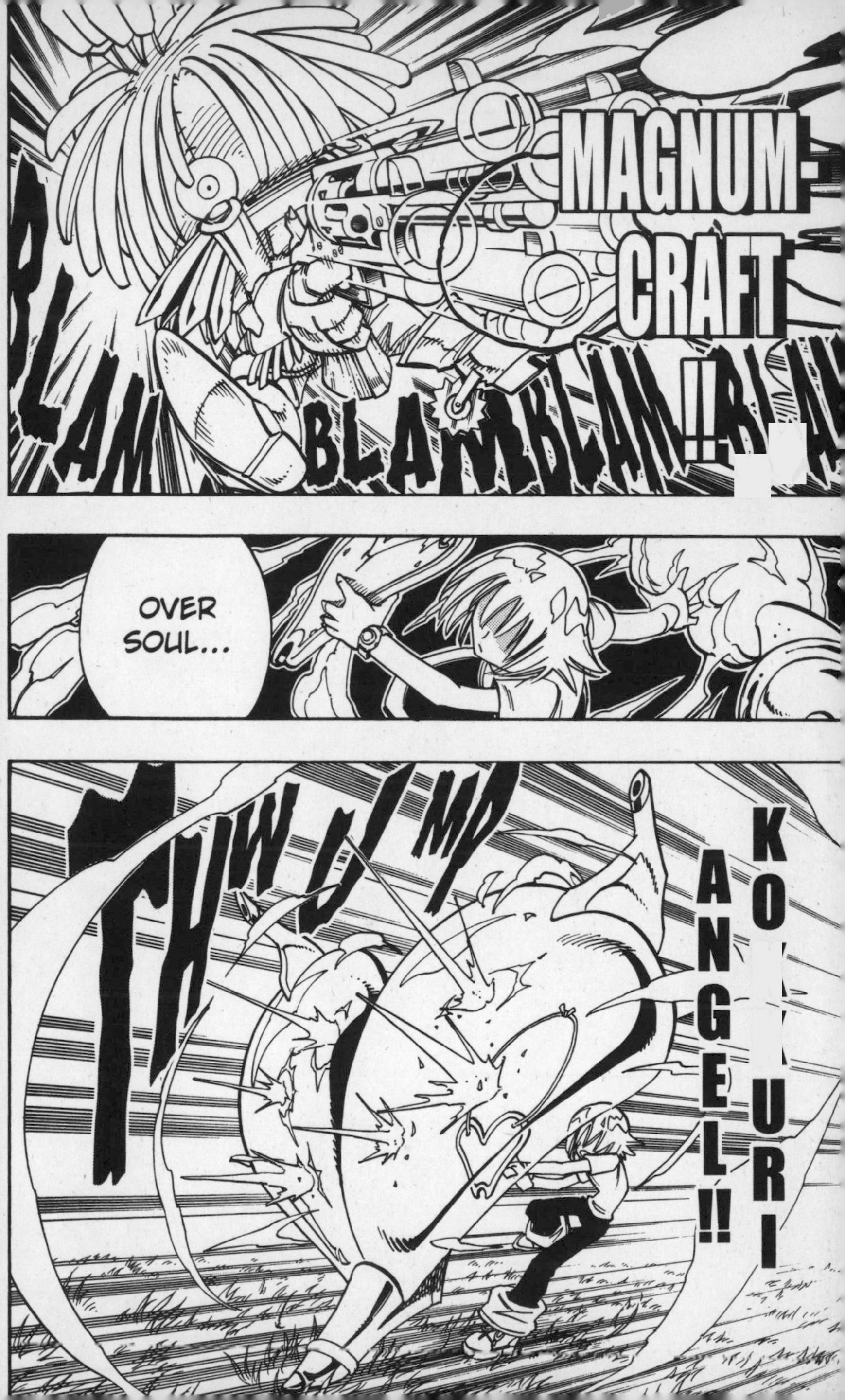
MAGNUM-CRAFT
BLAM BLAM!!
BLAM
OVER SOUL...
KOKKURI
ANGEL!!
THWUMP

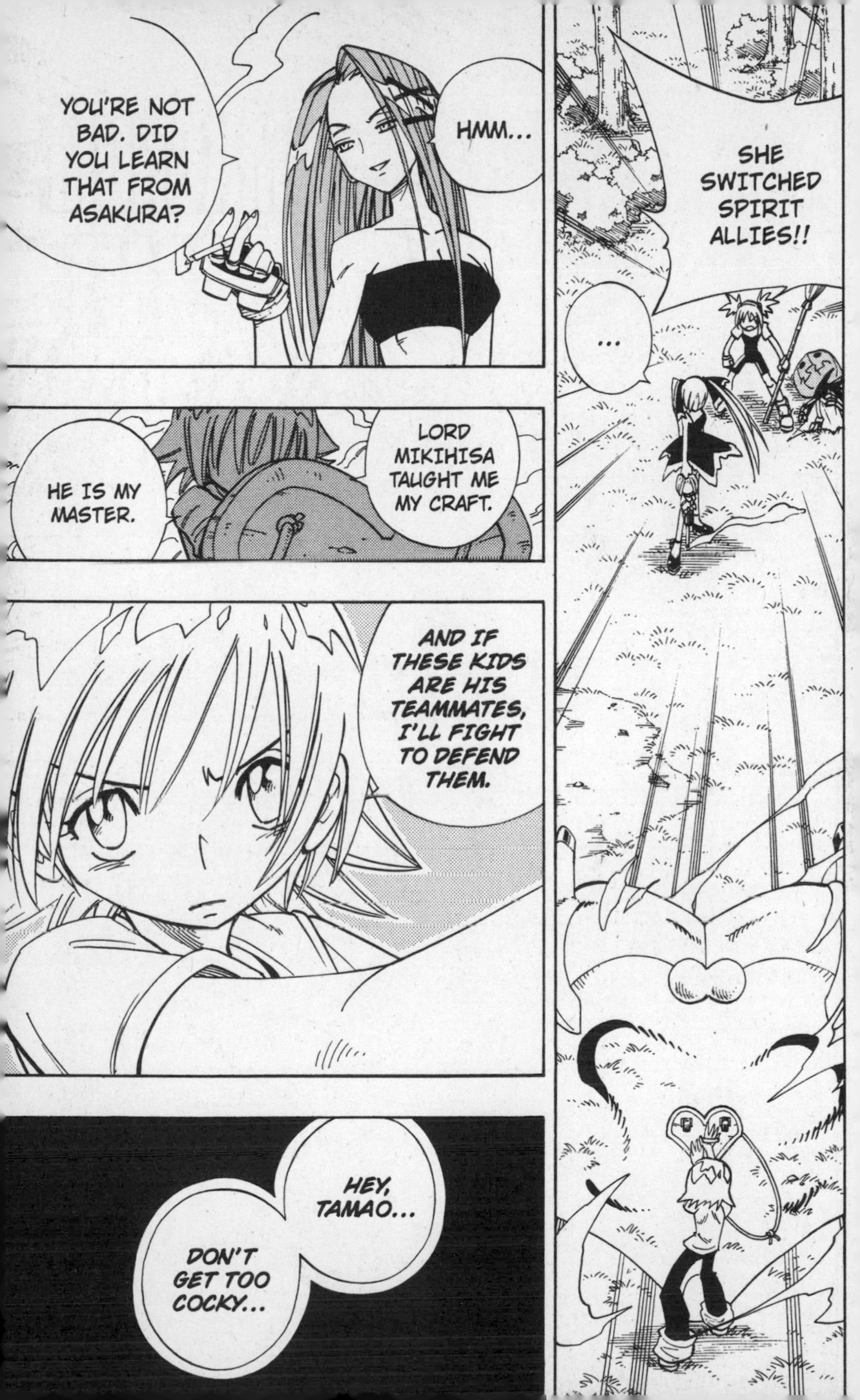
SHE SWITCHED SPIRIT ALLIES!!
...
HMM...
YOU'RE NOT BAD. DID YOU LEARN THAT FROM ASAKURA?
LORD MIKIHISA TAUGHT ME MY CRAFT.
HE IS MY MASTER.
AND IF THESE KIDS ARE HIS TEAMMATES, I'LL FIGHT TO DEFEND THEM.
HEY, TAMAO...
DON'T GET TOO COCKY...

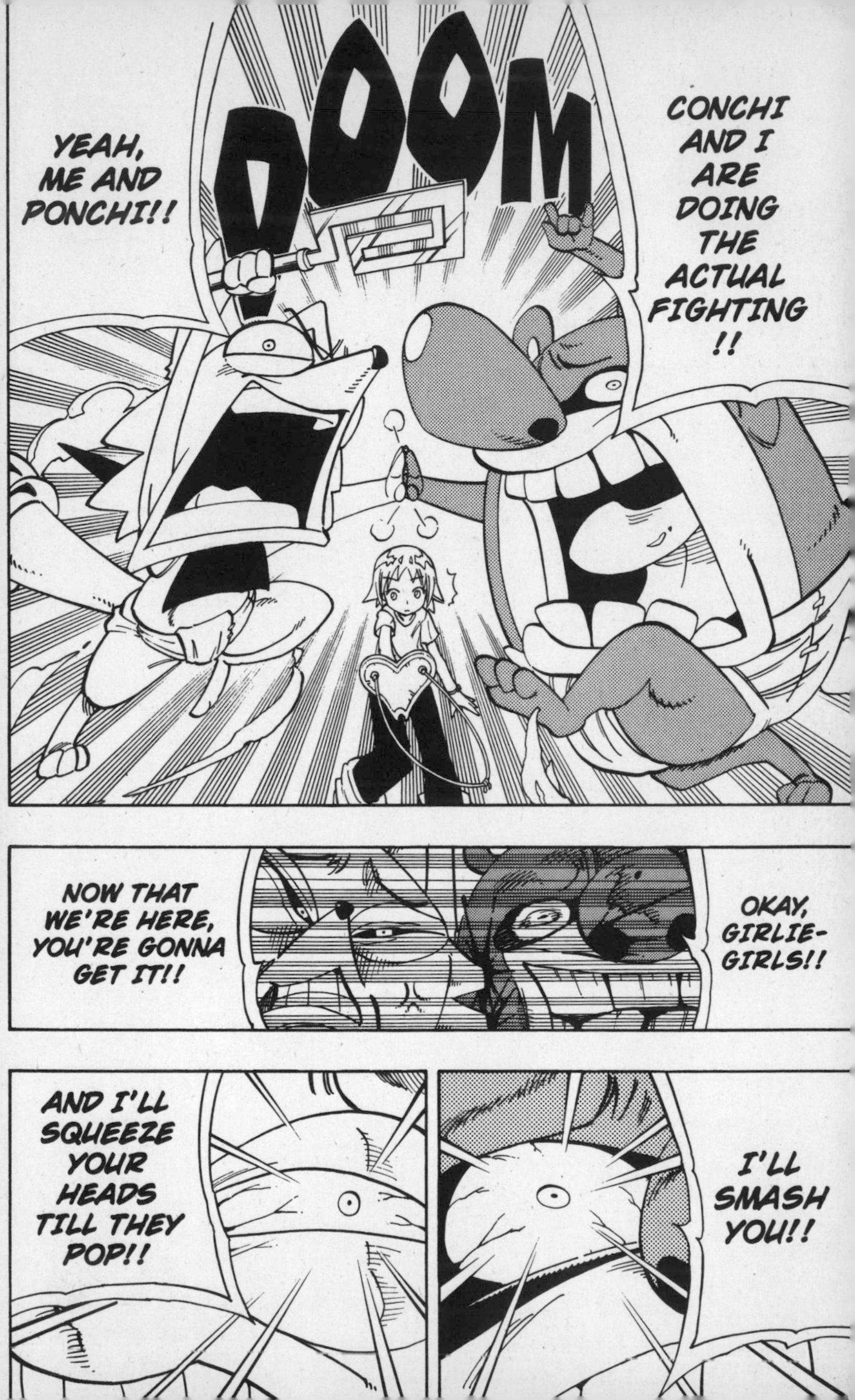
CONCHI AND I ARE DOING THE ACTUAL FIGHTING!!
DOOM
YEAH, ME AND PONCHI!!
OKAY, GIRLIE-GIRLS!!
NOW THAT WE'RE HERE, YOU'RE GONNA GET IT!!
I'LL SMASH YOU!!
AND I'LL SQUEEZE YOUR HEADS TILL THEY POP!!

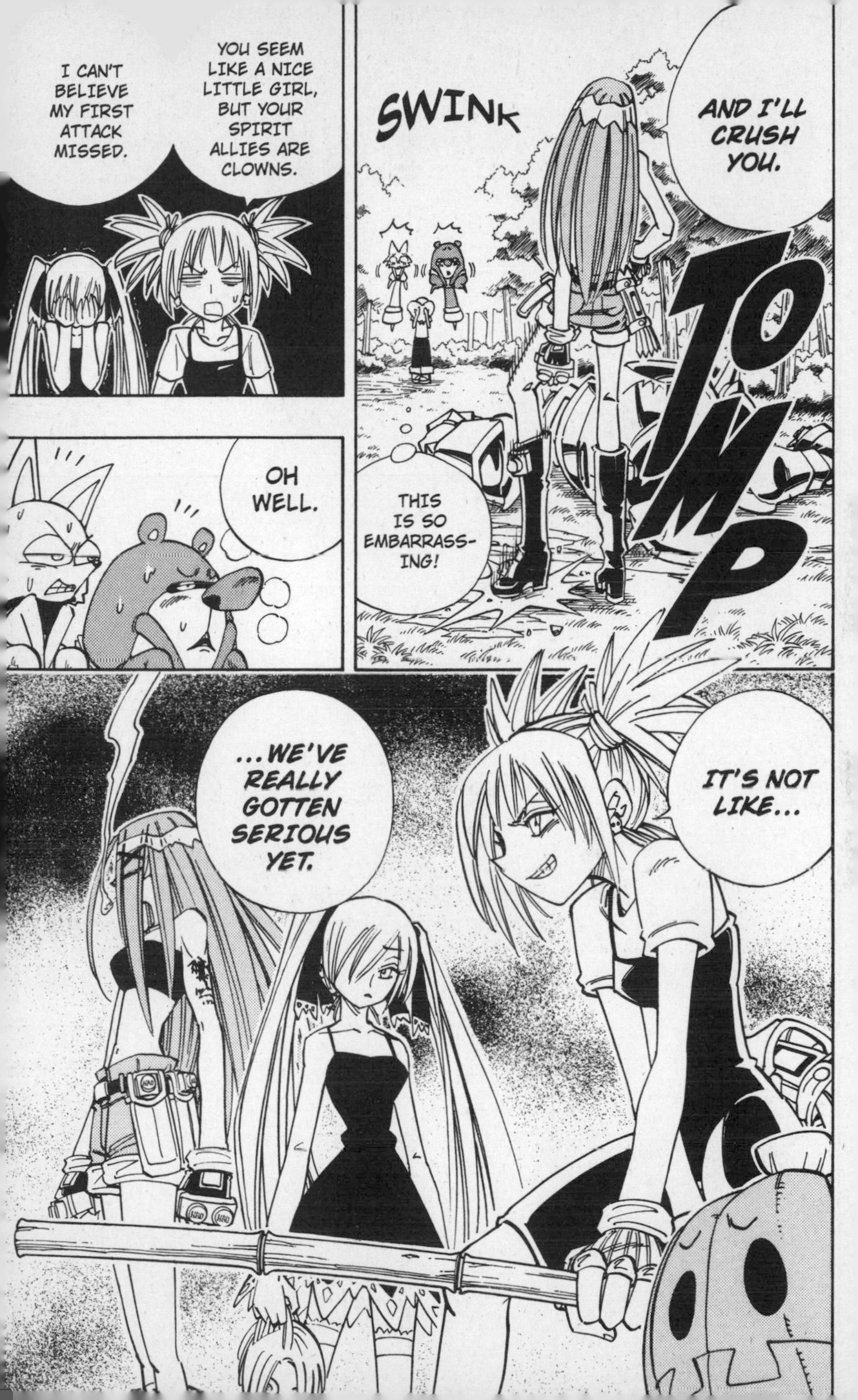
AND I'LL CRUSH YOU.
SWINK
TOMP
THIS IS SO EMBARRASSING!
YOU SEEM LIKE A NICE LITTLE GIRL, BUT YOUR SPIRIT ALLIES ARE CLOWNS.
I CAN'T BELIEVE MY FIRST ATTACK MISSED.
OH WELL.
IT'S NOT LIKE...
...WE'VE REALLY GOTTEN SERIOUS YET.

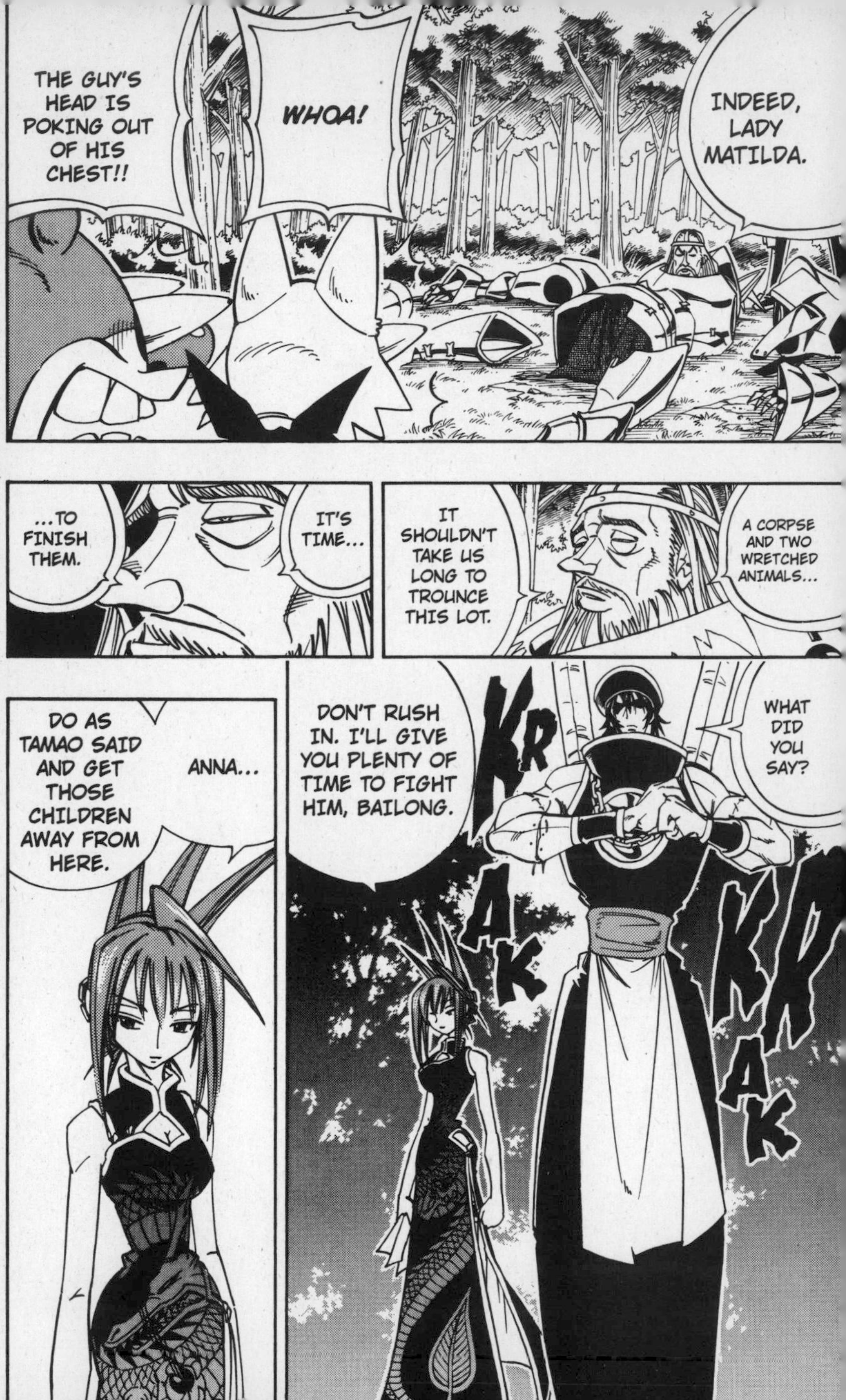
INDEED, LADY MATILDA.
WHOA!
THE GUY'S HEAD IS POKING OUT OF HIS CHEST!!
A CORPSE AND TWO WRETCHED ANIMALS...
IT SHOULDN'T TAKE US LONG TO TROUNCE THIS LOT.
IT'S TIME...
...TO FINISH THEM.
WHAT DID YOU SAY?
KRAK
KRAK
DON'T RUSH IN. I'LL GIVE YOU PLENTY OF TIME TO FIGHT HIM, BAILONG.
ANNA...
DO AS TAMAO SAID AND GET THOSE CHILDREN AWAY FROM HERE.

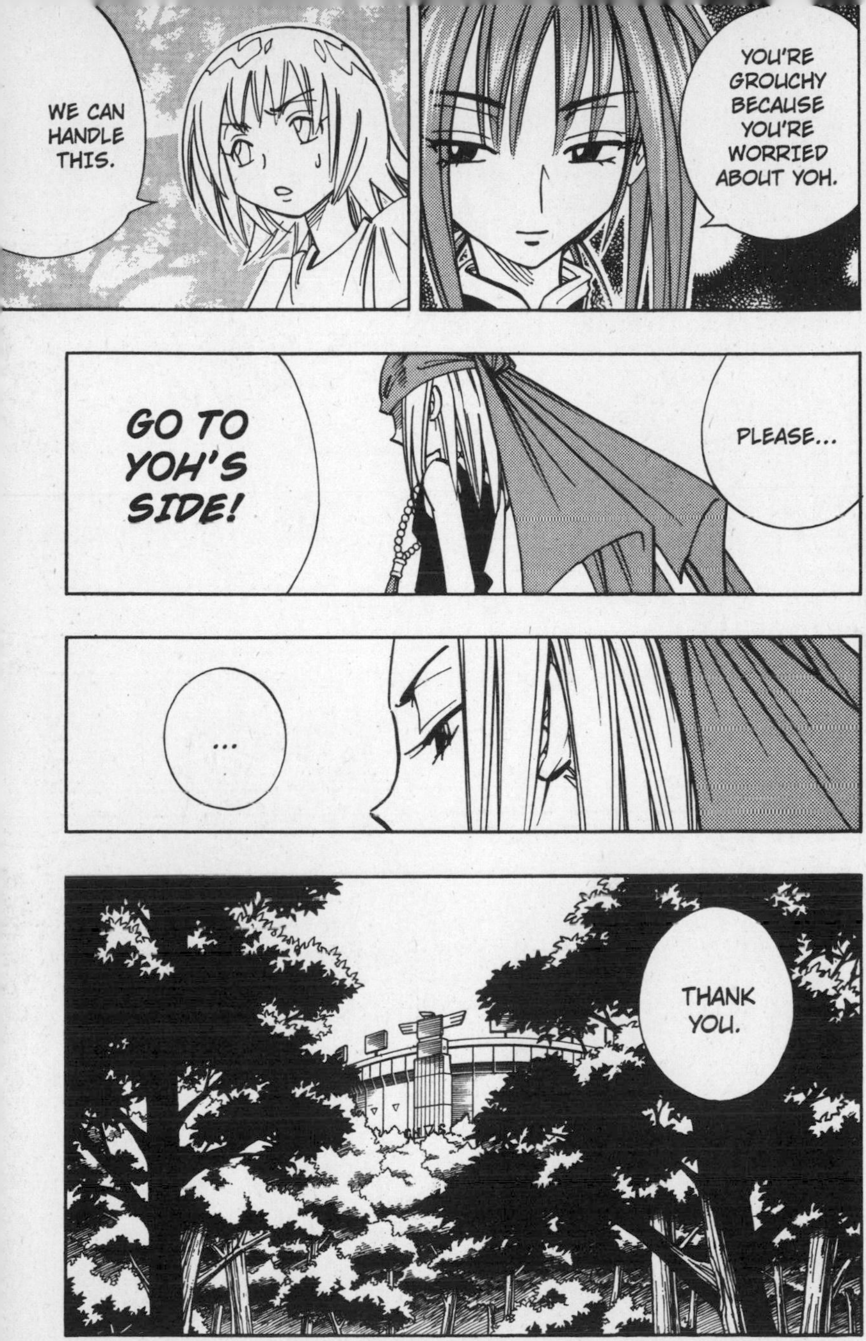
YOU'RE GROUCHY BECAUSE YOU'RE WORRIED ABOUT YOH.
WE CAN HANDLE THIS.
PLEASE...
GO TO YOH'S SIDE!
...
THANK YOU.

SHAMAN KING CHARACTER FILE No.93

セイラーム ルドセブ

SALERM **REDSEB**

2001
(JAN)

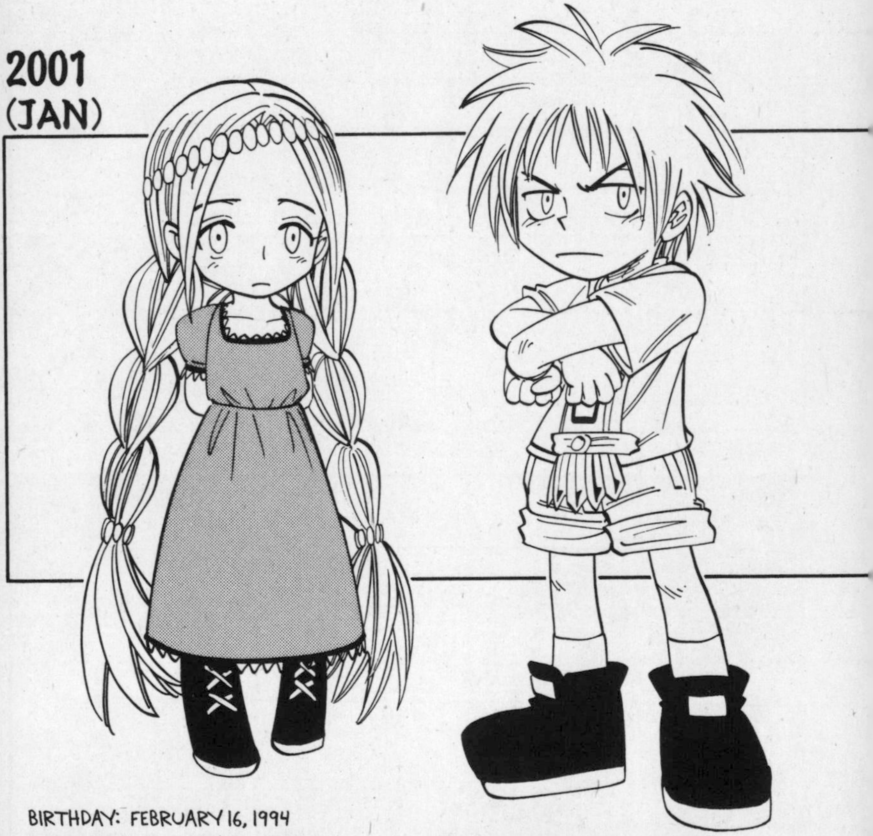

BIRTHDAY: FEBRUARY 16, 1994
ASTROLOGICAL SIGN: AQUARIUS
BLOOD TYPE: O
AGE: 6

BIRTHDAY: AUGUST 15, 1992
ASTROLOGICAL SIGN: LEO
BLOOD TYPE: O
AGE: 8

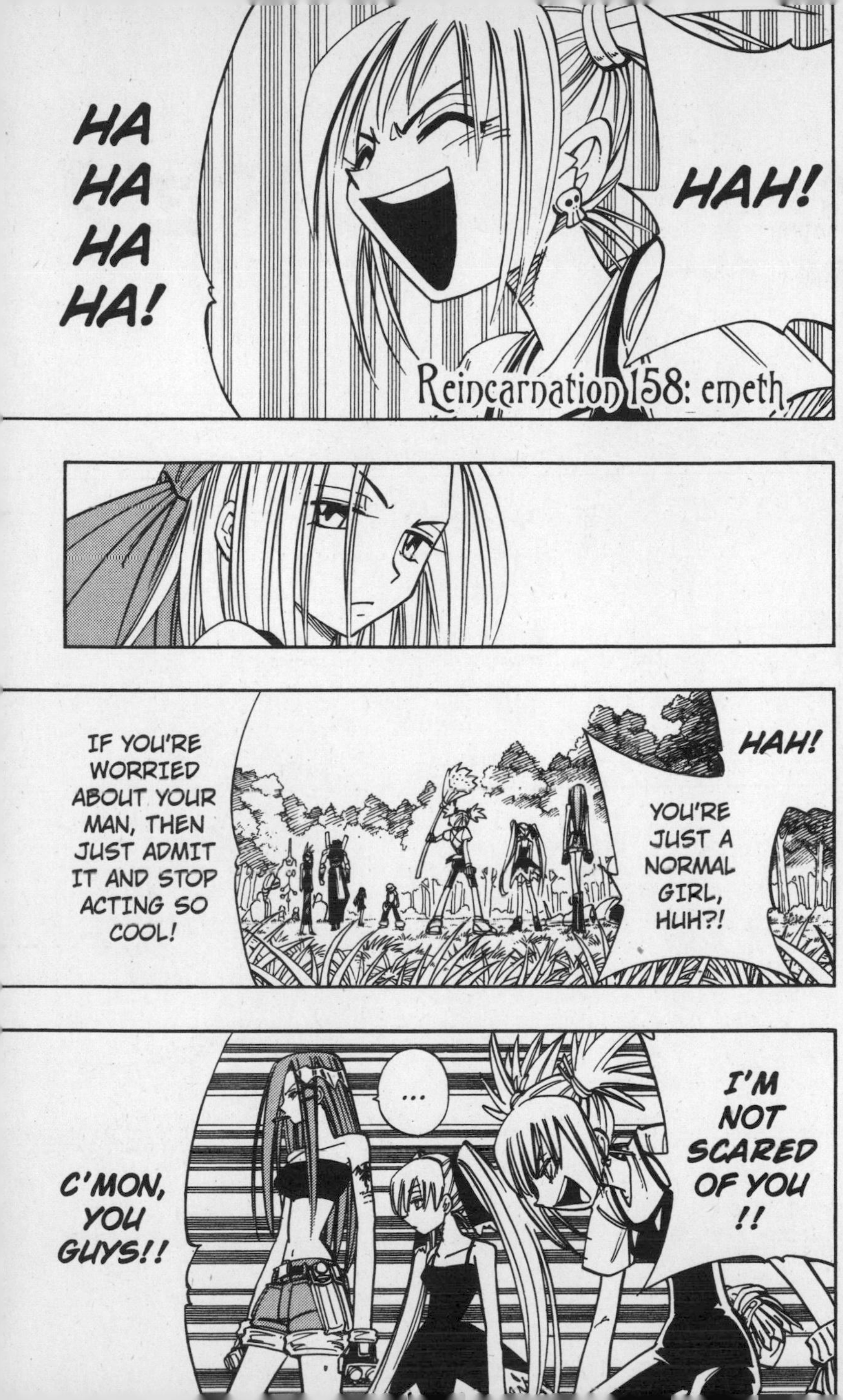
HAH!
HA HA HA HA!
Reincarnation 158: emeth
HAH!
YOU'RE JUST A NORMAL GIRL, HUH?!
IF YOU'RE WORRIED ABOUT YOUR MAN, THEN JUST ADMIT IT AND STOP ACTING SO COOL!
I'M NOT SCARED OF YOU!!
...
C'MON, YOU GUYS!!

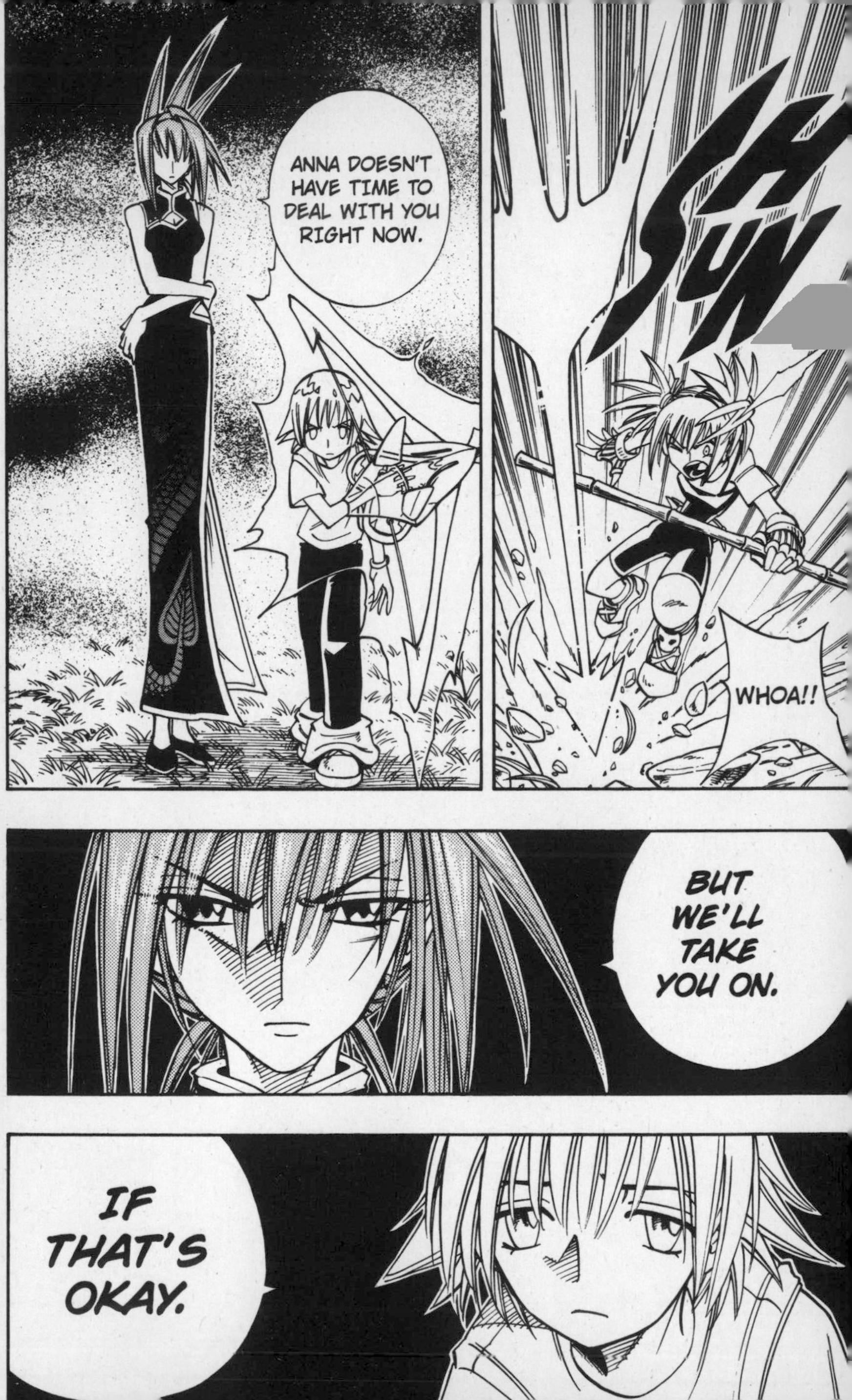
SHUN
WHOA!!
ANNA DOESN'T HAVE TIME TO DEAL WITH YOU RIGHT NOW.
BUT WE'LL TAKE YOU ON.
IF THAT'S OKAY.

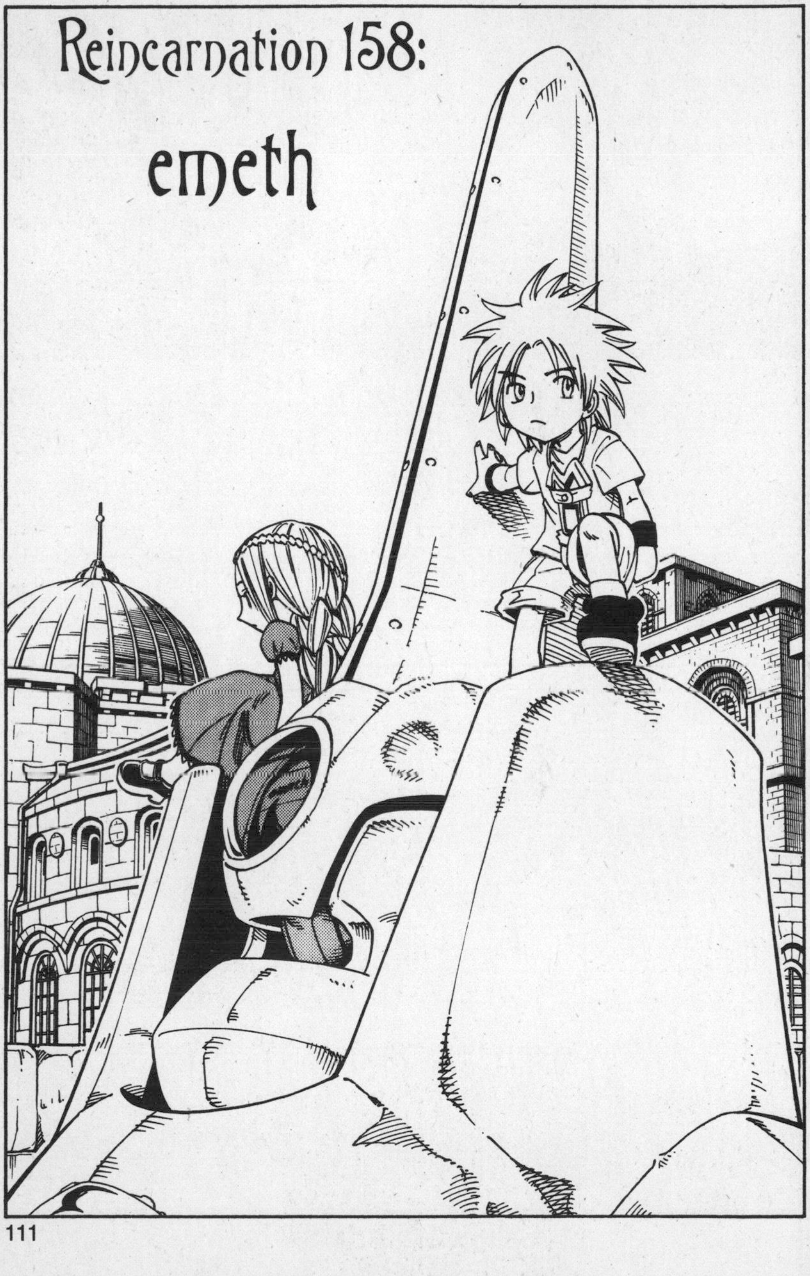
Reincarnation 158:
emeth

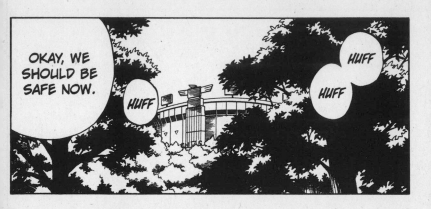

HUFF
HUFF
HUFF
OKAY, WE SHOULD BE SAFE NOW.
THANKS...
...FOR COMING WITH US.
DON'T THANK ME.
I DIDN'T DO IT FOR YOU.
YOU'RE BREATHING SO HARD.
ARE YOU SURE YOU'RE...

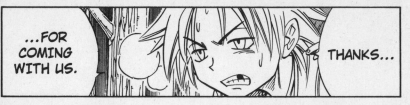

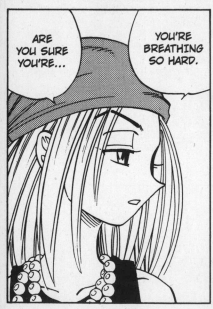

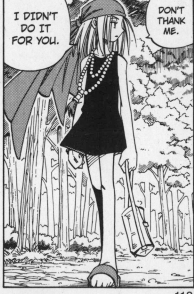

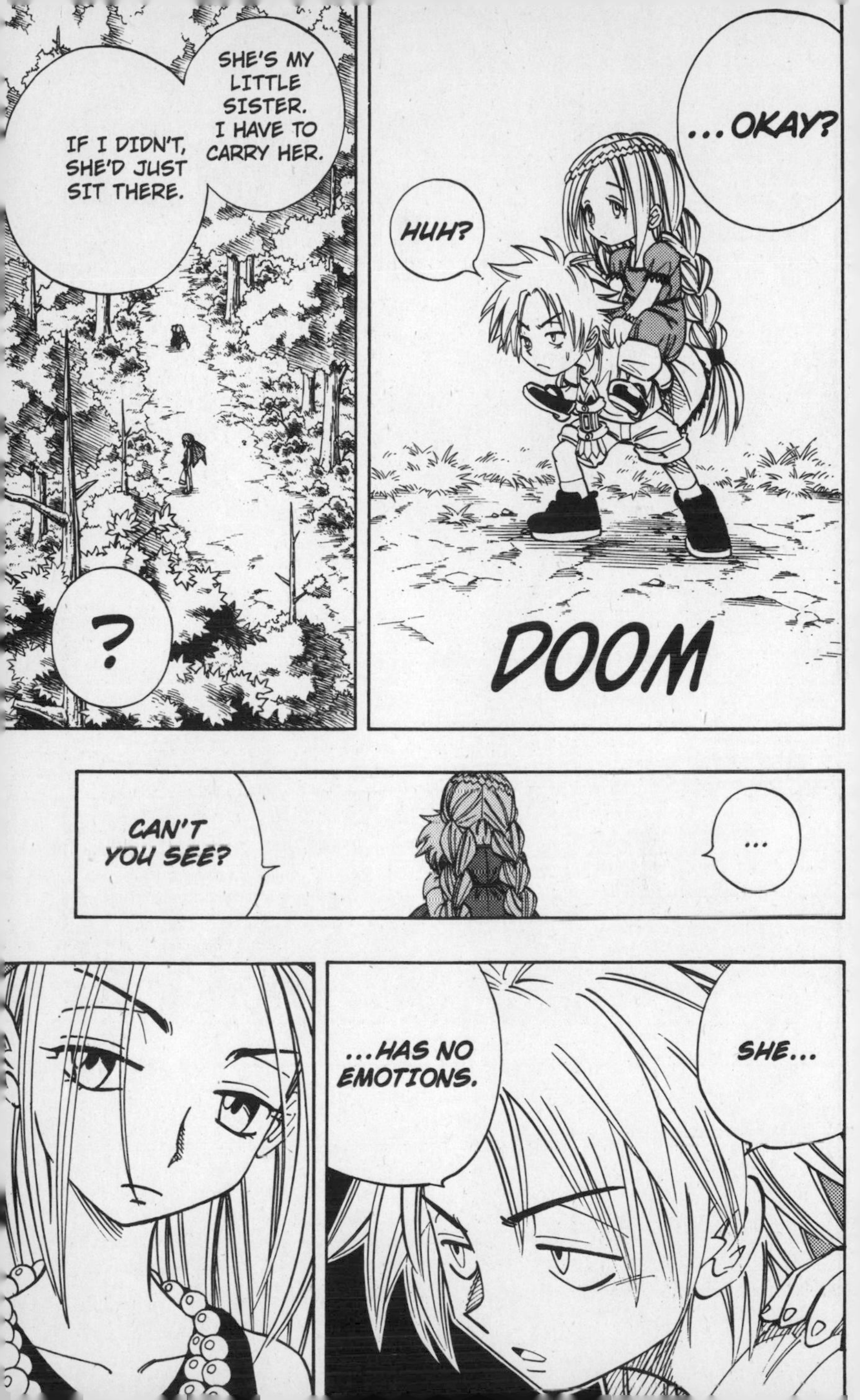
...OKAY?
HUH?
DOOM
SHE'S MY LITTLE SISTER. I HAVE TO CARRY HER.
IF I DIDN'T, SHE'D JUST SIT THERE.
?
...
CAN'T YOU SEE?
SHE...
...HAS NO EMOTIONS.

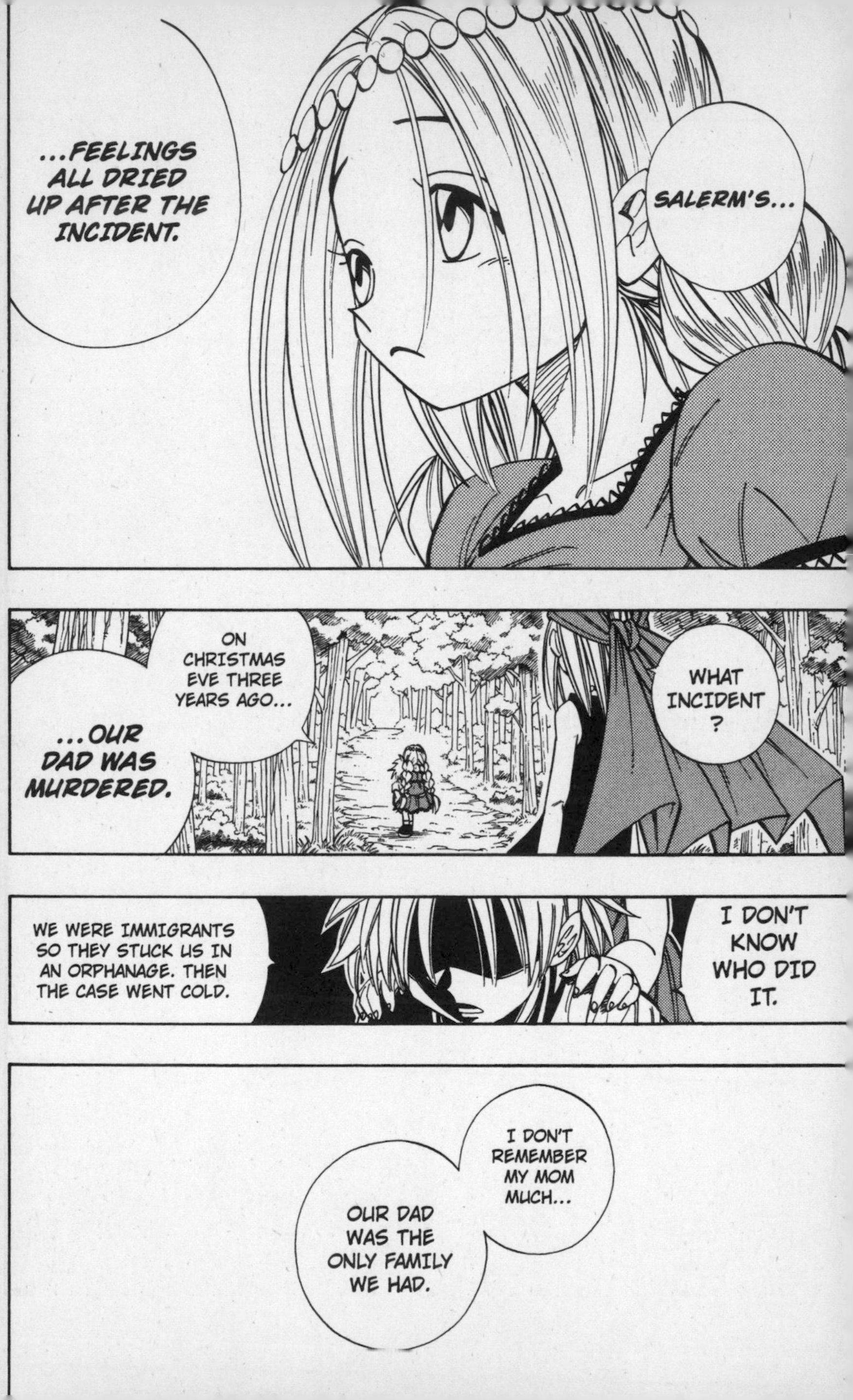
SALERM'S...
...FEELINGS ALL DRIED UP AFTER THE INCIDENT.
WHAT INCIDENT?
ON CHRISTMAS EVE THREE YEARS AGO...
...OUR DAD WAS MURDERED.
I DON'T KNOW WHO DID IT.
WE WERE IMMIGRANTS SO THEY STUCK US IN AN ORPHANAGE. THEN THE CASE WENT COLD.
I DON'T REMEMBER MY MOM MUCH...
OUR DAD WAS THE ONLY FAMILY WE HAD.

READ THIS WAY

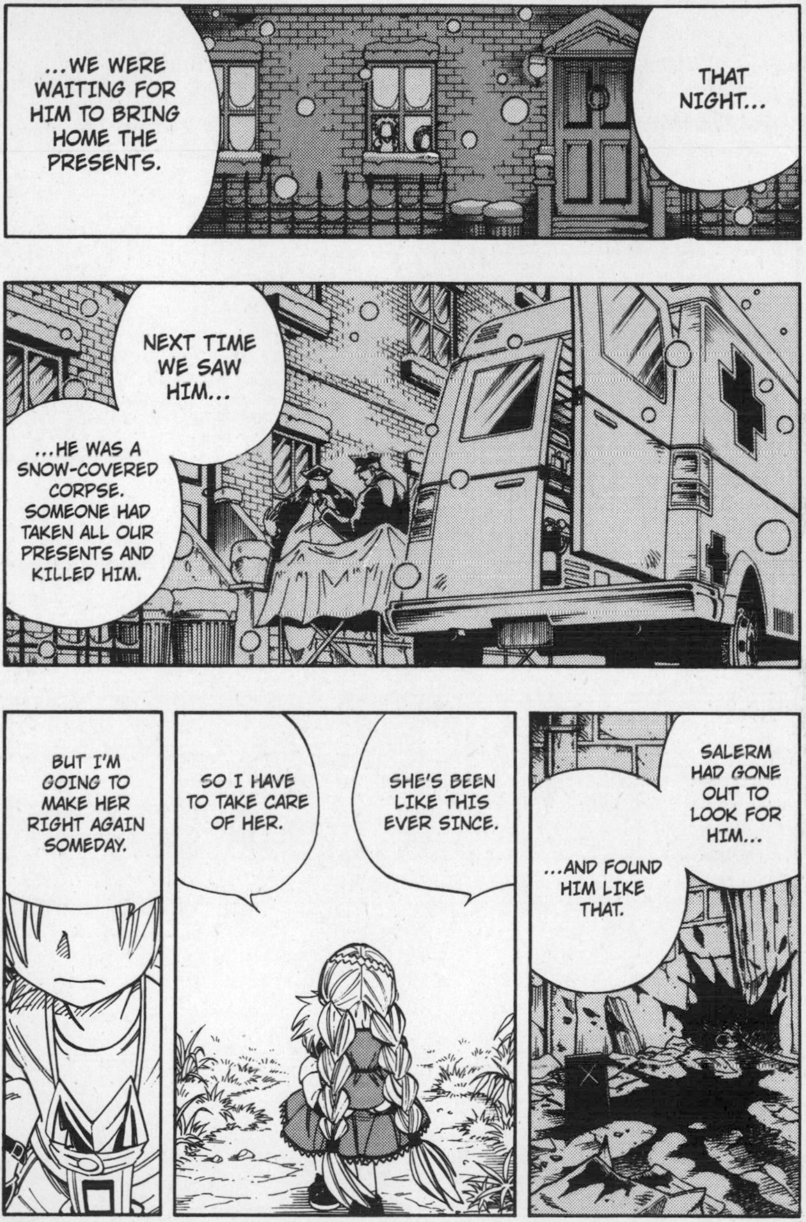
THAT NIGHT...
...WE WERE WAITING FOR HIM TO BRING HOME THE PRESENTS.
NEXT TIME WE SAW HIM...
...HE WAS A SNOW-COVERED CORPSE. SOMEONE HAD TAKEN ALL OUR PRESENTS AND KILLED HIM.
SALERM HAD GONE OUT TO LOOK FOR HIM...
...AND FOUND HIM LIKE THAT.
SHE'S BEEN LIKE THIS EVER SINCE.
SO I HAVE TO TAKE CARE OF HER.
BUT I'M GOING TO MAKE HER RIGHT AGAIN SOMEDAY.

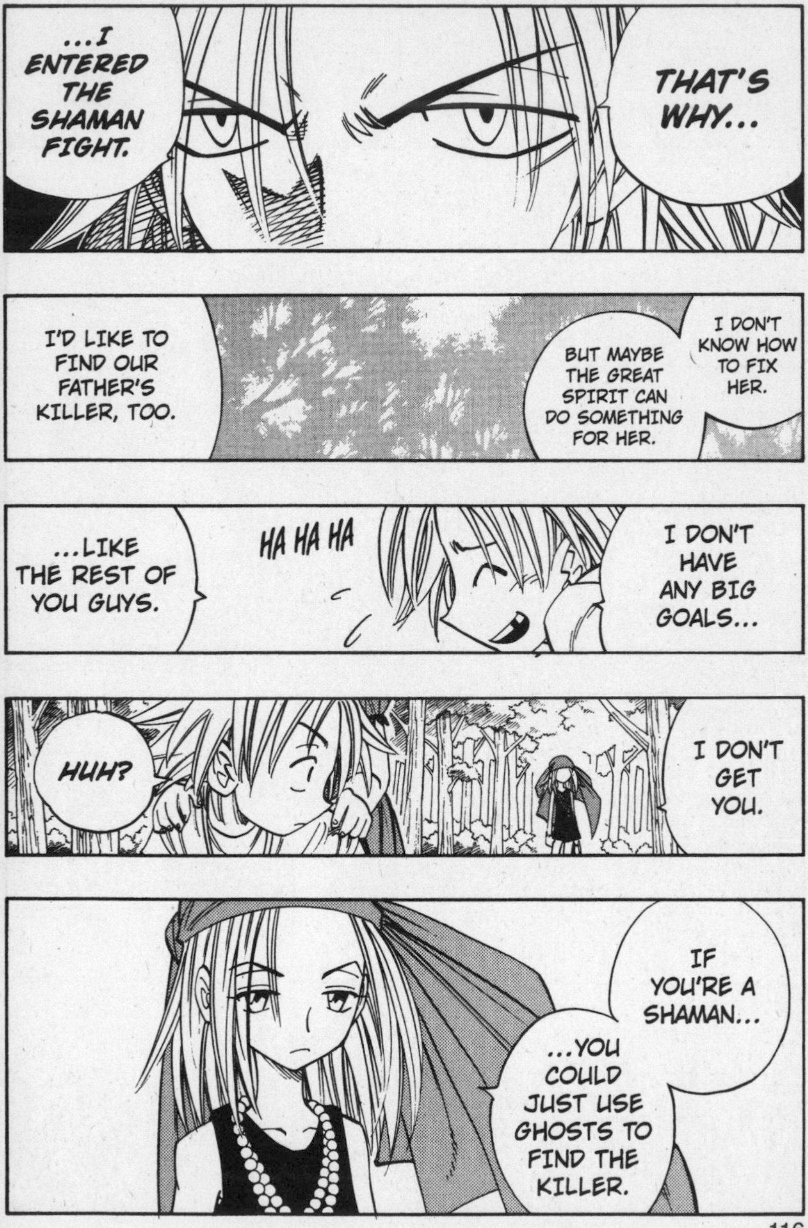
THAT'S WHY...
...I ENTERED THE SHAMAN FIGHT.
I DON'T KNOW HOW TO FIX HER.
BUT MAYBE THE GREAT SPIRIT CAN DO SOMETHING FOR HER.
I'D LIKE TO FIND OUR FATHER'S KILLER, TOO.
I DON'T HAVE ANY BIG GOALS...
HA HA HA
...LIKE THE REST OF YOU GUYS.
I DON'T GET YOU.
HUH?
IF YOU'RE A SHAMAN...
...YOU COULD JUST USE GHOSTS TO FIND THE KILLER.

READ THIS WAY

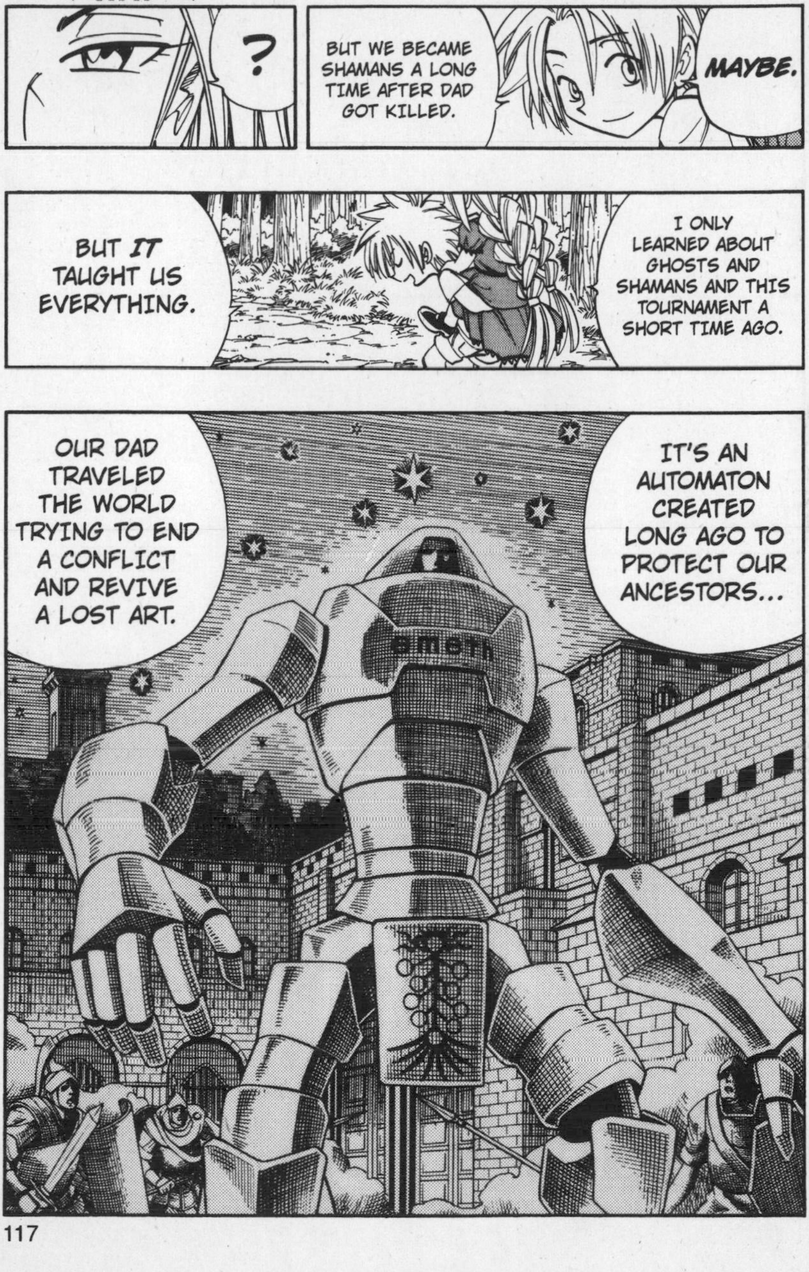
MAYBE.
BUT WE BECAME SHAMANS A LONG TIME AFTER DAD GOT KILLED.
?
I ONLY LEARNED ABOUT GHOSTS AND SHAMANS AND THIS TOURNAMENT A SHORT TIME AGO.
BUT *IT* TAUGHT US EVERYTHING.
IT'S AN AUTOMATON CREATED LONG AGO TO PROTECT OUR ANCESTORS...
OUR DAD TRAVELED THE WORLD TRYING TO END A CONFLICT AND REVIVE A LOST ART.
emeth

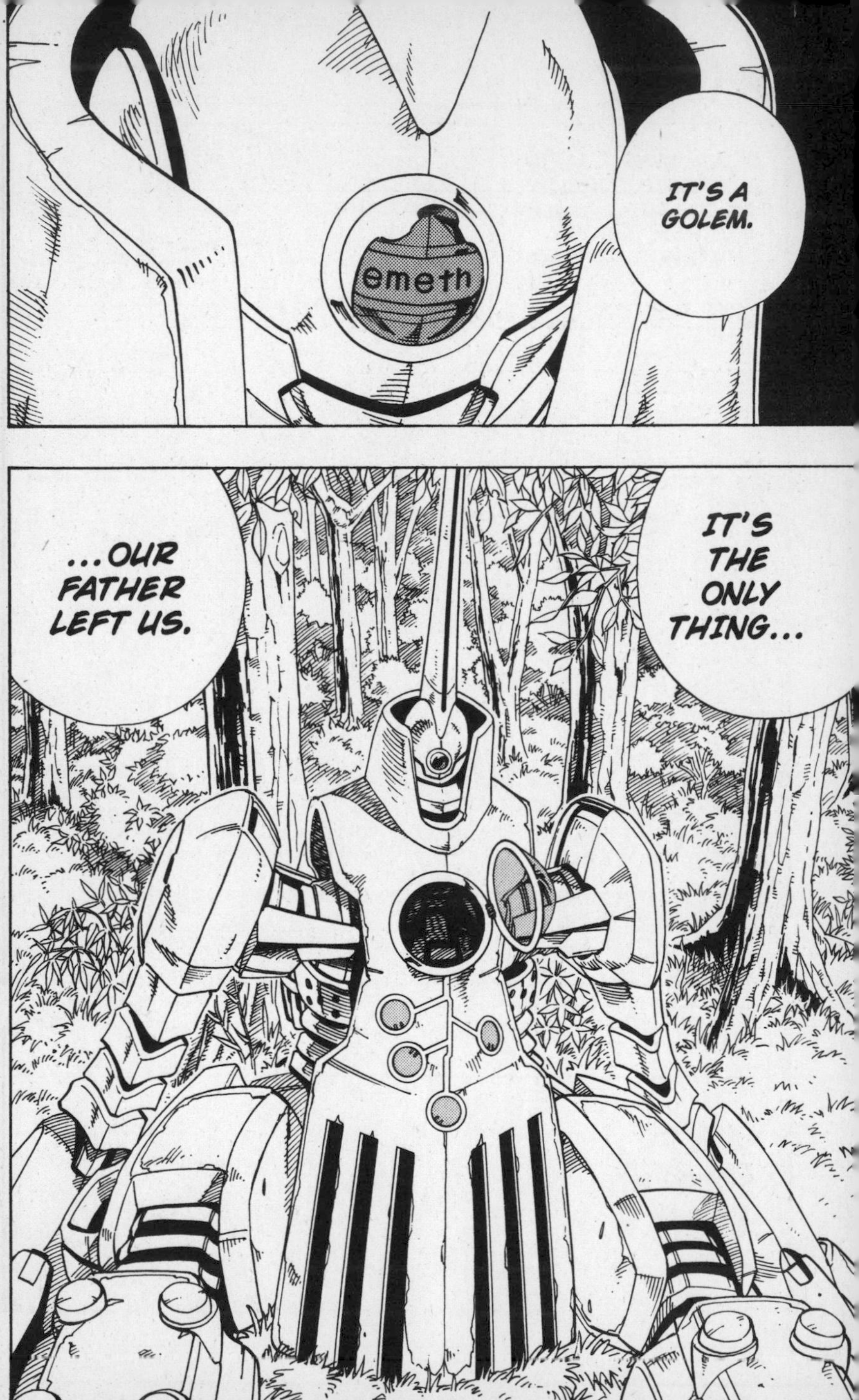
emeth
IT'S A GOLEM.
IT'S THE ONLY THING...
...OUR FATHER LEFT US.

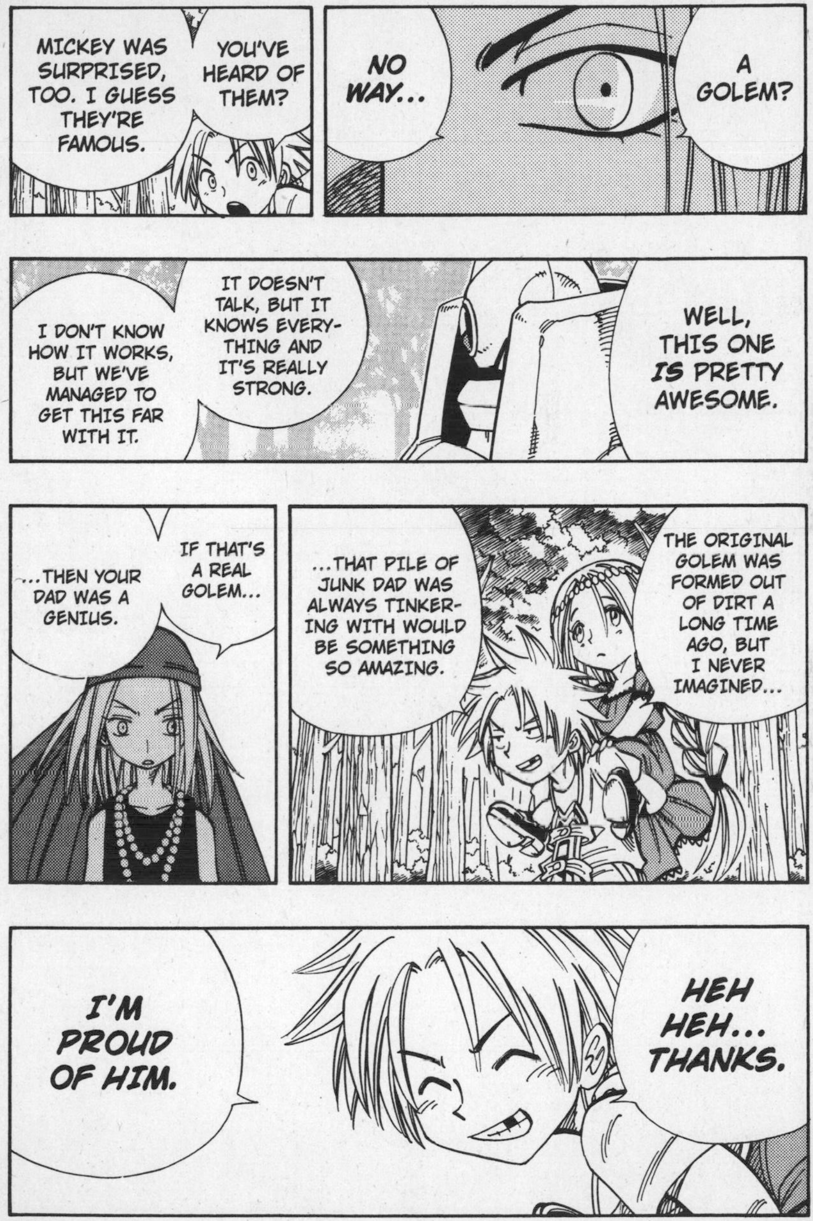
A GOLEM?
NO WAY...
YOU'VE HEARD OF THEM?
MICKEY WAS SURPRISED, TOO. I GUESS THEY'RE FAMOUS.
WELL, THIS ONE IS PRETTY AWESOME.
IT DOESN'T TALK, BUT IT KNOWS EVERYTHING AND IT'S REALLY STRONG.
I DON'T KNOW HOW IT WORKS, BUT WE'VE MANAGED TO GET THIS FAR WITH IT.
THE ORIGINAL GOLEM WAS FORMED OUT OF DIRT A LONG TIME AGO, BUT I NEVER IMAGINED...
...THAT PILE OF JUNK DAD WAS ALWAYS TINKERING WITH WOULD BE SOMETHING SO AMAZING.
IF THAT'S A REAL GOLEM...
...THEN YOUR DAD WAS A GENIUS.
HEH HEH... THANKS.
I'M PROUD OF HIM.

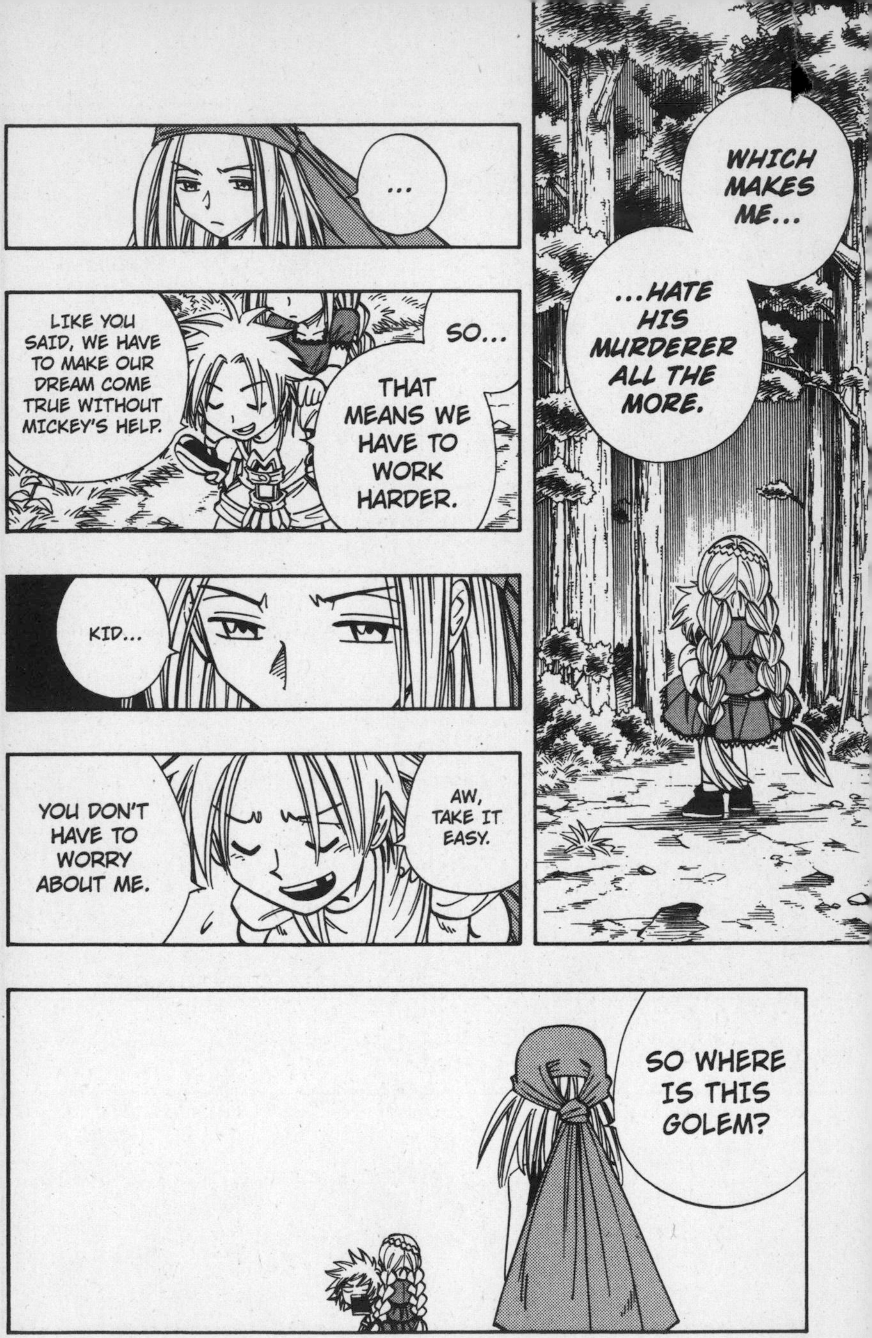
WHICH MAKES ME...
...HATE HIS MURDERER ALL THE MORE.
...
SO...
THAT MEANS WE HAVE TO WORK HARDER.
LIKE YOU SAID, WE HAVE TO MAKE OUR DREAM COME TRUE WITHOUT MICKEY'S HELP.
KID...
AW, TAKE IT EASY.
YOU DON'T HAVE TO WORRY ABOUT ME.
SO WHERE IS THIS GOLEM?

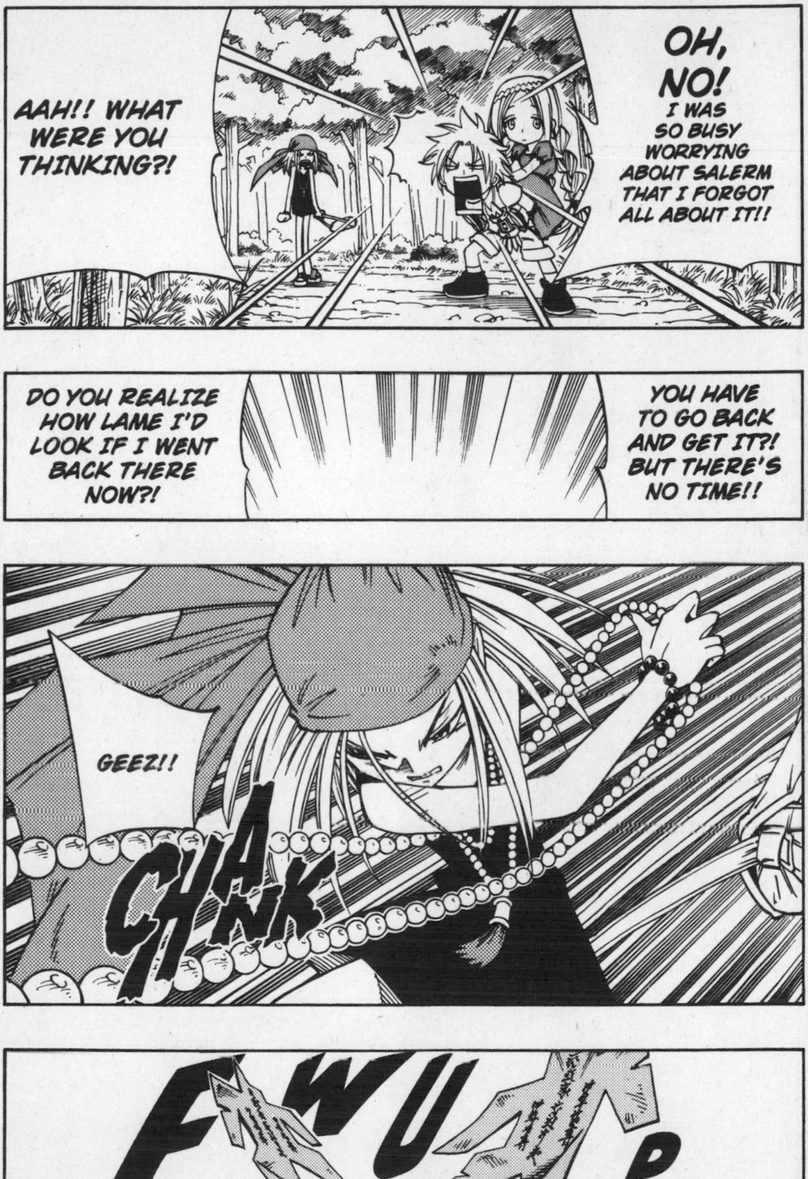
OH, NO! I WAS SO BUSY WORRYING ABOUT SALERM THAT I FORGOT ALL ABOUT IT!!
AAH!! WHAT WERE YOU THINKING?!
YOU HAVE TO GO BACK AND GET IT?! BUT THERE'S NO TIME!!
DO YOU REALIZE HOW LAME I'D LOOK IF I WENT BACK THERE NOW?!
GEEZ!!
CHAK
FWUP

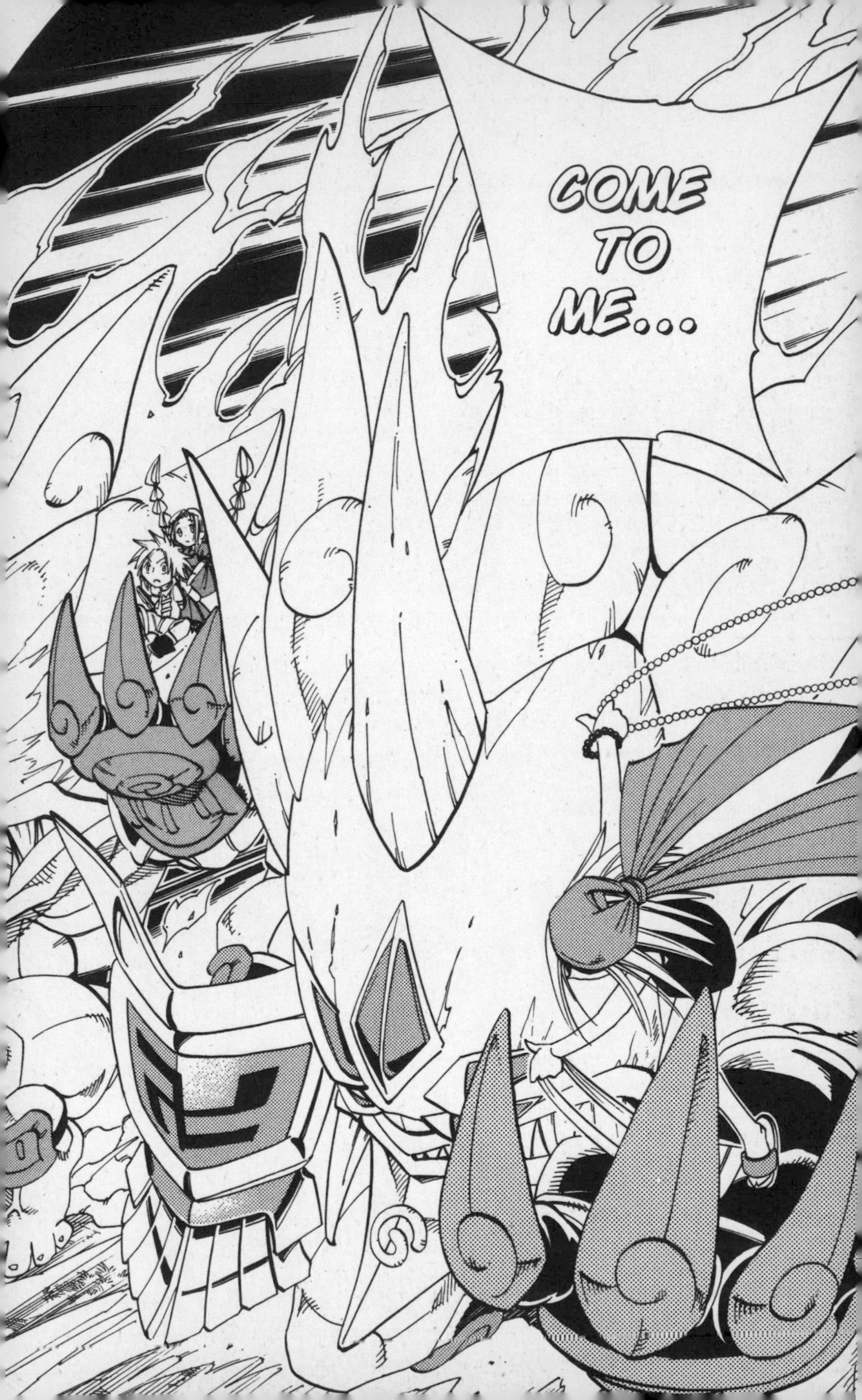
COME TO ME...

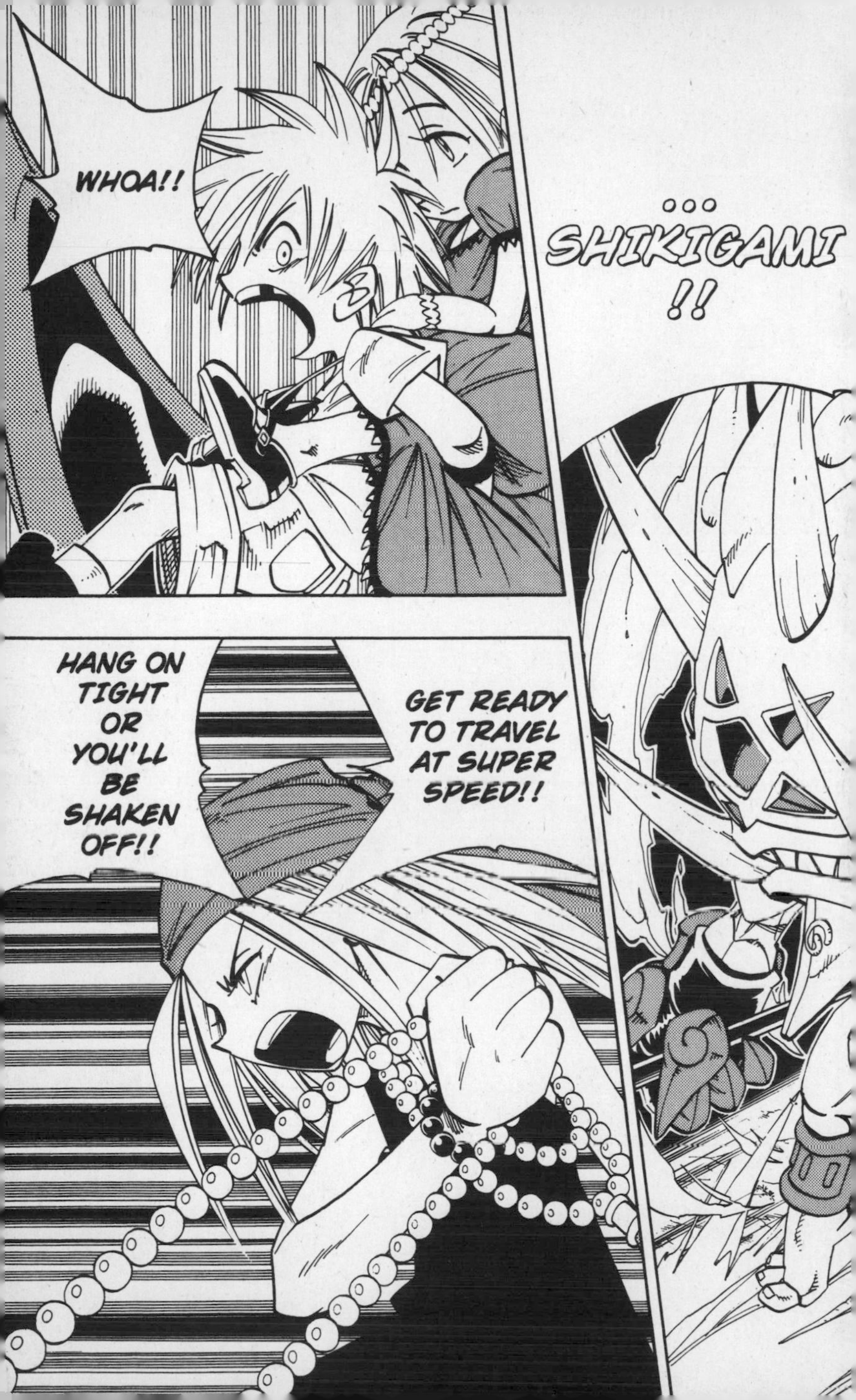
...SHIKIGAMI !!
WHOA!!
GET READY TO TRAVEL AT SUPER SPEED!!
HANG ON TIGHT OR YOU'LL BE SHAKEN OFF!!

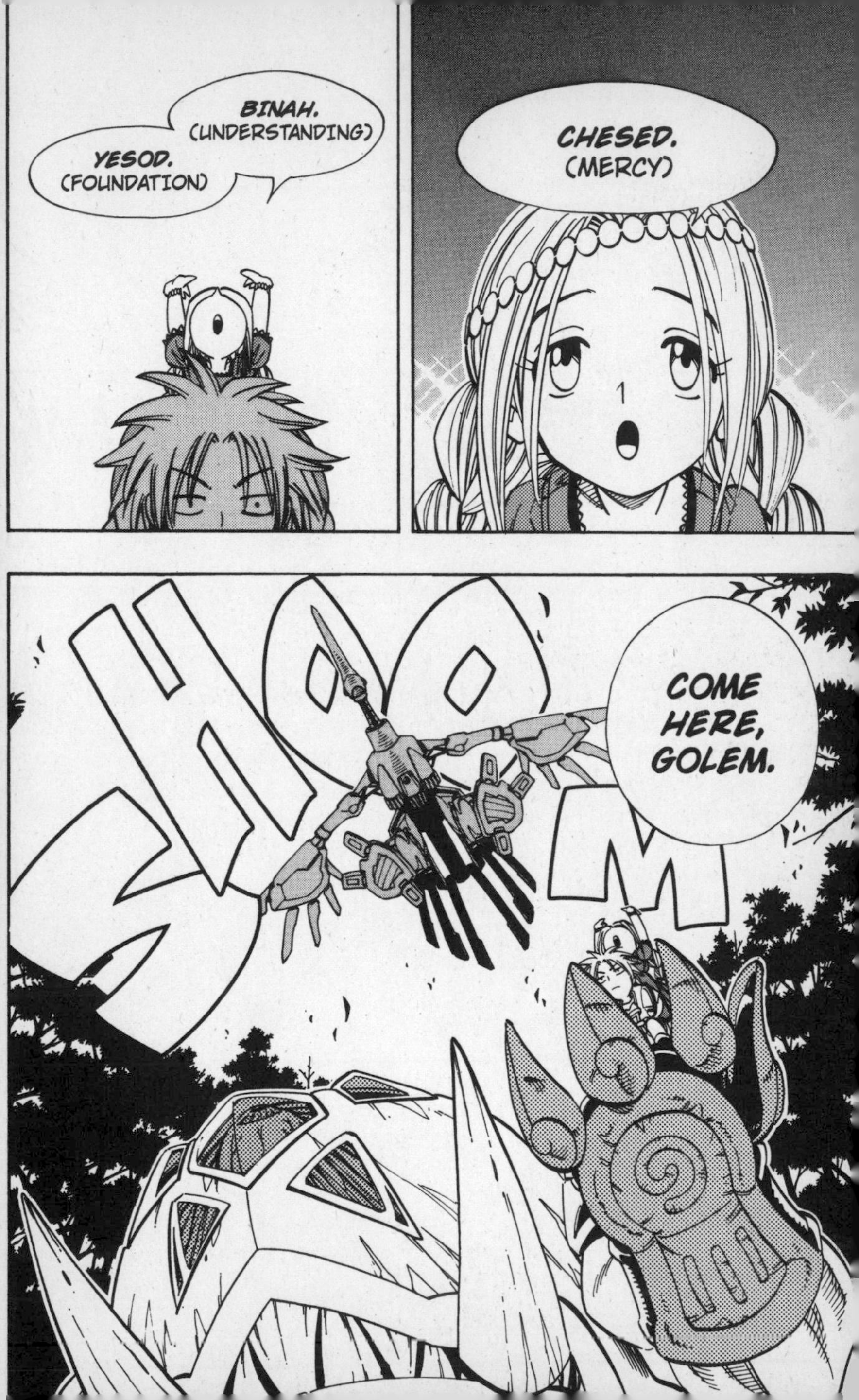
CHESED. (MERCY)
BINAH. (UNDERSTANDING)
YESOD. (FOUNDATION)
COME HERE, GOLEM.
SHOOM

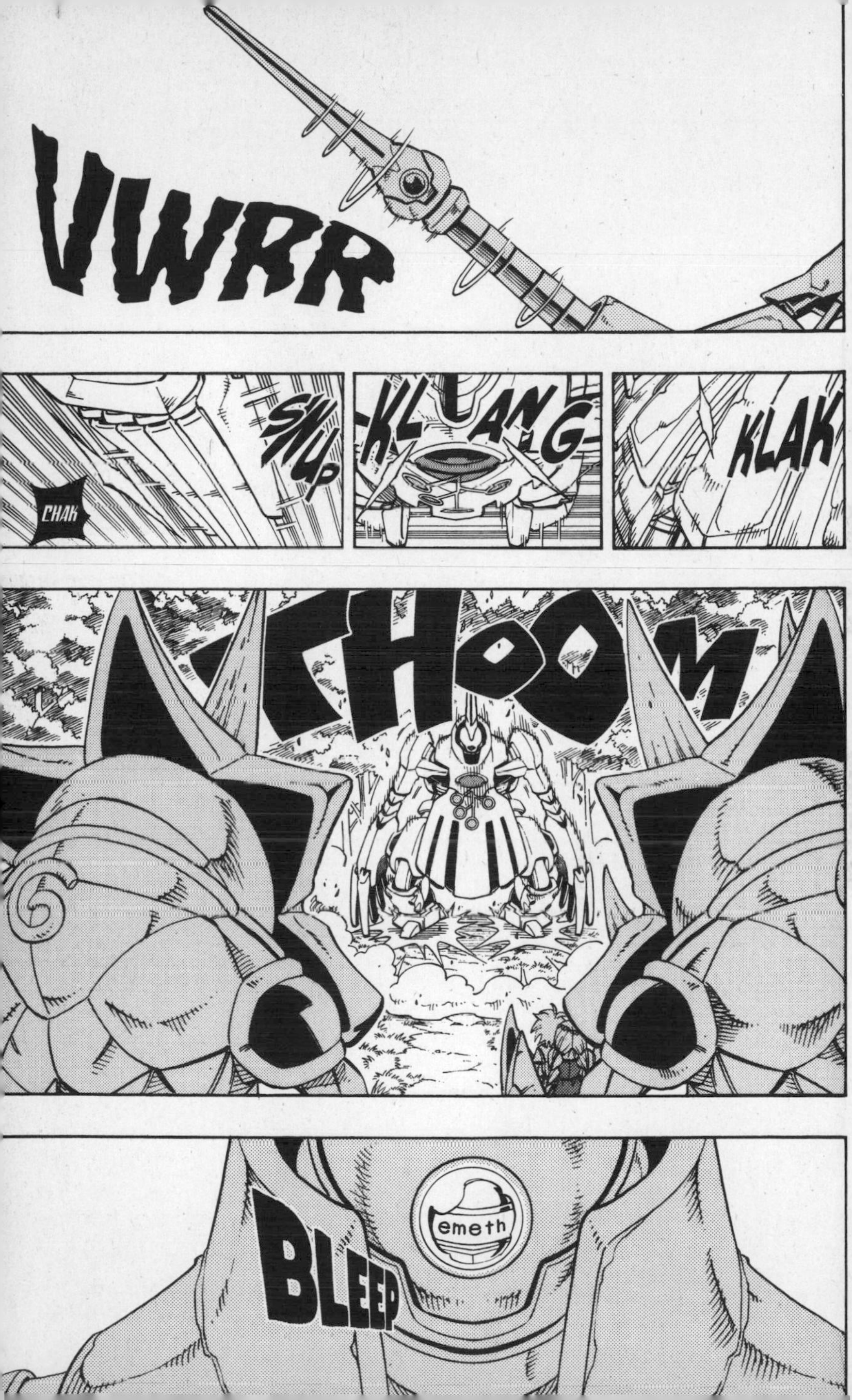
VWRR
KLAK
KLANG
SNUP
CHAK
CHOOM
emeth
BLEEP

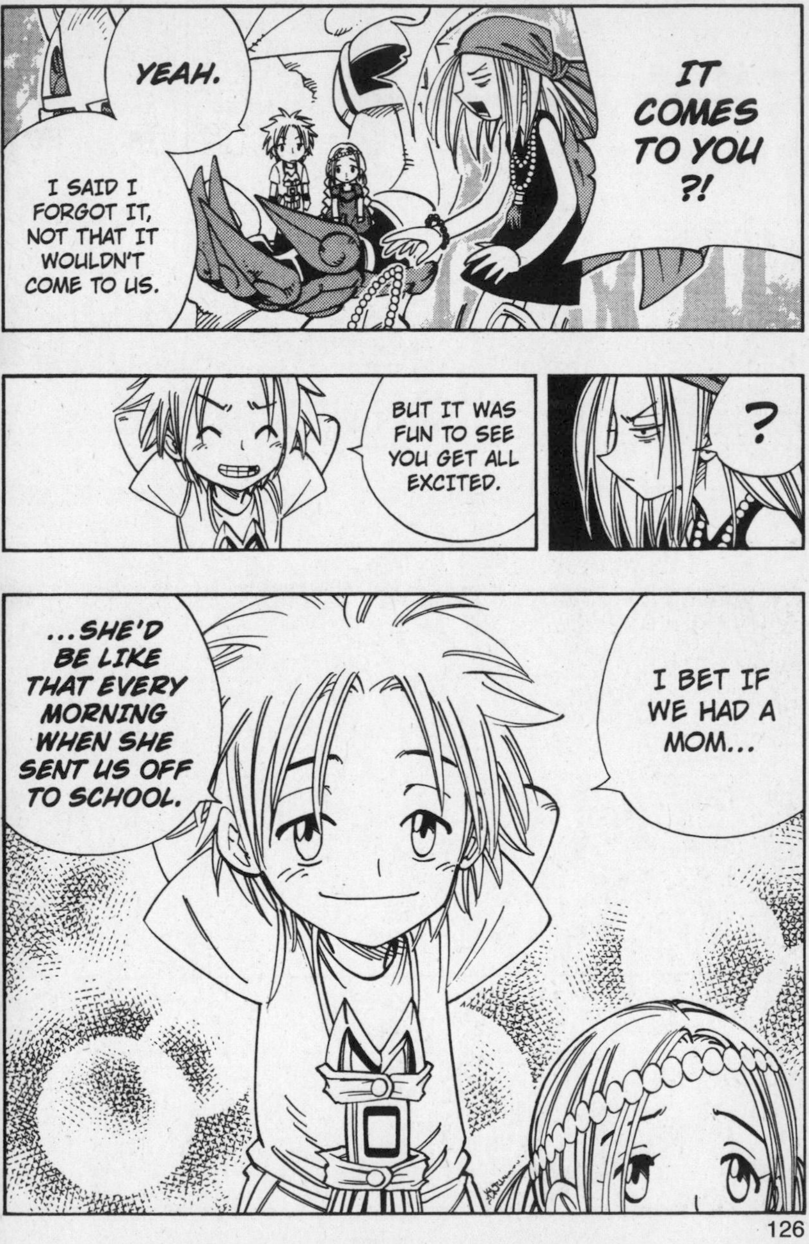
IT COMES TO YOU ?!
YEAH.
I SAID I FORGOT IT, NOT THAT IT WOULDN'T COME TO US.
?
BUT IT WAS FUN TO SEE YOU GET ALL EXCITED.
I BET IF WE HAD A MOM...
...SHE'D BE LIKE THAT EVERY MORNING WHEN SHE SENT US OFF TO SCHOOL.

READ THIS WAY

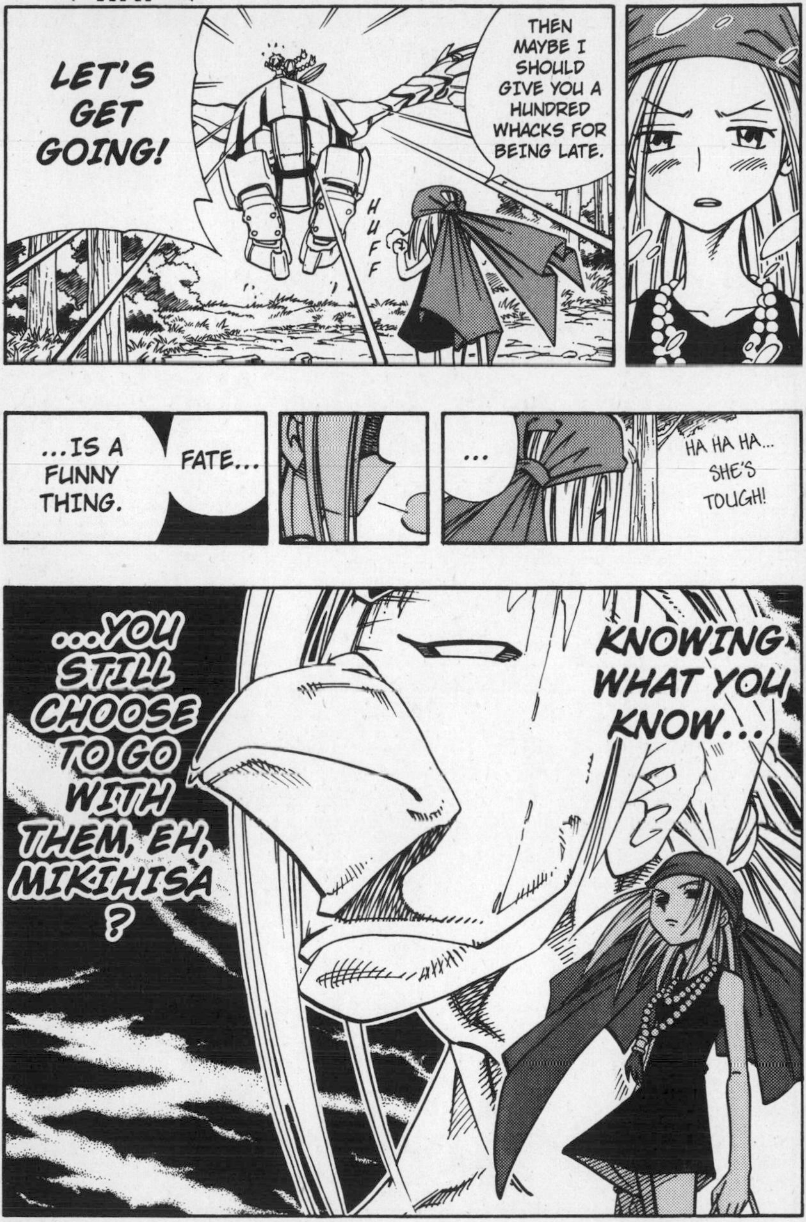
THEN MAYBE I SHOULD GIVE YOU A HUNDRED WHACKS FOR BEING LATE.
LET'S GET GOING!
HUFF
HA HA HA... SHE'S TOUGH!
...
FATE...
...IS A FUNNY THING.
KNOWING WHAT YOU KNOW...
...YOU STILL CHOOSE TO GO WITH THEM, EH, MIKIHISA?

SHAMAN KING CHARACTER FILE No.94

2001
(JAN)

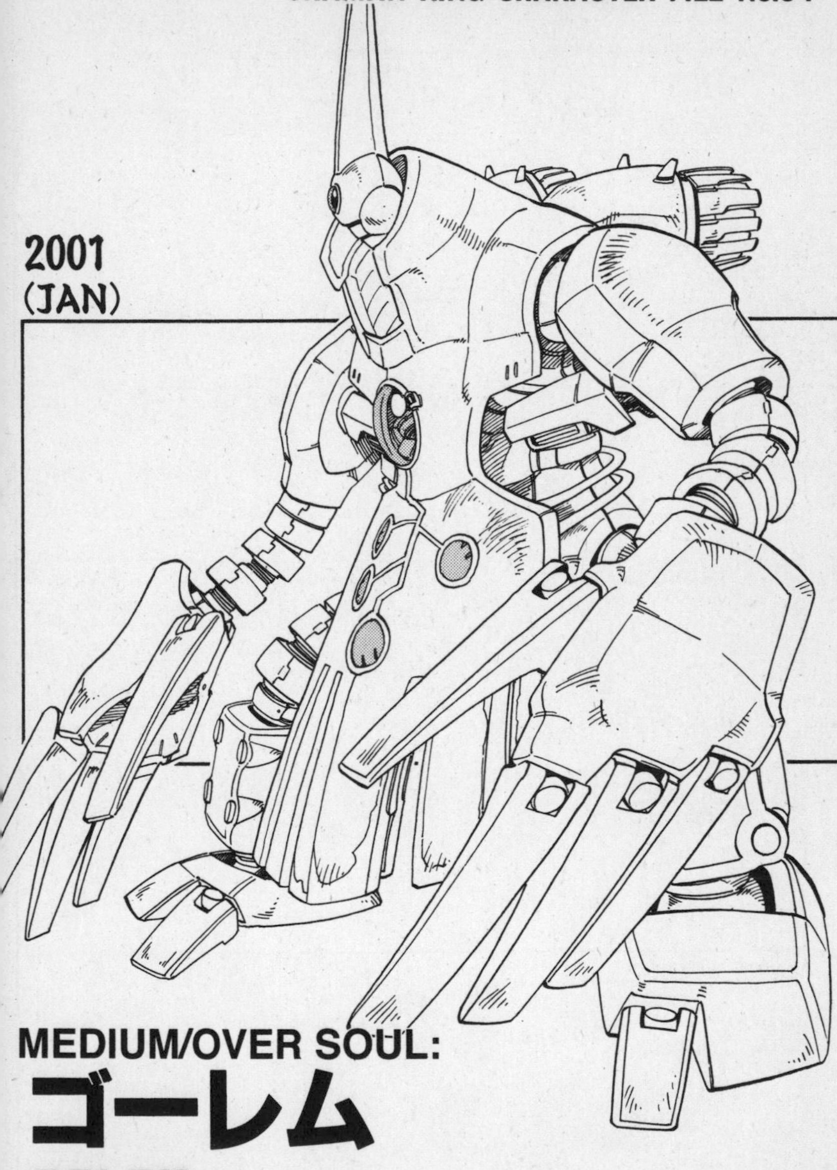

MEDIUM/OVER SOUL:

ゴーレム

GOLEM

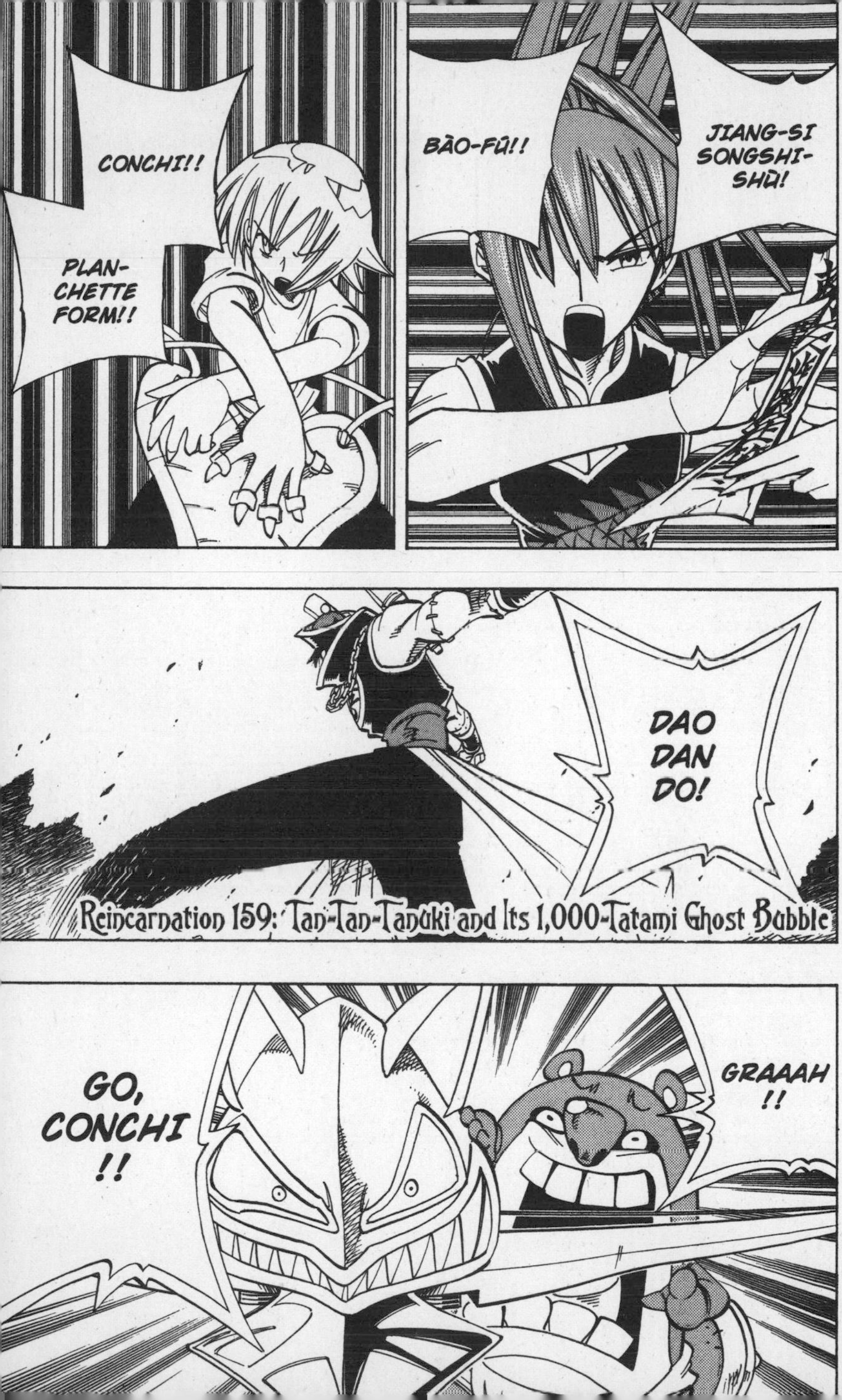
JIANG-SI SONGSHI-SHÙ!
BÀO-FÛ!!
CONCHI!!
PLANCHETTE FORM!!
DAO DAN DO!
Reincarnation 159: Tan-Tan-Tanuki and Its 1,000-Tatami Ghost Bubble
GRAAAH!!
GO, CONCHI!!

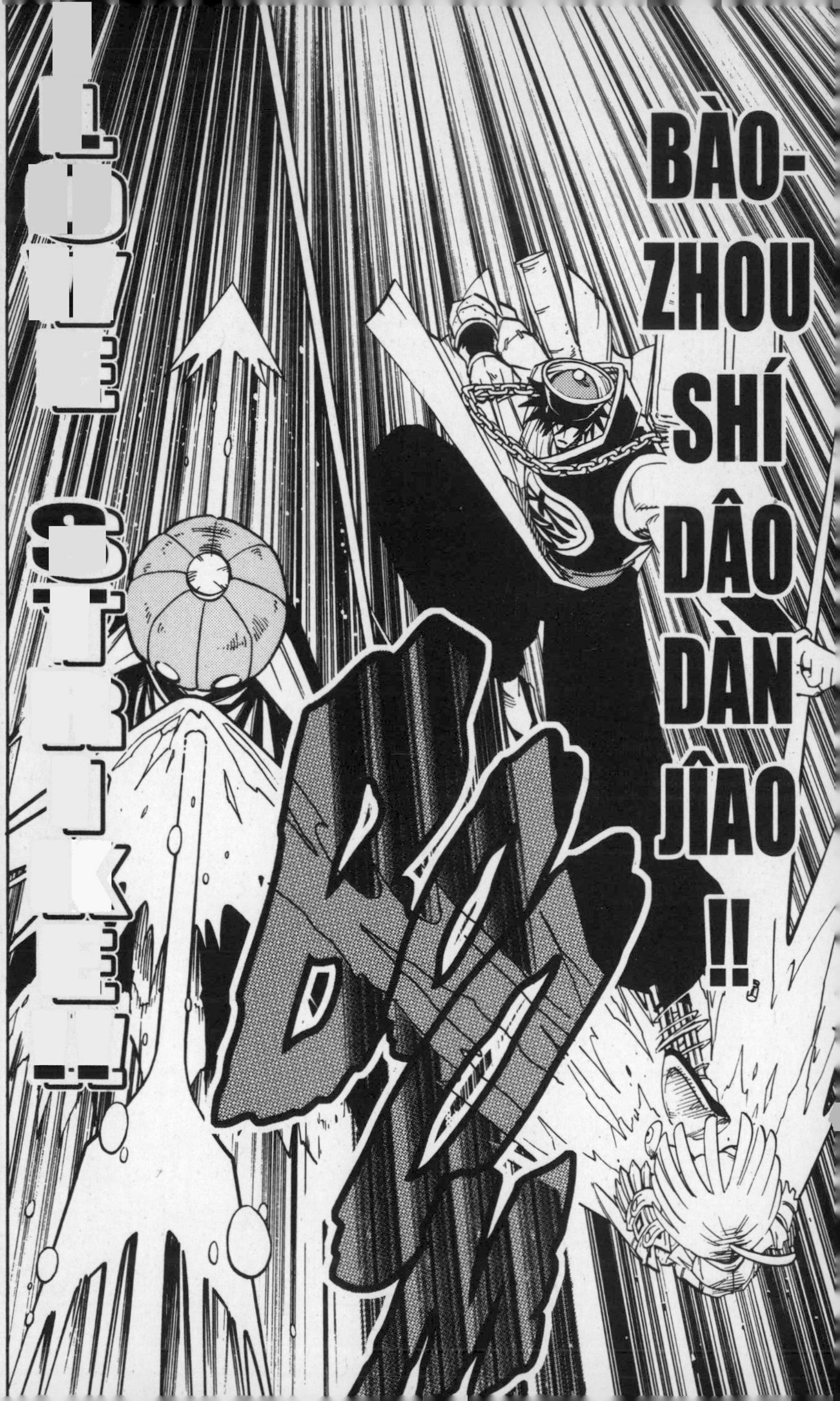
BÀO-ZHOU SHÍ DÂO DÀN JÎAO !!

Reincarnation 159: Tan-Tan-Tanuki and Its 1,000-Tatami Ghost Bubble

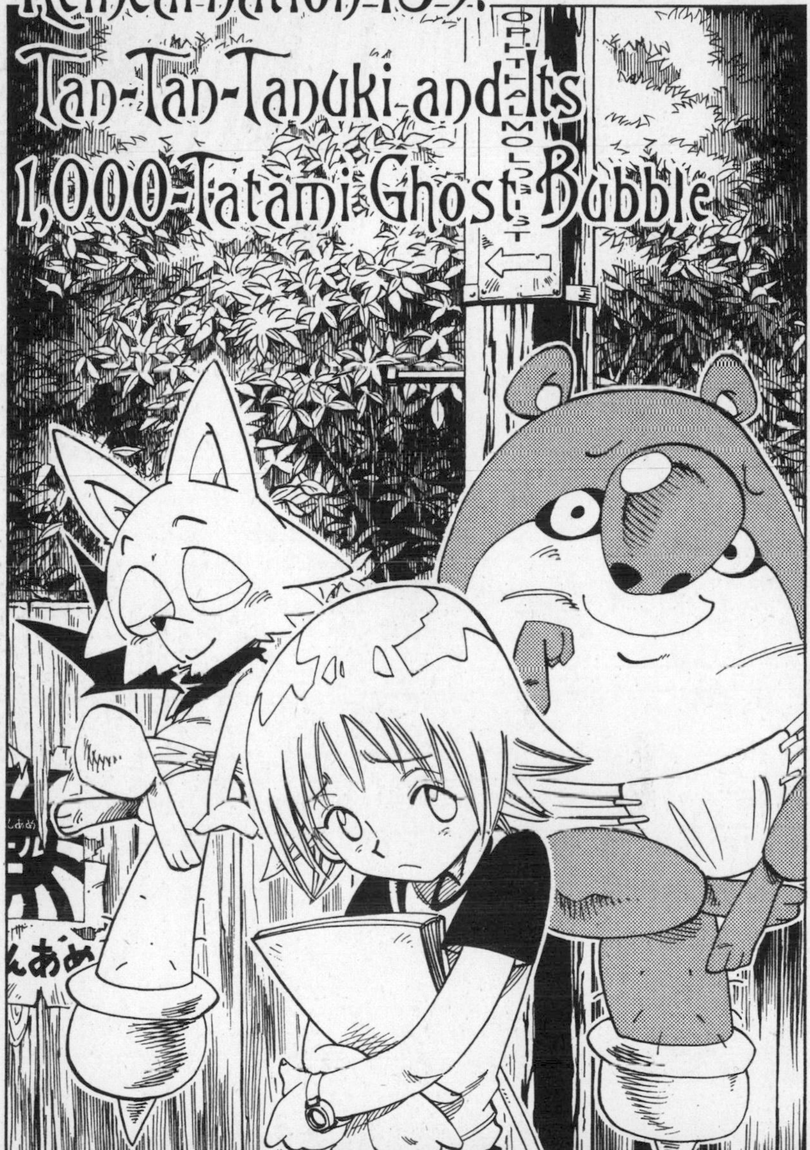
OPHTHALMOLOGIST

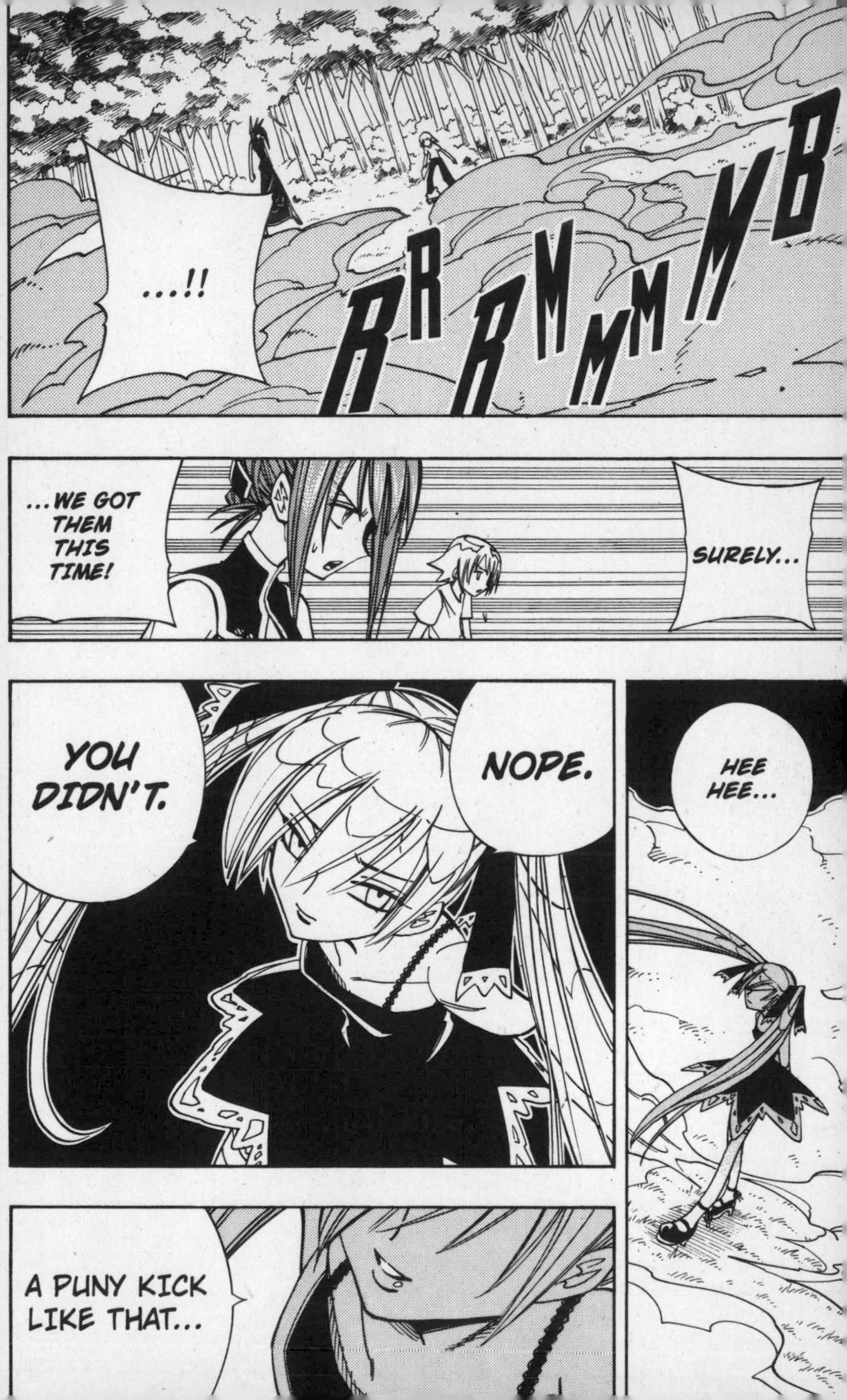
...!!
SURELY...
...WE GOT THEM THIS TIME!
HEE HEE...
NOPE.
YOU DIDN'T.
A PUNY KICK LIKE THAT...

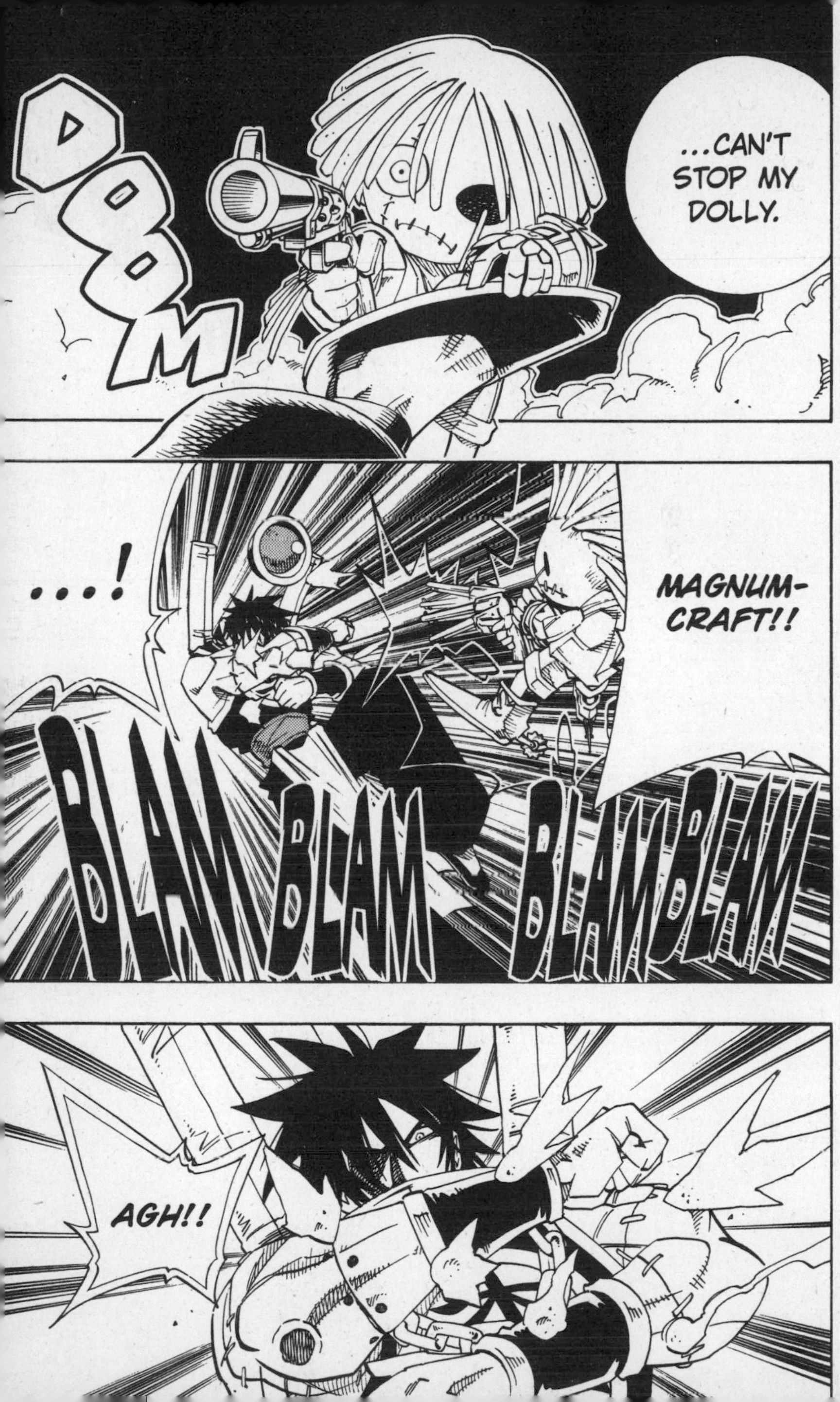
...CAN'T STOP MY DOLLY.
DOOM
MAGNUM-CRAFT!!
...!
BLAM BLAM BLAM BLAM
AGH!!

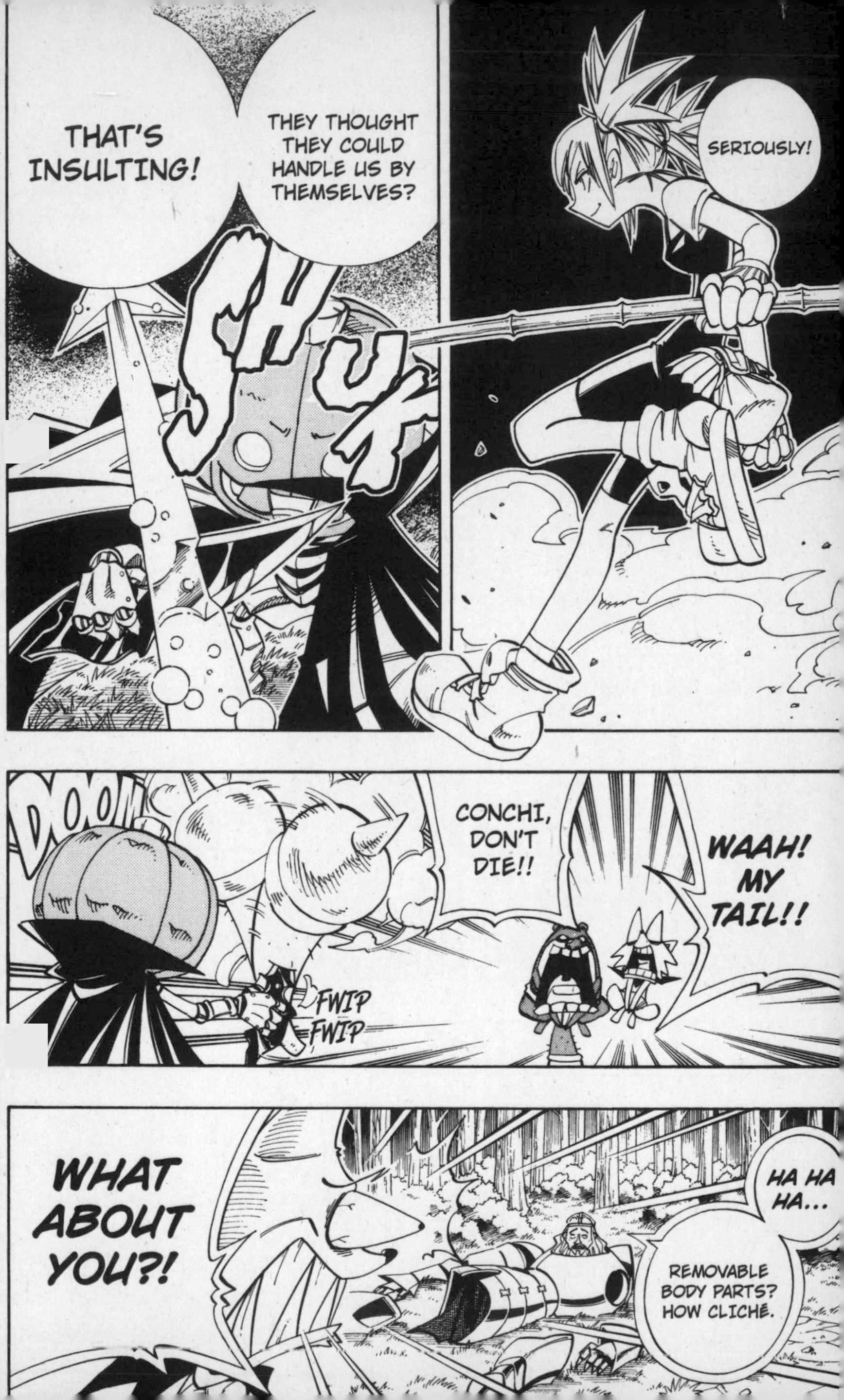
SERIOUSLY!
THEY THOUGHT THEY COULD HANDLE US BY THEMSELVES?
THAT'S INSULTING!
SHUK
WAAH! MY TAIL!!
CONCHI, DON'T DIE!!
DOOM
FWIP FWIP
HA HA HA...
REMOVABLE BODY PARTS? HOW CLICHÉ.
WHAT ABOUT YOU?!

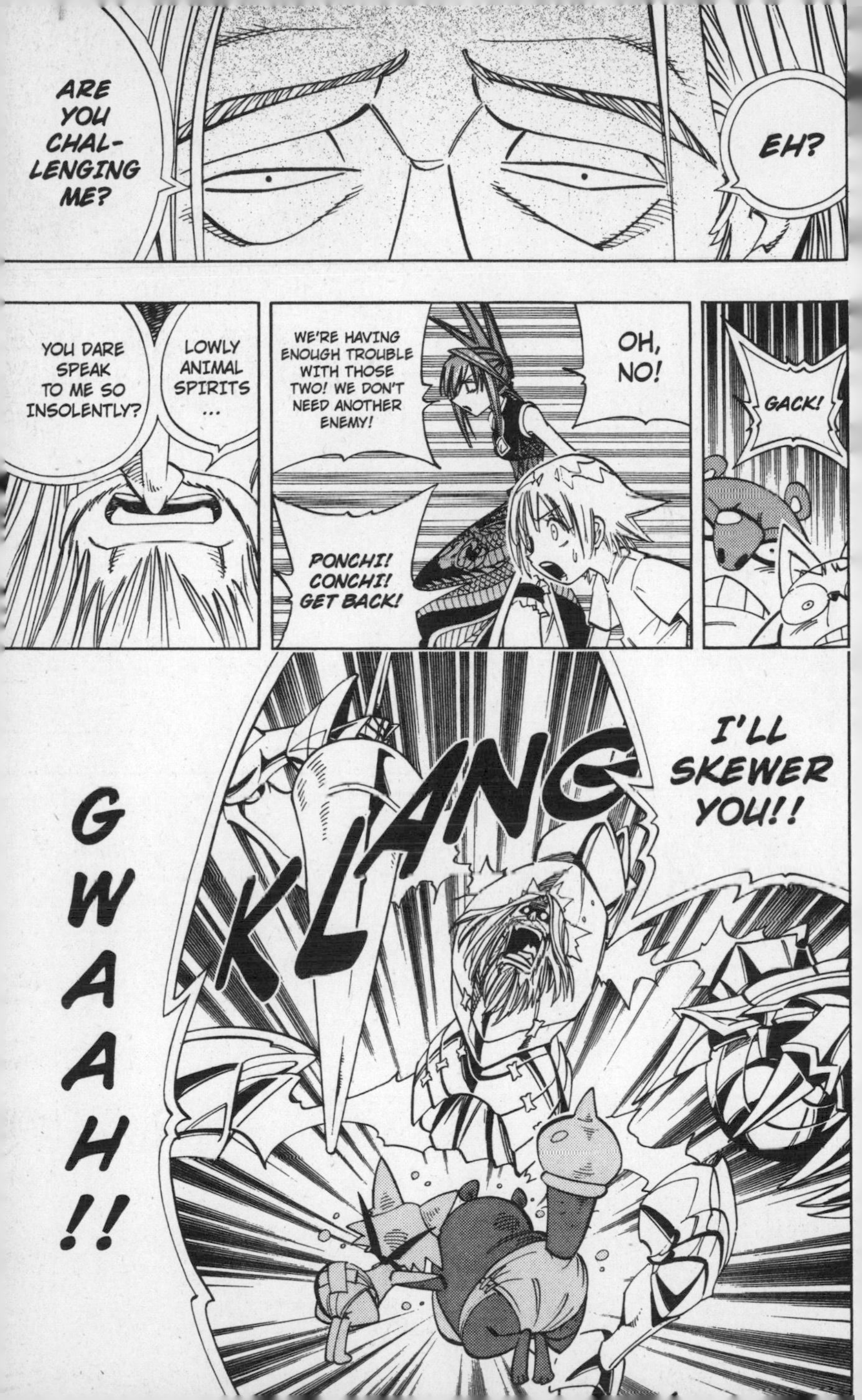
EH?
ARE YOU CHAL-LENGING ME?
GACK!
OH, NO!
WE'RE HAVING ENOUGH TROUBLE WITH THOSE TWO! WE DON'T NEED ANOTHER ENEMY!
PONCHI! CONCHI! GET BACK!
LOWLY ANIMAL SPIRITS ...
YOU DARE SPEAK TO ME SO INSOLENTLY?
I'LL SKEWER YOU!!
KLANG
GWAAAH!!

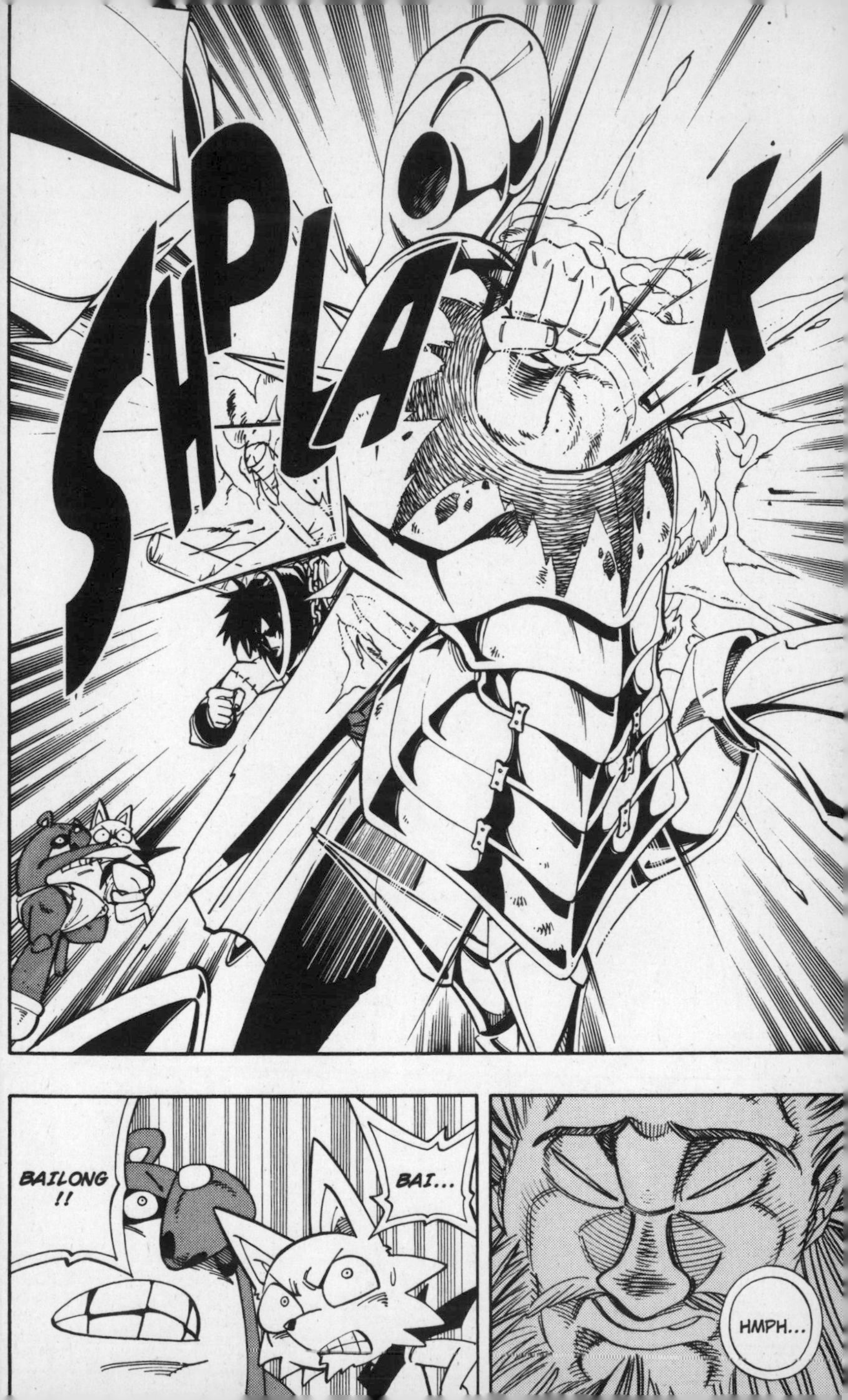
SHPLACK
HMPH...
BAI...
BAILONG !!

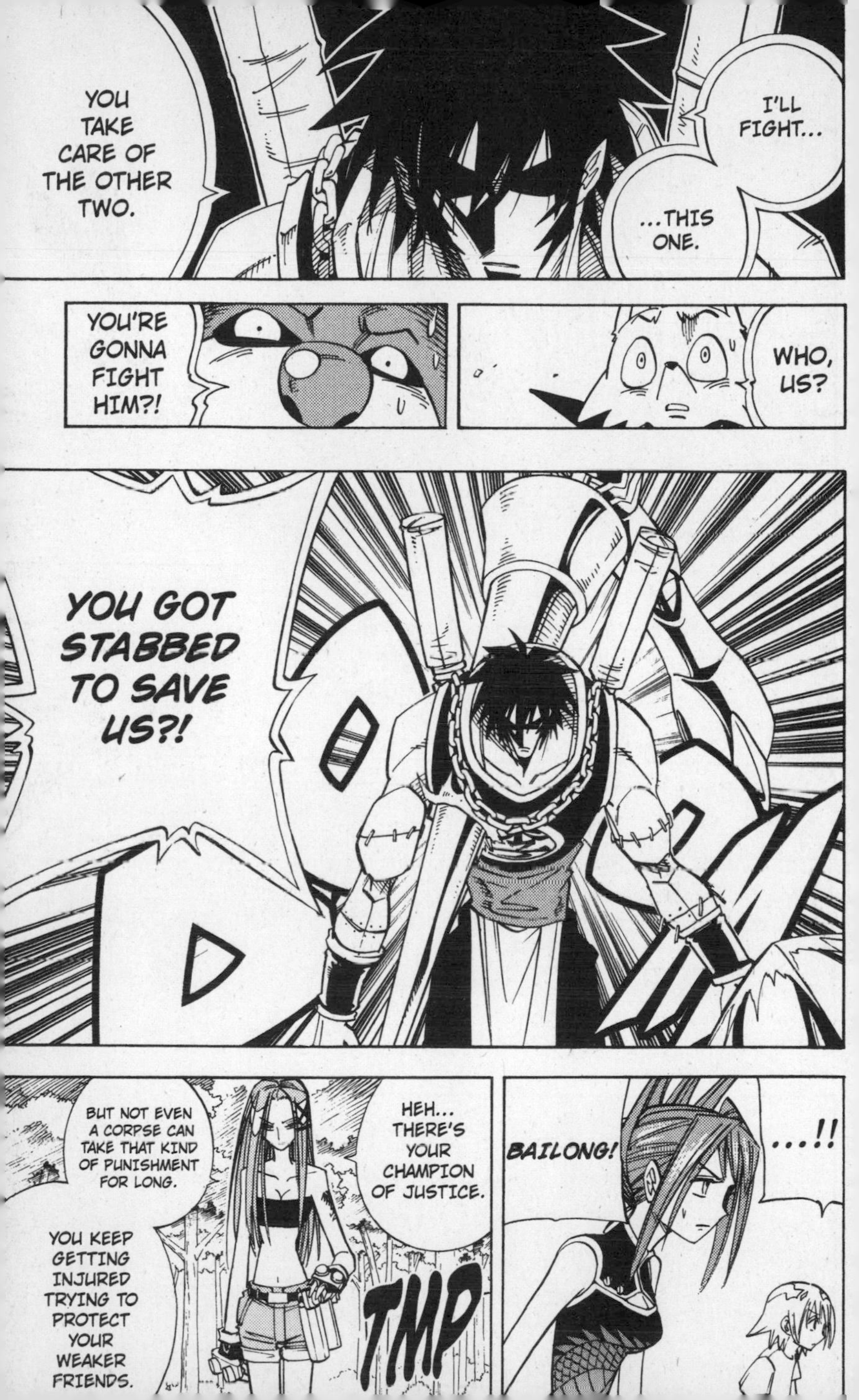

I'LL FIGHT...
...THIS ONE.
YOU TAKE CARE OF THE OTHER TWO.
WHO, US?
YOU'RE GONNA FIGHT HIM?!
YOU GOT STABBED TO SAVE US?!
...!!
BAILONG!
HEH... THERE'S YOUR CHAMPION OF JUSTICE.
BUT NOT EVEN A CORPSE CAN TAKE THAT KIND OF PUNISHMENT FOR LONG.
YOU KEEP GETTING INJURED TRYING TO PROTECT YOUR WEAKER FRIENDS.
TMP

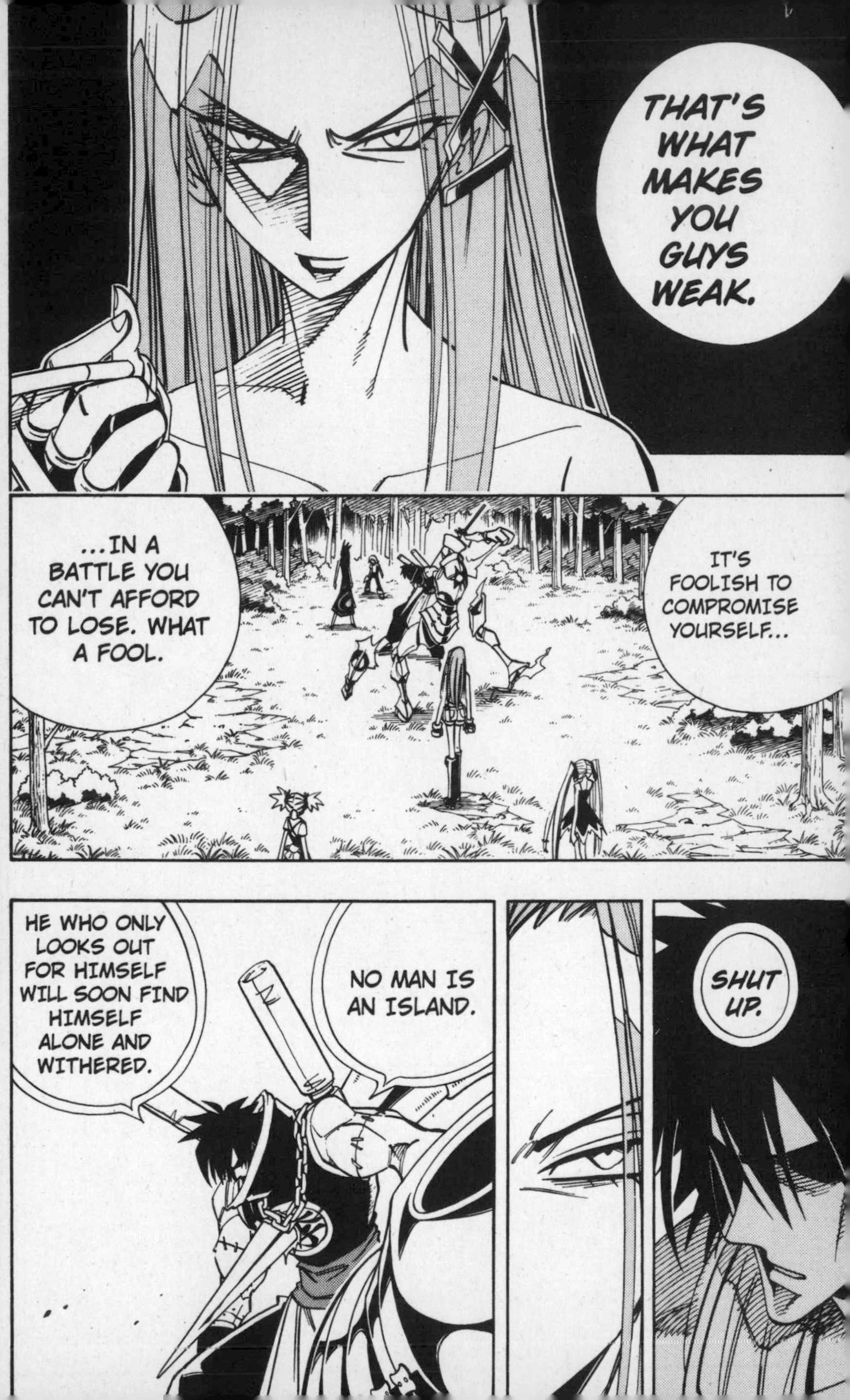
THAT'S WHAT MAKES YOU GUYS WEAK.
IT'S FOOLISH TO COMPROMISE YOURSELF...
...IN A BATTLE YOU CAN'T AFFORD TO LOSE. WHAT A FOOL.
SHUT UP.
NO MAN IS AN ISLAND.
HE WHO ONLY LOOKS OUT FOR HIMSELF WILL SOON FIND HIMSELF ALONE AND WITHERED.

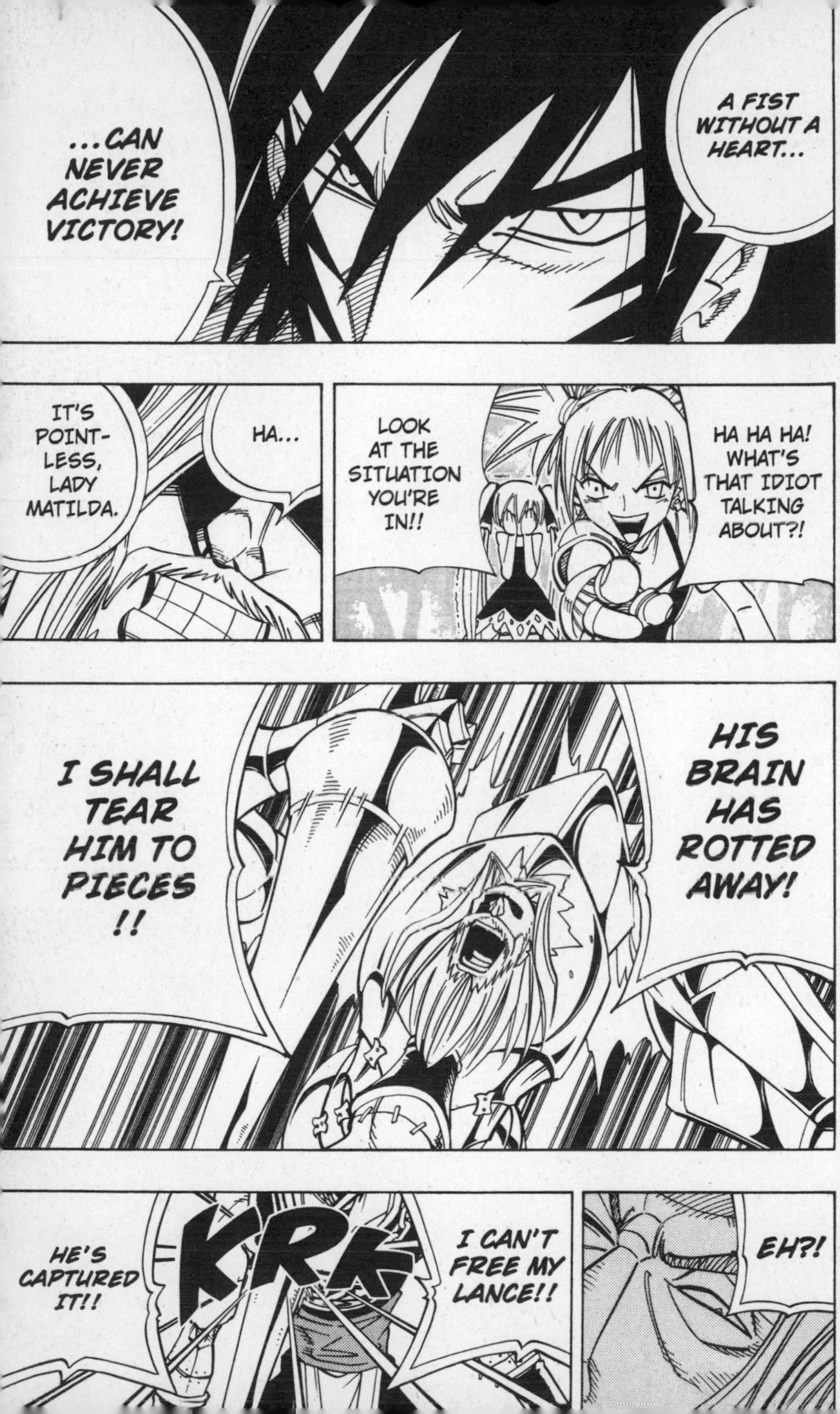
A FIST WITHOUT A HEART...
...CAN NEVER ACHIEVE VICTORY!
HA HA HA! WHAT'S THAT IDIOT TALKING ABOUT?!
LOOK AT THE SITUATION YOU'RE IN!!
HA...
IT'S POINTLESS, LADY MATILDA.
HIS BRAIN HAS ROTTED AWAY!
I SHALL TEAR HIM TO PIECES!!
EH?!
I CAN'T FREE MY LANCE!!
KRK
HE'S CAPTURED IT!!

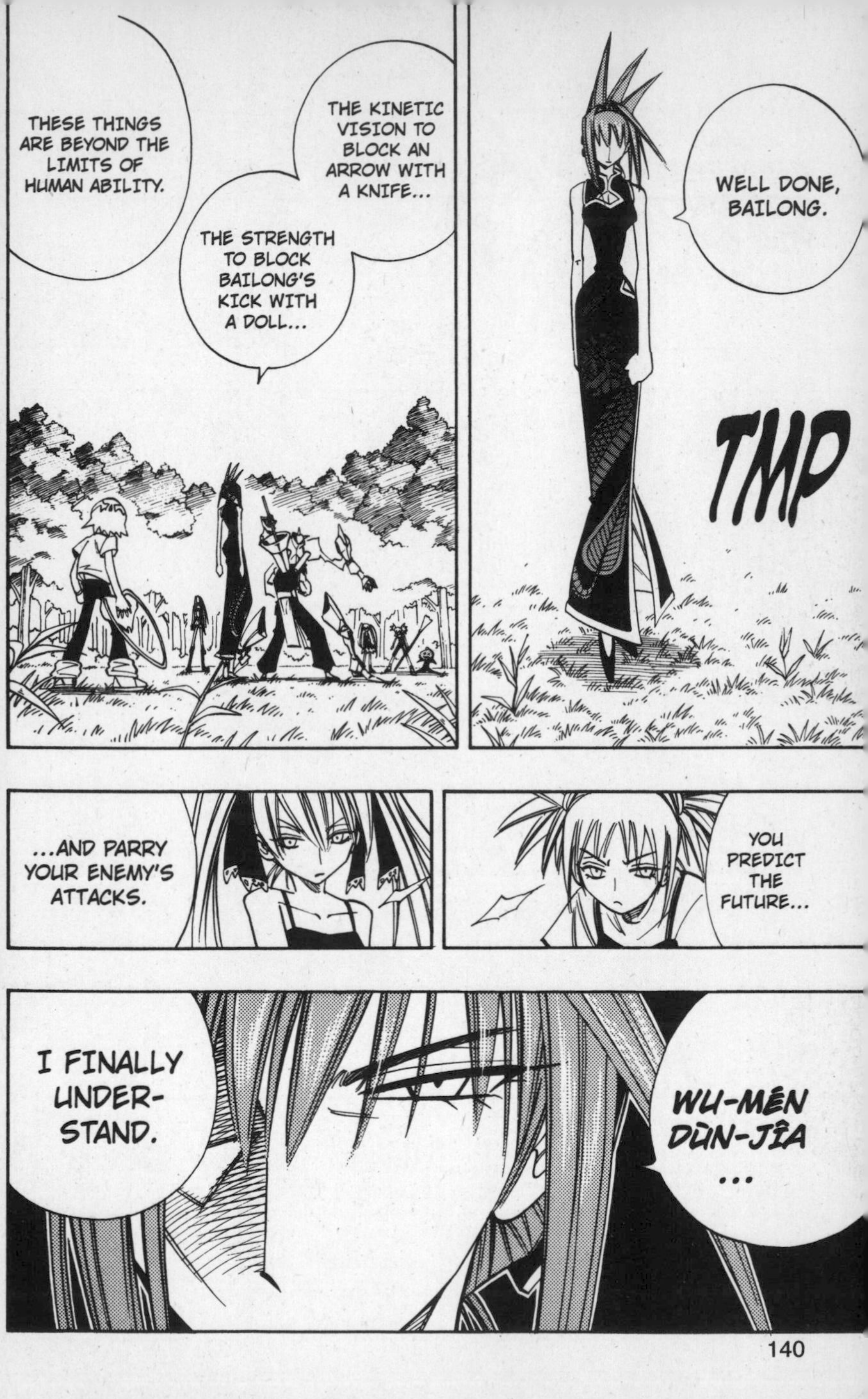
WELL DONE, BAILONG.
TMP
THE KINETIC VISION TO BLOCK AN ARROW WITH A KNIFE...
THE STRENGTH TO BLOCK BAILONG'S KICK WITH A DOLL...
THESE THINGS ARE BEYOND THE LIMITS OF HUMAN ABILITY.
YOU PREDICT THE FUTURE...
...AND PARRY YOUR ENEMY'S ATTACKS.
WU-MÉN DŪN-JĪA ...
I FINALLY UNDER-STAND.

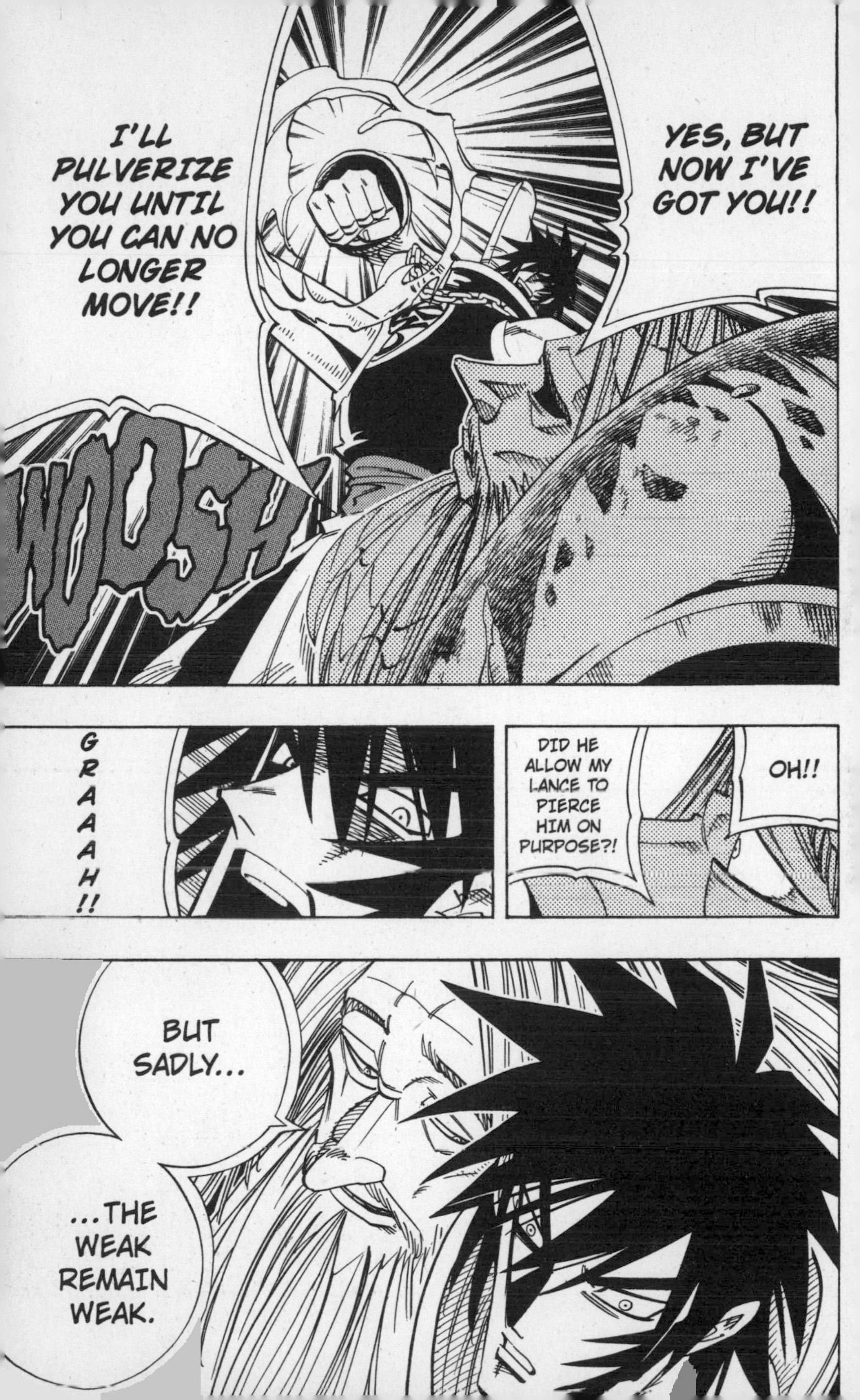
YES, BUT NOW I'VE GOT YOU!!
I'LL PULVERIZE YOU UNTIL YOU CAN NO LONGER MOVE!!
WOOSH
OH!!
DID HE ALLOW MY LANCE TO PIERCE HIM ON PURPOSE?!
GRAAAAH!!
BUT SADLY...
...THE WEAK REMAIN WEAK.

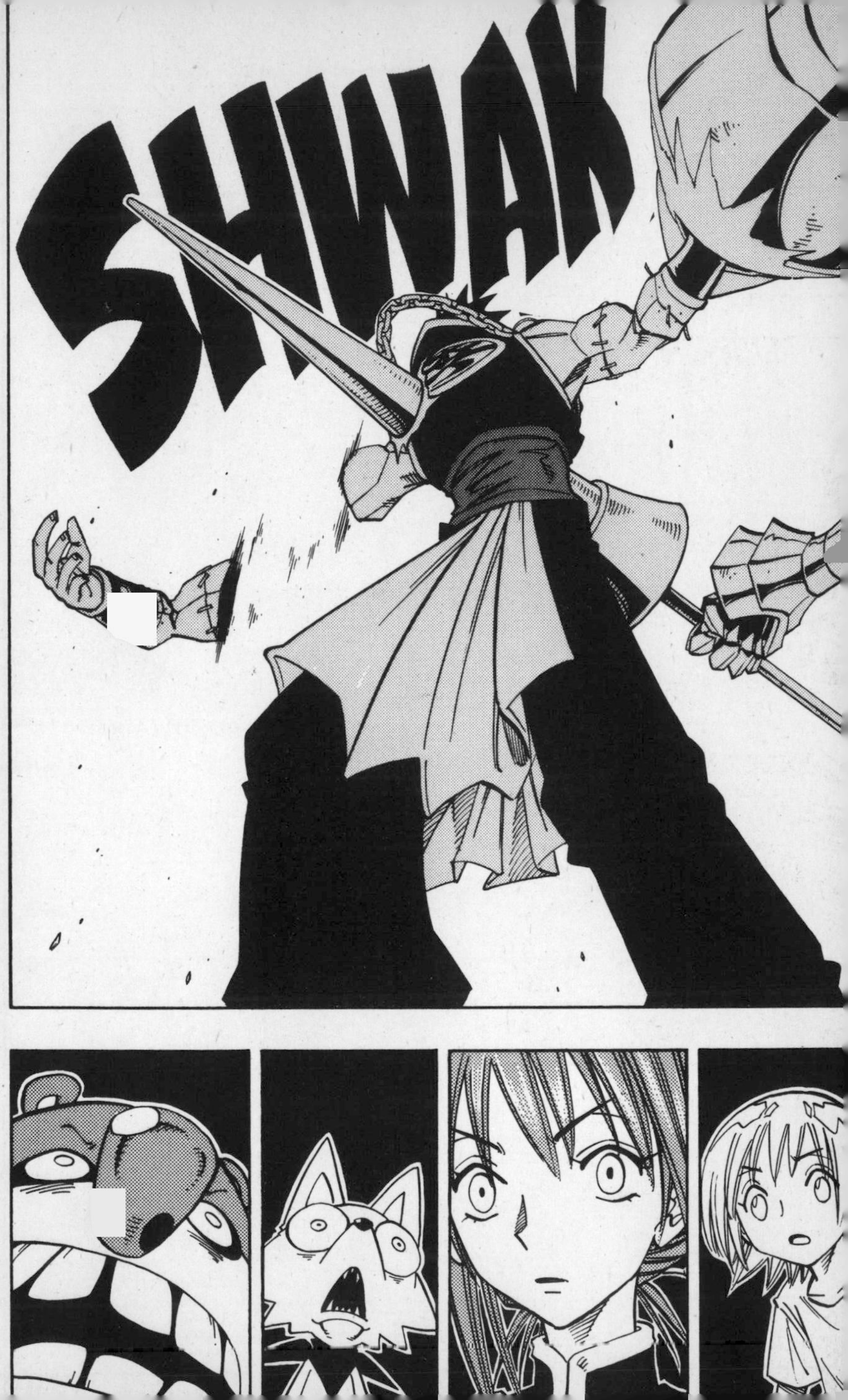
SHWAK

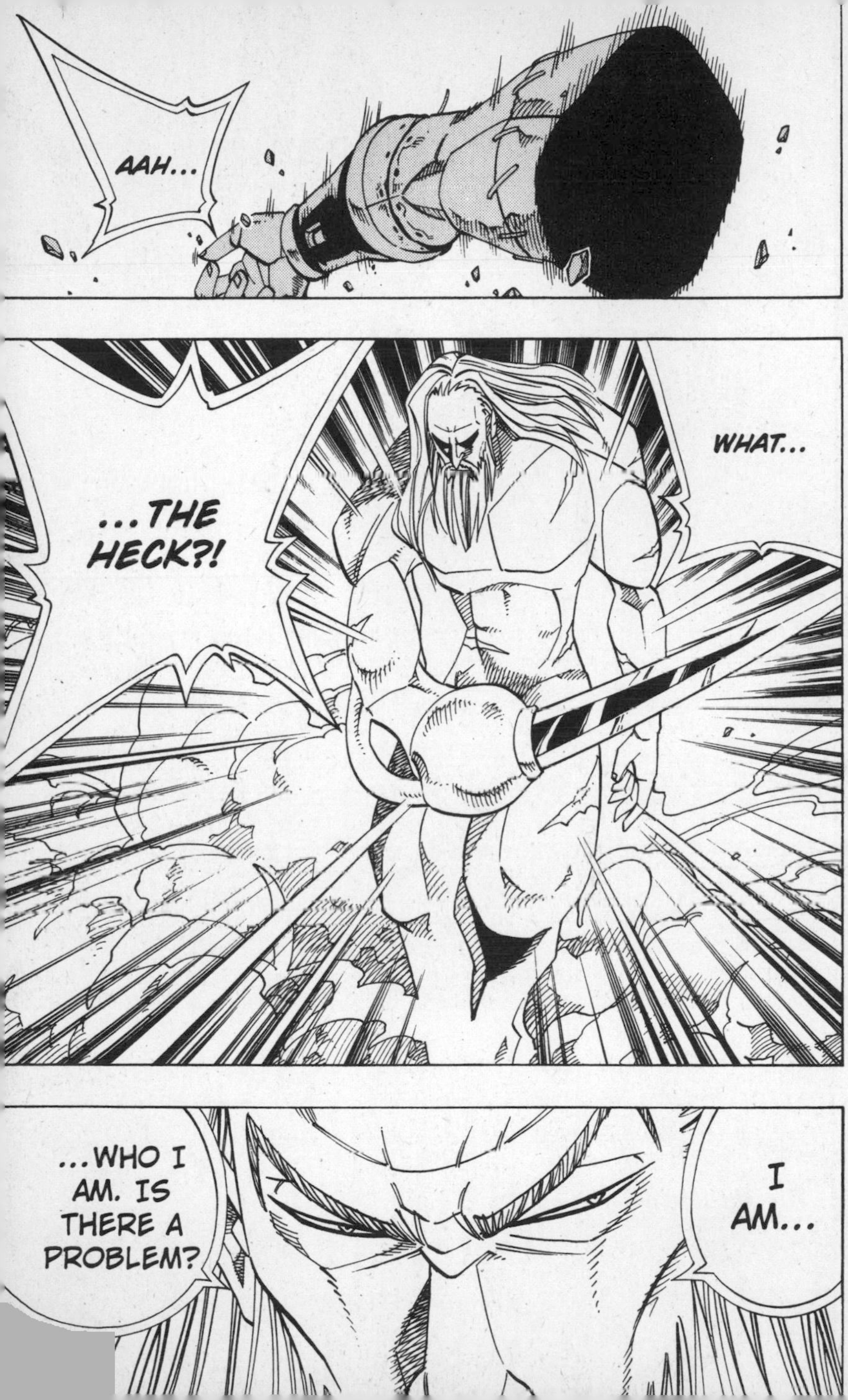
AAH...
WHAT...
...THE HECK?!
I AM...
...WHO I AM. IS THERE A PROBLEM?

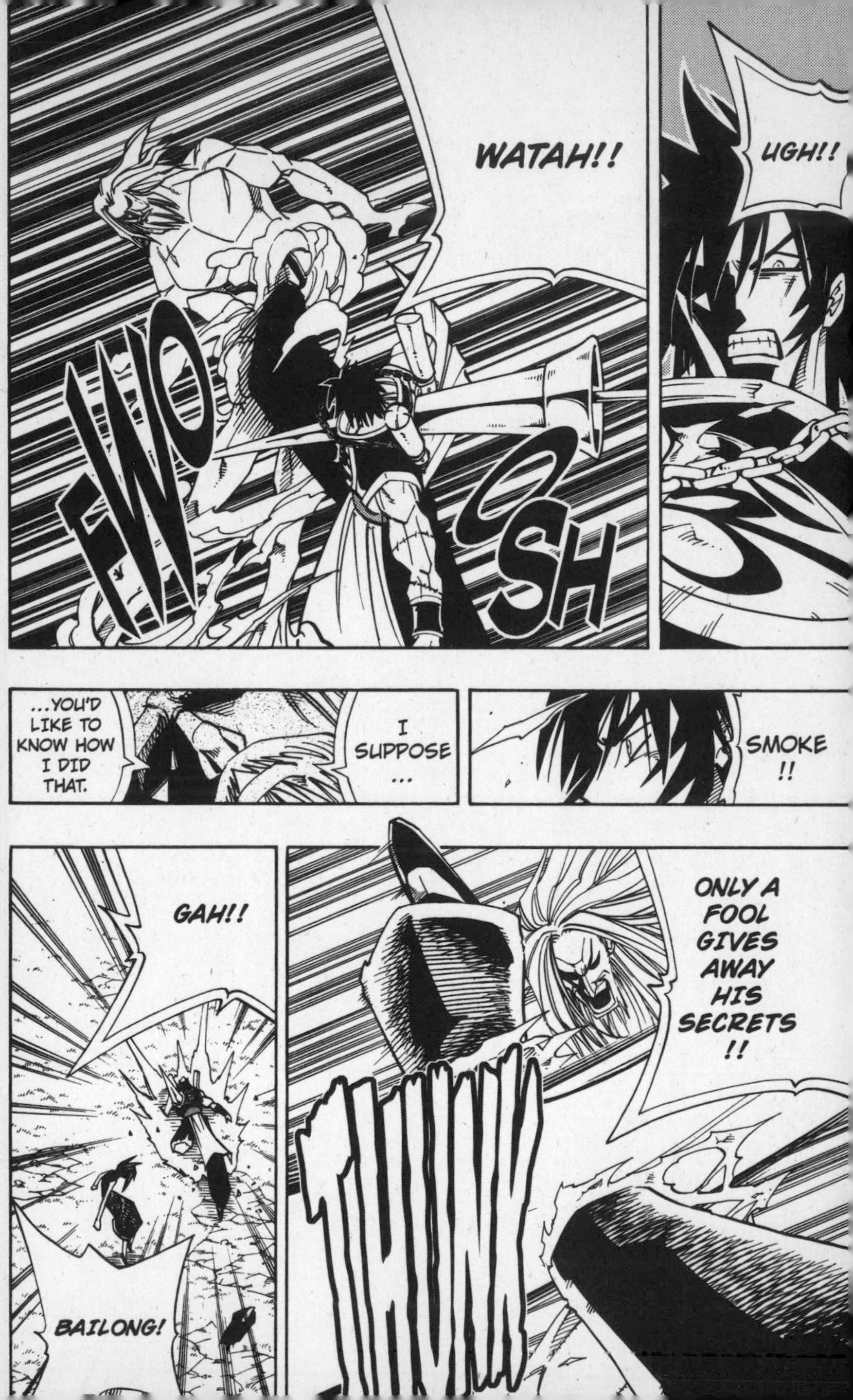
UGH!!
WATAH!!
FWOOSH
SMOKE !!
I SUPPOSE ...
...YOU'D LIKE TO KNOW HOW I DID THAT.
ONLY A FOOL GIVES AWAY HIS SECRETS !!
THUNK
GAH!!
BAILONG!

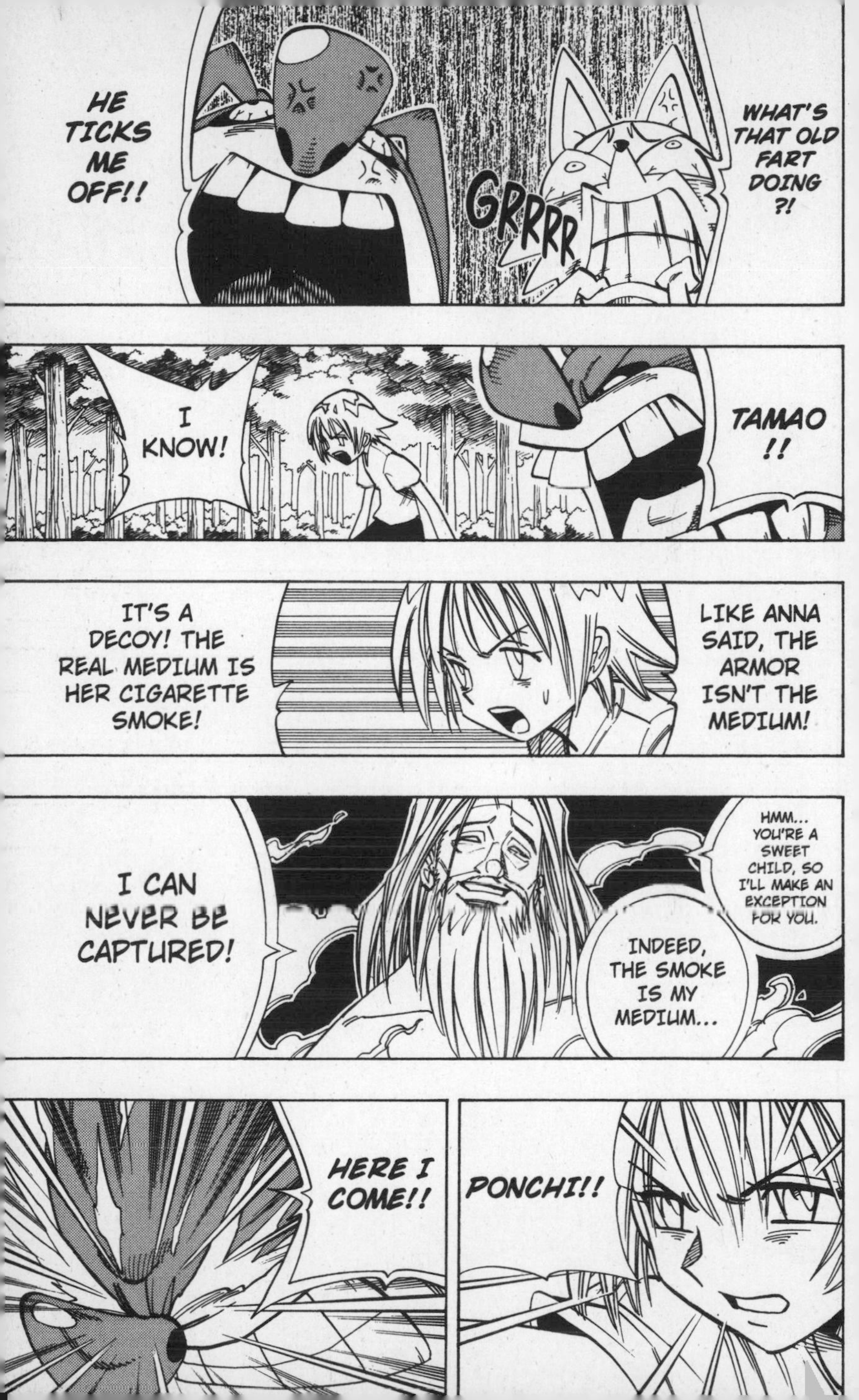
WHAT'S THAT OLD FART DOING?!
GRRRR
HE TICKS ME OFF!!
TAMAO!!
I KNOW!
LIKE ANNA SAID, THE ARMOR ISN'T THE MEDIUM!
IT'S A DECOY! THE REAL MEDIUM IS HER CIGARETTE SMOKE!
HMM... YOU'RE A SWEET CHILD, SO I'LL MAKE AN EXCEPTION FOR YOU.
INDEED, THE SMOKE IS MY MEDIUM...
I CAN NEVER BE CAPTURED!
PONCHI!!
HERE I COME!!

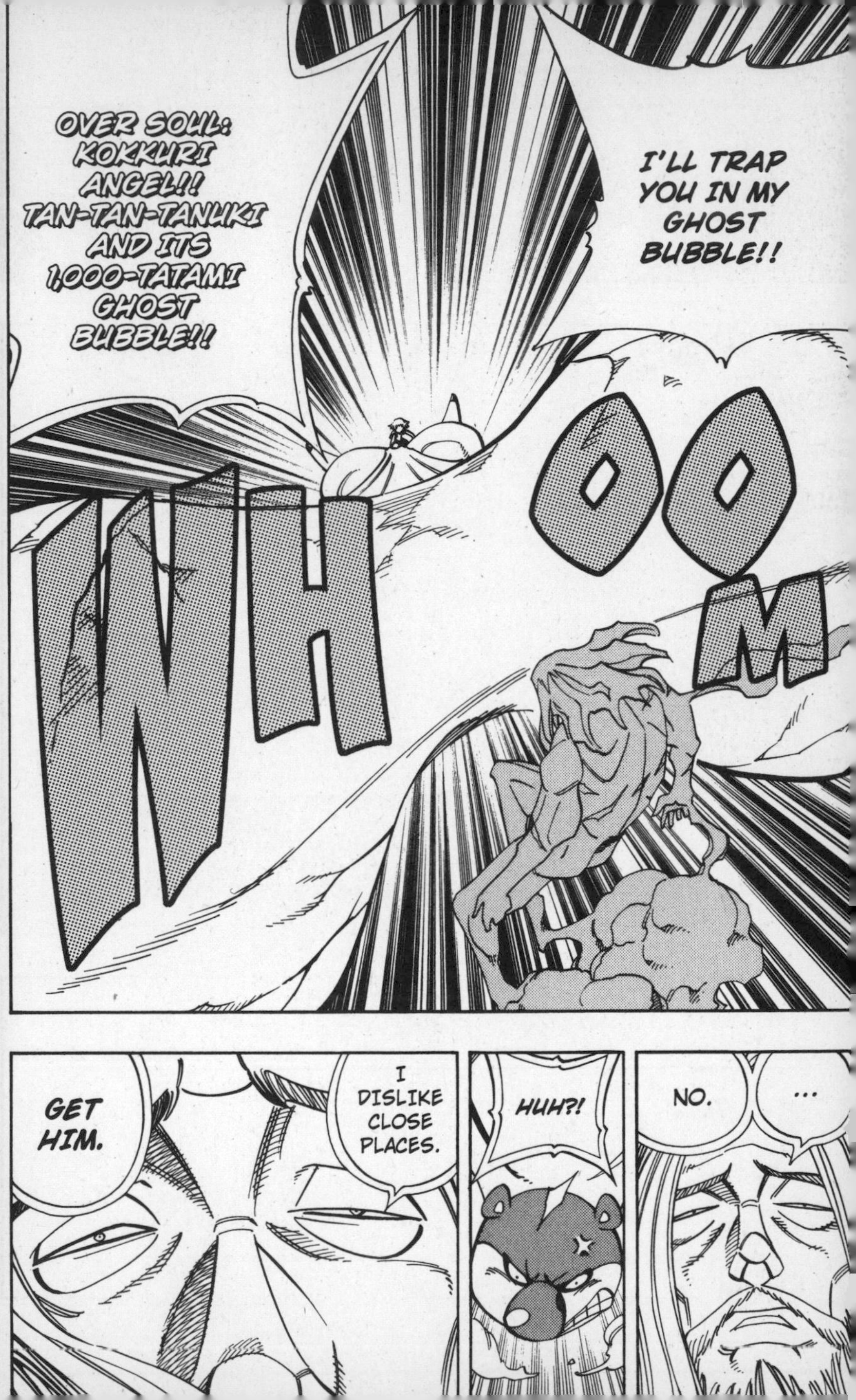
I'LL TRAP YOU IN MY GHOST BUBBLE!!
OVER SOUL: KOKKURI ANGEL!! TAN-TAN-TANUKI AND ITS 1,000-TATAMI GHOST BUBBLE!!
WHOOM
...
NO.
HUH?!
I DISLIKE CLOSE PLACES.
GET HIM.

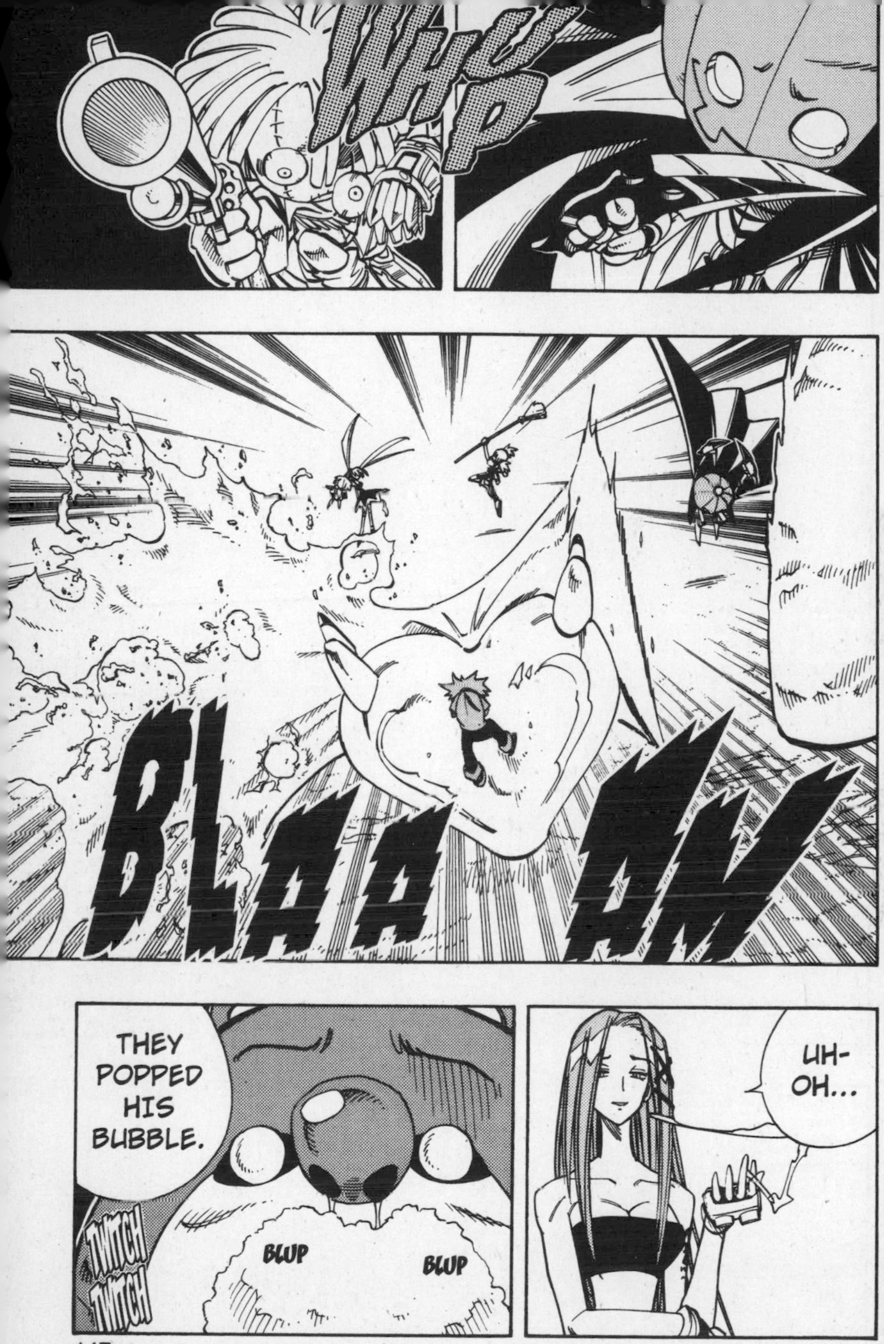
WHIP
BLAAAM
UH-OH...
THEY POPPED HIS BUBBLE.
BLUP
BLUP
TWITCH TWITCH

SHAMAN KING CHARACTER FILE No.95

2001
(JAN)

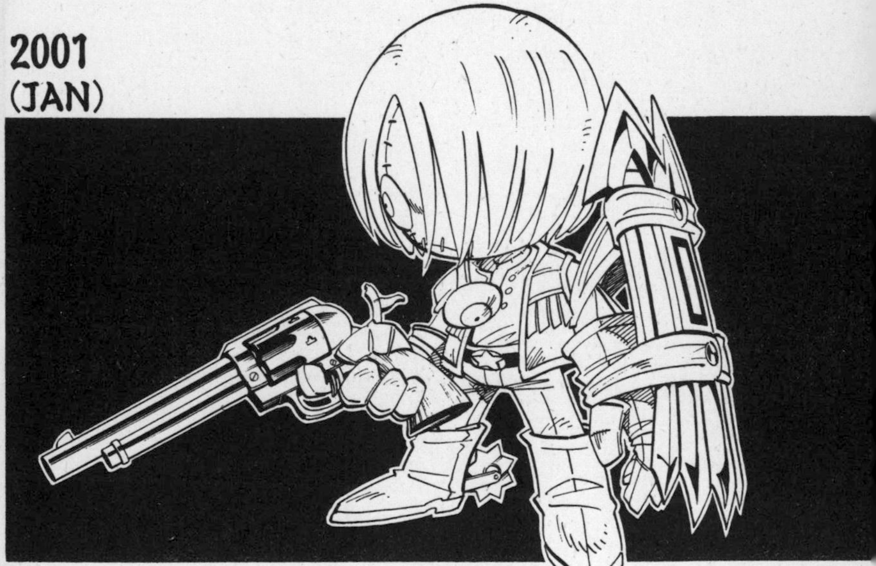

MEDIUM/OVER SOUL:

チャック

CHUCK

Reincarnation 160: The Mask Restored

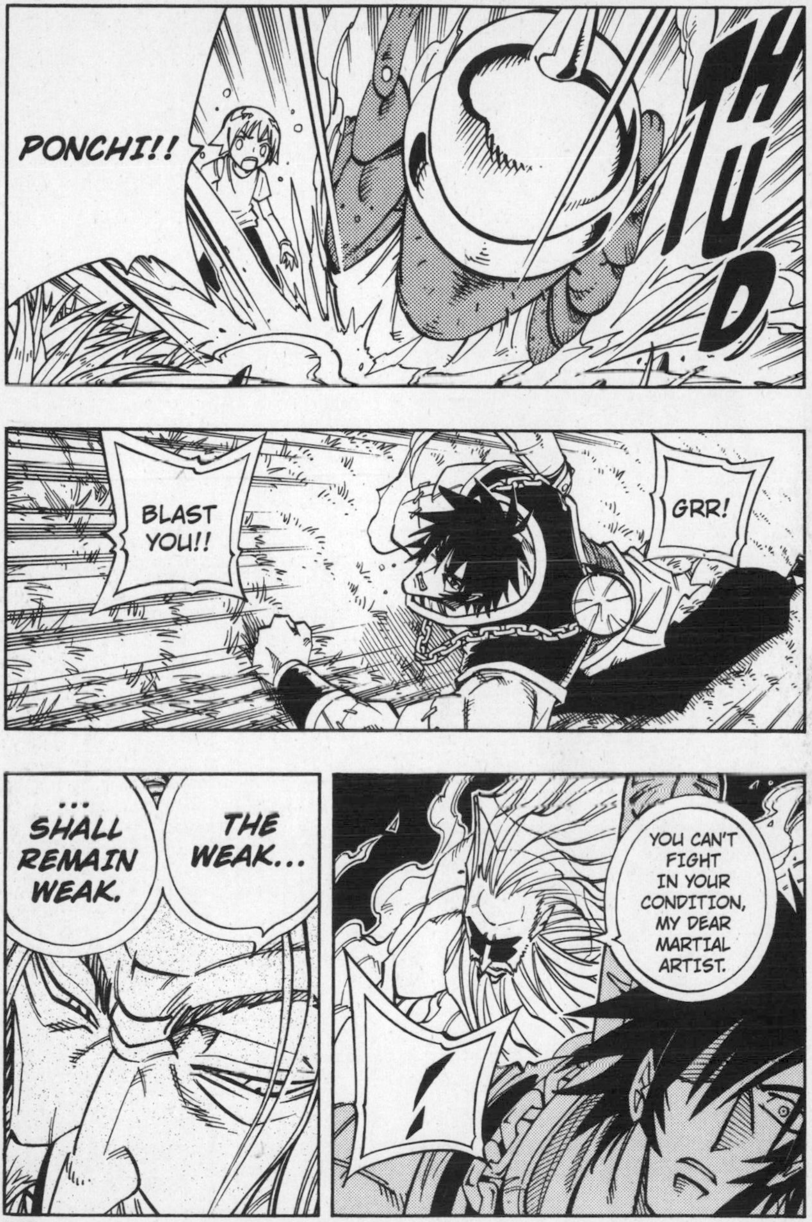
THUD
PONCHI!!
GRR!
BLAST YOU!!
YOU CAN'T FIGHT IN YOUR CONDITION, MY DEAR MARTIAL ARTIST.
!
THE WEAK...
... SHALL REMAIN WEAK.

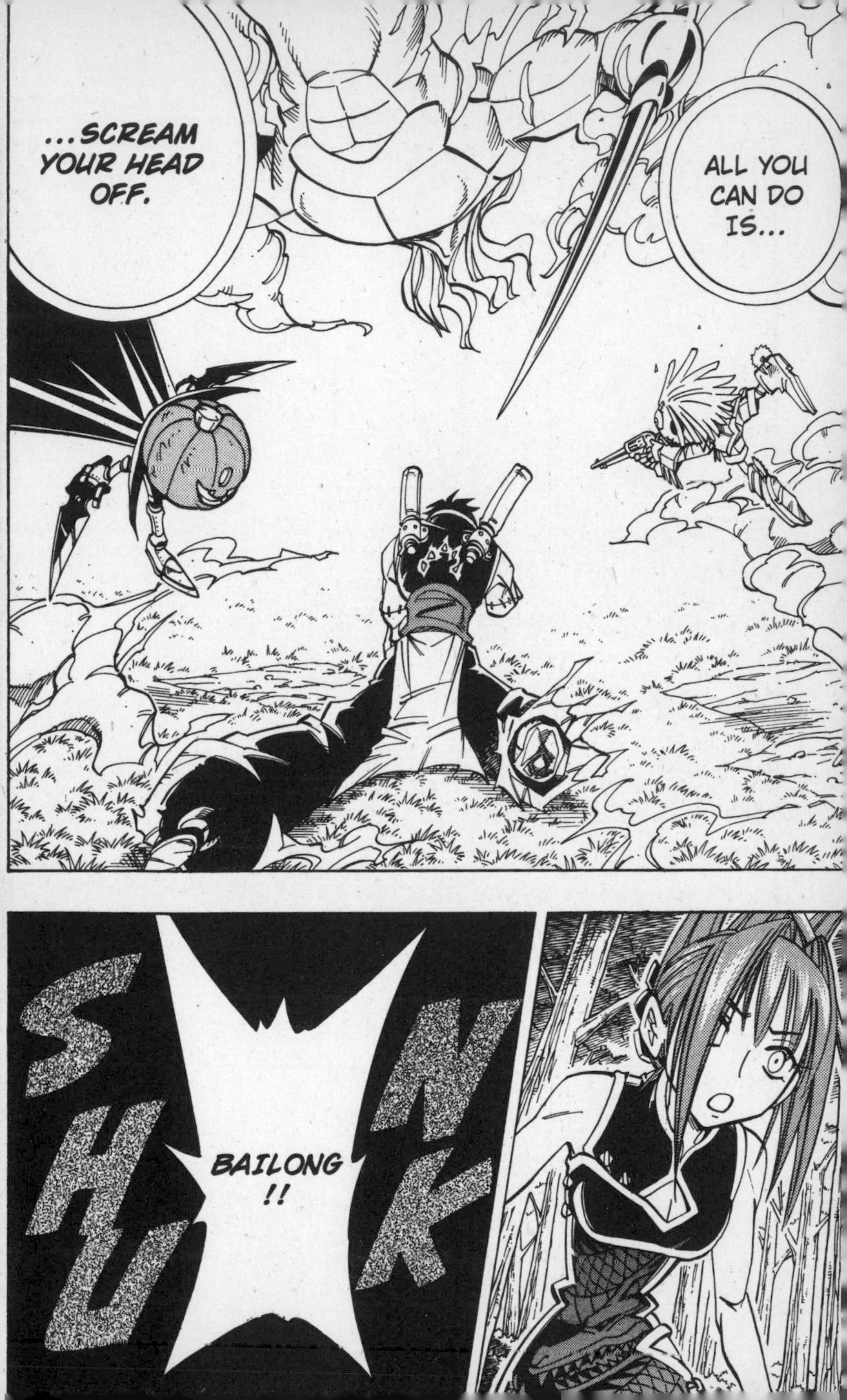
ALL YOU CAN DO IS...
...SCREAM YOUR HEAD OFF.
BAILONG!!
SHUNK

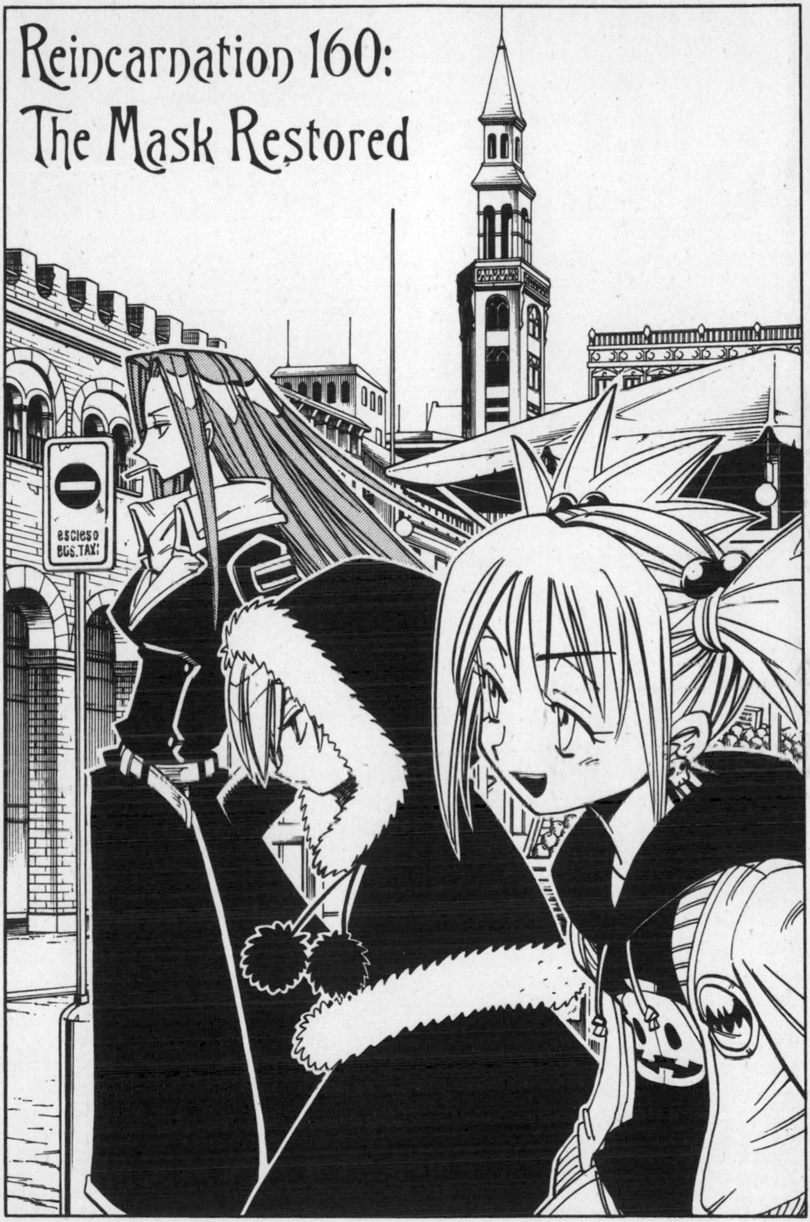
Reincarnation 160:
The Mask Restored
escleso
BUS.TAXI

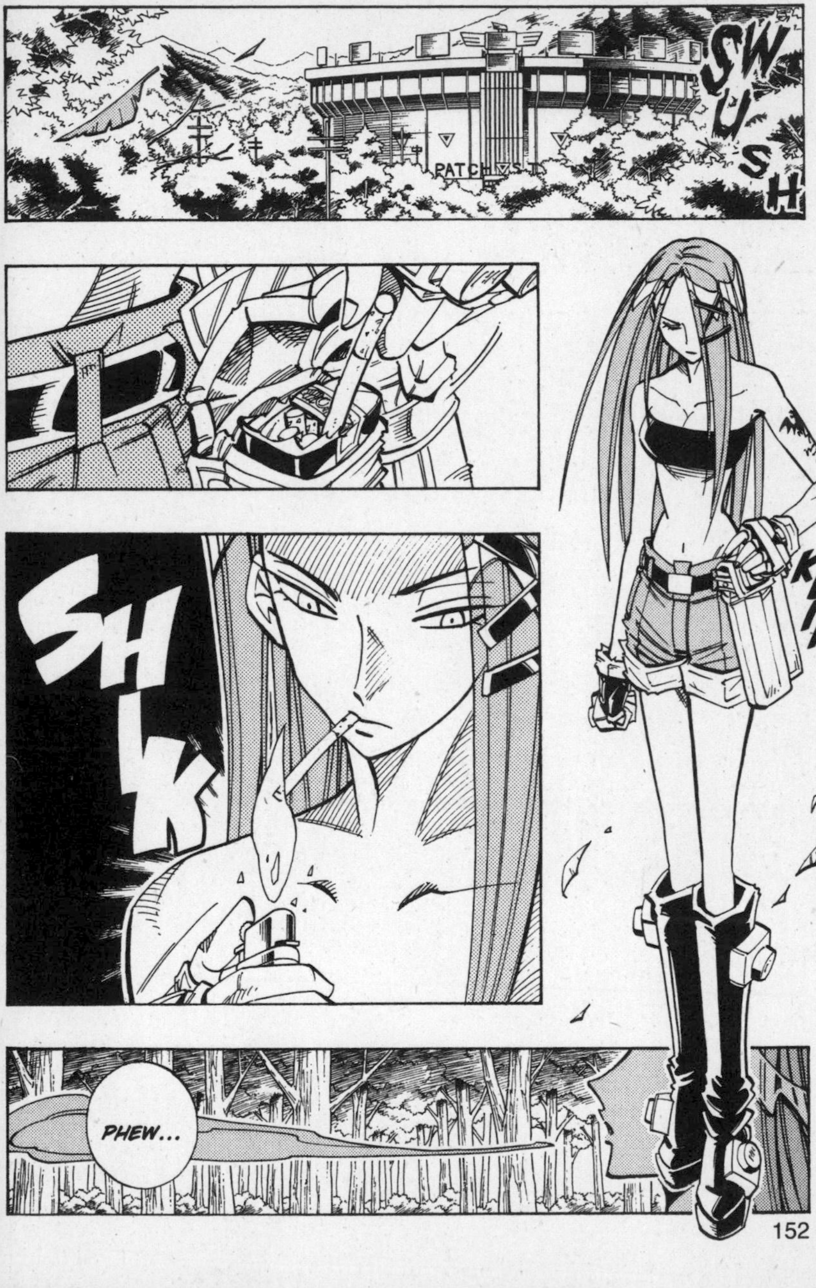
SWUSH
KLIK
SHK
PHEW...

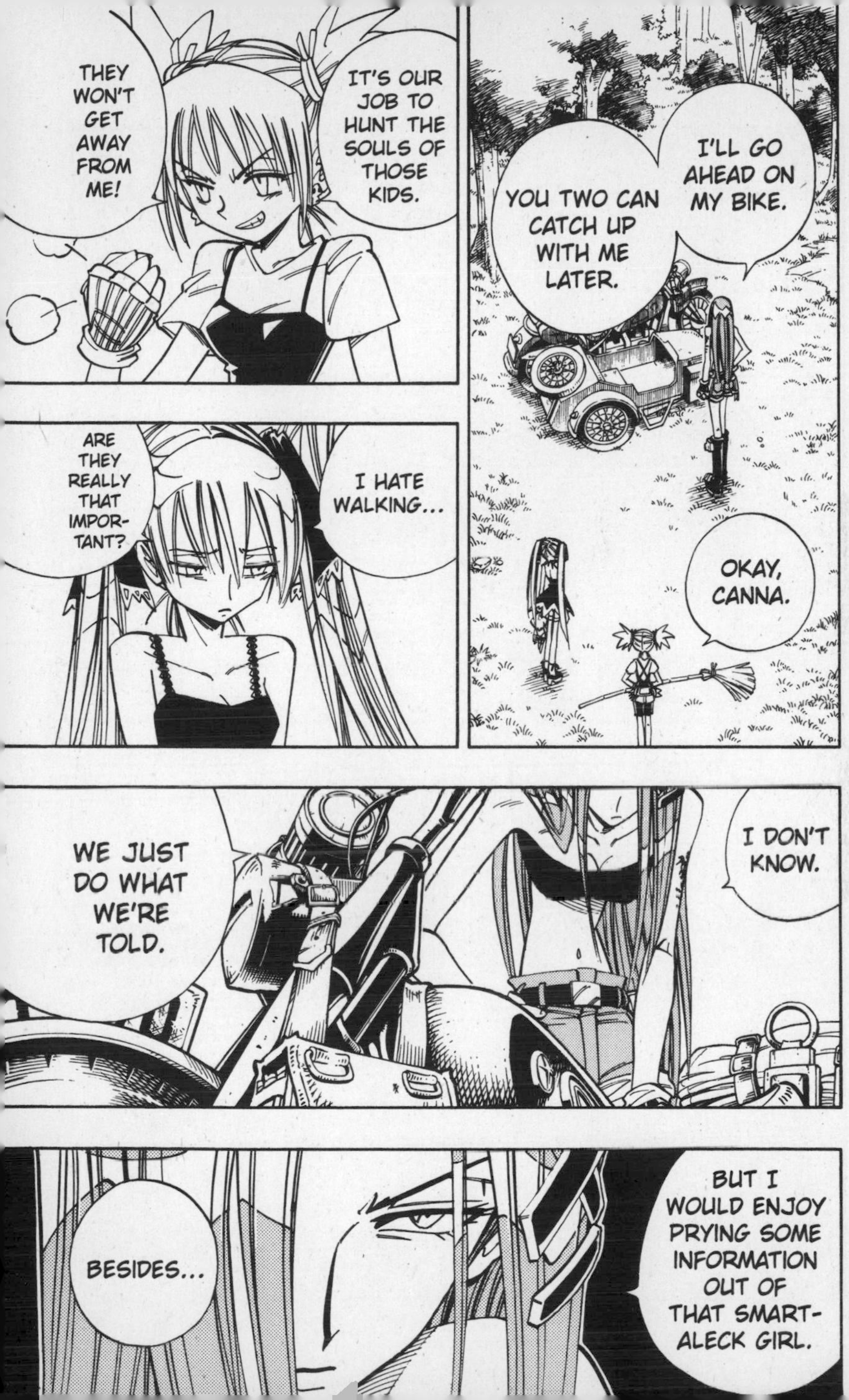
I'LL GO AHEAD ON MY BIKE.
YOU TWO CAN CATCH UP WITH ME LATER.
OKAY, CANNA.
IT'S OUR JOB TO HUNT THE SOULS OF THOSE KIDS.
THEY WON'T GET AWAY FROM ME!
I HATE WALKING...
ARE THEY REALLY THAT IMPOR-TANT?
I DON'T KNOW.
WE JUST DO WHAT WE'RE TOLD.
BUT I WOULD ENJOY PRYING SOME INFORMATION OUT OF THAT SMART-ALECK GIRL.
BESIDES...

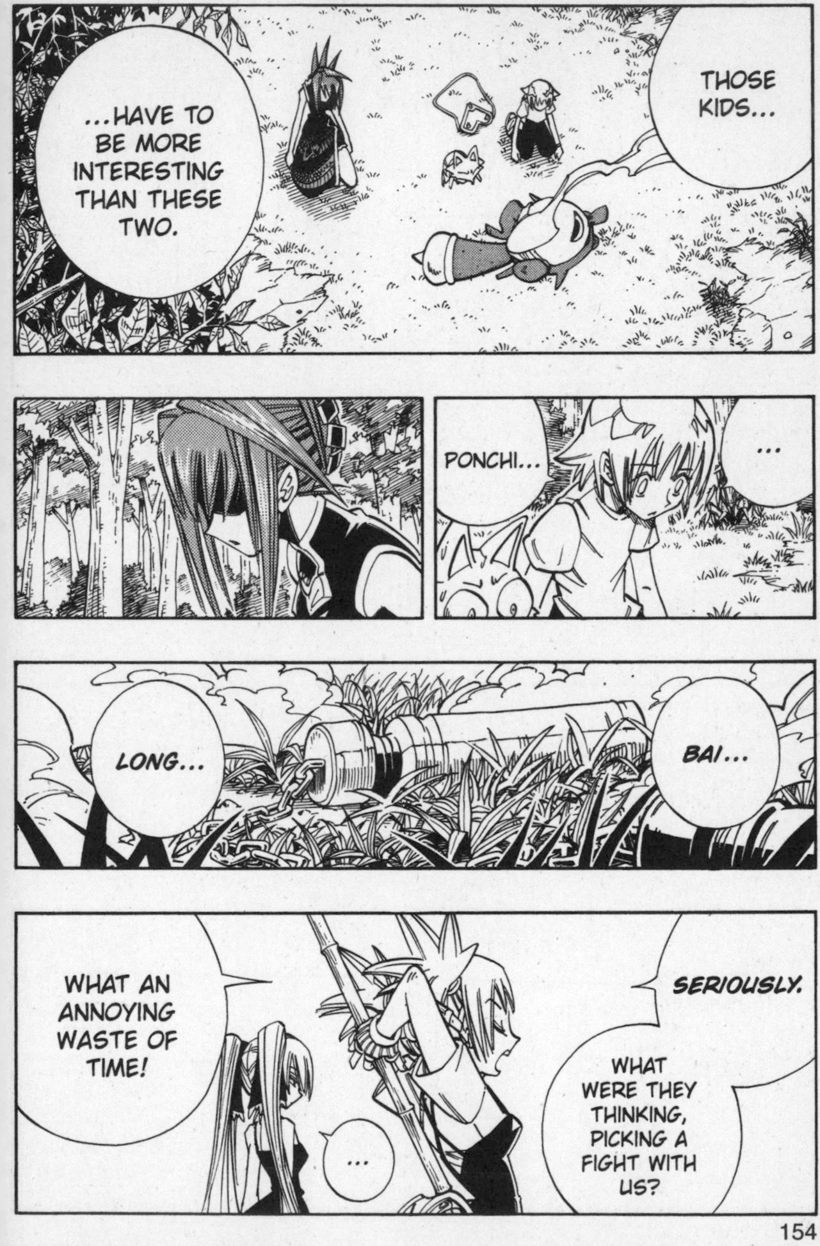
THOSE KIDS...
...HAVE TO BE MORE INTERESTING THAN THESE TWO.
...
PONCHI...
BAI...
LONG...
SERIOUSLY.
WHAT WERE THEY THINKING, PICKING A FIGHT WITH US?
WHAT AN ANNOYING WASTE OF TIME!
...

READ THIS WAY

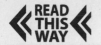

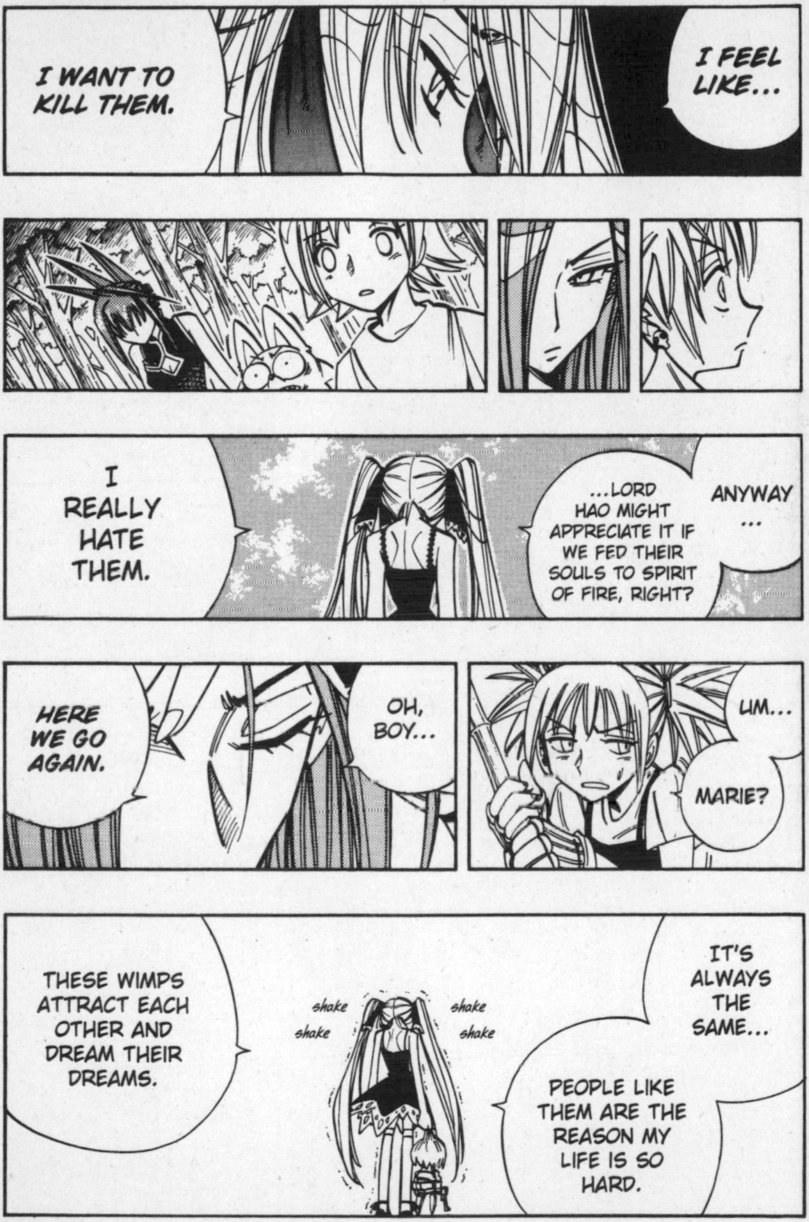
I FEEL LIKE...
I WANT TO KILL THEM.
ANYWAY...
...LORD HAO MIGHT APPRECIATE IT IF WE FED THEIR SOULS TO SPIRIT OF FIRE, RIGHT?
I REALLY HATE THEM.
UM...
MARIE?
OH, BOY...
HERE WE GO AGAIN.
IT'S ALWAYS THE SAME...
PEOPLE LIKE THEM ARE THE REASON MY LIFE IS SO HARD.
shake
shake
shake
shake
THESE WIMPS ATTRACT EACH OTHER AND DREAM THEIR DREAMS.

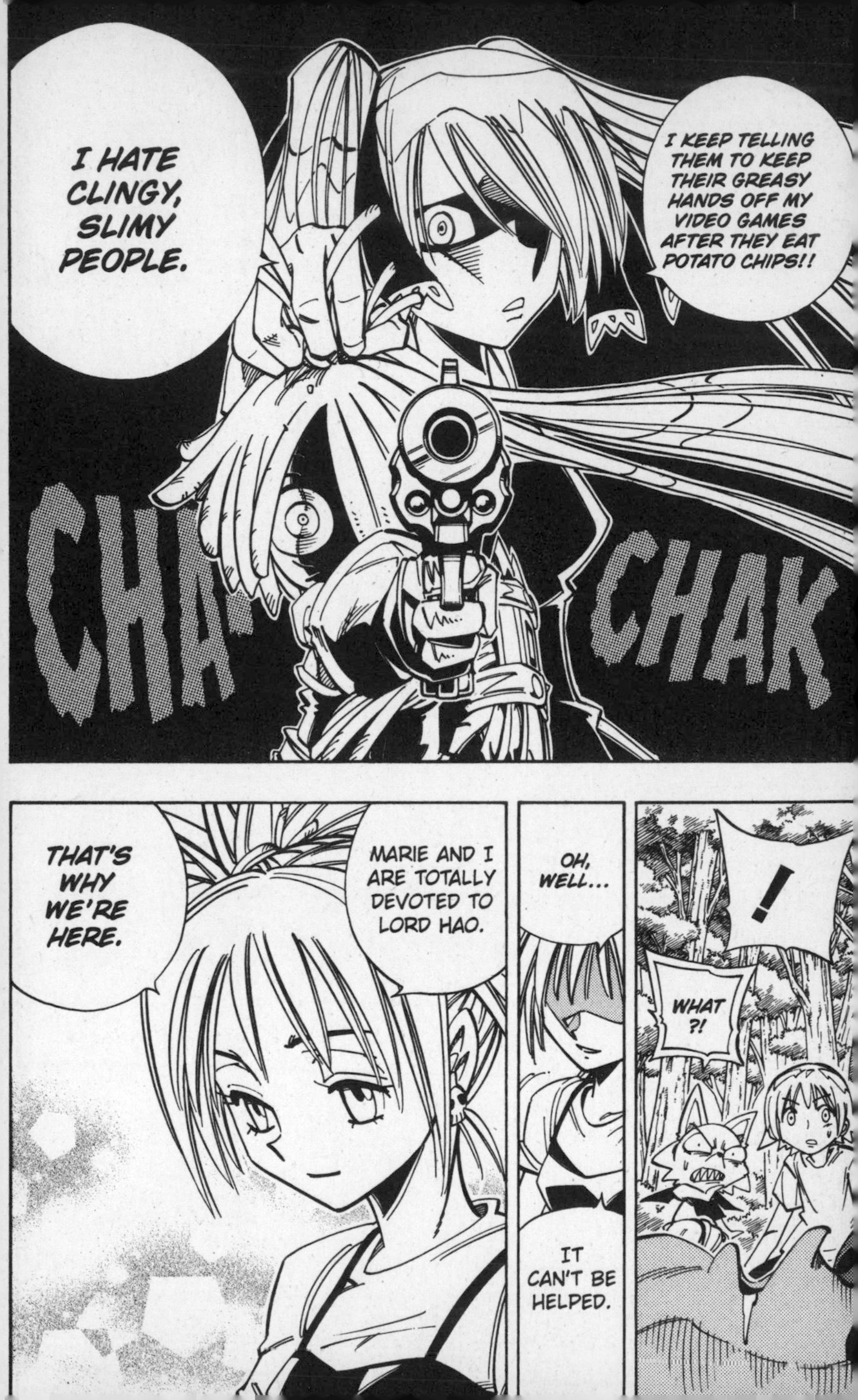
I KEEP TELLING THEM TO KEEP THEIR GREASY HANDS OFF MY VIDEO GAMES AFTER THEY EAT POTATO CHIPS!!
I HATE CLINGY, SLIMY PEOPLE.
CHA-
CHAK
!
WHAT?!
OH, WELL...
IT CAN'T BE HELPED.
MARIE AND I ARE TOTALLY DEVOTED TO LORD HAO.
THAT'S WHY WE'RE HERE.

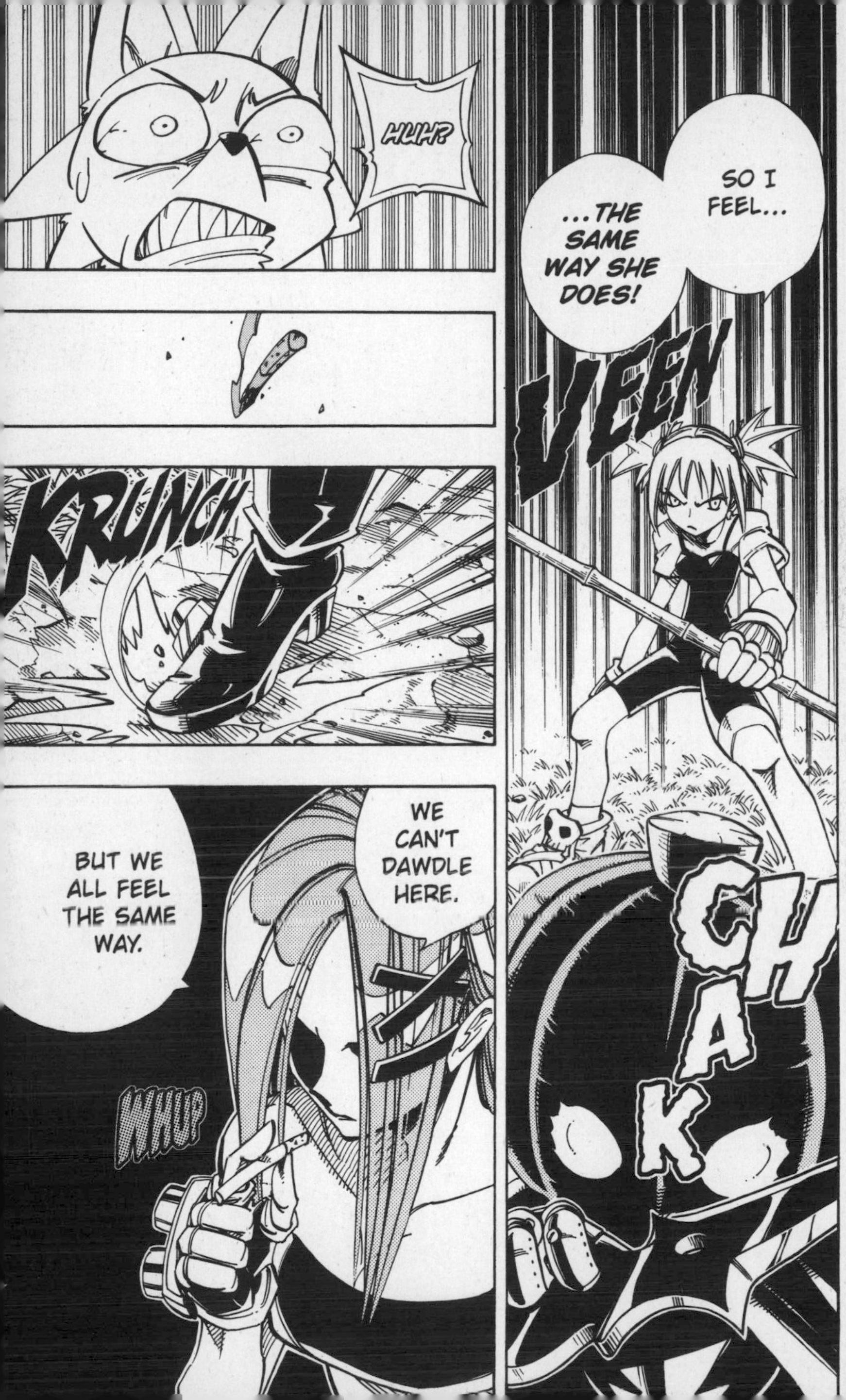
SO I FEEL...
...THE SAME WAY SHE DOES!
VEEN
CHAKA
HUH?
KRUNCH
WE CAN'T DAWDLE HERE.
BUT WE ALL FEEL THE SAME WAY.
WHUP

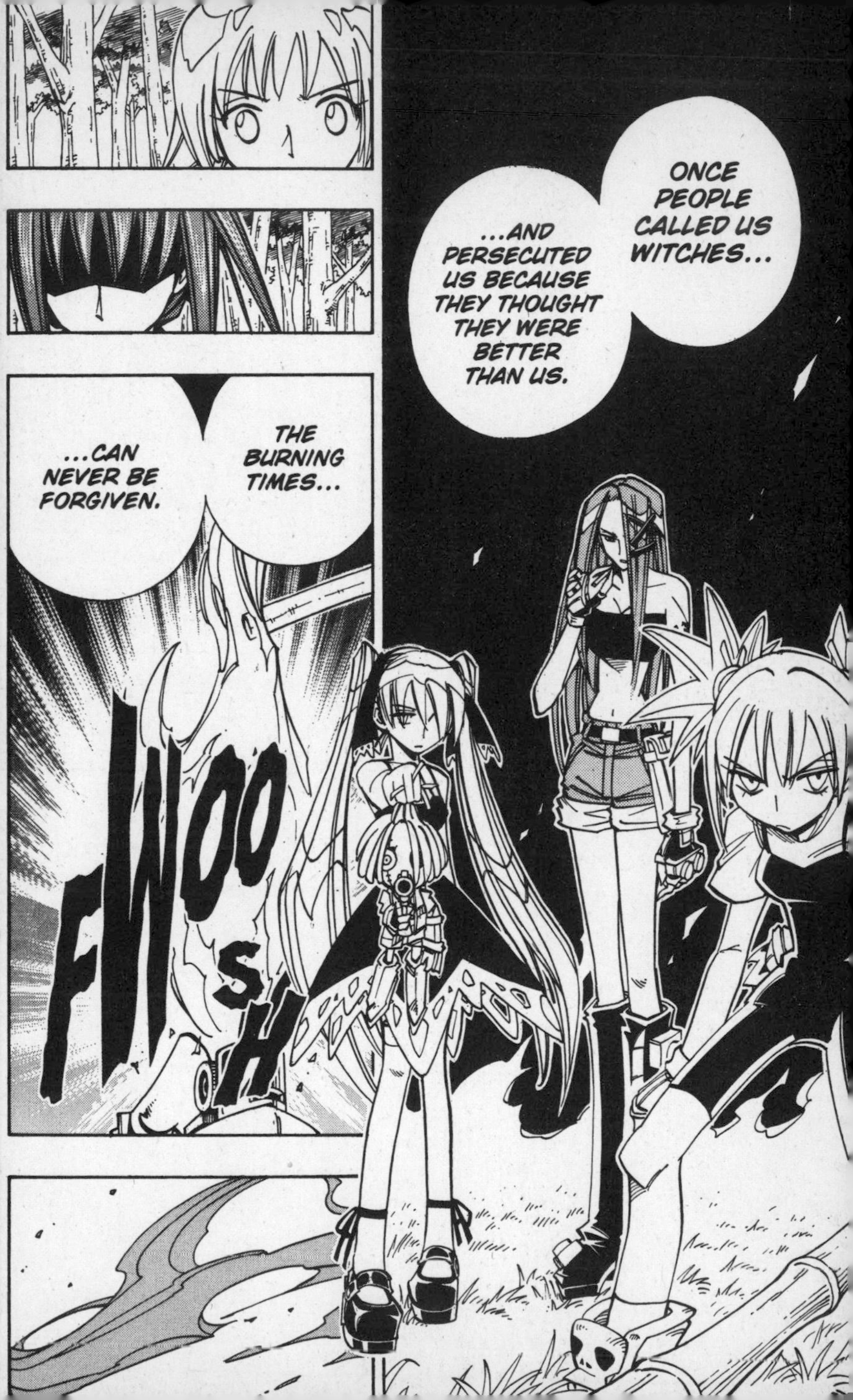
ONCE PEOPLE CALLED US WITCHES...
...AND PERSECUTED US BECAUSE THEY THOUGHT THEY WERE BETTER THAN US.
THE BURNING TIMES...
...CAN NEVER BE FORGIVEN.
FWOOSH

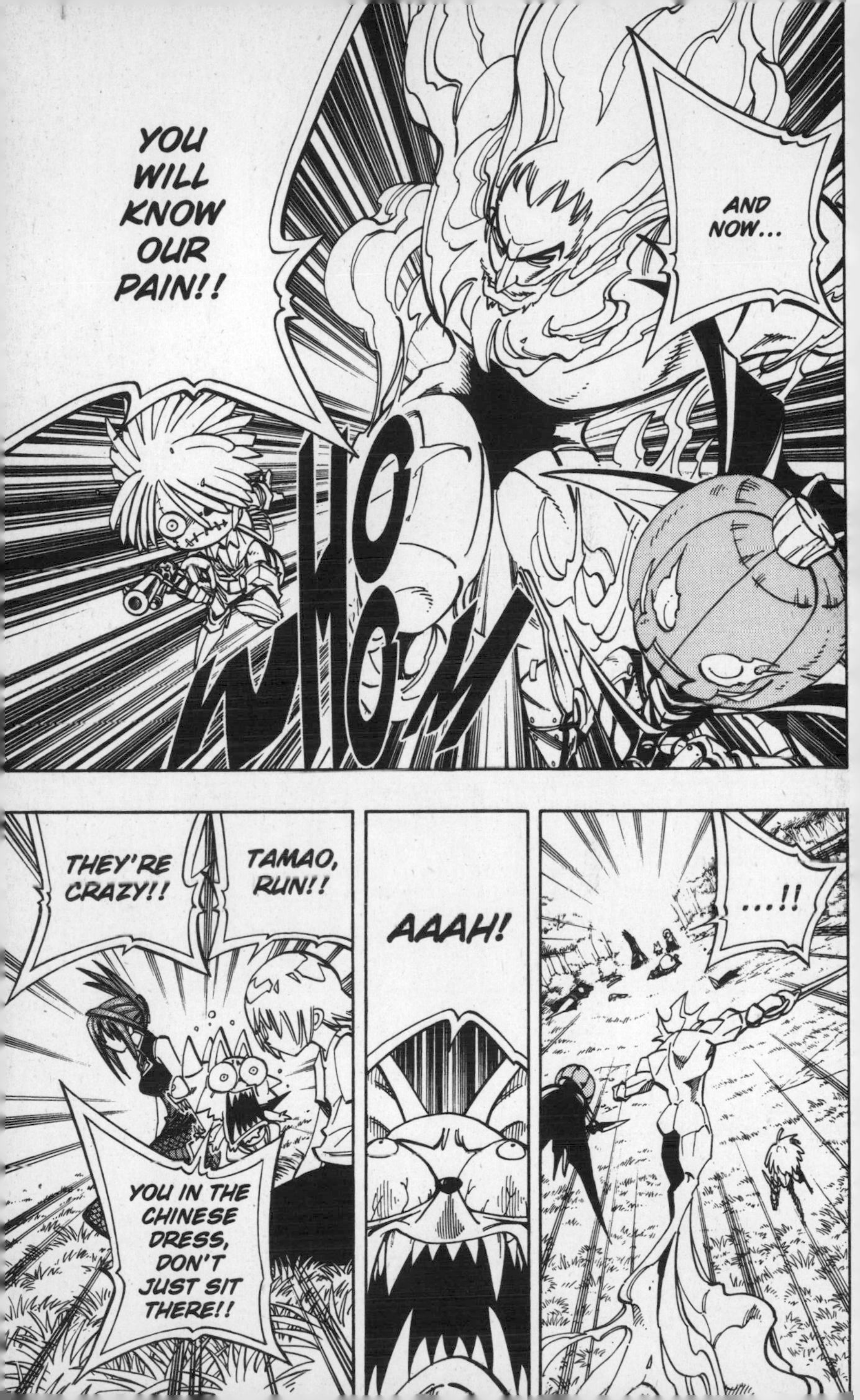
AND NOW...
YOU WILL KNOW OUR PAIN!!
WHOOM
...!!
AAAH!
TAMAO, RUN!!
THEY'RE CRAZY!!
YOU IN THE CHINESE DRESS, DON'T JUST SIT THERE!!

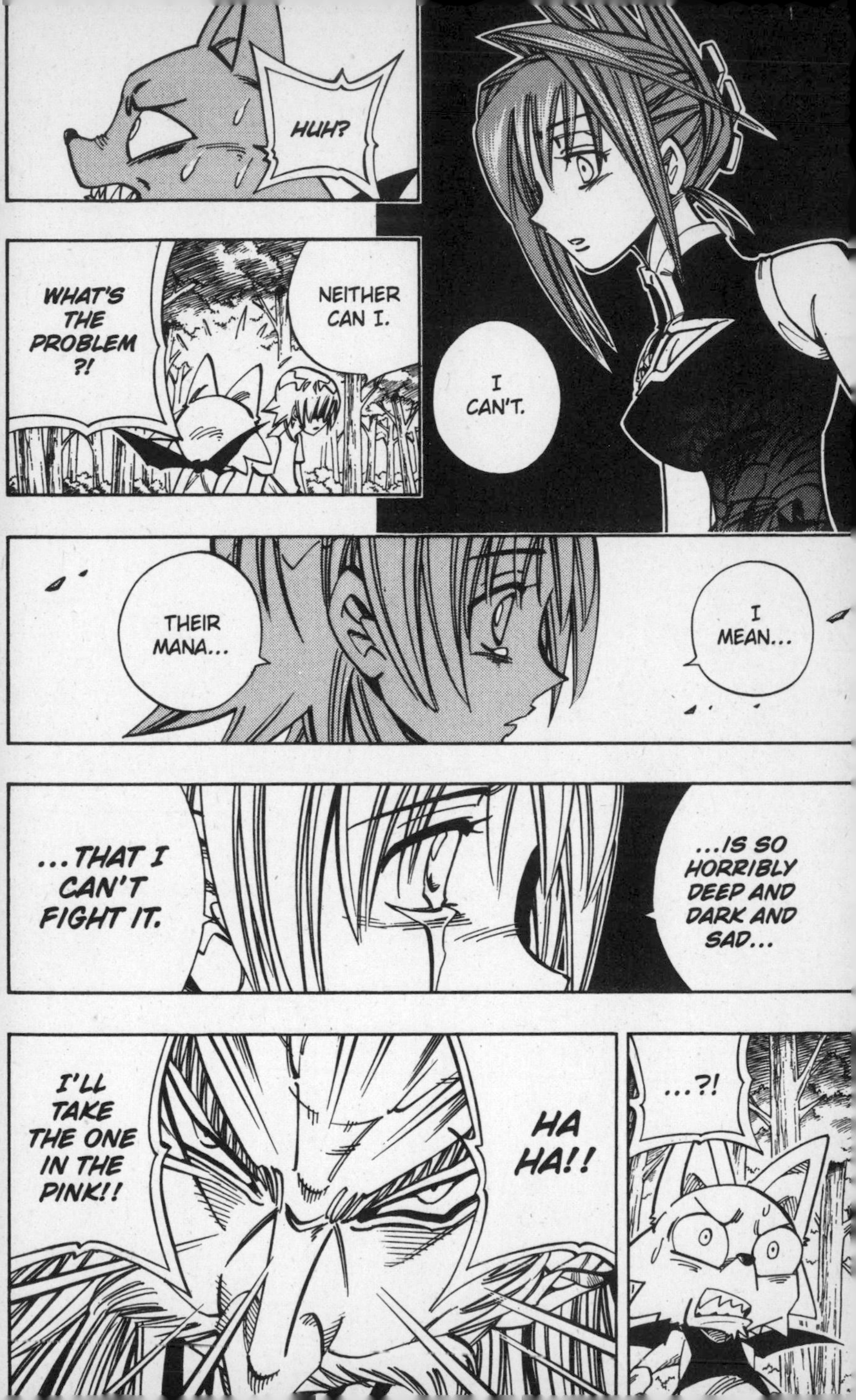
I CAN'T.
HUH?
NEITHER CAN I.
WHAT'S THE PROBLEM ?!
I MEAN...
THEIR MANA...
...IS SO HORRIBLY DEEP AND DARK AND SAD...
...THAT I CAN'T FIGHT IT.
...?!
HA HA!!
I'LL TAKE THE ONE IN THE PINK!!

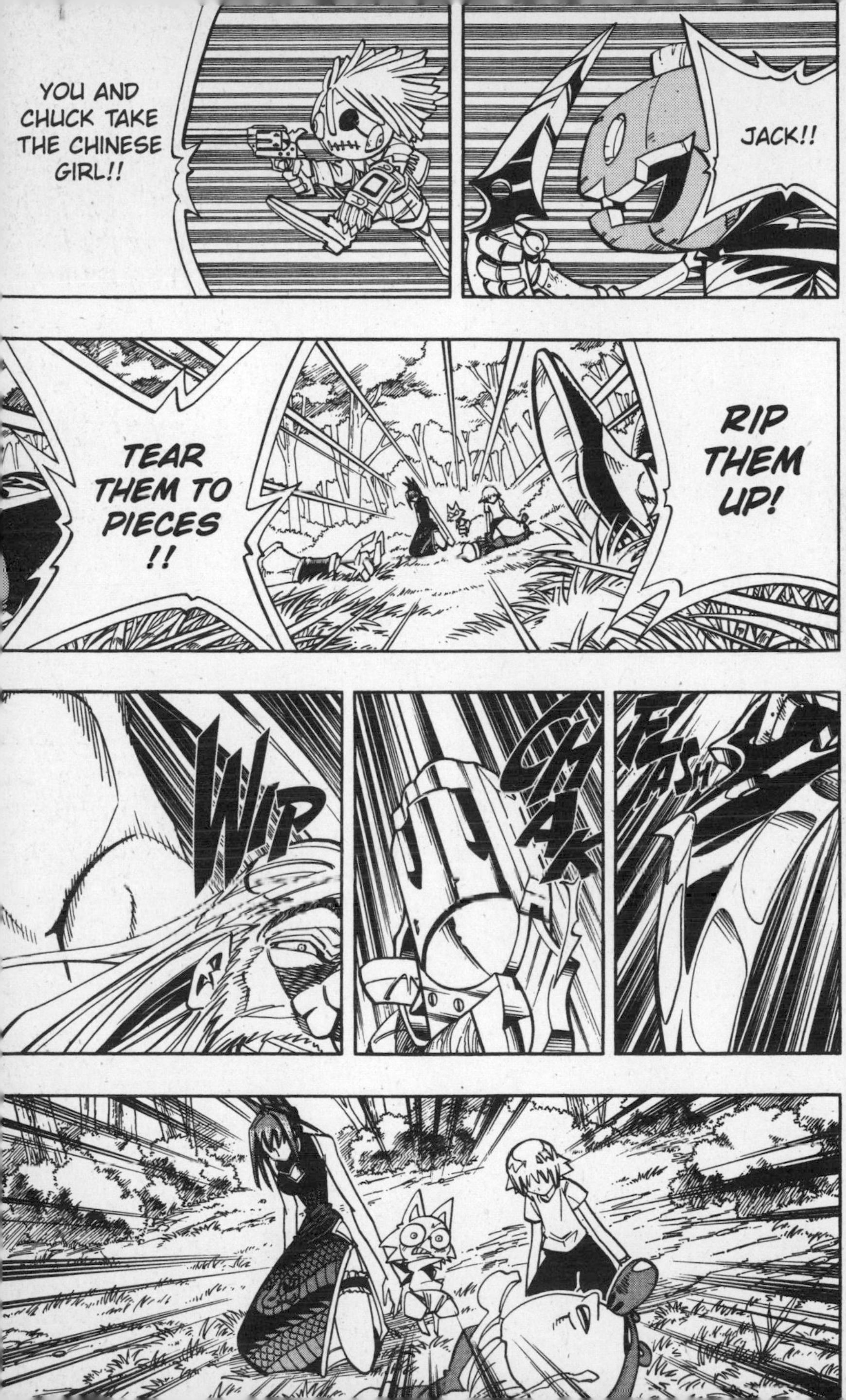
JACK!!
YOU AND CHUCK TAKE THE CHINESE GIRL!!
RIP THEM UP!
TEAR THEM TO PIECES !!

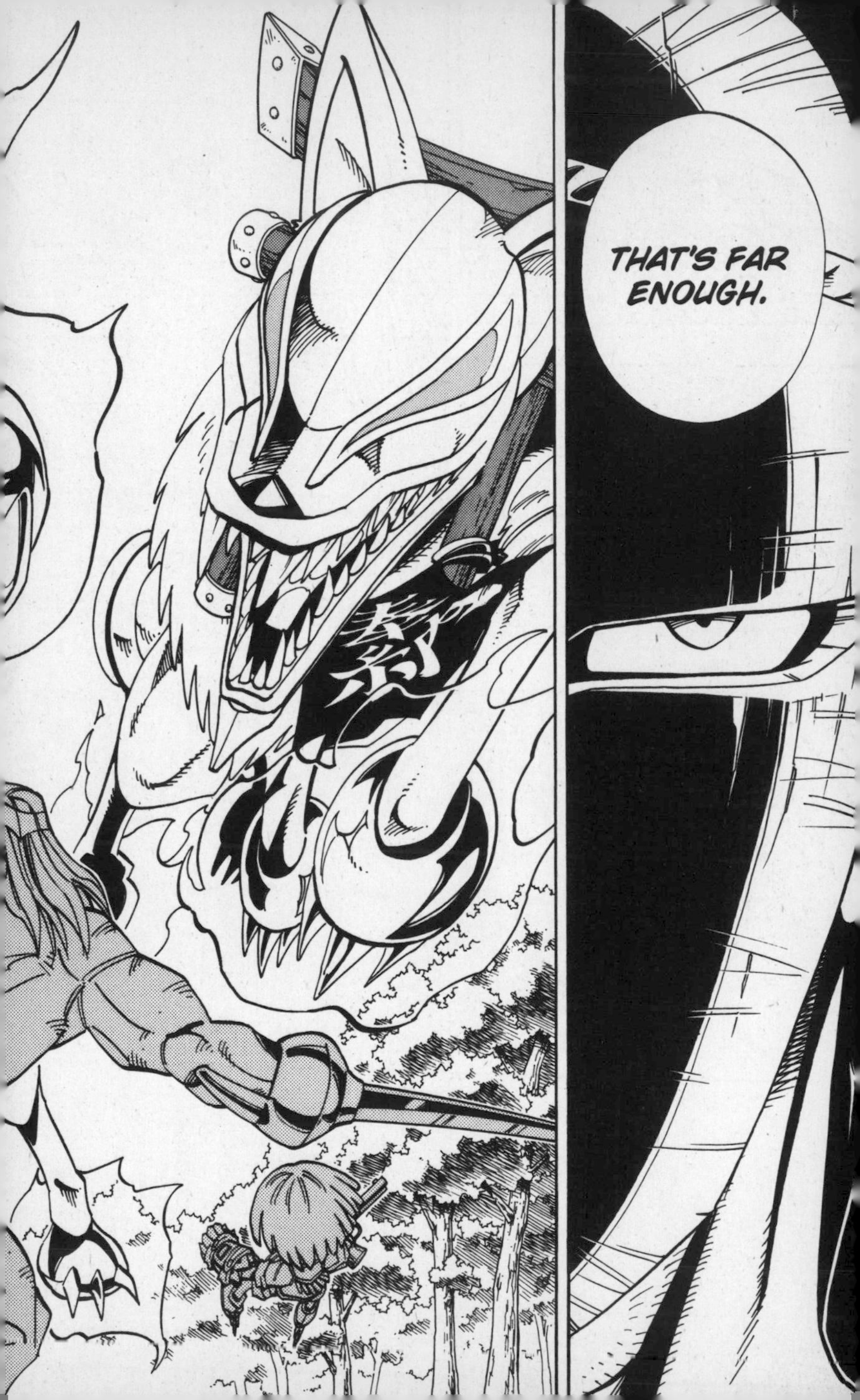
THAT'S FAR ENOUGH.

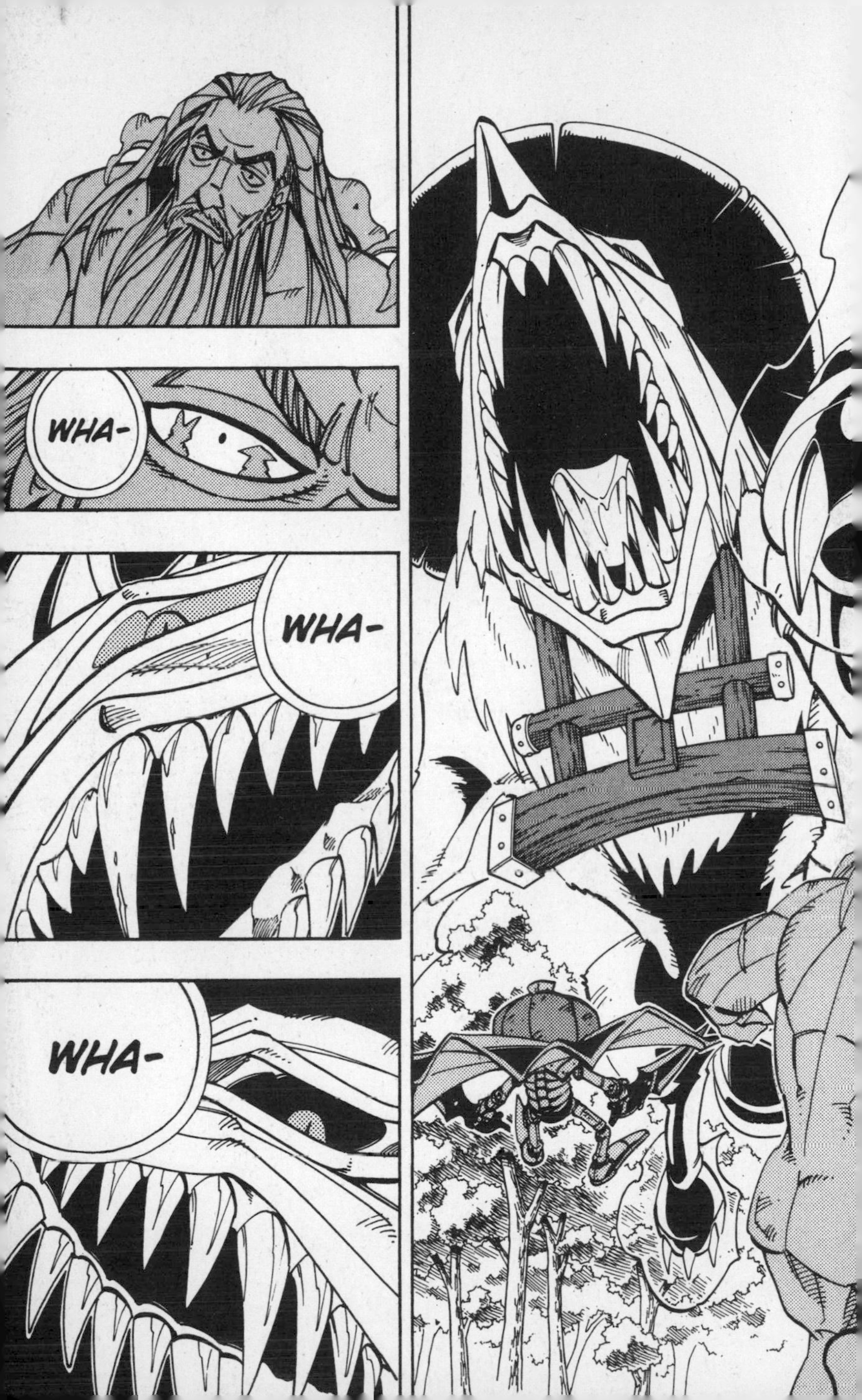
WHA-
WHA-
WHA-

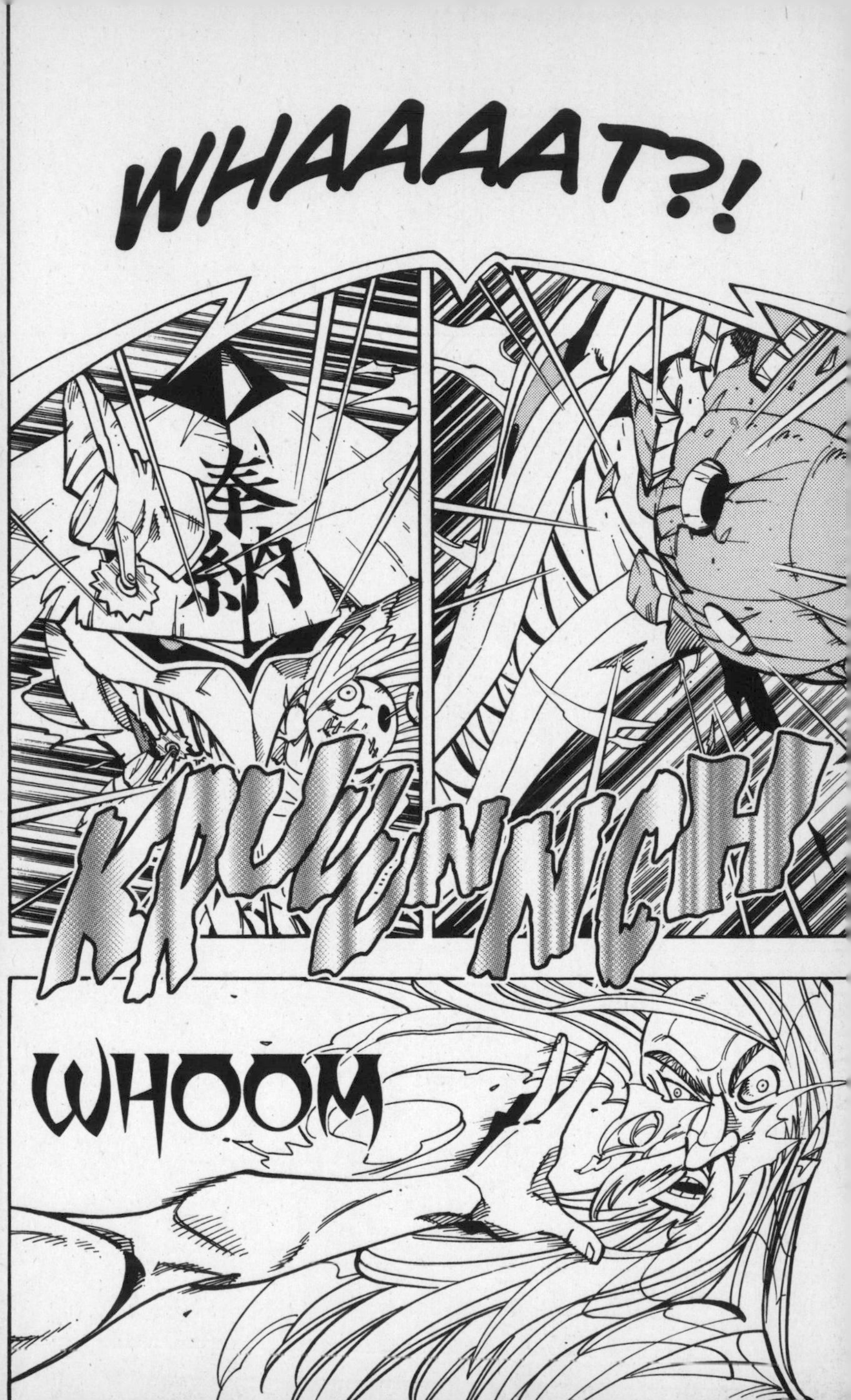
WHAAAAT?!
奉納
KRUUNNCH
WHOOM

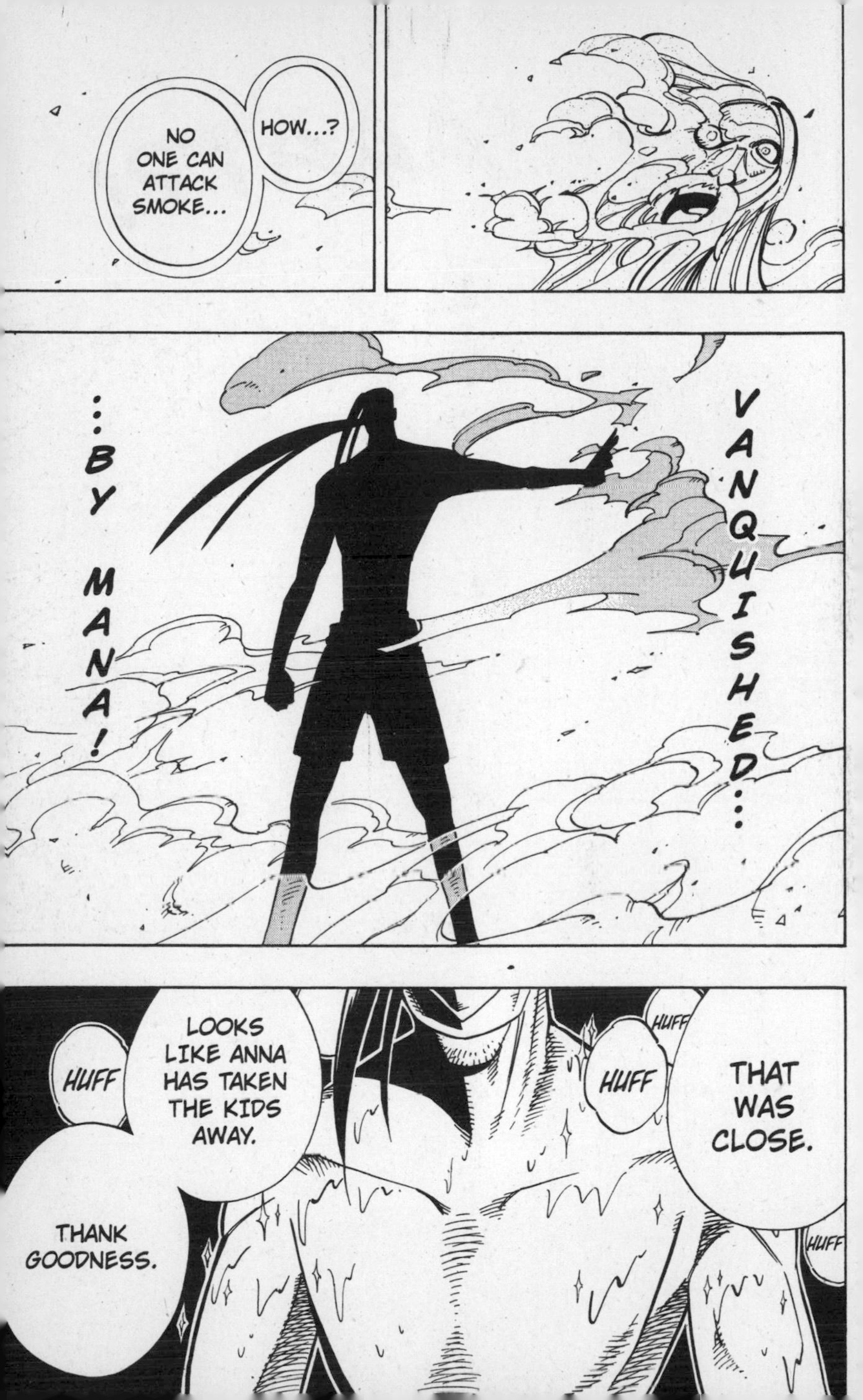
HOW...?
NO ONE CAN ATTACK SMOKE...
VANQUISHED...
...BY MANA!
HUFF
THAT WAS CLOSE.
HUFF
HUFF
LOOKS LIKE ANNA HAS TAKEN THE KIDS AWAY.
HUFF
THANK GOODNESS.

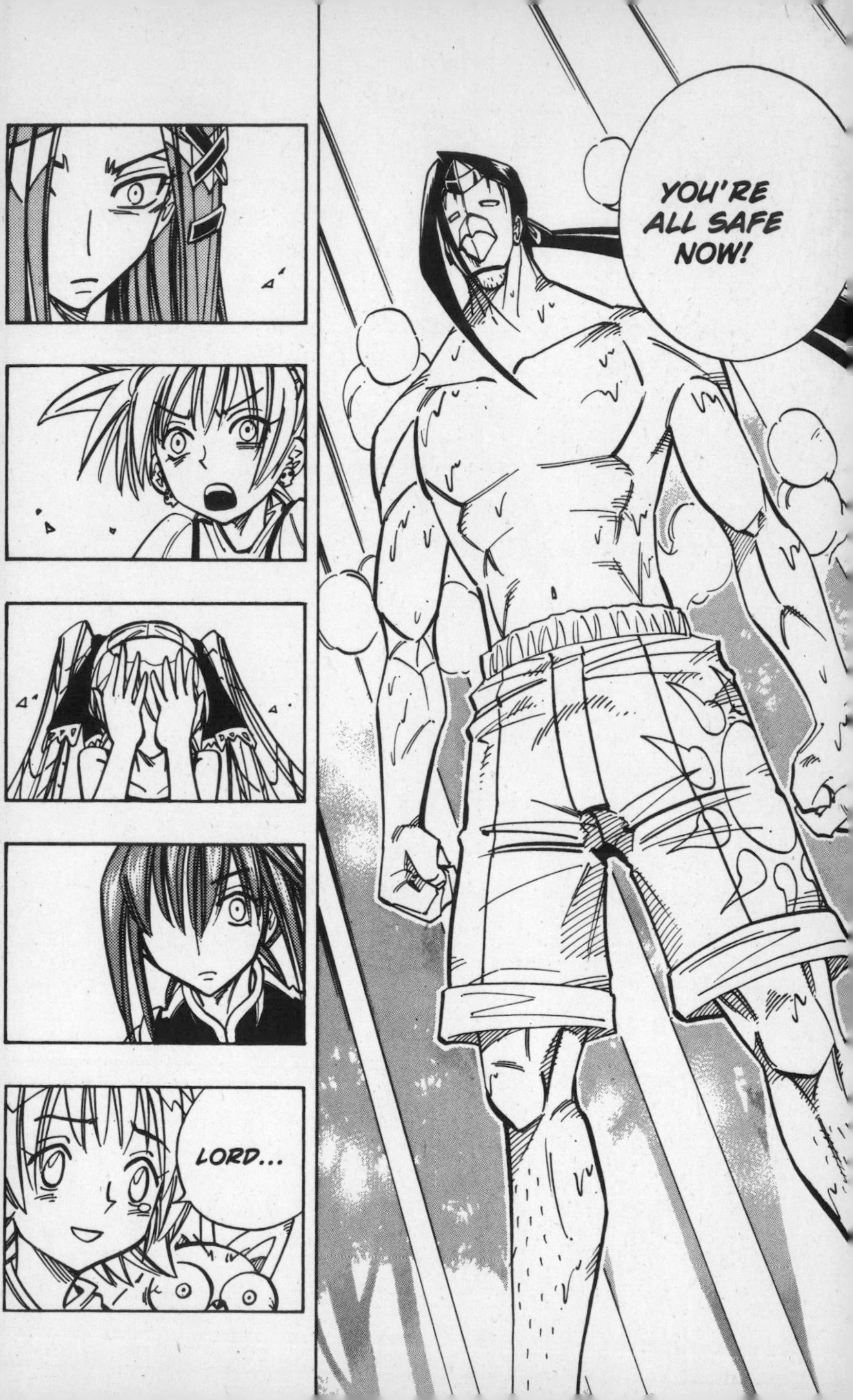
YOU'RE ALL SAFE NOW!
LORD...

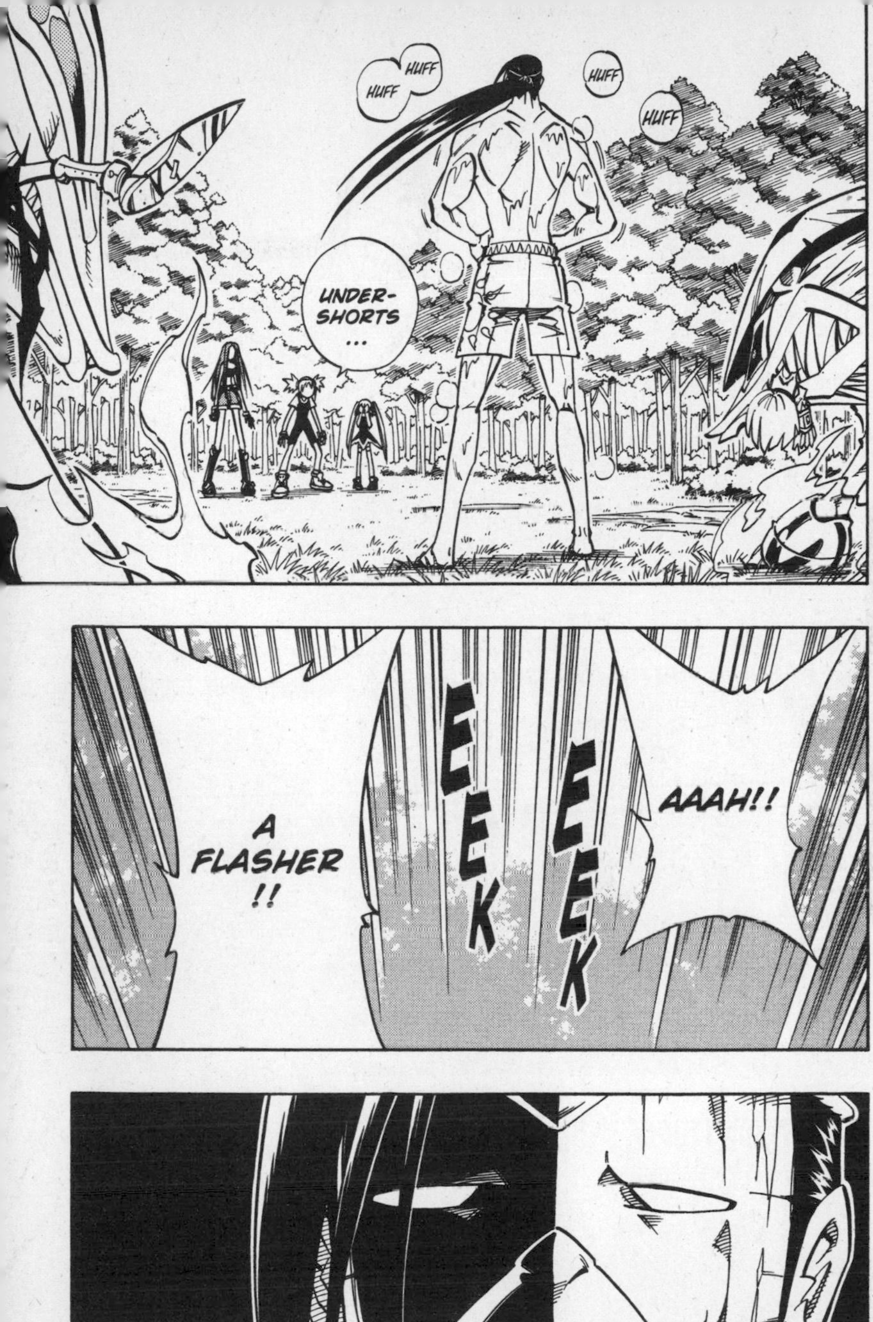
HUFF
HUFF
HUFF
HUFF
UNDER-SHORTS ...
AAAH!!
EEK
EEK
A FLASHER!!

SHAMAN KING CHARACTER FILE No.96

2001
(JAN)

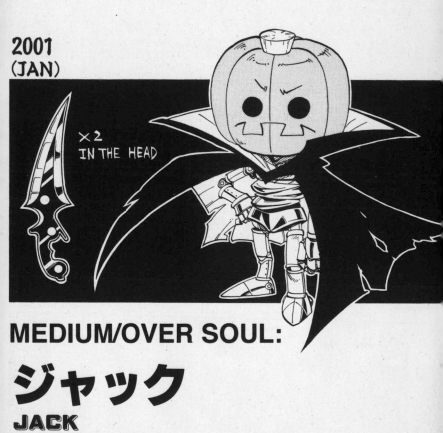

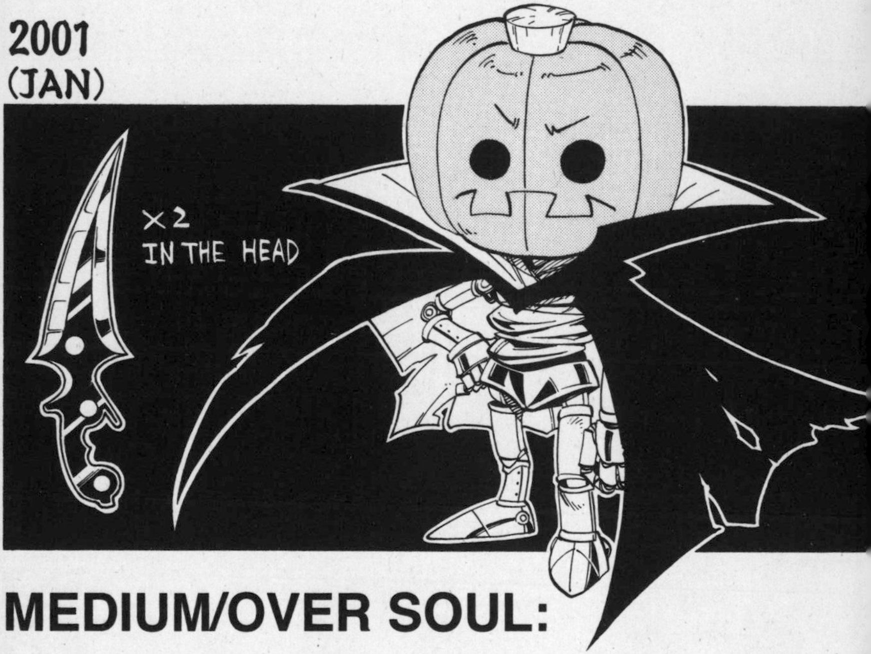
×2
IN THE HEAD

MEDIUM/OVER SOUL:

ジャック

JACK

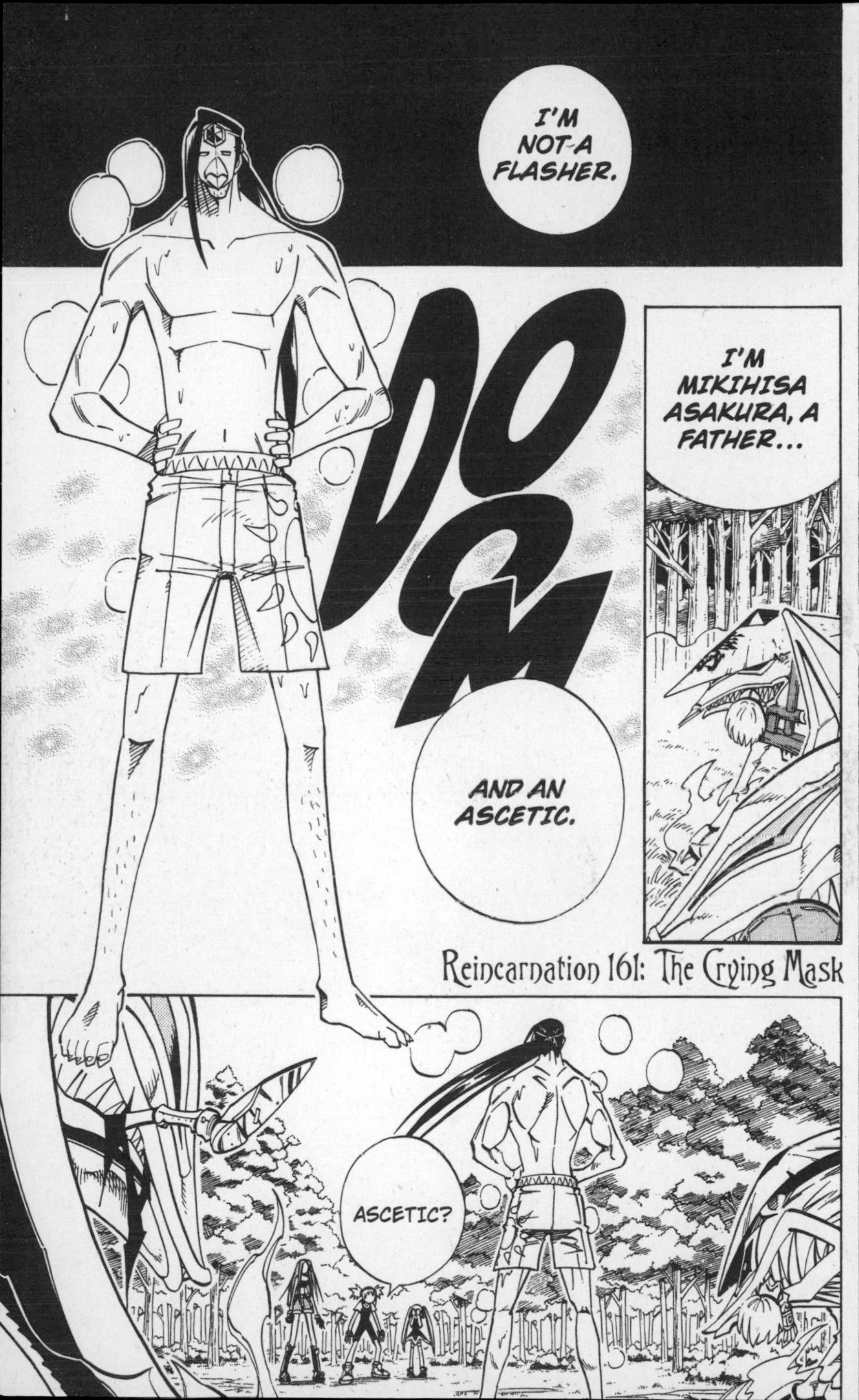
I'M NOT A FLASHER.
I'M MIKIHISA ASAKURA, A FATHER...
DOOM
AND AN ASCETIC.
Reincarnation 161: The Crying Mask
ASCETIC?

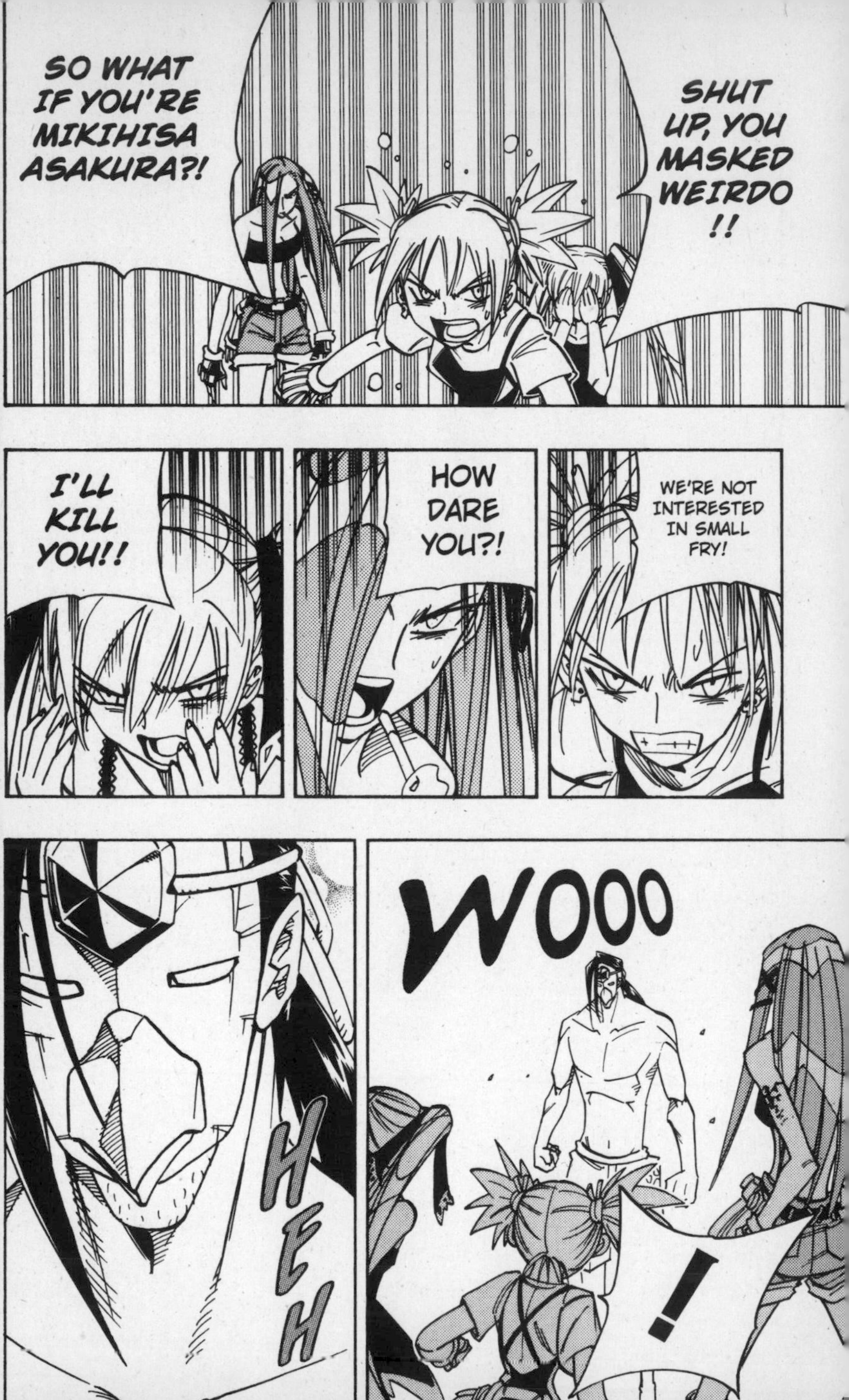
SHUT UP, YOU MASKED WEIRDO!!
SO WHAT IF YOU'RE MIKIHISA ASAKURA?!
WE'RE NOT INTERESTED IN SMALL FRY!
HOW DARE YOU?!
I'LL KILL YOU!!
WOOO
!
HEH HEH

Reincarnation 161: The Crying Mask

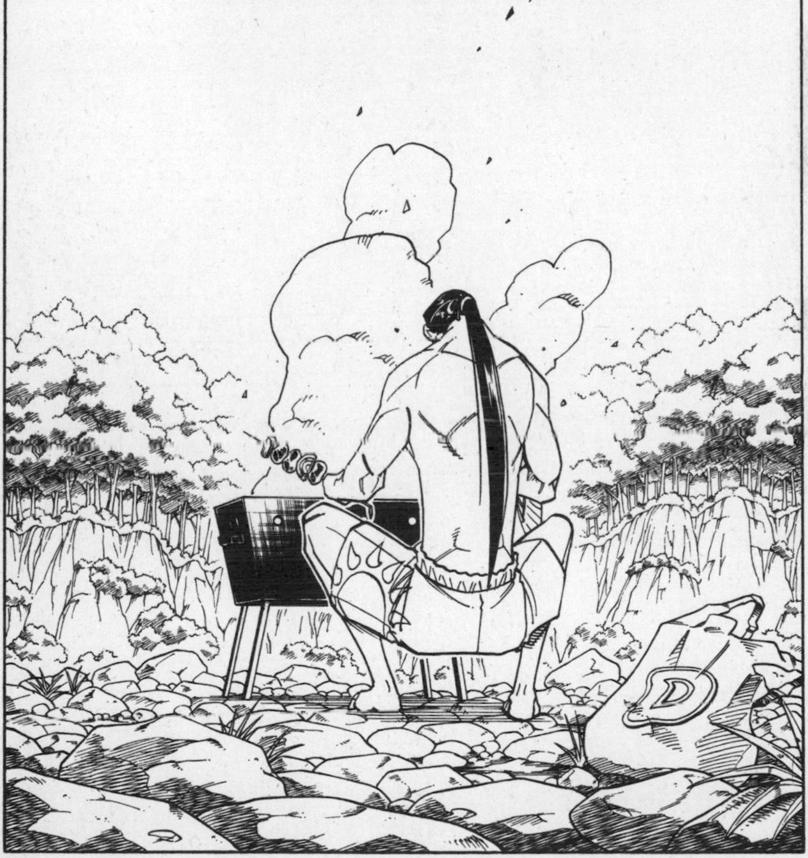

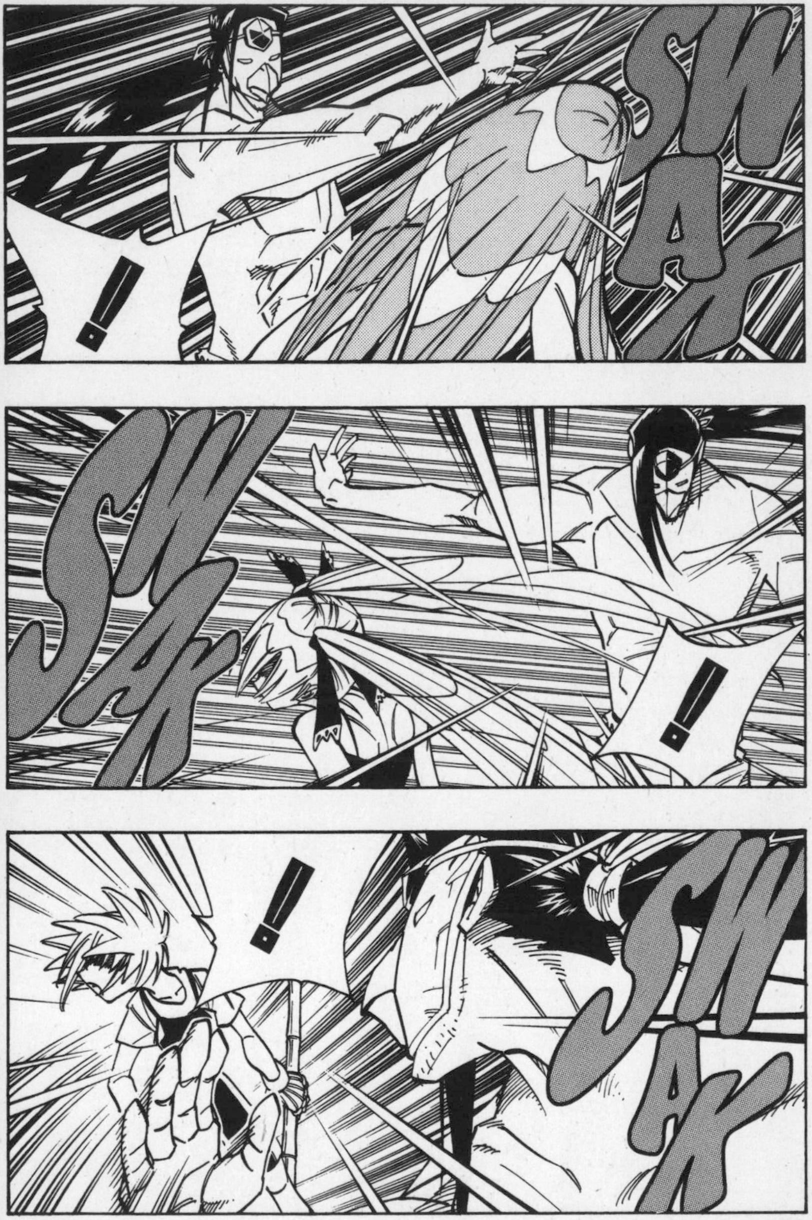
SHAK
!
!
SHAK
SHAK
!

READ THIS WAY

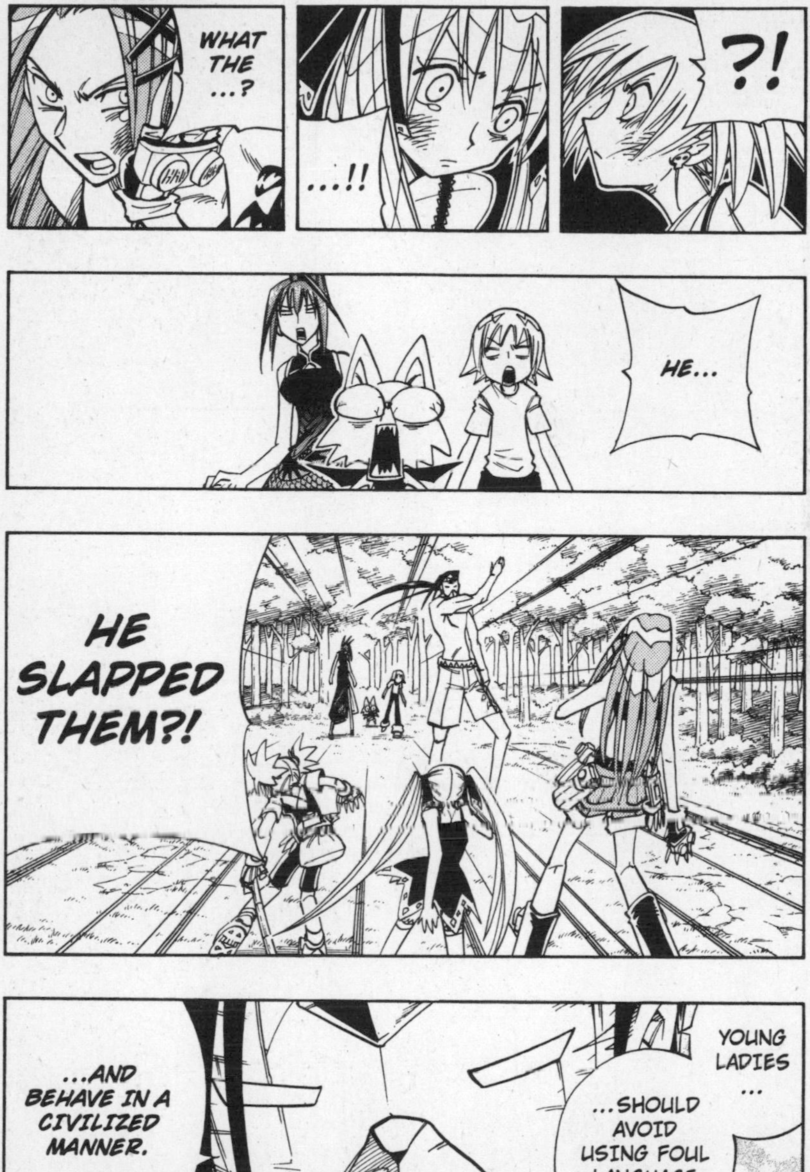
?!
...!!
WHAT THE ...?
HE...
HE SLAPPED THEM?!
YOUNG LADIES ...
...SHOULD AVOID USING FOUL LANGUAGE ...
...AND BEHAVE IN A CIVILIZED MANNER.

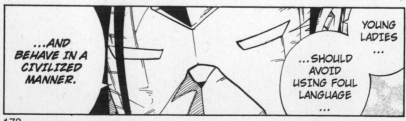

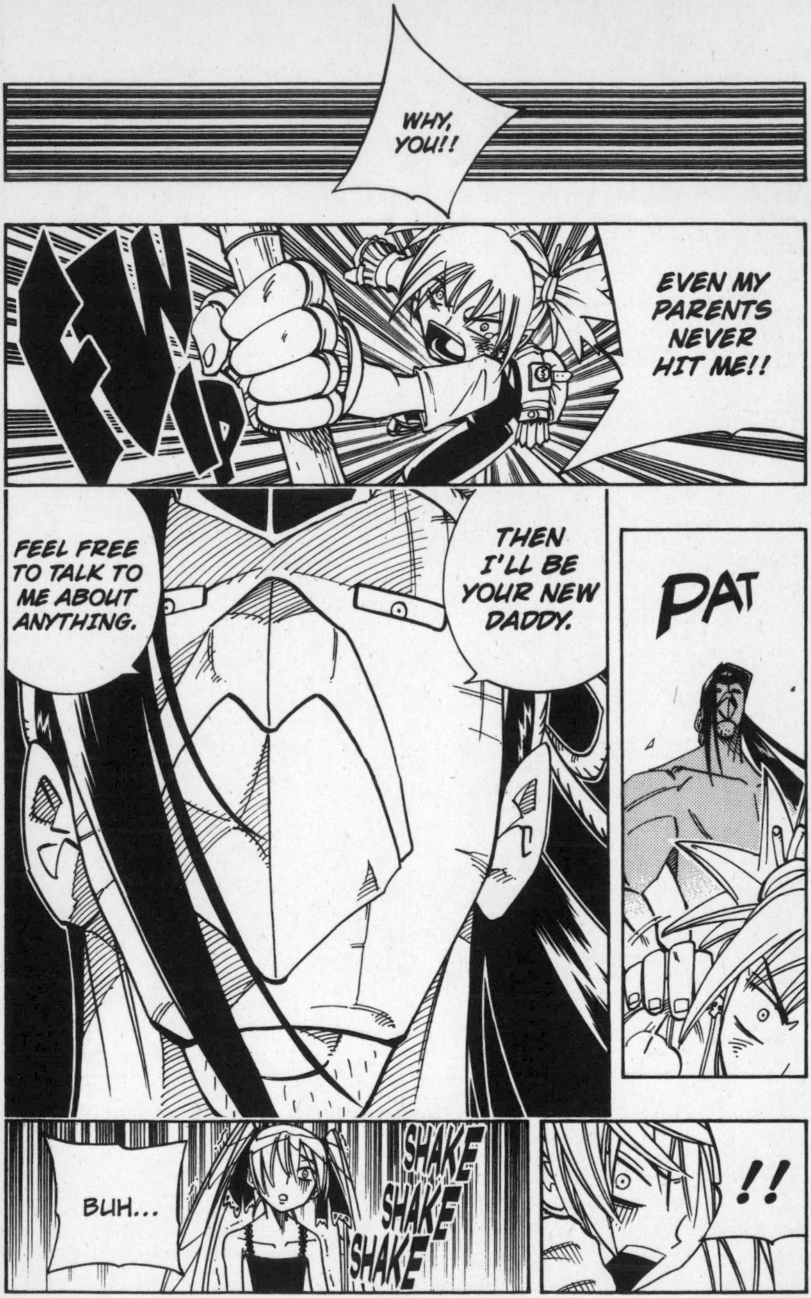
WHY, YOU!!
EVEN MY PARENTS NEVER HIT ME!!
PAT
THEN I'LL BE YOUR NEW DADDY.
FEEL FREE TO TALK TO ME ABOUT ANYTHING.
!!
SHAKE SHAKE SHAKE
BUH...

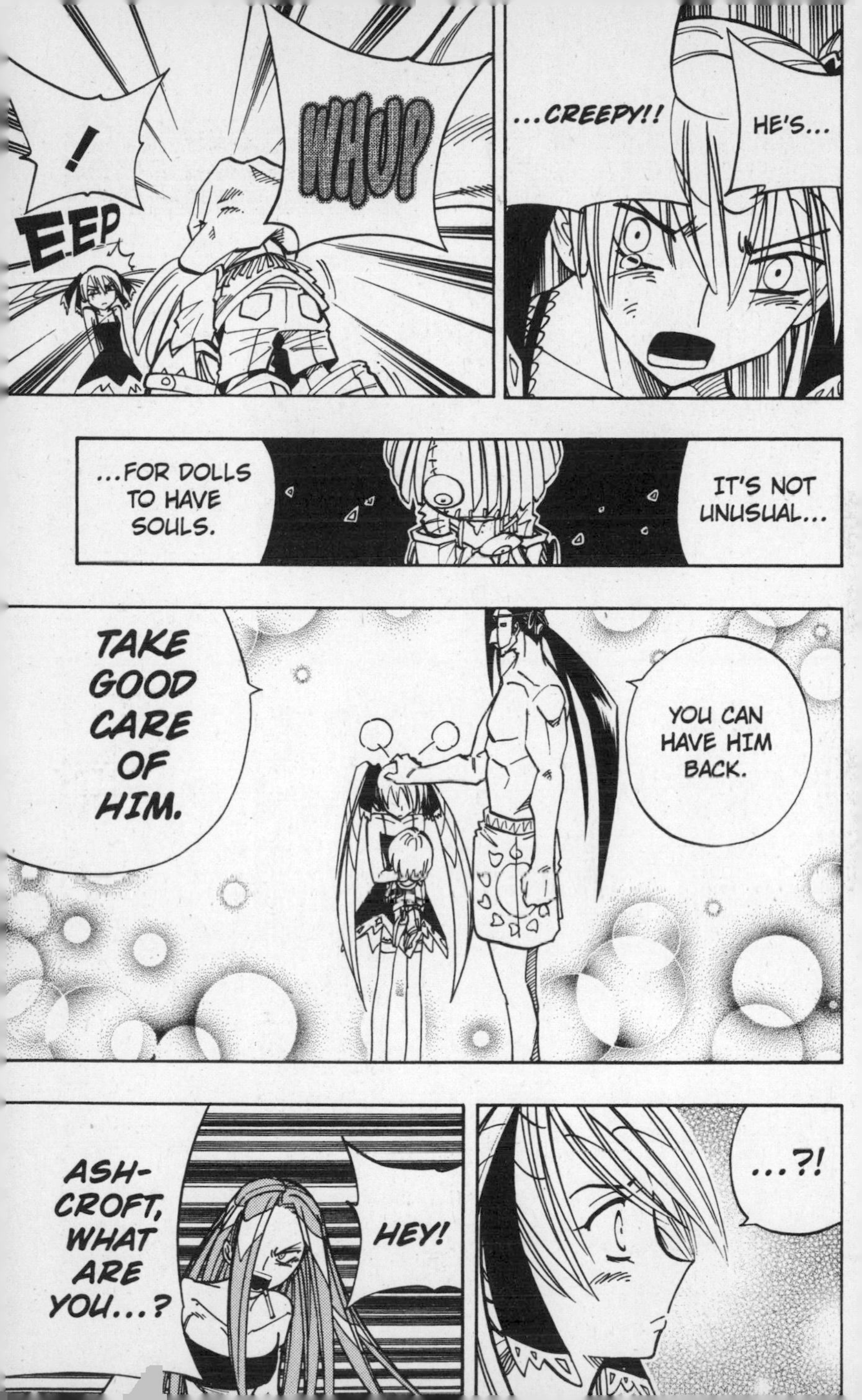
HE'S...
...CREEPY!!
WHUP
!
EEP
IT'S NOT UNUSUAL...
...FOR DOLLS TO HAVE SOULS.
YOU CAN HAVE HIM BACK.
TAKE GOOD CARE OF HIM.
...?!
HEY!
ASH-CROFT, WHAT ARE YOU...?

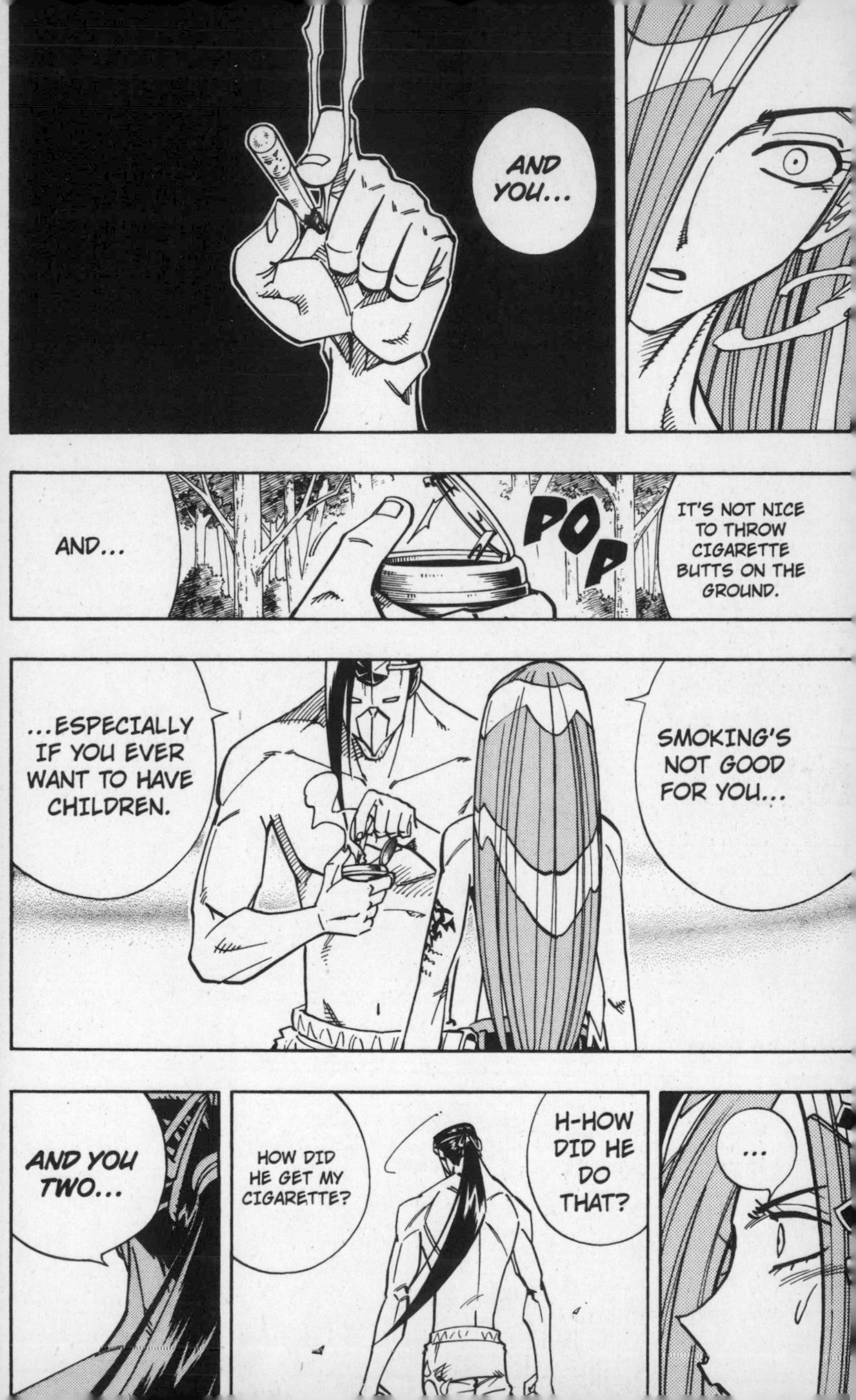
AND YOU...
IT'S NOT NICE TO THROW CIGARETTE BUTTS ON THE GROUND.
POP
AND...
SMOKING'S NOT GOOD FOR YOU...
...ESPECIALLY IF YOU EVER WANT TO HAVE CHILDREN.
...
H-HOW DID HE DO THAT?
HOW DID HE GET MY CIGARETTE?
AND YOU TWO...

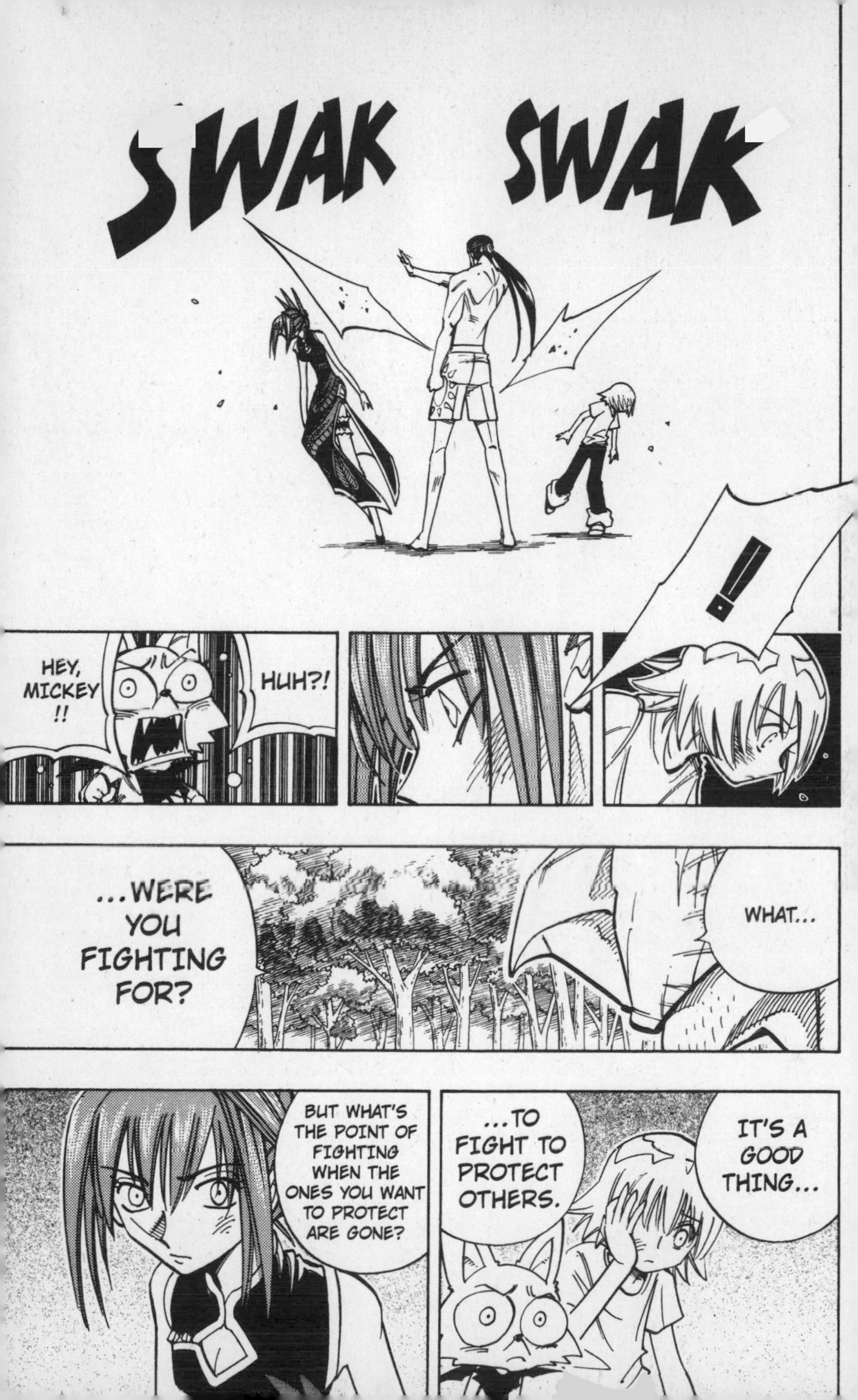
SWAK SWAK
!
HUH?!
HEY, MICKEY!!
WHAT...
...WERE YOU FIGHTING FOR?
IT'S A GOOD THING...
...TO FIGHT TO PROTECT OTHERS.
BUT WHAT'S THE POINT OF FIGHTING WHEN THE ONES YOU WANT TO PROTECT ARE GONE?

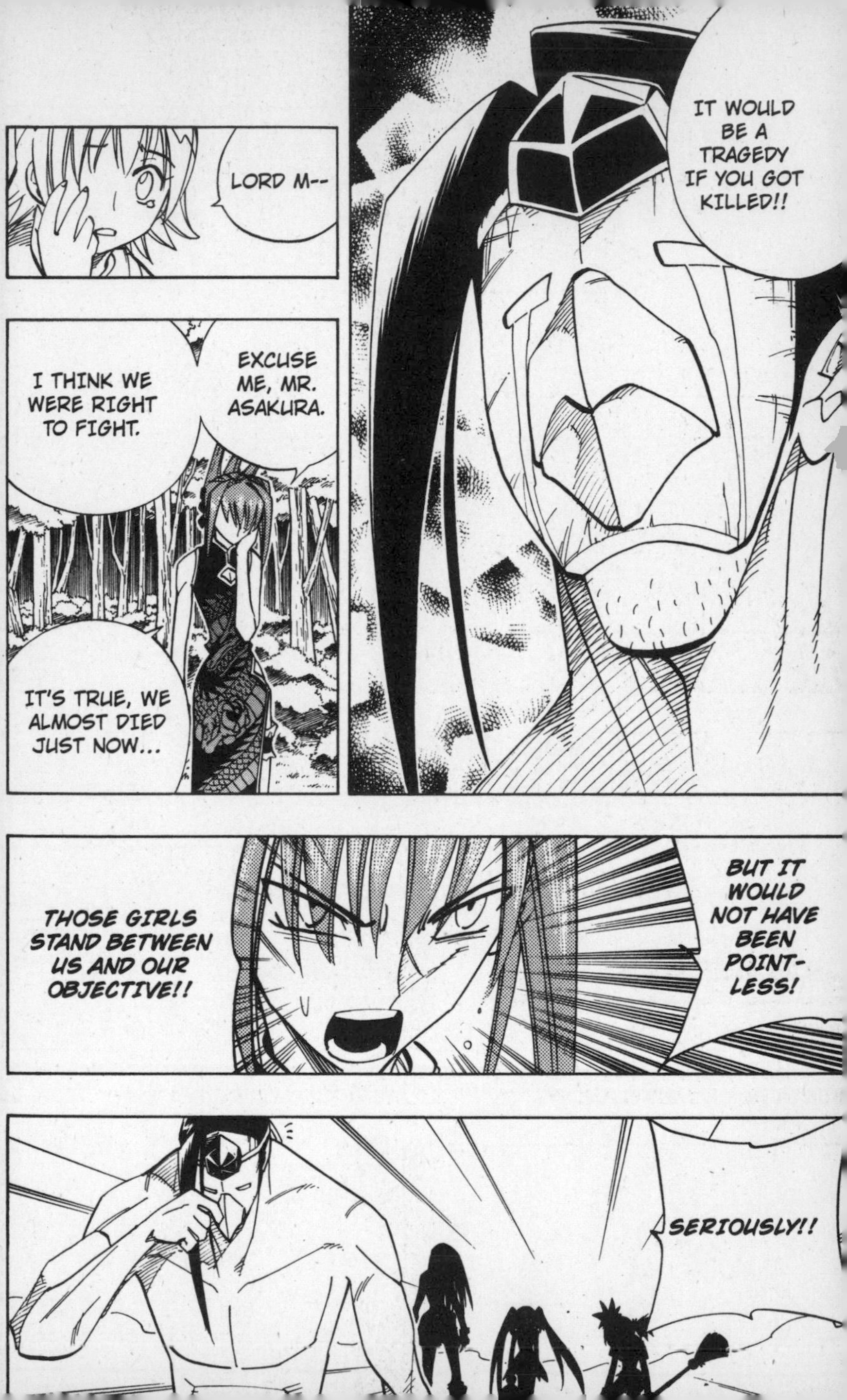
IT WOULD BE A TRAGEDY IF YOU GOT KILLED!!
LORD M--
EXCUSE ME, MR. ASAKURA.
I THINK WE WERE RIGHT TO FIGHT.
IT'S TRUE, WE ALMOST DIED JUST NOW...
BUT IT WOULD NOT HAVE BEEN POINT-LESS!
THOSE GIRLS STAND BETWEEN US AND OUR OBJECTIVE!!
SERIOUSLY!!

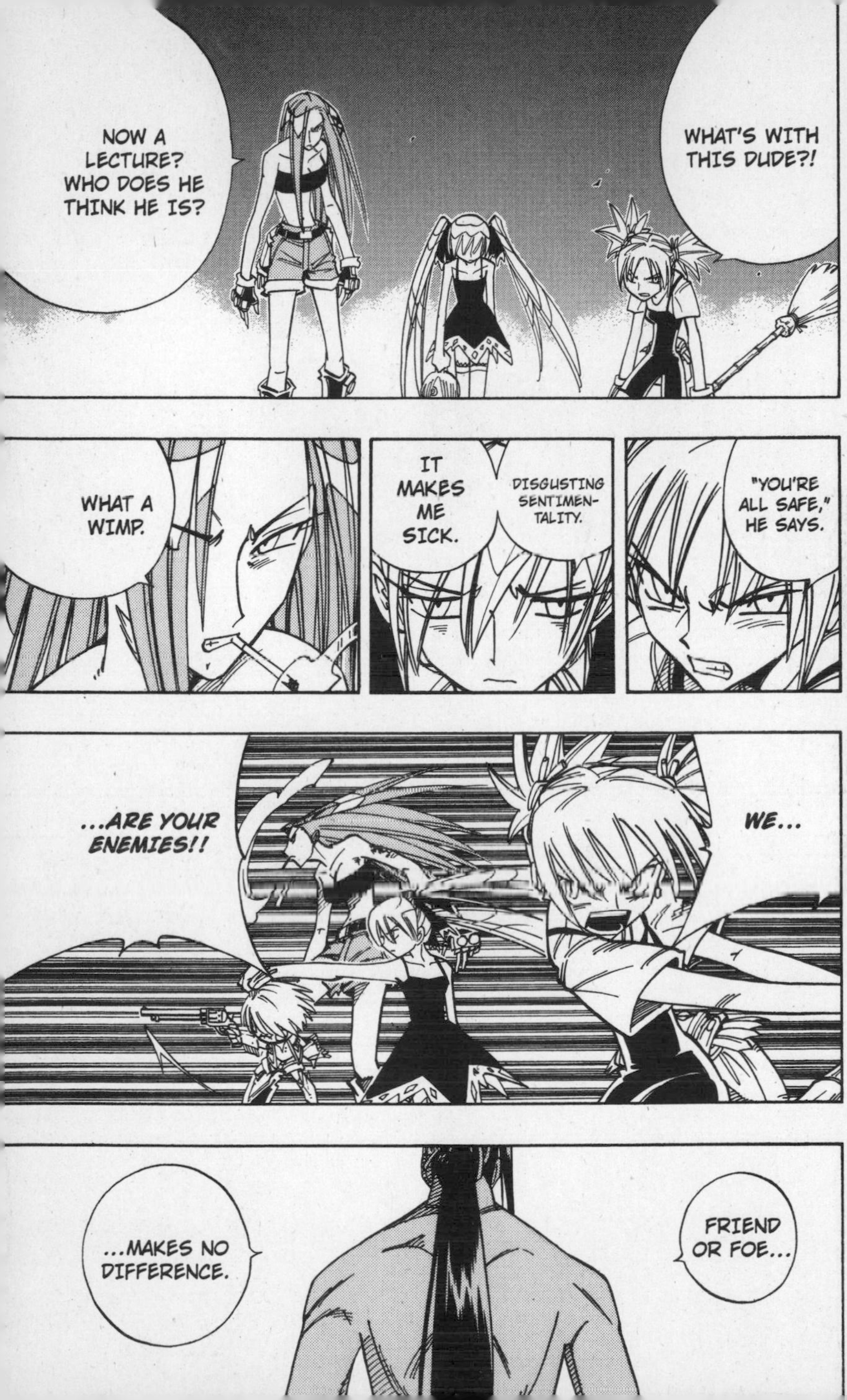
WHAT'S WITH THIS DUDE?!
NOW A LECTURE? WHO DOES HE THINK HE IS?
"YOU'RE ALL SAFE," HE SAYS.
DISGUSTING SENTIMENTALITY.
IT MAKES ME SICK.
WHAT A WIMP.
WE...
...ARE YOUR ENEMIES!!
FRIEND OR FOE...
...MAKES NO DIFFERENCE.

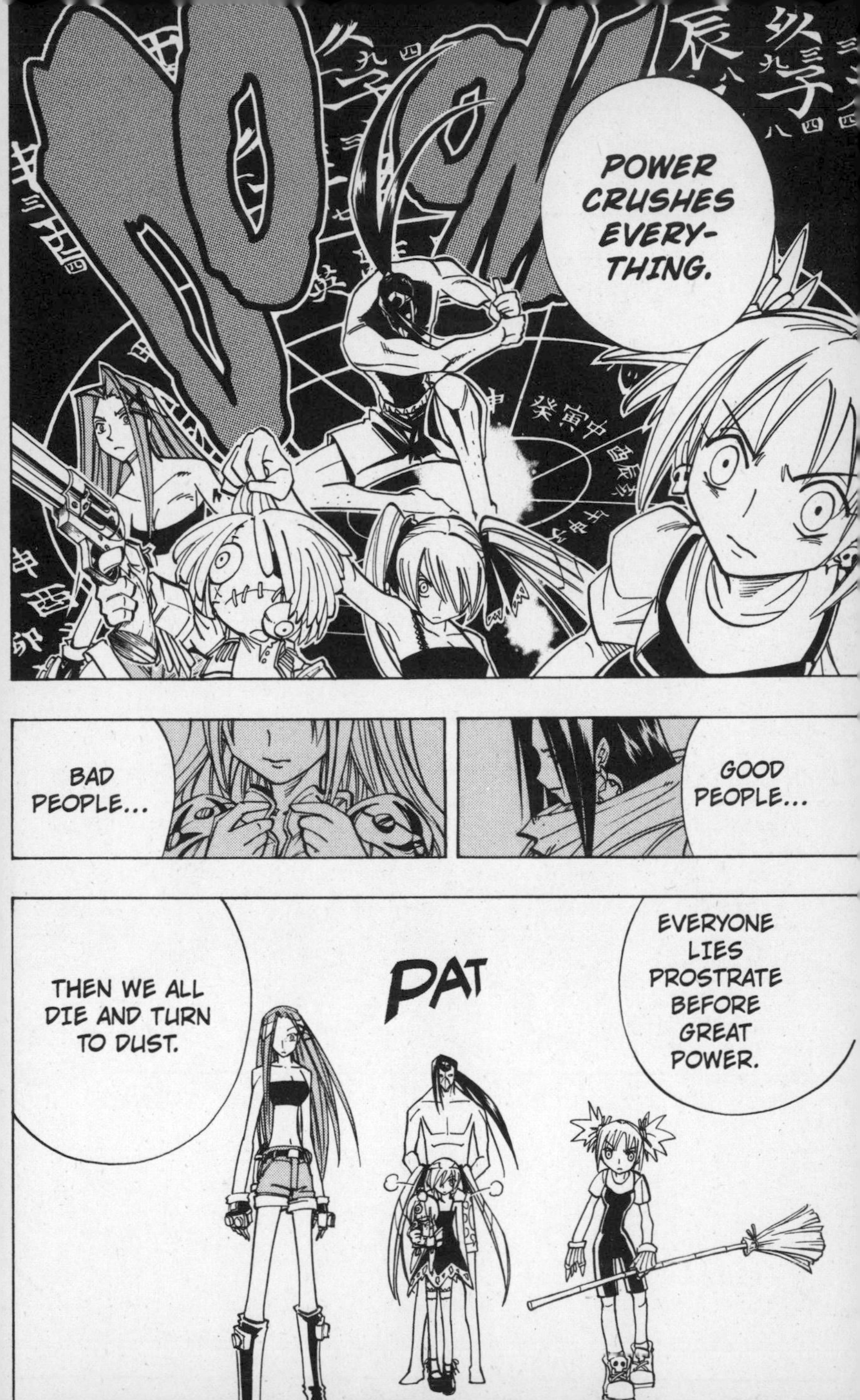
POWER CRUSHES EVERY-THING.
GOOD PEOPLE...
BAD PEOPLE...
EVERYONE LIES PROSTRATE BEFORE GREAT POWER.
PAT
THEN WE ALL DIE AND TURN TO DUST.

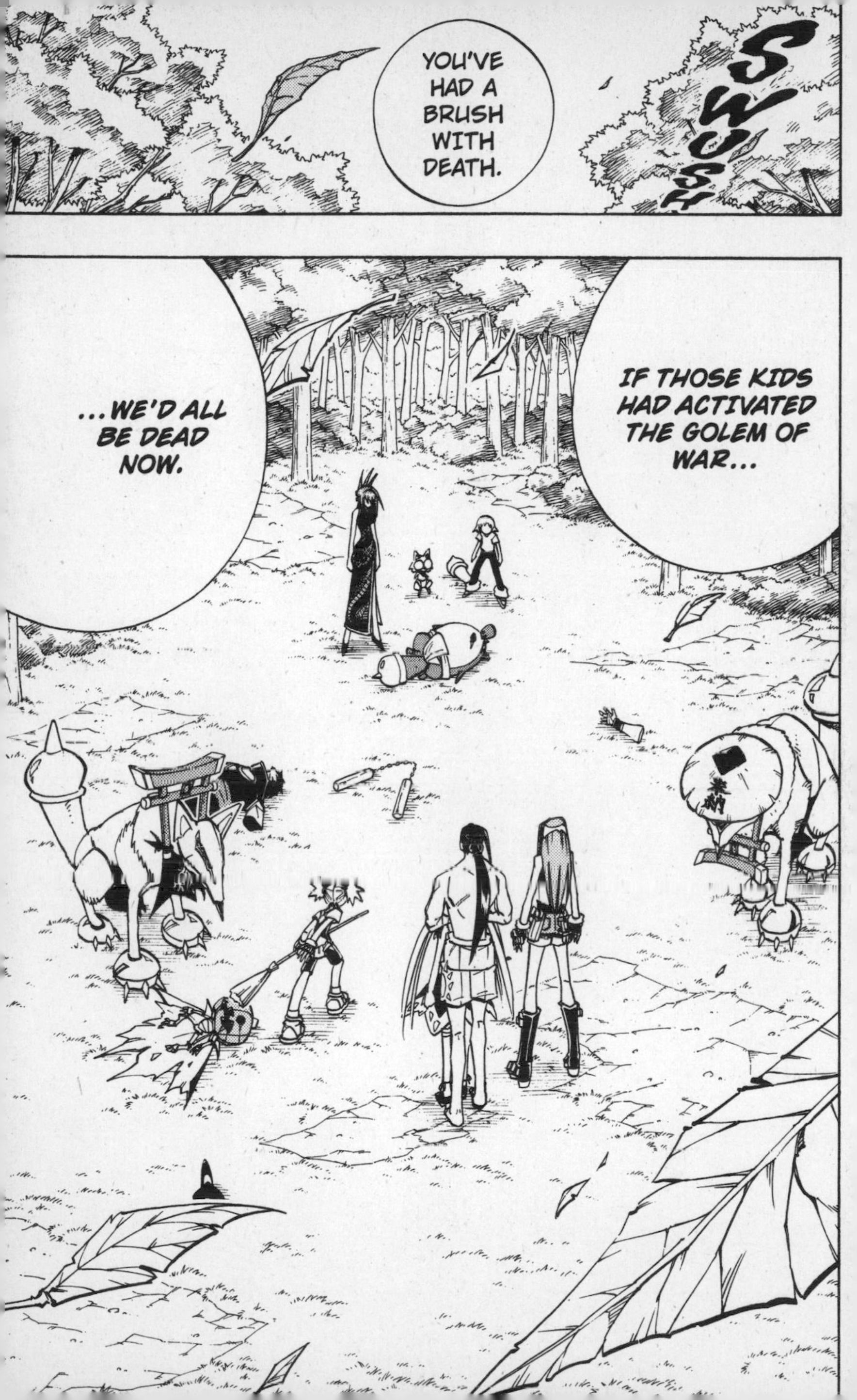
SWOOSH
YOU'VE HAD A BRUSH WITH DEATH.
IF THOSE KIDS HAD ACTIVATED THE GOLEM OF WAR...
...WE'D ALL BE DEAD NOW.

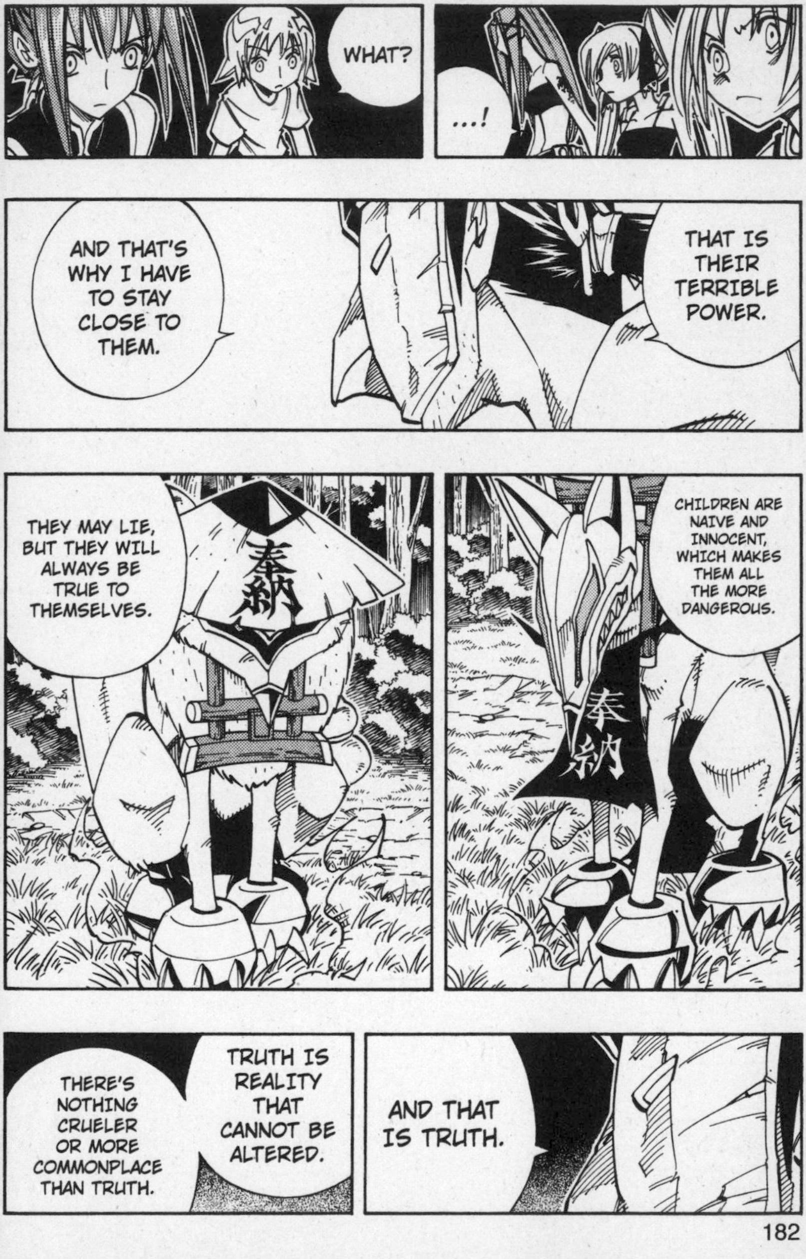

...!
WHAT?
THAT IS THEIR TERRIBLE POWER.
AND THAT'S WHY I HAVE TO STAY CLOSE TO THEM.
CHILDREN ARE NAIVE AND INNOCENT, WHICH MAKES THEM ALL THE MORE DANGEROUS.
THEY MAY LIE, BUT THEY WILL ALWAYS BE TRUE TO THEMSELVES.
AND THAT IS TRUTH.
TRUTH IS REALITY THAT CANNOT BE ALTERED.
THERE'S NOTHING CRUELER OR MORE COMMONPLACE THAN TRUTH.

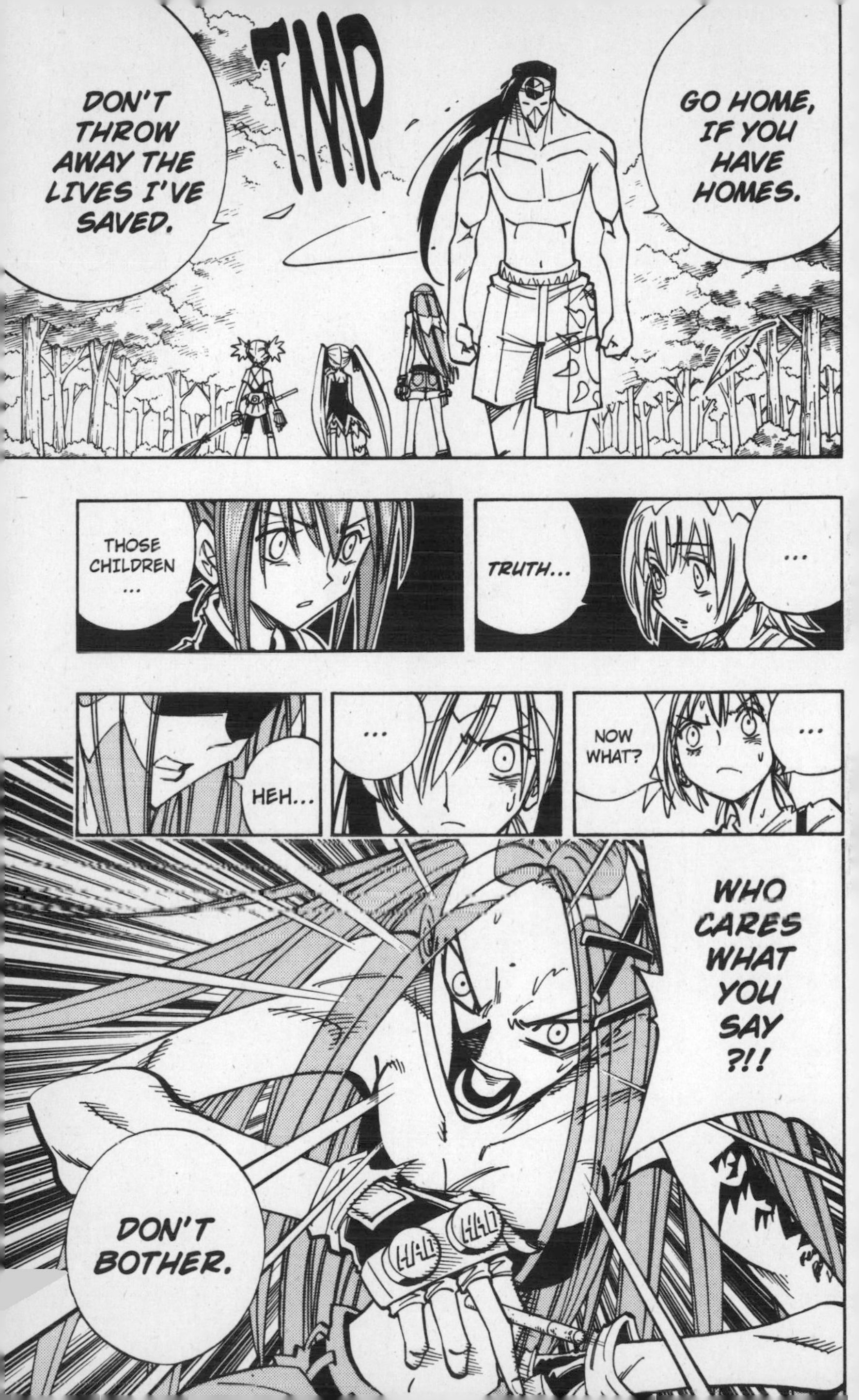
GO HOME, IF YOU HAVE HOMES.
TMP
DON'T THROW AWAY THE LIVES I'VE SAVED.
...
TRUTH...
THOSE CHILDREN ...
...
NOW WHAT?
...
HEH...
WHO CARES WHAT YOU SAY ?!!
DON'T BOTHER.

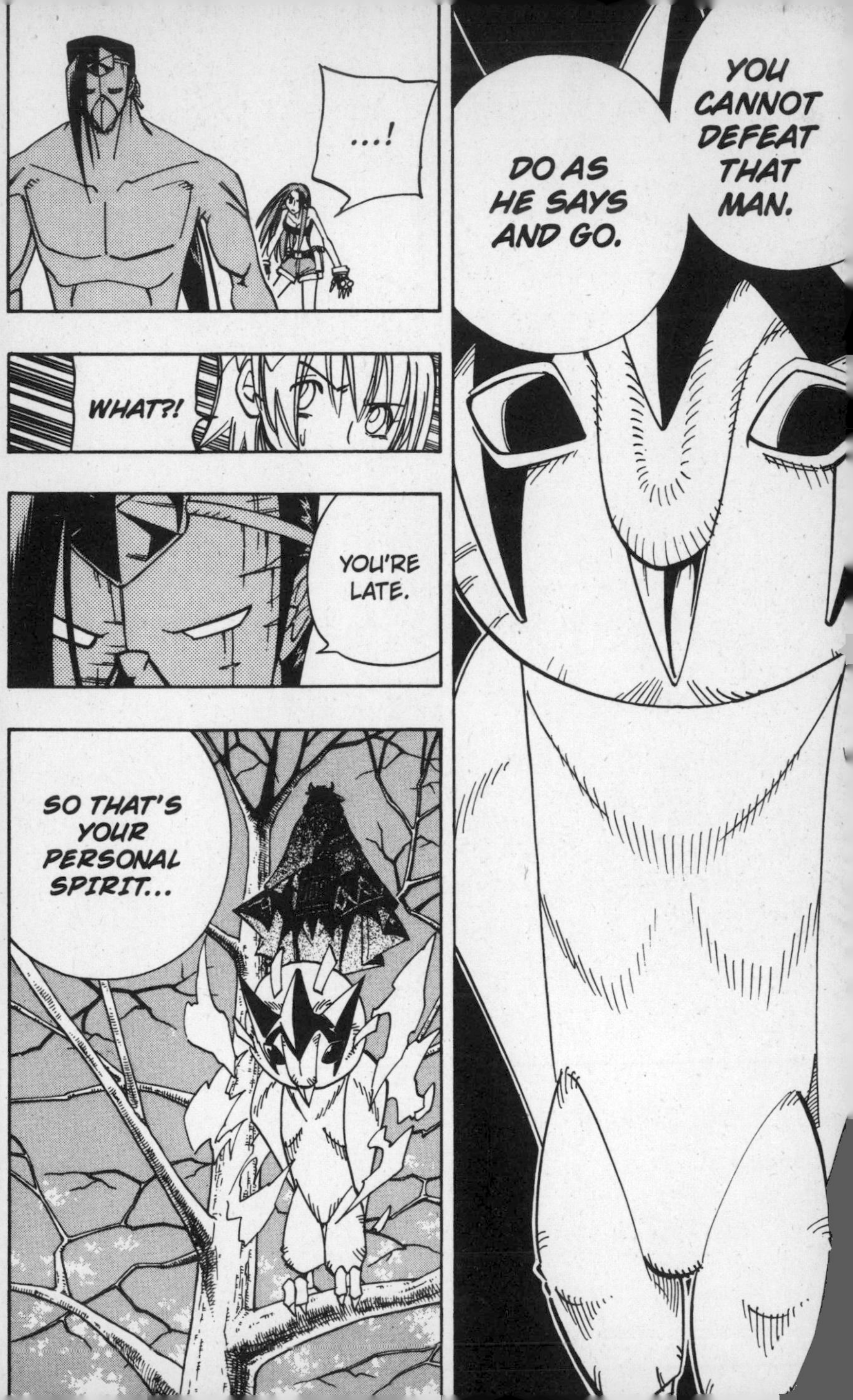
YOU CANNOT DEFEAT THAT MAN.
DO AS HE SAYS AND GO.
...!
WHAT?!
YOU'RE LATE.
SO THAT'S YOUR PERSONAL SPIRIT...

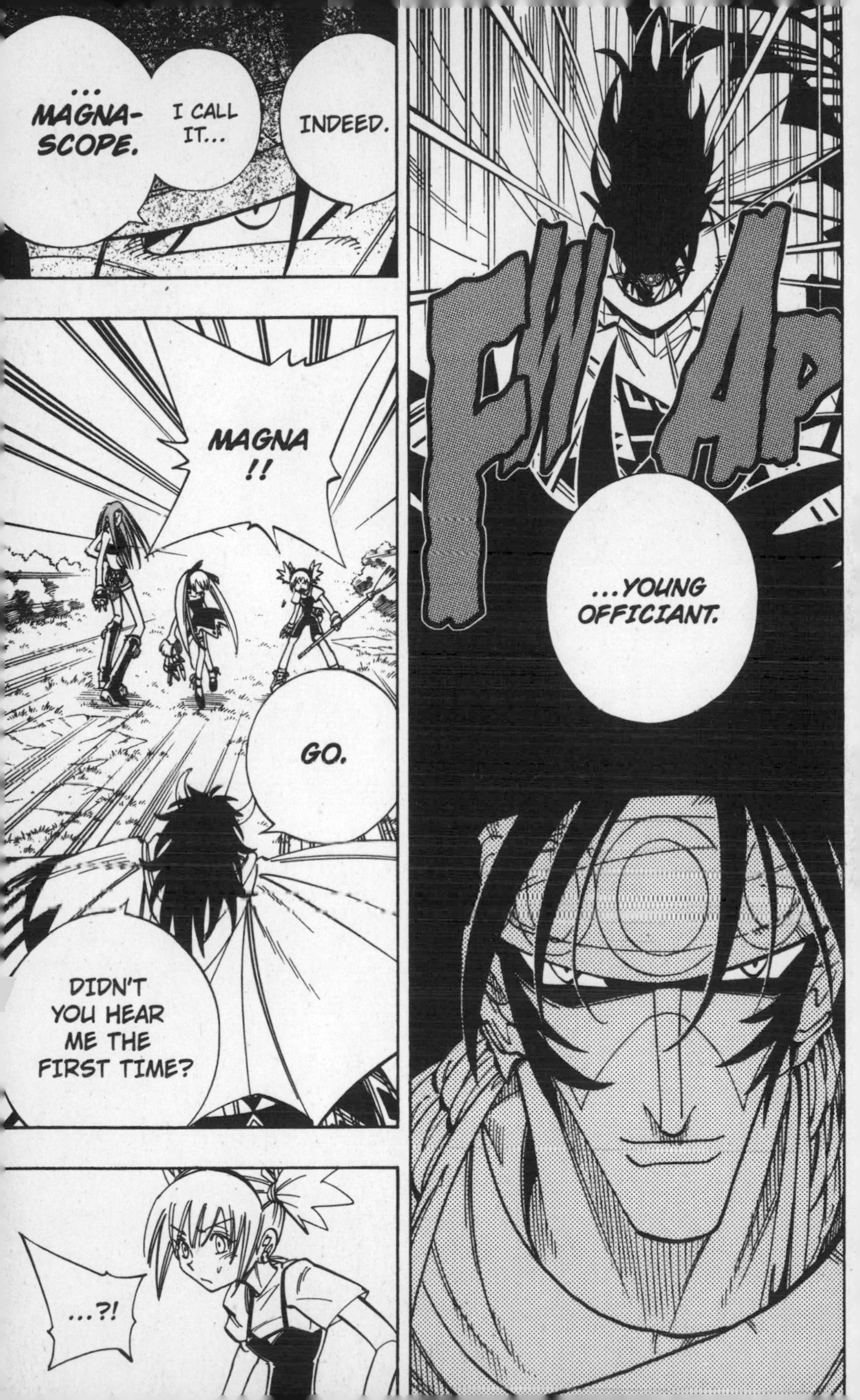
FWAP
...YOUNG OFFICIANT.
INDEED.
I CALL IT...
...MAGNA-SCOPE.
MAGNA!!
GO.
DIDN'T YOU HEAR ME THE FIRST TIME?
...?!

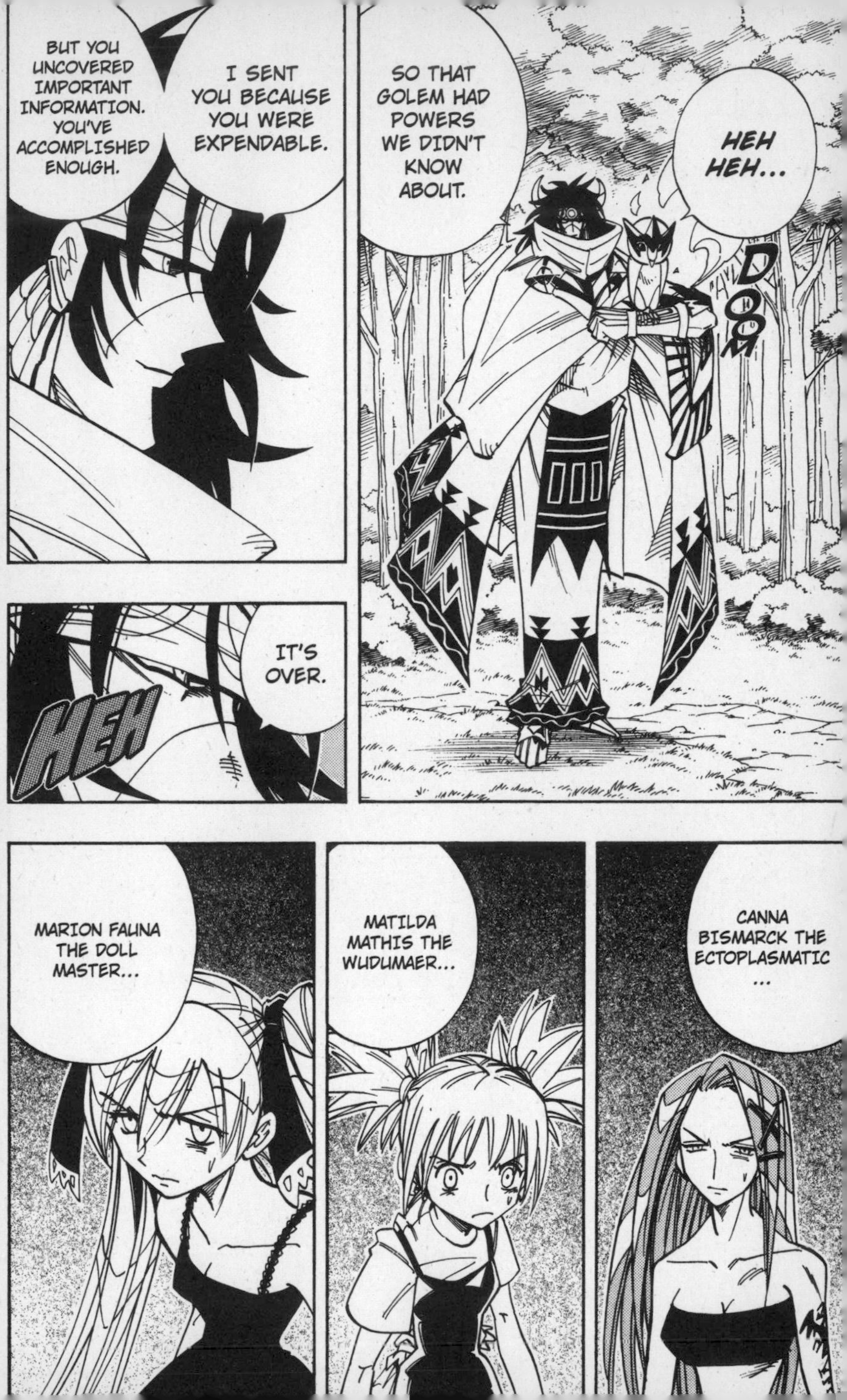
HEH HEH...
DOOM
SO THAT GOLEM HAD POWERS WE DIDN'T KNOW ABOUT.
I SENT YOU BECAUSE YOU WERE EXPENDABLE.
BUT YOU UNCOVERED IMPORTANT INFORMATION. YOU'VE ACCOMPLISHED ENOUGH.
IT'S OVER.
HEH
CANNA BISMARCK THE ECTOPLASMATIC ...
MATILDA MATHIS THE WUDUMAER...
MARION FAUNA THE DOLL MASTER...

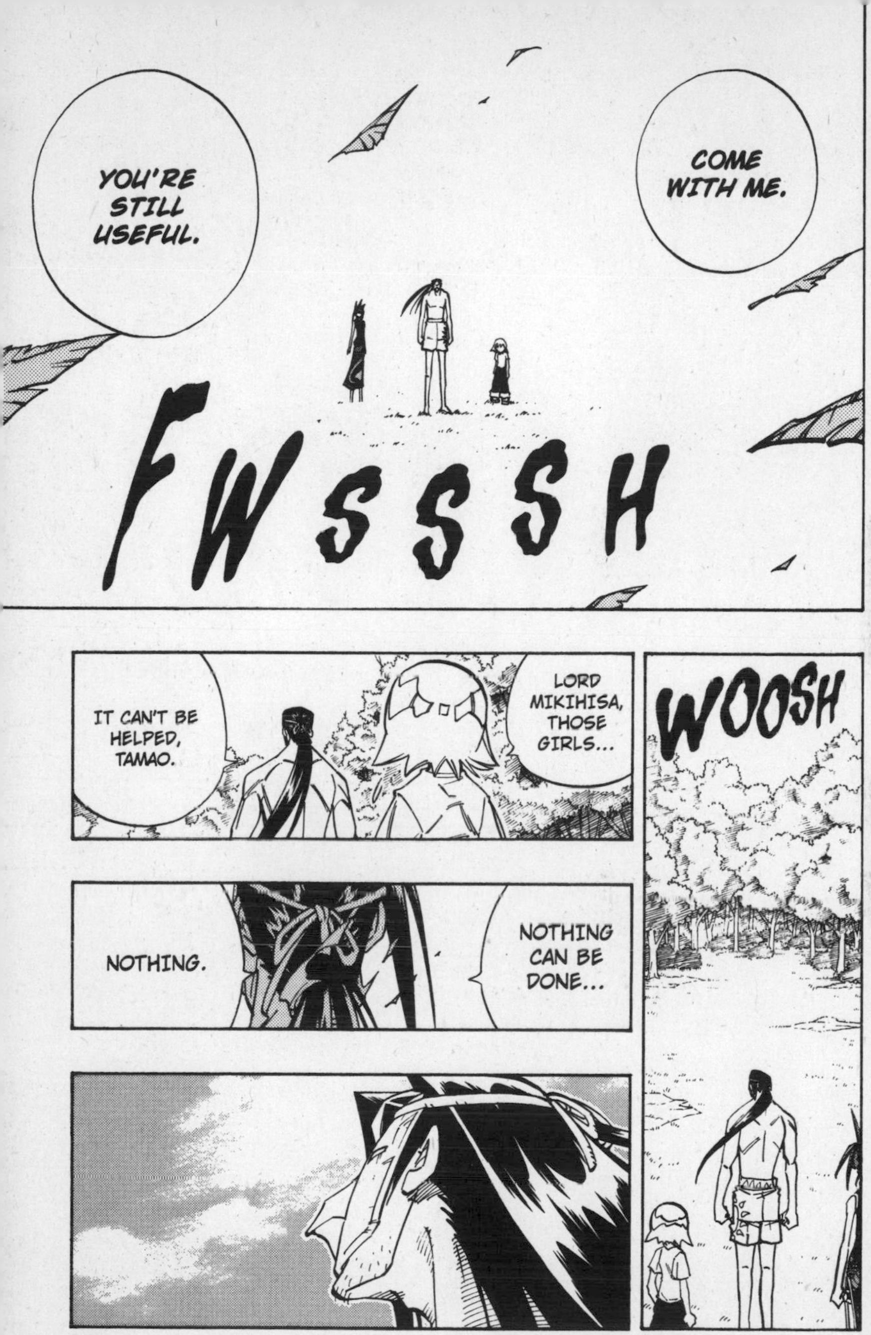
COME WITH ME.
YOU'RE STILL USEFUL.
FWSSSH
WOOSH
LORD MIKIHISA, THOSE GIRLS...
IT CAN'T BE HELPED, TAMAO.
NOTHING CAN BE DONE...
NOTHING.

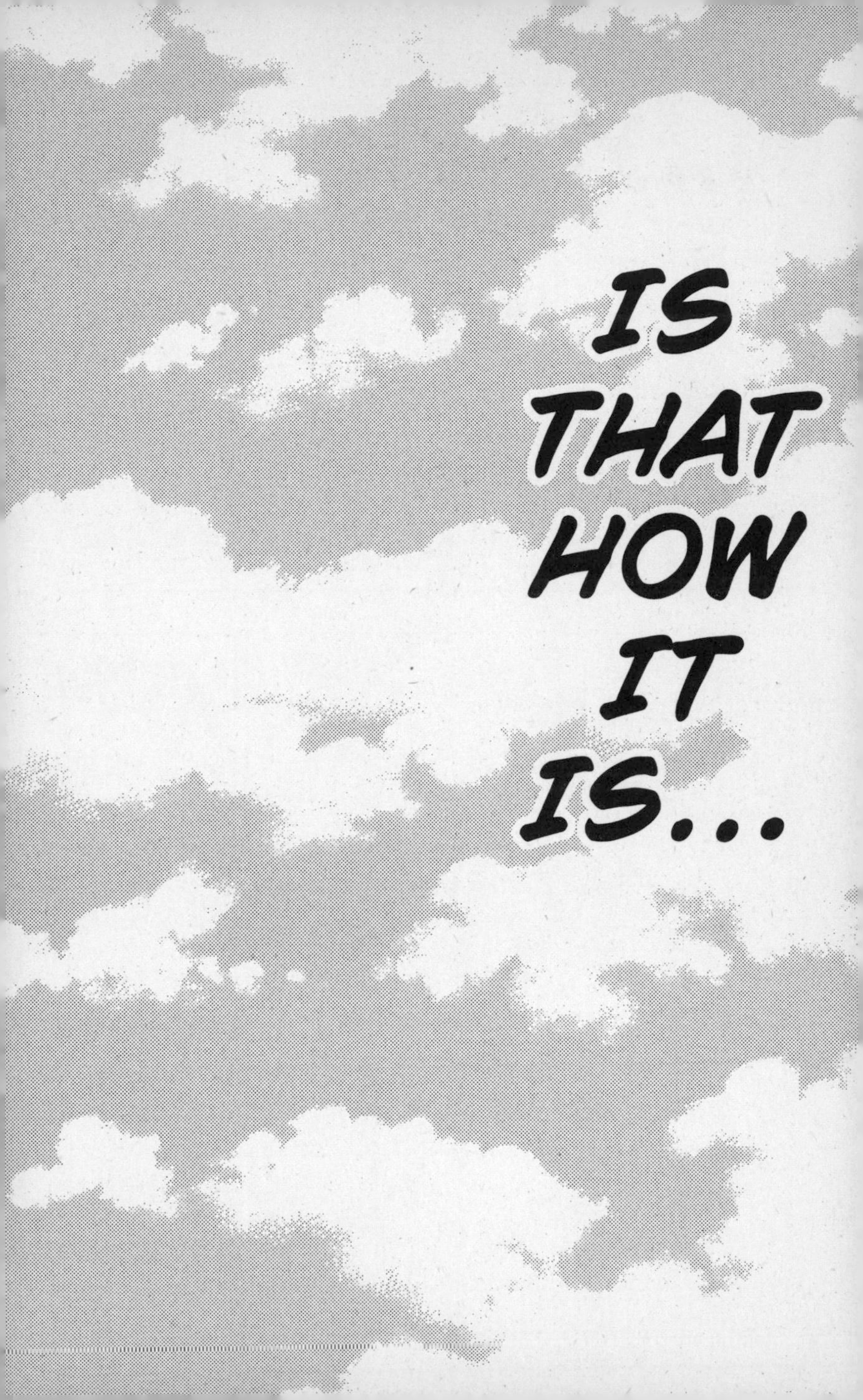
IS THAT HOW IT IS...

...YOH?

SHAMAN KING CHARACTER FILE No.97

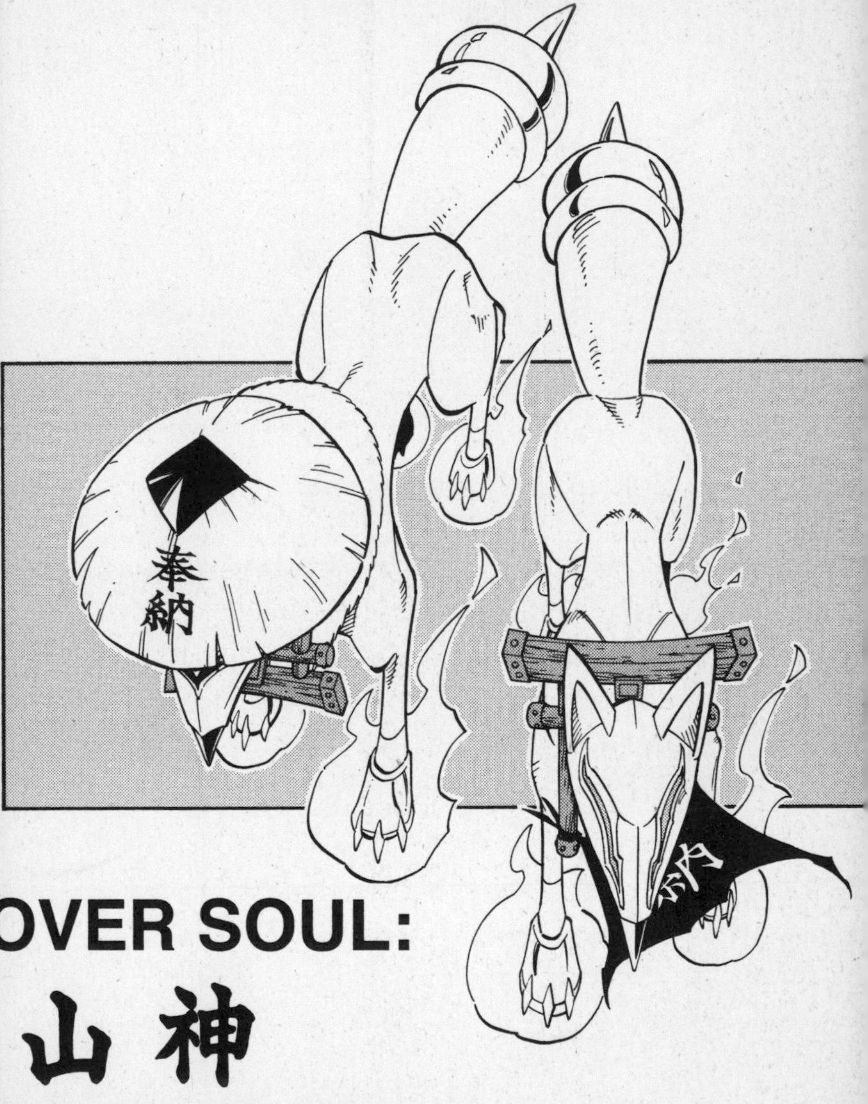
奉納

OVER SOUL:
山神
MOUNTAIN SPIRITS

IN THE NEXT VOLUME...

The unthinkable has happened—Yoh has withdrawn from the Shaman Fight! What happens now? To understand Yoh's future we must revisit his past, back to when he and Anna first met. How did their acquaintance shape Yoh's fate, and what terrible secret still burns between them?

AVAILABLE NOVEMBER 2008!

BONUS! Attach this sticker to the back of the entry form that's also in this product.

SLAM DUNK

This sticker goes on the 40th anniversary poster from SHONEN JUMP magazine!

Find out how to get the collectible poster (while supplies last) by visiting www.shonenjump.com/wsj40.

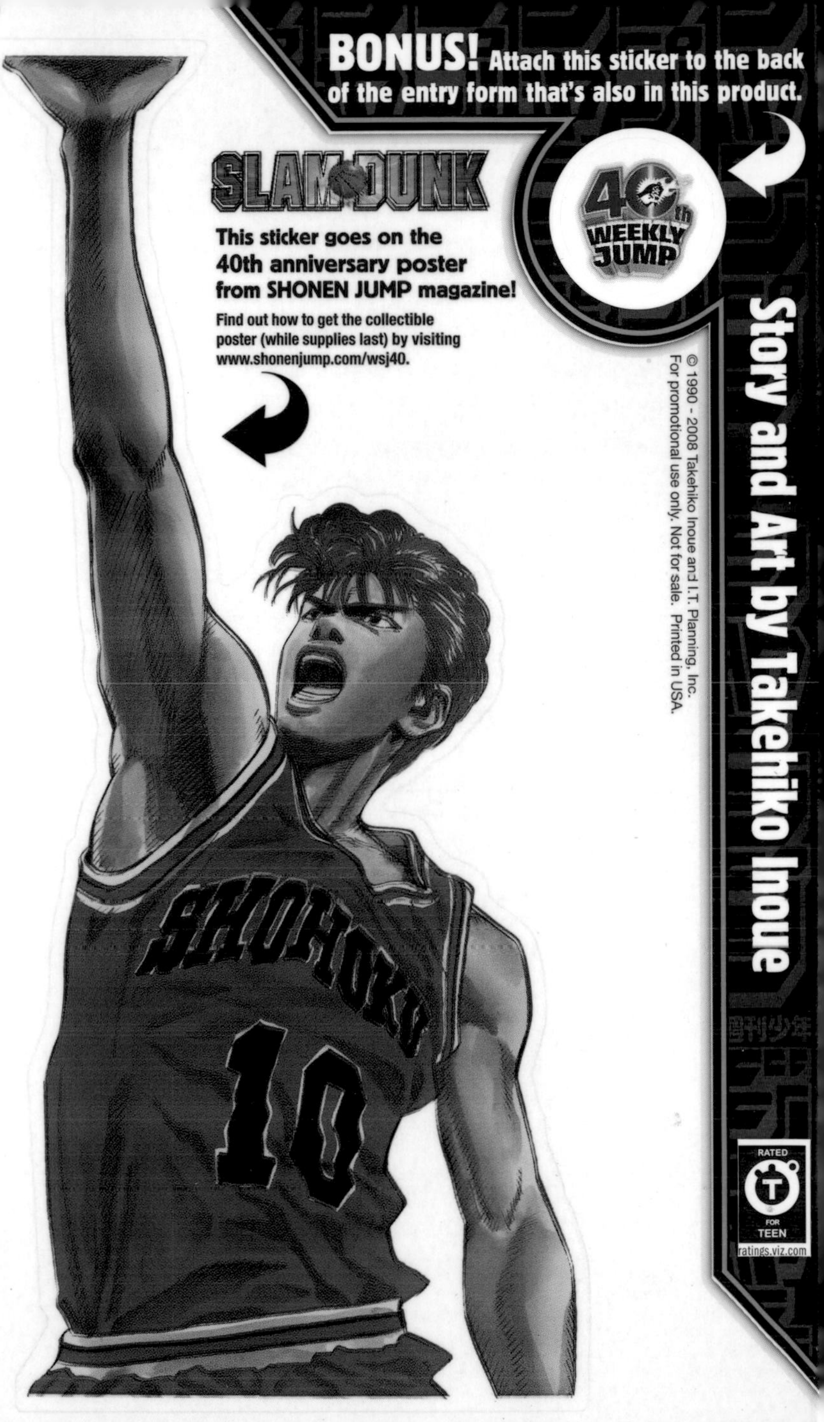
SHOHOKU
10

40th WEEKLY JUMP

Story and Art by Takehiko Inoue

RATED T FOR TEEN
ratings.viz.com

WIN A TRIP TO JAPAN!

The year 2008 marks the 40th anniversary of *Weekly Shonen Jump*, the biggest manga magazine in Japan and the source for the English-language edition of *SHONEN JUMP*. *Weekly Shonen Jump* is the birthplace of the greatest manga artists and stories, and for 40 years has given the world amazing manga, including *NARUTO*, *BLEACH* and *SLAM DUNK*, to name just a few.

To celebrate this incredible milestone, we are giving away a trip for one winner and a friend to Japan to attend Jump Festa 2009 (Dec. 20-21, 2008), the ULTIMATE convention for everything SHONEN JUMP!

To enter, fill out the entry form that's also in this product and mail it in an envelope for a chance to win:
- A 6 day/5 night trip to Japan for you and a friend in December 2008
- Coach airfare and 5 nights hotel and accommodations
- Two-day passes for two to Jump Festa 2009 (December 20-21, 2008)

Visit www.shonenjump.com/wsj40
for complete sweepstakes rules and details!

WIN A TRIP TO JAPAN
through the SHONEN JUMP Experience Sweepstakes!

The year 2008 marks the 40th anniversary of *Weekly Shonen Jump*, the biggest manga magazine in Japan and the source for the English-language edition of *SHONEN JUMP*. *Weekly Shonen Jump* is the birthplace of the greatest manga artists and stories, and for 40 years has given the world amazing manga, including *NARUTO*, *BLEACH* and *SLAM DUNK*, to name just a few.

To celebrate this incredible milestone, we are giving away a
trip for one winner and a friend to Japan to attend Jump Festa 2009 (Dec. 20-21, 2008),
the ULTIMATE convention for everything SHONEN JUMP!

(Entries must be postmarked by October 15, 2008 in order to qualify.)

(Please print clearly)

Name: _____

Street Address: _____

City: _____ State: _____ Postal Code: _____

Country: _____ Date of Birth (01/01/2000): _____

Phone number: _____

For mailing address information, visit www.shonenjump.com/wsj40.

BONUS!

Whether or not you win the sweepstakes, you can still get a GIFT!

COLLECT THREE (3) of the special bonus ***Weekly Shonen Jump*** stickers, stick them all on this form, enter your information on the other side, and mail this in for a surprise gift!* (ARV $10.00)

PLACE STICKER HERE

PLACE STICKER HERE

PLACE STICKER HERE

* While supplies last. Submissions must be postmarked by 10/15/08 and received by 10/31/08 in order to qualify. All three special round stickers must be mailed in on the same card in order to qualify for the surprise gift. Limit two submissions for surprise gift allowed per household. Allow 6-8 weeks from submission deadline for shipment of gift. No mechanical reproduction or copies of form or sticker allowed. Illegible or incomplete submissions will not be honored. Sponsor is not responsible for lost, late, mutilated, misdirected, or postage due mail or submissions. Void where prohibited.

VIZ media

www.viz.com